BOOK 2 – ECONOMICS AND FINANCIAL STATEMENT ANALYSIS

READINGS AND LEARNING OUTCOME STATEMENTS

READINGS

The following material is a review of the Economics and Financial Statement Analysis principles designed to address the learning outcome statements set forth by CFA Institute.

LEARNING OUTCOME STATEMENTS (LOS)

The CFA Institute Learning Outcome Statements are listed below. These are repeated in each topic review; however, the order may have been changed in order to get a better fit with the flow of the review.

STUDY SESSION 4

The topical coverage corresponds with the following CFA Institute assigned reading:

14. **Economic Growth**
    The candidate should be able to:
    a. discuss the preconditions for economic growth. (page 10)
    b. distinguish among saving and investment in new capital, investment in human capital, and investments in new technologies and the way each contributes to economic growth. (page 11)
    c. discuss labor productivity and the productivity curve, and the effects of changes in capital stock and/or technology on the productivity curve. (page 12)
    d. discuss the "One-Third Rule," and how this rule can be used to explain productivity growth slowdown and speedup. (page 13)
    e. compare and contrast the classical growth theory, the neoclassical growth theory, and the new growth theory. (page 15)

The topical coverage corresponds with the following CFA Institute assigned reading:

15. **Regulation and Antitrust Policy in a Globalized Economy**
    The candidate should be able to:
    a. discuss the objectives of regulation and the concepts of cost-of-service regulation and rate-of-return regulation. (page 28)
    b. discuss the benefits of social regulation. (page 28)
    c. analyze negative side effects of regulation. (page 29)
    d. distinguish between the different types of regulators' behavior. (page 29)
    e. discuss the cost of regulation and the effects of deregulation. (page 30)

The topical coverage corresponds with the following CFA Institute assigned reading:

16. **Trading with the World**
    The candidate should be able to:
    a. discuss opportunity cost associated with trade, how countries can gain from international trade, how countries determine whether to import, export, or produce goods and services, and explain the gains of trade for all parties. (page 36)
    b. compare and contrast tariffs, non-tariff barriers, quotas, and voluntary export restraints with respect to international trade. (page 39)
    c. discuss the advantages and disadvantages of protection for each party, and explain the main reasons for trade restriction. (page 41)

The topical coverage corresponds with the following CFA Institute assigned reading:

17. **International Finance**
    The candidate should be able to:
    a. explain the different components of the balance of payments accounts, the transactions recorded for import and export on the different accounts, and how the three sector balances are related. (page 47)
    b. explain the law of demand and the law of supply for foreign exchange, and how changes in demand and supply occur. (page 48)

   c. discuss the influence of supply and demand on the exchange rate, and why exchange rates can be volatile. (page 50)

   d. distinguish between purchasing power and interest rate parity. (page 51)

   e. discuss how and why intervention by a central bank in the exchange market may be required. (page 52)

The topical coverage corresponds with the following CFA Institute assigned reading:

18. **Foreign Exchange**

The candidate should be able to:

   a. define direct and indirect methods of foreign exchange quotations and convert direct (indirect) foreign exchange quotations into indirect (direct) foreign exchange quotations. (page 58)

   b. calculate and interpret the spread on a foreign currency quotation and explain how spreads on foreign currency quotations can differ as a result of market conditions, bank/dealer positions, and trading volume. (page 59)

   c. calculate and interpret currency cross rates, given two spot exchange quotations involving three currencies. (page 61)

   d. distinguish between the spot and forward markets for foreign exchange. (page 65)

   e. calculate and interpret the spread on a forward foreign currency quotation and explain how spreads on forward foreign currency quotations can differ as a result of market conditions, bank/dealer positions, trading volume, and maturity/length of contract. (page 66)

   f. calculate and interpret a forward discount or premium and express it as an annualized rate. (page 67)

   g. explain interest rate parity and illustrate covered interest arbitrage. (page 69)

   h. calculate the profit on a triangular arbitrage opportunity, given the bid-ask quotations for the currencies of three countries involved in the arbitrage. (page 75)

   i. distinguish between spot and forward transactions, and calculate the annualized forward premium/discount for a given currency and infer whether the currency is "strong" or "weak." (page 67)

The topical coverage corresponds with the following CFA Institute assigned reading:

19. **Foreign Exchange Parity Relations**

The candidate should be able to:

   a. explain how exchange rates are determined in a flexible or floating exchange rate system. (page 84)

   b. explain the role of each component of the balance-of-payments accounts. (page 85)

   c. explain how current account deficits or surpluses and financial account deficits or surpluses affect an economy. (page 86)

   d. describe the factors that cause a nation's currency to appreciate or depreciate. (page 86)

   e. explain how monetary and fiscal policies affect the exchange rate and balance-of-payments components. (page 87)

   f. describe a fixed exchange rate and a pegged exchange rate system. (page 88)

   g. discuss absolute purchasing power parity and relative purchasing power parity, and calculate the end-of-period exchange rate implied by purchasing power parity, given the beginning-of-period exchange rate and the inflation rates. (page 89)

   h. discuss the international Fisher relation and calculate and interpret 1) interest rates exactly and by linear approximation, given expected inflation rates and the assumption that the international Fisher relation holds, 2) the real interest rate, given interest rates and inflation rates and the assumption that the international Fisher relation holds, and 3) the international Fisher relation, and its linear approximation, between interest rates and expected inflation rates. (page 92)

i. discuss the theory of uncovered interest rate parity, and explain the theory's relationship to other exchange rate parity theories, and calculate and interpret the expected change in the exchange rate, given interest rates and the assumption that uncovered interest rate parity holds. (page 95)

j. discuss the foreign exchange expectation relation between the forward exchange rate and the expected spot exchange rate, and calculate and interpret the expected change in the exchange rate, given the forward exchange rate discount or premium, and discuss the implications of a foreign currency risk premium. (page 96)

k. calculate the forward exchange rate, given the spot exchange rate and risk-free interest rates, using 1) interest rate parity, and 2) its linear approximation. (page 98)

l. discuss the implication of the parity relationships combined. (page 99)

m. explain the roles of absolute purchasing power parity and relative purchasing power parity in exchange rate determination. (page 100)

n. discuss the elements of balance of payments and their role in exchange rate determination. (page 101)

o. discuss the asset markets approach to pricing exchange rate expectations. (page 101)

p. calculate the short-term and the long-run exchange rate effects of a sudden and unexpected increase in the money supply. (page 102)

The topical coverage corresponds with the following CFA Institute assigned reading:

20. **Measuring Economic Activity**
The candidate should be able to:

a. distinguish between the different measures of economic activity and their components. (page 116)

b. distinguish between GDP at market prices and GDP at factor cost, and explain the adjustments made. (page 118)

c. discuss the difference between current and constant prices, and the GDP deflator. (page 118)

STUDY SESSION 5

The topical coverage corresponds with the following CFA Institute assigned reading:

21. **Analysis of Intercorporate Investments**
The candidate should be able to:

a. distinguish whether a debt security or equity security should be classified as held-to-maturity, available-for-sale, or as a trading security. (page 126)

b. calculate and analyze the effect of marketable securities classification on the financial statements and financial ratios under SFAS 115. (page 127)

c. calculate and analyze the mark-to-market investment return on a marketable securities portfolio under SFAS 115. (page 131)

d. distinguish, given various ownership and/or control levels and relevant accounting standards, whether the cost method, equity method, proportionate consolidation method, or consolidation method should be used, and analyze and contrast the earnings effects of using the cost method, equity method, consolidation method, and proportionate consolidation method on a company's financial statements and financial ratios. (page 133)

e. analyze a reportable segment under SFAS 131, and evaluate the uses and limitations of segment data. (page 141)

f. calculate financial ratios for the reportable segments of a company, and interpret the level and trend of each ratio. (page 143)

The topical coverage corresponds with the following CFA Institute assigned reading:

22.   **Mergers, Acquisitions, and Other Intercorporate Investments**
The candidate should be able to:
   a.   compare and contrast U.S. and international accounting for mergers, acquisitions, and other intercorporate investments. (page 158)
   b.   evaluate the impact of the purchase versus pooling methods on reported financial results. (page 159)
   c.   distinguish between cost investments, equity investments, proportionately consolidated investments, and consolidated investments. (page 163)
   d.   determine when income should be recognized on investments that are accounted for using the cost method. (page 166)
   e.   describe the reporting of market value increases and decreases in the financial statements for cost-method investments. (page 167)
   f.   identify situations when companies should apply the equity and consolidation methods of accounting for investments. (page 165)
   g.   explain the implications of proportionate consolidation methods for the evaluation of leverage, profitability, and return on assets (ROA). (page 167)

The topical coverage corresponds with the following CFA Institute assigned reading:

23.   **Variable Interest Entities, Intercompany Debt, Consolidated Cash Flows, and Other Issues**
The candidate should be able to:
   a.   describe the form of, characteristics of, and rationale for establishing VIEs. (page 175)
   b.   describe the conditions under which a VIE must be consolidated. (page 176)

STUDY SESSION 6

The topical coverage corresponds with the following CFA Institute assigned reading:

24.   **Understanding Retirement Benefit Accounting and Disclosures for Financial Analysis**
The candidate should be able to:
   a.   explain the types of post-employment benefit plans and the implications for financial reports. (page 184)
   b.   describe the components of a company's defined-benefit pension expense and explain the impact of plan assumptions on that pension expense. (page 192)
   c.   explain the measures of a defined-benefit pension plan's liabilities, including the projected benefit obligation, accumulated benefit obligation, and vested benefit obligation. (page 186)
   d.   explain the impact on financial statements of U.S. generally accepted accounting principles (U.S. GAAP) and international financial reporting standards (IFRS) for pension and other post-employment benefits that permit some items to be reported in the footnotes rather than being reflected in the financial statements themselves. (page 195)
   e.   calculate the underlying economic liability (or asset) of a company based upon pension and other post-employment benefit disclosures. (page 199)
   f.   calculate the underlying economic pension and other post-employment expense (income) based upon disclosures after removing the effect of amortized items and smoothing mechanisms. (page 207)

The topical coverage corresponds with the following CFA Institute assigned reading:

25. **FAS 123(R)—Accounting for Stock-Based Compensation: Happy Anniversary?**
   The candidate should be able to:
   a. explain the key features of stock option accounting in the United States. (page 228)
   b. describe the differences between the U.S. and international standards of accounting for stock options. (page 232)

The topical coverage corresponds with the following CFA Institute assigned reading:

26. **Analysis of Multinational Operations**
   The candidate should be able to:
   a. distinguish between the impact of changes in local currency sales and changes in exchange rates on the translated sales of the subsidiary and parent company. (page 237)
   b. distinguish among the local currency, the functional currency, and the reporting currency. (page 239)
   c. compare and contrast the all-current (translation) method and the temporal (remeasurement) method. (page 239)
   d. analyze and evaluate the effects of the all-current and temporal methods on the parent company's balance sheet and income statement. (page 243)
   e. distinguish whether the all-current or the temporal method is appropriate in various scenarios. (page 244)
   f. calculate the translation effects of the all-current and temporal methods of foreign currency translation. (page 246)
   g. translate a subsidiary's balance sheet and income statement into the parent company's currency, using the all-current method and the temporal method. (page 247)
   h. analyze how the translation of a subsidiary's financial statements will affect the subsidiary's financial ratios. (page 257)
   i. compare and contrast the effect of using the temporal method and the all-current method on the parent company's financial ratios. (page 261)
   j. analyze foreign currency disclosures in the footnotes to financial statements. (page 267)
   k. illustrate and analyze alternative accounting methods for subsidiaries operating in hyperinflationary economies. (page 271)

STUDY SESSION 7

The topical coverage corresponds with the following CFA Institute assigned reading:

27. **Accounting Shenanigans on the Cash Flow Statement**
   The candidate should be able to analyze and discuss the following ways to manipulate the cash flow statement:
   - stretching out payables. (page 284)
   - financing of payables. (page 284)
   - securitization of receivables. (page 284)
   - using stock buybacks to offset dilution of earnings. (page 284)

The topical coverage corresponds with the following CFA Institute assigned reading:

28. **Financial Reporting Quality: Red Flags and Accounting Warning Signs**
   The candidate should be able to:
   a. describe incentives that might induce a company's management to overreport or underreport earnings. (page 293)
   b. describe activities that will result in a low quality of earnings. (page 294)
   c. describe the "fraud triangle". (page 294)

   d. describe the risk factors related to incentives and pressures that may lead to fraudulent accounting. (page 295)

   e. describe the risk factors related to opportunities that may lead to fraudulent accounting. (page 296)

   f. describe the risk factors related to attitudes and rationalizations that may lead to fraudulent accounting. (page 297)

   g. describe common accounting warning signs and methods of detecting each. (page 298)

   h. describe the accounting warning signs related to the Enron accounting scandal. (page 300)

   i. describe the accounting warning signs related to the Sunbeam accounting scandal. (page 301)

The topical coverage corresponds with the following CFA Institute assigned reading:

29.   The Lessons We Learn

The candidate should be able to:

   a. distinguish among the various definitions of earnings (e.g., EBITDA, operating earnings, net income, etc.). (page 307)

   b. illustrate how trends in cash flow from operations can be more reliable than earnings trends. (page 308)

   c. provide a simplified description of the accounting treatment for derivatives being used:

- to hedge exposure to changes in the value of assets and liabilities. (page 308)
- to hedge exposure to variable cash flow. (page 308)
- to hedge a foreign currency exposure of an investment in a foreign corporation. (page 308)

The topical coverage corresponds with the following CFA Institute assigned reading:

30.   Analysis of Financial Statements: A Synthesis

The candidate should be able to:

   a. analyze and evaluate the balance sheet for assets and liabilities that are not recorded, and for assets and liabilities for which the amounts shown on the balance sheet differ from their current values. (page 315)

   b. analyze and evaluate the balance sheet for the current value of assets and liabilities. (page 317)

   c. compute a company's normal operating earnings and comprehensive income. (page 322)

   d. analyze and interpret:

- the effect on reported financial results and ratios of a company's choices of accounting methods and assumptions. (page 327)
- the effect on reported financial results and ratios of changes in accounting methods and assumptions. (page 327)
- the effects of balance sheet modifications and earnings normalization on a company's financial statements, financial ratios, and overall financial condition. (page 327)

ECONOMIC GROWTH

EXAM FOCUS

This topic review covers the variables that affect the economic growth process along with three theories that provide insight into the key drivers of economic growth. There are important links here to the equity valuation material. You should be able to integrate this material with the equity valuation concepts in Study Session 11 (particularly LOS 40.d) and, in the country analysis component of global industry analysis, identify countries that are expected to experience higher economic growth.

WARM-UP: ECONOMIC GROWTH

Economic growth is measured as the percentage change in real gross domestic product (GDP) per labor hour. GDP per labor hour is also called **labor productivity**, because it measures the amount of output a country produces for each hour of labor used as an input. Labor productivity is discussed in LOS 14.c.

economic growth = %Δ real GDP/labor hour = growth in labor productivity

The terms economic growth and growth in labor productivity are used interchangeably throughout this topic review.

Professor's Note: Real GDP is a measure of a country's inflation-adjusted output of goods and services and, because output must equal income in an economy, also a measure of a country's inflation-adjusted income. Therefore, GDP is also a measure of the standard of living. See the topic review of Measuring Economic Activity in this study session for a more complete discussion of GDP.

PRECONDITIONS FOR ECONOMIC GROWTH

LOS 14.a: Discuss the preconditions for economic growth.

A suitable **incentive system** is the most important precondition for a society to realize economic growth. The three social institutions that are critical to the development of incentives are markets, property rights, and monetary exchange. Collectively, these three social institutions create incentives for people to specialize in the production of goods in which they have a comparative advantage, trade for those products in which they do not, save the profits from trading, and invest those savings to discover new technologies.

Markets facilitate the exchange of information between buyers and sellers and enable them to conduct business with each other. Market prices send information to buyers and sellers that give them the incentive to adjust the quantities they supply or demand. In order for markets to be effective, property rights and monetary exchange are required.

Property rights are laws and regulations that govern the ownership, use, and sale of goods, services, and factors of production (e.g., land, labor, and equipment). Property rights pertain to physical assets, intellectual property (such as patents and copyrights), and financial claims. If property rights are properly established and enforced, people will be assured that no government will seize their savings and investments.

Monetary exchange provides for the efficient exchange of goods and services, including the transfer of private property from one individual to another.

 Professor's Note: A specific form of political organization (e.g., democracy) is not one of the necessary pre-conditions for economic growth. Countries with communist and authoritarian governments have also experienced economic growth.

KEY FACTORS THAT DRIVE ECONOMIC GROWTH

LOS 14.b: Distinguish among saving and investment in new capital, investment in human capital, and investments in new technologies and the way each contributes to economic growth.

With the proper incentives in place, economic growth occurs as people specialize in activities for which they have a comparative advantage and then trade with one another. As specialization and trading evolve, people acquire increasingly more goods and services in exchange for their labor, gross domestic product (GDP) per person increases, and the standard of living rises. However, in order for economic growth to continue, societies must also have incentives that encourage three activities: (1) savings and investment in new capital, (2) investment in human capital, and (3) discovery of new technologies.

Saving and investment in new capital increase labor productivity (which is economic growth) by increasing the level of capital per worker (i.e., "machines per worker").

Investment in human capital is the investment in people's skills and knowledge, and it is a key driver of economic growth. Both productivity improvements and technological advances derive from investment in human capital. Some fundamental examples of human capital include written language and scientific knowledge. A more subtle form of human capital is the knowledge that workers gain by repeating the same tasks and acquiring experience.

The **discovery of new technologies** contributes to sustained economic growth by making human capital and physical capital more productive. Research and development is the primary driver of the discovery of new technologies. While the most widespread and powerful technologies represent developments in human capital (written and spoken language, science, and mathematics), most technological progress involves improvements in the productivity of physical capital.

 Professor's Note: The material discussed in the next two LOS are part of the area of economics called growth accounting.

THE PRODUCTIVITY CURVE

LOS 14.c: Discuss labor productivity and the productivity curve, and the effects of changes in capital stock and/or technology on the productivity curve.

Labor productivity, as we discussed in the warm up to this topic review, is calculated by dividing real GDP by aggregate labor hours, and is thus quantified as real GDP per labor hour. The growth rate of labor productivity (i.e., economic growth) changes over time. In order to evaluate what drives these changes, the growth rate of labor productivity may be decomposed into two factors: (1) growth in physical capital per labor hour and technological change, and (2) the influence of each can be evaluated separately.

Technological change includes everything that contributes to labor productivity growth except those things that are included in the growth of physical capital. Technological change is largely dependent on growth in human capital because technology only advances as long as knowledge advances.

The **productivity curve** is the curve that results when labor productivity (real GDP per labor hour) is plotted against capital per labor hour at a given state of technology. The productivity curve shows how real GDP per labor hour changes as capital per labor hour changes, holding technology constant. Figure 1 illustrates two productivity curves under two different but constant states of technology. Two important properties of productivity curves can be seen in Figure 1:

1. *Growth in capital per labor hour causes movement along a productivity curve.* Real GDP per labor hour increases as capital per labor hour increases (at a given state of technology.) Referring to the lower productivity curve in Figure 1 labeled "Less technology," an increase in capital from C_0 to C_1 along the curve results in an increase in labor productivity from LP_0 to LP_1. This increase in labor productivity represents real economic growth.

2. *Technological growth causes the productivity curve to shift upwards.* Real GDP per labor hour increases as the state of technology increases at any given level of capital per labor hour. In Figure 1, this is illustrated by the vertical distance LP_0 to LP_1 at C_0, or LP_1 to LP_2 at C_1.

The **law of diminishing returns** applies to productivity curves. This means that at a given level of technology, as more and more capital per labor hour is added, the increase in real GDP per labor hour gets smaller and smaller. For example, the increase in real GDP per labor hour resulting from a given $10 increase in capital per labor hour will be greater than the increase in real GDP per labor hour from an additional $10 increase in capital per labor hour.

Figure 1: Productivity Curve

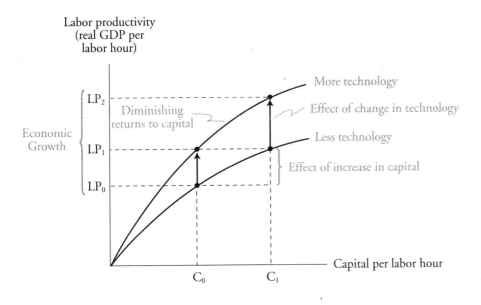

LOS 14.d: Discuss the "One-Third Rule," and how this rule can be used to explain productivity growth slowdown and speedup.

In a healthy economy, productivity growth is always positive. However, the productivity growth rate is not constant. From one time period to the next, productivity growth may speed up or slow down.

The **"One-Third Rule"** states that at a given level of technology, on average, a 1% increase in capital per labor hour results in a one third of 1% increase in real GDP per labor hour. The "One-Third Rule" can be used to divide a change in productivity growth into two components: (1) that which is attributable to a change in capital per labor hour (i.e., movement along a productivity curve); and (2) that which is attributable to technological change (i.e., shifts in a productivity curve).

Example: One-third rule applied to productivity speedup

Assume that real GDP per labor hour grew by 5% over the past five years while capital per labor hour grew by 4.5%. Use the "One-Third Rule" to estimate the amount of real GDP per labor hour growth attributable to the increase in capital and the amount attributable to technological change.

Answer:

According to the one-third rule, capital has contributed one third of 4.5% toward the increase in real GDP per labor hour, or 1.5% (1/3 × 4.5%). This component results from the movement along the productivity curve. The remaining 3.5% (5% – 1.5%) growth in real GDP per labor hour is attributable to technological change. This component results from the shift in the productivity curve. These two effects are illustrated in the following figure.

Productivity Curve

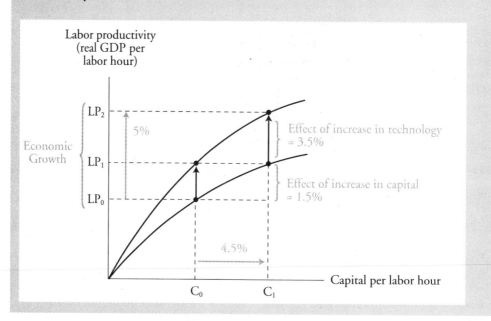

Productivity slowdowns result when technology is applied to deal with issues other than increasing productivity. For example, energy price shocks cause R&D to be diverted from productivity improvement to finding technologies that increase fuel efficiency, which contributes little to real economic growth. Also, technology applied to improving environmental quality creates benefits that are not measured as part of GDP and therefore don't contribute to economic growth.

The key methods for increasing economic growth (i.e., **productivity speedup**) include the following:

- *Encourage savings*, which leads to capital accumulation. Tax incentives are commonly used to encourage private savings.
- *Encourage basic R&D* to develop technological advances that are public goods. The problem is that a capital market will devote too few resources to basic research because the benefits must be shared and the returns are too low. Therefore, government policy must create incentives for basic research.
- *Stimulate international trade* to realize the gains from specialization.
- *Improve the quality of education* by investing in human capital. Once again, government tax policy can provide incentives in this area.

GROWTH THEORIES

LOS 14.e: Compare and contrast the classical growth theory, the neoclassical growth theory, and the new growth theory.

Growth theories have been developed to evaluate the relationship between the factors that affect economic growth. We will compare and contrast three popular growth theories: (1) classical growth theory, (2) neoclassical growth theory, and (3) new growth theory.

Classical Growth Theory

Classical growth theory contends that growth in real GDP is not permanent. When real GDP per person rises above what is referred to as the **subsistence level**, a population explosion occurs, and GDP per person is driven back to the subsistence level.

What classical economists believe is that technological advances lead to increased investment in new capital, which increases labor productivity (in Figure 2, the economy moves from Point 1 to Point 2). With increased labor productivity, new businesses start and the demand for labor increases. This puts upward pressure on real wages and employment increases, which is good news.

However, classical economists also argue that increased real wages lead to a population explosion, which drives real GDP back to its original level (in Figure 2, the economy moves from Point 2 to Point 3). This argument is based on the concept of a **subsistence real wage**, which is defined as the minimum real wage necessary to support life. Whenever real wages are below the subsistence real wage, some people will not survive and the population will decline. When real wages are greater than the subsistence real wage, the population will increase. The increase in the number of workers from the population boom leads to diminishing returns to labor and, eventually, decreased labor productivity. The implication of the classical view is that no matter how much technology advances, real wages will eventually be driven back to the subsistence level and no permanent productivity growth or improvement in the standard of living will occur.

Figure 2: Classical Growth Theory

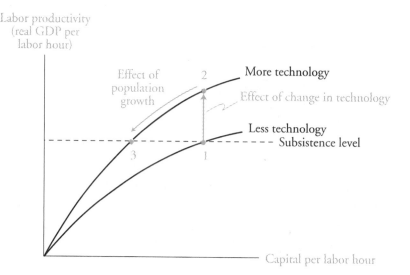

 Professor's Note: The key to classical growth theory is the population explosion that occurs whenever real GDP per labor hour increases above the subsistence level will eventually eliminate any gains from increased labor productivity.

Neoclassical Growth Theory

Neoclassical growth theory holds that without technological change, no long-term growth in real GDP will occur. Neoclassical economists believe that changes in technology lead to increased saving and investment, which causes capital per labor hour to grow.

The big difference between the neoclassical theory and the classical theory is the neoclassical treatment of population growth. Unlike the classical economists, neoclassical economists believe that population growth is not simply a matter of adjustments centered on the subsistence real wage rate.

Neoclassical economists argue that the most important economic influence on population growth is the *opportunity cost* to women for entering the workplace. As real wages for women rise and their job opportunities expand, the opportunity cost of staying home and raising children increases. As the opportunity cost of having children increases, birth rates decline, and population growth slows.

Don't forget that population growth is not only dependent on the birth rate; it is also a function of the death rate. Neoclassical economists argue that as technology advances and productivity increases, incomes rise and more is spent on healthcare. The increased spending on healthcare ultimately increases life expectancy, which causes population growth to increase.

As technology advances in a neoclassical world, both the birth rate and death rate decrease. As it turns out, these opposing economic forces on population growth essentially offset each other. *The bottom line is that population growth is independent of economic growth in the neoclassical model.*

Neoclassical economists argue that technology drives economic growth, but technological growth is not influenced by economic growth. Technological advances in a neoclassical framework occur through a process of trial and error. When the results of R&D are successful, technology grows rapidly. When R&D is not successful, the rate of technological growth slows.

A key assumption of neoclassical growth theory is that there is a **target rate of return** that people use as a benchmark when making their savings decisions. The target rate of return is represented in Figure 3 as the slope of the dashed straight lines labeled "target rate of return." The actual real interest rate at any point is the slope of the line tangent to the productivity curve at that point.

Figure 3: Neoclassical Growth Theory

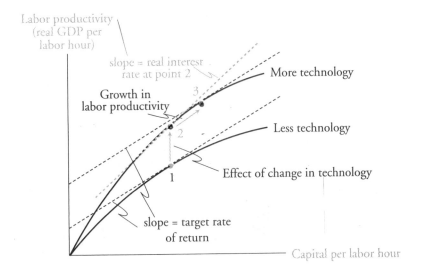

Professor's Note: Although this may seem a little confusing, remember that a return is basically income divided by invested capital. The slope of that line in Figure 3 is "real GDP per labor hour" divided by "capital per labor hour." You should recognize the result, real GDP divided by capital, as a form of a return measure.

Improvements in technology lead to an increase in labor productivity (the economy moves from Point 1 to Point 2 in Figure 3). Remember that the slope of the productivity curve at the point where the economy is operating is equal to the real rate of return. At Point 2, the real interest rate exceeds the target rate of return (i.e., the slope of the dashed blue line tangent to the curve at Point 2 is greater than the slope of the dashed black line). At that point, savings will be sufficient to support an increase in the growth of capital per labor hour. When this occurs, technology will advance, and new profit opportunities will be created. Existing business will expand, new business will be formed, and investment and savings will increase further. The economy will experience prosperity and growth in labor productivity (the economy moves from Point 2 to Point 3 in Figure 3).

Neoclassical economists believe that economic growth will decline if and only if technology stops advancing. *Unlike classical growth theory*, there is no population growth to slow economic growth.

The primary reason why technology may stop growing is because ultimately, real interest rates adjust. Initially, the high returns from technological change will increase savings and the accumulation of capital. Up to a point, capital accumulation supports further technological advances. However, capital accumulation eventually leads to diminishing returns, which lowers real interest rates. The lower real rates result in decreased savings and a decline in the rate of capital accumulation. Ultimately, technological growth declines and economic growth stops. In Figure 3, growth stops at Point 3, when the real interest rate is equal to the target rate of return.

New Growth Theory

New growth theory is based on two properties of market economies: (1) discoveries are the result of choices, and (2) discoveries lead to profit and competition eliminates profit.

New growth theory, like neoclassical growth theory, contends that the discovery of new products and techniques that lead to technological advancement is the result of luck. However, unlike the neoclassical theory, the rate at which discoveries are made depends on the number of people looking for new technologies and how large the incentive (i.e., the return on the investment) is to find them.

Competition threatens profits, and profits are what drive technological change, so there is an ongoing search to discover technologies that will increase profit by lowering costs, or produce better products that can be sold at higher prices.

There are two other assumptions that are important to new growth theory:

1. Discoveries are public capital goods.
2. The law of diminishing returns does not apply to knowledge capital.

A **public good** is a good that is available to everyone, and its use by one person does not restrict its use by others. The interstate highway system in the U.S. is an example of a public good.

Knowledge capital is also a public good. As the benefits of a new discovery become interwoven in a society, free resources become available to everyone. Knowledge is a free resource because it has no opportunity cost. That is, nothing must be sacrificed when it is used.

Knowledge capital is a special type of public good because it is not subject to the law of diminishing returns. In a production model, increasing the contribution of labor with a fixed amount of equipment will result in diminishing returns. Likewise, diminishing returns are realized when the amount of equipment is increased while holding labor constant. But, increasing knowledge capital makes both labor and equipment more productive.

The proposition that knowledge is not subject to the law of diminishing returns is a key element of new growth theory. The implication is that, unlike the classical or neoclassical growth theories, there is no mechanism to stop economic growth in a new growth theory framework. Under neoclassical theory, capital accumulation leads to decreased real interest rates, which stifles economic growth. To the contrary, under the new growth theory, a decrease in real interest rates will intensify peoples' incentive to discover new products and methods in order to earn higher profits. However, there is also an offsetting effect on real interest rates. As discovery occurs, real interest rates rise (and stay consistently above the target rate of return), and real GDP per labor hour grows indefinitely (from Point 1 to Point 2 to Point 3 in Figure 4).

Figure 4: New Growth Theory

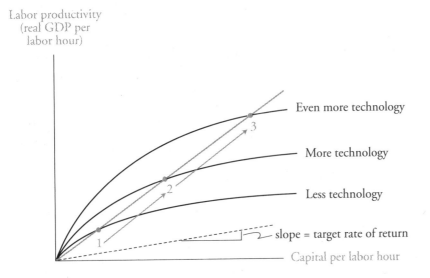

 Professor's Note: In Study Session 11, LOS 40.d, the new growth theory is called the endogenous growth model.

Notice in Figure 4 that, although the productivity curves exhibit diminishing returns to capital (where capital refers to physical capital, human capital, and technology), the new growth theory predicts that economic growth (growth in labor productivity) will equal growth in capital per labor hour.

The new growth theory describes the economy as a "perpetual motion economy," as shown in Figure 5. Innovation leads to new technologies and economic growth, which generate higher profits. The higher profits attract competition, which reduces profits. Lower profits provide the incentive to innovate in search of even newer technologies and more economic growth, and the cycle starts again.

Figure 5: New Growth Theory: The Perpetual Motion Economy

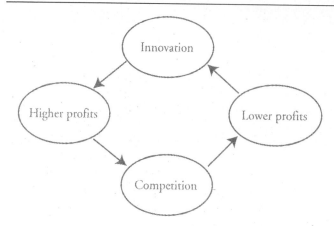

The key difference between the new growth theory and neoclassical theory is that neoclassical theory does not include the link between lower profits and the resulting incentive to innovate. Under the neoclassical model, lower profits do not provide an incentive for companies to innovate and develop new technologies.

KEY CONCEPTS

1. There are three social institutions that are preconditions to economic growth because they are critical to the development of incentives:
   - Market prices send information to buyers and sellers that give them the incentive to adjust the quantities they supply or demand.
   - Property rights are laws and regulations that govern ownership, use, and sale of goods, services, and factors of production.
   - Monetary exchange provides for the efficient exchange of goods and services.

2. Three activities are necessary to result in persistent economic growth:
   - Savings and investment in new capital increase labor productivity, which is defined as real GDP per labor hour. Saving and investment in new capital increases the level of capital per worker.
   - Investment in human capital is the investment in people's skills and knowledge, leading to productivity improvements and technological advances.
   - Discovery of new technologies contributes to sustained economic growth by making human capital and physical capital more productive.

3. The two factors that contribute to labor productivity growth (real GDP per labor hour) are growth in physical capital per labor hour and technological change.

4. Productivity curves are a plot of labor productivity (y-axis) against capital per labor hour (x-axis) at a given state of technology. Properties of productivity curves include:
   - Productivity increases as capital per labor hour increases, at a given state of technology. Growth in capital per labor hour causes movements along a productivity curve.
   - Productivity increases as the state of technology increases at any given level of capital per labor hour. Technological growth causes the productivity curve to shift upward.
   - Productivity curves exhibit the law of diminishing returns.

5. The "One-Third Rule" states that at a given level of technology, a 1% increase in capital per labor hour results in a one third of 1% increase in real GDP per labor hour. It can be used to decompose a change in productivity growth into two components attributable to:
   - Change in capital per labor hour.
   - Technological change.

6. Classical growth theory contends that growth in real GDP is temporary—real GDP per person rises above the subsistence level, a population explosion occurs, and GDP per person is driven back to the subsistence level.

7. Neoclassical growth theory holds that without technological change, no growth in real GDP will occur because changes in technology lead to increased saving and investment, which causes capital per labor hour to grow and the real rate of return to fall. When the real return falls to the target rate of return, economic growth stops. The main difference between the neoclassical theory and the classical theory is that neoclassical economists believe that population growth is independent of economic growth.

8. New growth theory argues that economic growth continues indefinitely as technology advances. This occurs because decreases in the real rate intensify the incentive to discover new products and methods, the discovery of which increases the real interest rate and keeps it above the target rate of return. According to the new growth theory, the economy is a perpetual motion machine: innovation leads to new technologies that produce higher profits; higher profits lead to competition, which reduces profits; the lower profits provide the incentive to innovate and develop even newer technologies.

CONCEPT CHECKERS

1. Which of the following is *least likely* to be associated with the incentive system that an economy must have as a precondition to experience economic growth?
   A. Human capital that promotes the discovery of new technologies.
   B. Markets that facilitate the exchange of information between buyers and sellers.
   C. Monetary exchange that facilitates the efficient exchange of goods and services.
   D. Property rights that govern the ownership, use, and exchange of physical and intellectual property.

2. Which of the following is *least likely* to be associated with the law of diminishing returns?
   A. Investment in labor.
   B. Investment in knowledge capital.
   C. Productivity curves.
   D. Investment in physical capital.

3. Which of the following is *most* closely associated with the classical theory of economic growth?
   A. A target rate of return.
   B. A subsistence real wage.
   C. Increased spending on health care.
   D. The opportunity cost of raising children.

4. Between 1965 and 1979, labor productivity increased from $12 per labor hour to $12.84 per labor hour. Over the same period, investment in new capital increased from $30 per labor hour to $31.05 per labor hour. The contribution of the increased investment in new capital and technological advancement toward economic growth over this period are *closest* to:

	Investment in new capital	Technological advancement
A.	1.17%	5.83%
B.	5.83%	1.17%
C.	5.83%	5.83%
D.	1.17%	1.17%

5. Which of the following *most accurately* represents a general property of a labor productivity curve?
   A. Movement along a productivity curve is caused by a change in capital per labor hour, holding all else constant.
   B. A shift in a labor productivity curve is caused by a change in capital per labor hour, holding all else constant.
   C. Movement along a labor productivity curve is caused by technological advancement, holding all else constant.
   D. A shift in a labor productivity curve is caused by a change in the population growth rate, holding technology constant.

6. Are the new growth and neoclassical growth theories supported by the premise that knowledge capital is **NOT** subject to the law of diminishing returns?

	New growth theory	Neoclassical growth theory
A.	Yes	Yes
B.	Yes	No
C.	No	Yes
D.	No	No

7. The two economic factors that are *most* important to the new theory of economic growth are:
    A. population growth and real interest rates.
    B. investment in new capital and real interest rates.
    C. the creation of knowledge capital and real interest rates.
    D. investment in health care and technological advancement.

CHALLENGE PROBLEMS

8. Refer to Figure 3, Neoclassical Growth Theory, from the topic review to answer this question. Assume that the target rate of return is 10%. What are the *most likely* values for the real interest rate at:

	Point 2?	Point 3?
A.	10%	15%
B.	10%	10%
C.	15%	10%
D.	15%	15%

9. Refer to Figure 3, Neoclassical Growth Theory, from the topic review to answer this question. What are the *most likely* values for growth in real GDP per labor hour at:

	Point 2?	Point 3?
A.	3%	3%
B.	3%	0%
C.	0%	3%
D.	0%	0%

10. Refer to Figure 4, New Growth Theory, from the topic review to answer this question. What are the *most likely* values for growth in real GDP per labor hour at:

	Point 2?	Point 3?
A.	3%	3%
B.	3%	0%
C.	0%	3%
D.	0%	0%

ANSWERS – CONCEPT CHECKERS

1. **A.** The three institutions that are critical to the development incentives that promote economic growth are markets, property rights, and monetary exchange. With these institutions in place, investment in human capital can lead to economic growth.

2. **B** Knowledge capital is a special type of public good that is not subject to the law of diminishing returns. Investment in labor and physical capital do exhibit diminishing returns, which are reflected in the shape of the productivity curve.

3. **B** Classical growth theory contends that growth in real GDP is temporary. Whenever real wages rise above the subsistence real wage, a population explosion occurs, and GDP per person is driven back to the subsistence level.

4. **A** According to the "One-Third Rule," at a given level of technology, a 1% increase in capital per labor hour results in a 1/3% increase in real GDP per labor hour. The percent change in capital per labor hour is 3.5% = (31.05/30) – 1. The increase in productivity due to the increase in capital per labor hour is 1/3 × 3.5% = 1.17%. Economic growth (growth in GDP per labor hour) is 7% = (12.84/12.00) – 1. The remainder of the increase in GDP per labor hour, 7% – 1.17% = 5.83%, is due to technology change.

5. **A** Productivity (GDP per labor hour) increases as capital per labor hour increases, at a given state of technology, resulting in movement along a productivity curve. Productivity increases as the state of technology increases at any given level of capital per labor hour, resulting in a shift in the productivity curve. Population growth is only relevant to economic growth under the classical theory, and will not result in a shift in a productivity curve.

6. **B** The idea that knowledge is not subject to the law of diminishing returns is the underpinning of new growth theory. The implication of this is that, unlike the neoclassical growth theory, there is no mechanism to stop economic growth.

7. **C** The new growth theory argues that productivity growth is a function of society's ability to discover new products and methods (i.e., the creation of knowledge capital) and real interest rates. A key part of new growth theory is that knowledge is not subject to the law of diminishing returns.

ANSWERS – CHALLENGE PROBLEMS

8. **C** According to the neoclassical growth theory, the real interest rate is equal to the slope of the line tangent to the productivity curve. At Point 2, the real interest rate is greater than the target rate of return (which is assumed to be 10%), while at Point 3, the real interest rate and the target rate of return are equal. Therefore, only Choice C is consistent with the 10% target rate of return.

9. **B** At Point 2, the real interest rate is greater than the target rate of return, so savings are sufficient to support an increase in the growth of capital per labor hour. When this occurs, technology will advance, new profit opportunities will be created, and investment and savings will increase further. As a result, labor productivity (real GDP per labor hour) will experience growth, so the growth rate must be greater than 0% at Point 2.

At Point 3, real interest rates adjust to the level of the target rate of return, capital accumulation stops, and the growth rate falls to 0%.

Only Choice B is consistent with a positive growth rate at Point 2 and a zero growth rate at Point 3.

10. **A**   Under the new growth theory as depicted in Figure 4, real GDP per labor hour will grow indefinitely at a positive rate because the real interest rate is consistently above the target rate of return. Only Choice A is consistent with a positive growth rate at both Point 2 and Point 3.

The following is a review of the Economics for Valuation principles designed to address the learning outcome statements set forth by CFA Institute®. This topic is also covered in:

REGULATION AND ANTITRUST POLICY IN A GLOBALIZED ECONOMY

Study Session 4

EXAM FOCUS

This topic review addresses the issue of how governments can influence a country's future economic growth through its regulation of certain industries. There is an important link to the global industry analysis material in Study Session 11. Analysis of heavily regulated industries requires an understanding of the economic analysis of government regulation. Focus your attention on the positive and negative effects of regulation on companies, industries, countries, and society as a whole.

WARM-UP: NATURAL MONOPOLIES

Natural monopolies occur when a single firm has the capacity to produce all of an industry's output at the lowest per-unit cost. This arises in industries where economies of large-scale production prevail, such as the electric utilities industry. Smaller, less efficient producers have higher long-run average costs, resulting in the most efficient producer emerging and dominating the industry. A monopolist will produce at a rate where marginal revenue equals its marginal cost and will charge the highest price that consumers are willing to pay for the quantity produced. This results in an inefficient market, because producers will charge (and consumers must pay) a higher price in a monopolistic market than they otherwise would in a competitive market.

Consider the following two scenarios: a natural monopolist operating in a completely unregulated market and the same monopolist operating in a highly regulated market. As stated earlier, a natural monopolist operating in an unregulated industry will charge the highest price that consumers are willing to pay. The end result is that consumers buy less of the product than they otherwise would in a competitive market. This is an economically inefficient allocation of resources because the price charged is higher than the opportunity cost to society.

In the second scenario, the government would force the natural monopolist to produce at an output level where price equals marginal cost. This would result in the value received by the consumer from the marginal unit to be equal to the marginal cost to society. The consequence of this approach is that the producers' average cost is greater than the price permitted to be charged, creating an economic loss for the producer. Sustaining losses over time would ultimately lead the producer to exit the industry. Therefore, as a practical matter, regulators of natural monopolies attempt to set their prices at a level where price is equal to long-run average cost. At this point, the average cost would include a profit component for the producer.

ECONOMIC REGULATION

LOS 15.a: Discuss the objectives of regulation and the concepts of cost-of-service regulation and rate-of-return regulation.

Government regulation can be categorized as either economic or social regulation:

- **Economic regulation** includes the regulation of natural monopolies and the regulation of competitive industries.
- **Social regulation** involves regulation across all industries.

One of the main objectives of economic regulation is for the controlling entity (i.e., governmental agency) to be able to dictate an industry-wide pricing policy for the firms within the industry. This serves a dual purpose: to prevent both excessive monopoly profits and predatory competitive practices.

The two prevalent methods of economic regulation of natural monopolies are cost-of-service regulation and rate-of-return regulation.

- **Cost-of-service regulation** involves the establishment of a pricing policy which sets the maximum price firms are permitted to charge customers, based upon industry-wide average costs to produce the product or service.
- **Rate-of-return regulation** permits producers and service providers in the regulated industry to establish their own prices, so long as those prices do not provide excessive returns to the producers/providers.

SOCIAL REGULATION

LOS 15.b: Discuss the benefits of social regulation.

Social regulation is a more qualitative, less quantitative concept than the economic regulation of natural monopolies that is applicable to all industries. It is based upon a wide variety of goals such as product quality, product safety, and the safety of employees in the workplace. In the United States, many regulatory agencies operate in specific industries and also on behalf of various interest groups. For example, the Food and Drug Administration (FDA) operates to ensure that U.S. consumers have safe food, drugs, and cosmetic products. Another U.S. regulatory body, the Environmental Protection Agency (EPA), was established to ensure that industries balance environmental concerns with their operating practices.

In almost all instances, increased regulation results in higher production costs, and those incremental costs are ultimately absorbed by the consumer. In addition, higher levels of regulation may have an unintended, negative impact on competition within an industry, because compliance with regulations may impose a disproportionately larger expense on smaller firms than on larger firms, thus negatively affecting their profitability.

However, the benefits of social regulation, although difficult to quantify, can be far-reaching and can positively affect society for years to come. Safer products, safer workplaces, and a cleaner environment are some of the positive outcomes of social regulation. The debate over the merits of social regulation typically focuses on the appropriate extent of the regulation and the accompanying complexity of the cost-benefit analysis, and not whether a governing body should utilize regulation at all.

EFFECTS OF REGULATION

LOS 15.c: Analyze negative side effects of regulation.

Firms subject to regulation (that will raise their costs of production and lower their profitability) may attempt to avoid the regulation or minimize the costs. A firm can conform to the letter, but not the intent, of the regulation through what is referred to as a **creative response**. For example, consider a law that requires employers in an industry to equally consider all qualified applicants for open positions within the firm, regardless of the applicants' gender, age or race. A firm may conform to the law by granting interviews to all applicants, but only extending job offers to men. In this instance, the firm may conform to the law by granting interviews to women, but not the intent of the law by only making job offers to men.

A **feedback effect** is a typical example of a creative response to regulation. It occurs when consumers' behavior is changed as a result of the new regulation. An example of a feedback effect would be if regulators required that automobiles utilize fuel more efficiently, consumers in turn may become less diligent in their effort to conserve fuel and drive more because their cost to drive per mile has decreased. The effect is to undermine the original intent of the regulation, which was to reduce fuel consumption.

LOS 15.d: Distinguish between the different types of regulators' behavior.

Regulators are selected and compensated by the applicable governing entity (i.e., federal or state government). In theory, regulators' actions are not influenced by the market or any of its participants. In reality, this is not always the case. There are two predominant theories of regulators' behavior that can help explain how regulation has at times both helped and harmed the consumer.

The **capture hypothesis** is based upon the assumption that, regardless of the original purpose behind its establishment, a regulatory body will, at some point in time, be influenced or even possibly controlled by the industry that is being regulated. The rationale behind the theory is that regulators will be selected from among the available pool of industry "experts" (people who have experience in the industry). Although no longer directly employed in the industry, these "experts," in their new roles as regulators, still have contacts and relationships with those in the industry, thus affecting the regulators' ability to render impartial decisions.

An additional bias in favor of industry participants is the fact that at a regulatory hearing, interested consumers and taxpayers will almost certainly be at a disadvantage to the opposing party, members of the industry. With a greater financial position at stake, industry participants are motivated to spend more resources to be better prepared at a regulatory hearing than the group of affected consumers, thus able to present a more persuasive argument to the regulators who are responsible for establishing the industry standards. Under the capture theory, only the interests of the industry participants are of concern to the regulatory agency.

The **share-the-gains, share-the-pains theory** is based upon the assumption that regulators will strive to satisfy all three interested parties: the legislators, the customers, and the regulated firms themselves. In contrast to the capture hypothesis, under this theory the regulators are not completely captured by the regulated firm; instead, regulators consider the consequences of their decisions from the standpoint of each of the three affected parties. For example, suppose an industry experiences a sudden and unexpected increase in fuel costs, which increases the cost of production. The share-the-gains, share-the-pains theory would predict that regulators would allow the regulated industry to pass along only part of the cost increase, and then only gradually over time. In the same scenario, the capture theory would anticipate that regulators would permit producers in the industry to pass through the bulk of the higher costs to consumers (or as much as consumers can tolerate) in a shorter period of time.

LOS 15.e: Discuss the cost of regulation and the effects of deregulation.

Although beneficial to society as a whole, increased regulation clearly causes higher costs of production for the regulated industry, which in turn leads to higher prices for the end consumer. However, it is generally agreed upon that there is no precise way to accurately assess the cost of regulation, although the general consensus is that it is large relative to the size of the total economy. The high cost of regulation has led to the discussion of **deregulation**, or the removal of existing regulations, among legislators and consumers alike.

There have been numerous proposals over the last 30 years to deregulate those U.S. industries that have, because of existing regulatory measures, little room for price competition or new entrants to the industry. Industries that have experienced varying degrees of deregulation include the airlines, financial institutions, and public utilities, such as natural gas and electricity.

The short-run effects of deregulation are typically negative and will differ based upon the industry's characteristics and the extent of the shift in regulation. Higher-cost producers may exit as excess profits decrease. Workers may be laid off or furloughed as a new production equilibrium is established. Consumers may experience a decrease in the quality of service or products they had formerly received, possibly in addition to increased prices. Unions will no longer experience the same level of stature in a less regulated environment. Some companies may go bankrupt, which displaces workers and negatively affects the communities in which companies operate.

In spite of these possible short-run negative impacts, deregulation has many positive, long-run benefits associated with it. Prices should eventually fall to the producers' marginal costs of production. Industries will become more competitive, because government-imposed barriers to entry will no longer discourage new entrants into the market. An increase in market participants will cause pricing to become more competitive.

According to the **theory of contestable markets**, if an industry's barriers to entry and exit are relatively low, the number of firms in an industry is not a determinant in whether consumers pay competitive prices. A contestable market will operate efficiently because any excess industry profits will induce new entrants into the market. Prices will be forced down to a level that will eliminate excess profits. Only those companies that can operate efficiently will be able to remain in the market.

KEY CONCEPTS

1. The main objective of economic regulation is to control the prices that the regulated firms are permitted to charge. Cost-of-service regulation requires the producers in the regulated industry to charge prices based upon the actual average cost of producing the product or providing the service to the consumer. Rate-of-return regulation permits producers in the regulated industry to formulate pricing policies that provide a competitive rate of return on their investment with no opportunities to earn a positive economic profit.

2. Social regulation is applicable to all industries, and its benefits include industry-wide improvements in such areas as product quality, product safety, and the safety of employees in the workplace.

3. There can be unintended negative effects of regulation, such as members of a regulated industry attempting to circumvent full compliance with the regulation, or the unforeseen consequences of consumers modifying their behavior in response to a regulation.

4. The capture hypothesis is based upon the assumption that regardless of the reason why a regulatory agency was established, it will eventually be influenced or "captured" by the industry that is being regulated. The share-the-gains, share-the-pains theory is based upon the assumption that regulators will strive to satisfy all three interested parties: the legislators, the customers, and the regulated firms themselves.

5. Although beneficial in many ways, increased regulation leads to higher costs of production for the regulated industry, which in turn leads to higher prices for the end consumer. The total cost of regulation is difficult to quantify. Deregulation typically has negative effects in the short term, but the long-run benefits include better service, more product variety, and lower costs.

CONCEPT CHECKERS

1. A regulatory commission that requires firms in the industry to charge prices that are close to the actual average costs of production is utilizing which of the following methods of regulation?
    A. Rate-of-return regulation.
    B. Cost-of-service regulation.
    C. Average cost regulation.
    D. Social regulation.

    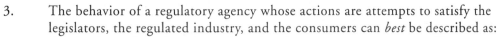

2. The main purpose of economic regulation by a government is to:
    A. encourage increased competition within an industry.
    B. promote higher product quality, increased product safety, and safer workplace conditions.
    C. preserve the profitability of existing industry participants.
    D. control the prices that regulated companies are allowed to charge.

3. The behavior of a regulatory agency whose actions are attempts to satisfy the legislators, the regulated industry, and the consumers can *best* be described as:
    A. the share-the-gains, share-the-pains theory.
    B. the feedback effect.
    C. the capture hypothesis.
    D. social regulation.

4. The *best* example of a *likely* long-term benefit to society of deregulation is:
    A. an increase in the power of unions in the deregulated industry.
    B. a shake out of higher-cost producers.
    C. lower prices that are closer to the producers' marginal cost.
    D. an increase in monopoly profits in the industry.

CHALLENGE PROBLEMS

Use the following data to answer Questions 5 and 6.

The Environmental Protection Agency (EPA), a U.S. regulatory agency that develops and enforces environmental standards, has recently imposed a new restriction on the tire industry, requiring that new tires produced in the U.S. utilize 20% more renewable resources than previously required.

5. The new government regulation is *most appropriately* classified as an example of:
    A. the capture hypothesis, because several high-ranking officials of the EPA are former environmental lobbyists.
    B. social regulation, because its primary goal is for a better quality of life through a less polluted environment.
    C. economic regulation, because higher-cost producers will be forced to exit the industry.
    D. rate of return regulation, because industry participants will still achieve a normal, competitive rate of return.

6. Tire Empire, a leading U.S. manufacturer of tires, decides to move its manufacturing operations abroad, which will decrease its production costs by significantly more than its increased distribution costs. Tire Empire's strategy is *best* described as:
    A. creative response.
    B. capture hypothesis.
    C. feedback effect.
    D. deregulation.

ANSWERS – CONCEPT CHECKERS

1. **B** Cost-of-service regulation establishes pricing policies for the industry based upon the actual average costs of the products or services.

2. **D** Economic regulation seeks to prevent both monopoly profits and predatory competition by controlling prices charged to consumers.

3. **A** A regulator that attempts to distribute the burden of regulation upon the three main interested parties is acting in accordance with the share-the-gains, share-the-pains theory.

4. **C** In the short term, price may temporarily increase as the market seeks a new level of equilibrium. However, a long-term benefit is that increased competition will decrease monopoly profits and drive prices down toward the producers' marginal cost.

ANSWERS – CHALLENGE PROBLEMS

5. **B** The most obvious goal of the regulation would be to conserve natural resources, which would align most closely with social regulation's focus on a better quality of life.

6. **A** Tire Empire is technically complying with the law by simply moving its manufacturing operations out of the U.S. However, the move undermines the spirit of the law by not utilizing a greater amount of renewable resources, which would benefit the environment in the U.S. as well as globally.

The following is a review of the Economics for Valuation principles designed to address the learning outcome statements set forth by CFA Institute®. This topic is also covered in:

TRADING WITH THE WORLD

Study Session 4

EXAM FOCUS

This topic was in the Level 1 curriculum last year and was moved to Level 2 for the 2008 season. You should understand the principle of comparative advantage as that is the basis of the case for free trade. Make sure you understand the difference between the effects of tariffs and the effects of quotas, and how restrictions on trade in general decrease the wealth of a country. Know who gains and who loses from trade restrictions and that trade restrictions are considered to be primarily driven by the political activity of those who stand to gain from specific trade restrictions.

THE GAINS FROM INTERNATIONAL TRADE

LOS 16.a: Discuss opportunity cost associated with trade, how countries can gain from international trade, how countries determine whether to import, export, or produce goods and services, and explain the gains of trade for all parties.

Comparative advantage refers to the lowest *opportunity cost* to produce a product.

The **law of comparative advantage** holds that *trading partners can be made better off if they specialize* in the production of goods for which they are the low-opportunity-cost producer (have a comparative advantage) and trade for those goods for which they are the high-opportunity-cost producer. A country gains (i.e., it realizes expanded consumption possibilities) from international trade when it *exports* those goods for which it has a comparative advantage and *imports* those goods for which it does *not*.

An example will illustrate the gains from trade in terms of expanded consumption opportunities for two countries. Figures 1 and 2 show the production possibility frontiers (PPF) for two countries, Alton and Borton, for two generic goods, food and machinery.

©2008 Schweser

Figure 1: Production Possibility Frontier for Alton

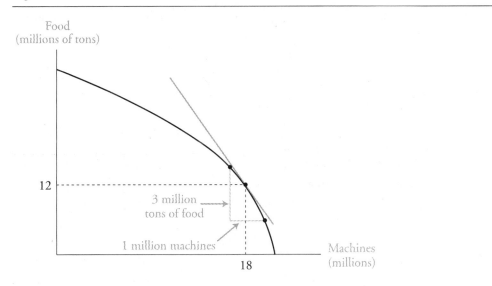

Figure 2: Production Possibility Frontier for Borton

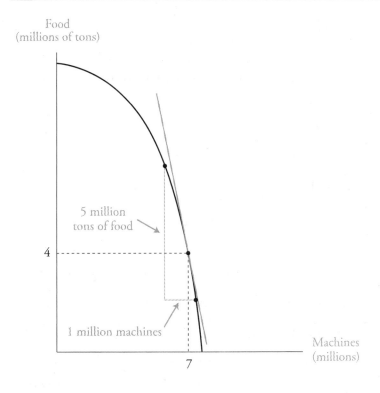

Without trade, Alton chooses to produce 12 million tons of food and 18 million units of machinery, while Borton chooses to produce 4 million tons of food and 7 million machines. The slope of the each country's PPF at its chosen production point represents the opportunity cost of food in terms of machinery. Given their possible production levels of the two goods, the opportunity cost of producing a unit of one good can be expressed in terms of how many units of the other good they must give up to produce it.

For Alton, the opportunity cost of producing another million units of machinery is 3 million tons of food, while for Borton, the opportunity cost of producing another million units of machinery is 5 million tons of food. The opportunity costs of food are simply the reciprocals of these amounts. For Alton, the opportunity cost of producing another million tons of food is 1/3 million units of machinery, and for Borton, the opportunity cost of producing another million tons of food is 1/5 million units of machinery. We say that Alton has a comparative advantage in the production of (the lowest opportunity cost of producing) machinery and that Borton has a comparative advantage in the production of food. If one country has a lower opportunity cost of producing one good, the other country must have a comparative advantage in the production of the other good in our simple example. Next we will show that, as long as their opportunity costs of production differ, trade will allow both countries to consume more than they can without trade.

Since Alton has a comparative advantage in the production of machinery, it will be advantageous for Alton to produce more machinery and to trade with Borton for food. For example, Alton could produce 2 million more units of machinery and 6 million tons less food. Borton could produce 6 million more tons of food and, given that their opportunity cost of a million tons of food is 1/5 of a million units of machinery, produce 1.2 million fewer units of machinery.

Professor's Note: I realize these are not realistic trade-offs because the PPFs are curved and we're using the approximate slope (trade-off) at a point. The results would be qualitatively the same if we used 6 tons of food and 1.2 units of machinery in our examples. Using these smaller amounts, the curvature of the PPF would not be significant, and the slope would be an accurate estimate of the actual trade-off in production.

The table in Figure 3 illustrates the total output of both countries with and without specialization and trade.

Figure 3: Gain From Trade

	Without Trade		*With Trade*	
	Machinery	*Food*	*Machinery*	*Food*
Alton	18 million	12 million tons	20 million	6 million tons
Borton	7 million	4 million tons	5.8 million	10 million tons
Total	25 million	16 million tons	25.8 million	16 million tons

When each country specializes in the good for which they have a comparative advantage and trades with the other, there are clear gains in our example. Total food production can remain at 16 million tons while the total output of machinery is increased by 0.8 million units. Alton will export machinery, since they are the low (opportunity) cost producer of machinery, and import food from Borton. Borton has a comparative advantage in the production of food, and will export food to Alton and import Alton-produced machinery.

How the gains from specialization and trade will be shared between the two countries is not determined here, but clearly there is a possible exchange that will allow both countries to enjoy a combination of food and machinery that they could not reach on their own without trade. In terms of our PPF graphs, each country can consume at a point *outside* its PPF through specialization and trade. That's the important point here, as long as opportunity costs differ, two countries can both benefit from trade.

WARM UP: CONSUMER AND PRODUCER SURPLUS

Recall from Level 1 that the consumer surplus is the difference between the total value to consumers of the quantity of a good or service consumed and the total amount consumers pay for that production. The producer surplus is the difference between the total cost of producing the output of a good or service and the total amount received for that output. The equilibrium quantity produced and consumed in well-functioning unregulated competitive markets is the quantity for which the sum of consumer surplus and producer surplus is maximized. This point is illustrated in Figure 4.

Figure 4: Consumer and Producer Surplus

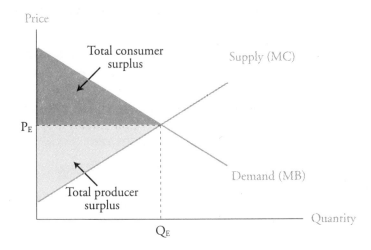

BARRIERS TO TRADE

LOS 16.b: Compare and contrast tariffs, non-tariff barriers, quotas, and voluntary export restraints with respect to international trade.

Although the gains from trade are very apparent, countries erect barriers to trade, including tariffs and quotas, and sometimes impose voluntary export restraints (VER).

Tariffs

A *tariff* is a tax imposed on imported goods while a *quota* is a limitation on the quantity of goods imported.

Tariffs benefit domestic producers because the level of imports will be reduced due to an effective increase in the price of the good. For example, if the world price of semiconductors is $40, and domestic producers can only profitably meet domestic semiconductor demand at a price of $45, foreign producers have a comparative advantage. Hence, domestic producers will not be able to compete in their own domestic semiconductor market. However, if the government places a $10 tariff on imported semiconductors, domestic producers will become competitive with foreign producers in the domestic market, and domestic semiconductor production will rise compared to the level of production without tariffs. Tariffs will also benefit the government, because it will collect the $10 tax (tariff) on all foreign semiconductors sold in the domestic market.

In Figure 5, without trade restrictions the equilibrium price is $45/ton and the equilibrium quantity is 90 million tons. With the imposition of a tariff of $20/ton, the supply curve shifts up by the amount of the tariff to "S + tariff." The equilibrium price paid by domestic consumers increases to $60/ton and the quantity imported decreases to 75 million tons. The amount of the tariff revenue is the tariff ($20/ton) times the quantity imported (75 million tons). Note that the gains from trade (equal to the sum of producer and consumer surplus) are reduced by more than the amount of the tariff revenue. While the tariff revenue is collected by the domestic government, the triangle of the lost gains from trade in excess of the tariff revenues represents a loss in the overall value produced by the exchange of goods and is a deadweight loss.

Figure 5: Effects of a Tariff

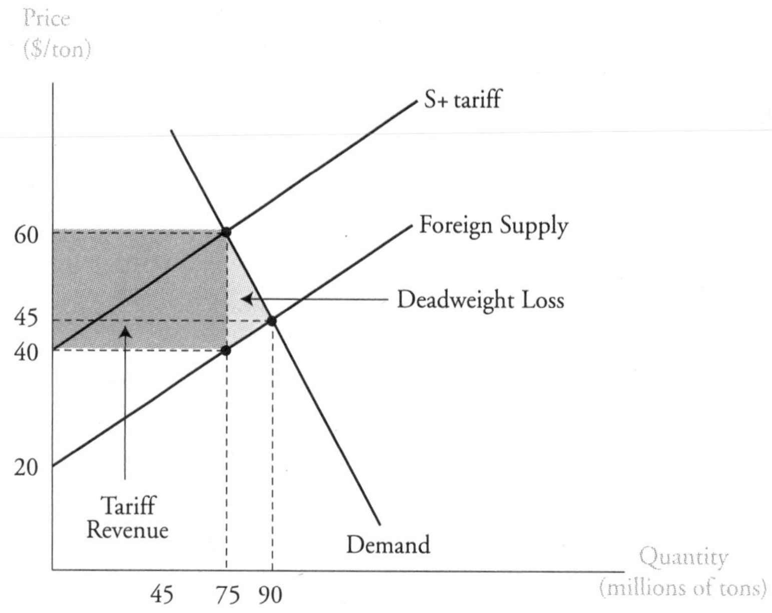

Quotas

A quota has an effect very similar to that of a tariff. Under a quota system, importers in the domestic country are given licenses to import specific amounts of a foreign-produced good. The supply of imported goods is reduced, and a lower supply means a higher price and reduction in the equilibrium domestic quantity. Clearly, domestic producers benefit from the quota because competition from foreign producers is reduced.

In Figure 6 we illustrate the effects of a quota. In order to illustrate the difference between the effects of a quota and an equivalent tariff, we have set the quota amount equal to 75 million tons, the equilibrium quantity exchanged when there is a $20 tariff (Figure 5). With the supply fixed at the quota amount of 75 million tons, the equilibrium price is $60/ton, as with the $20 tariff. Wealth is transferred from domestic consumers (lost consumer surplus) to those producers with allocations of some of the quota amount. The deadweight loss is the same with the quota and with the tariff, the price paid by domestic consumers is the same with the quota and with the tariff, but the revenue under the tariff collected by the domestic government is now part of foreign producer surplus. Those that gain the right to export some of the quota amount have received a valuable right. The way in which export amounts are allocated among foreign producers will determine who gets these gains in producer surplus.

Figure 6: Effects of a Quota

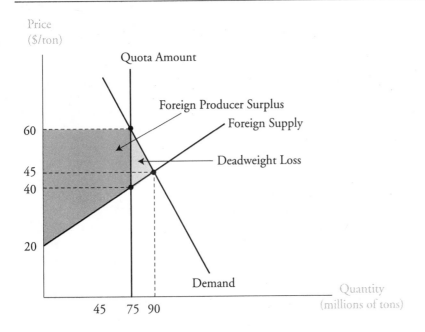

Voluntary export restraints (VER) are agreements by exporting countries to voluntarily limit the quantity of goods they will export to an importing country. The primary difference between VERs and quotas is that the gains that accrue to those with import licenses under a quota system are received by the firms in the exporting countries that hold export permits under a VER system. It is probably common that the foreign government officials who determine which exporters get permits find ways to receive some of the value of these licenses.

REASONS FOR TRADE RESTRICTIONS

LOS 16.c: Discuss the advantages and disadvantages of protection for each party, and explain the main reasons for trade restriction.

It is reasonable at this point to ask why trade restrictions are as common as they are, given that free trade appears to offer societal gains to all countries. While trade restrictions have fallen over recent decades, they are still prevalent and significant in such products as sugar, textiles, footwear, meat, and metals, among others.

The primary forces underlying trade restrictions are twofold. Governments like tariff revenue, and domestic producers affected by lower-cost imports use political means to gain protection from foreign competition. In developing countries, the ability to collect income tax revenue is restricted by both the lack of financial records and problems of compliance. This makes tariff revenue an attractive alternative.

In theory, the benefits of free trade could be used to compensate domestic producers that lose as a result of free trade. This, however, is problematic and seldom done. The affected parties, such as domestic steel producers and steel workers or domestic textile manufacturers and textile workers, have a strong incentive to use their votes and political contributions to gain protection in the form of tariffs, quotas, or voluntary export restraints.

A variety of arguments are made for trade restrictions to hide the reality that they are imposed to benefit one group at the expense of the entire economy and its citizens. Whether they are defended on the basis of saving jobs, protecting workers from competition with low-wage countries, temporarily protecting a developing "infant" industry, lower environmental protection standards in exporting countries, or preventing the "exploitation" of less-developed countries, most economists agree that trade restrictions benefit specific groups at the expense of the whole economy.

Some arguments commonly made to support trade restrictions that have some support among economists are:

- *Developing industries (infant industries) should be protected while they get up to world standards of productivity and quality.* There are two problems with this argument. First, the benefits of a developing industry mainly accrue to the firms and workers in those industries and not to the overall population. Second, it is argued that a government subsidy to the industry as it develops would be a much more economically efficient way to gain any benefits that are expected to accrue to the whole economy when the industry becomes globally competitive.
- *Exporters should be prohibited from selling goods abroad at less than production cost (anti-dumping argument).* It is difficult to estimate production costs, and just the fact that a foreign firm sells at a lower price in the export market than in its own domestic market is not evidence of dumping as it is usually defined. Even if a foreign firm managed to drive domestic firms out of business, there could still be foreign competition from other countries, and domestic firms could re-enter the business if the foreign firm subsequently raised prices.
- *Industries associated with national defense should be protected by trade restrictions so they will exist domestically in case of war.* One problem with this argument is that it is hard to find an industry that does not contribute, or cannot potentially contribute, to national defense. From an economic efficiency perspective, it is better for the government to subsidize strategic industries judged essential to national defense directly, rather than impose costs on all domestic consumers by imposing trade restrictions.

Other arguments for trade restrictions that have very little support among economists are:

- *Trade barriers protect jobs.* Part of the popularity of trade restrictions stems from their ability to protect easily identifiable jobs and the high wage levels in these jobs. Tariffs or quotas on imported steel will protect domestic steelworkers' jobs and benefit domestic steel producers. However, in the long run, trade restrictions cannot protect the *net* number of jobs in the country. The number of jobs protected by import restrictions will be offset by jobs lost in other industries in general (that would sell less because more is spent on higher-priced imported goods) and in the import/export industry. Import/export firms will be unable to sell the overpriced domestic product abroad or import and sell the lower-priced, restricted foreign-made product.

- *Trade restrictions create jobs.* In the short run maybe, but in the long run, no. First of all, trade restrictions prevent your trading partners from developing the purchasing power needed to buy import goods from you, thus depressing your own export industry. Secondly, the higher price of the protected domestic goods dampens domestic aggregate purchasing power, taking sales away from other domestic products. Finally, some jobs that would have been created in the import industry are never created.

- *Trade with low-wage countries depresses wage rates in high-wage countries.* The belief that trading with low-wage countries depresses wages is based on a misunderstanding of the law of comparative advantage. A high hourly wage does not necessarily mean high per-unit labor costs. Labor productivity must be considered. The worker's skill level, the amount of invested capital, and production methods may produce labor costs per unit of output below those found in low-wage countries. Consider the law of comparative advantage. When each country produces goods for which it has a comparative advantage, both countries will benefit. High-wage countries will have an advantage in high-tech manufacturing, and low-wage countries will have an advantage in labor-intensive goods. When both produce the goods in which they have a comparative advantage, total output and the availability of goods will increase.

In summary, tariffs benefit domestic producers, workers in protected industries, and governments, at the expense of domestic consumers and workers outside the protected industry. Quotas benefit domestic producers, workers in protected industries, and those with import licenses, at the expense of domestic consumers and workers outside the protected industry. VERs benefit domestic producers, workers in protected industries, and those with export licenses or the power to grant them, at the expense of domestic consumers and workers outside the protected industry.

KEY CONCEPTS

1. If two countries have different opportunity costs of producing goods, each will have a comparative advantage in some goods, and trade will increase the total production and consumption possibilities in both countries, improving economic welfare.

2. International trade will tend to increase domestic supply as imports are available and increase domestic demand because exports will be possible.

3. Tariffs are taxes on imports. Quotas restrict physical amounts of imports by granting import licenses. Voluntary export restraints are agreements by exporting countries to limit exports to an importing country. An exporting country gives export licenses for specific quantities to its exporting firms.

4. Trade barriers reduce the possible consumption for a country's citizens.

5. Tariffs benefit domestic producers, workers in protected industries, and government, at the expense of domestic consumers.

6. Quotas benefit domestic producers, workers in protected industries, and import license holders, at the expense of domestic consumers.

7. Voluntary export restraints benefit domestic producers, workers in protected industries, and export license holders, at the expense of domestic consumers.

8. In general, trade restrictions arise from a desire by government for tariff revenue and from economically motivated political activity by the domestic groups who will gain from protection from foreign competition.

9. Of the reasons commonly used to support trade restrictions, national defense arguments, infant industry arguments, and anti-dumping arguments may have some validity, but the goals of maintaining these industries are likely reached in a more economically efficient manner by direct government subsidy than by imposing costs on all domestic consumers and the entire economy.

10. Other arguments for trade restrictions are not supported by economic theory.

CONCEPT CHECKERS

1. Which of the following statements about international trade is *least accurate*? If two countries have different opportunity costs of production for two goods, by engaging in trade:
    A. both countries can increase their total consumption.
    B. each country gains by importing the good for which it has a comparative advantage.
    C. each country can achieve a level of consumption outside its domestic production possibility frontier.
    D. the low opportunity cost producer of each good will export to the high opportunity cost producer of that good.

2. The *least likely* result of import quotas and voluntary export restraints is:
    A. increased revenue for the government.
    B. a decrease in the quantity of imports of the product.
    C. an increase in the domestic price of the product.
    D. a shift in production toward higher-cost suppliers.

3. Consider the following statements about the imposition of trade restrictions.

    Statement 1: Trade restrictions are needed to ensure the existence of industries needed for national defense and to protect developing industries until they grow to a competitive size.

    Statement 2: Developing industries should be protected until they become competitive and trade restrictions will prevent trade with low-wage countries from depressing the wages of high-wage trading partners.

    Do economists generally support:

	Statement 1?	Statement 2?
A.	Yes	Yes
B.	Yes	No
C.	No	Yes
D.	No	No

4. Which of the following groups would be *most* harmed by the imposition of a tariff on steel imports?
    A. Domestic steel producers.
    B. The national government.
    C. Workers in the domestic auto industry.
    D. Workers in the domestic steel industry.

ANSWERS – CONCEPT CHECKERS

1. **B** Each country gains by *exporting* the good for which it has a comparative advantage.

2. **A** Import quotas and voluntary export restraints, unlike tariffs, do not generate tax revenue. The other choices describe effects that result from all trade restrictions, including tariffs, quotas, and VERs.

3. **B** Economists generally support Statement 1. Trade restrictions (1) to ensure the existence of industries producing goods important to national defense, (2) to offer temporary protection of developing industries, and (3) to prevent countries from exporting products at less than their production costs, all have more support among economists than other arguments put forward as reasons for restricting trade. It can be argued, however, that direct subsidies to such industries would be a more efficient way to achieve these ends than restricting trade.

   Economists generally do not support Statement 2 because it contains the argument that trade with low-wage countries depresses wages in the home country.

4. **C** Imposing a tariff on steel imports benefits domestic steel producers and workers by increasing the domestic price of steel, and benefits the national government by increasing tax (tariff) revenue. However, the increase in the domestic price of steel would increase costs in industries that use significant amounts of steel, such as the automobile industry. The resulting increase in the price of automobiles reduces the quantity of automobiles demanded and ultimately reduces employment in that industry.

INTERNATIONAL FINANCE

EXAM FOCUS

This topic review was in the Level 1 curriculum last year and was moved to Level 2 for the 2008 season. You need to know the basics of the balance of payments accounts and to understand the factors that can shift the demand for one currency in terms of another. Focus on the fact that an exchange rate is the equilibrium "price" of a currency, why exchange rates can be volatile even with little change in trading volume, and how this volatility can be reduced by central bank intervention. Don't worry too much about purchasing power and interest rate parity here, they are covered in more detail in the two topic reviews that follow.

BALANCE OF PAYMENTS ACCOUNTING

LOS 17.a: Explain the different components of the balance of payments accounts, the transactions recorded for import and export on the different accounts, and how the three sector balances are related.

Balance-of-payments (BOP) accounting is a method used to keep track of transactions between a country and its international trading partners. It includes government transactions, consumer transactions, and business transactions. The balance-of-payments accounts reflect all payments and liabilities to foreigners and all payments and liabilities from foreigners. The BOP equation is:

current account + capital account + official reserve account = 0

The **current account** measures the exchange of merchandise goods, services, investment income, and unilateral transfers (gifts to and from other nations). The *current account balance* is the net exchange of goods and services, investment income, and unilateral transfers.

The **capital (or financial) account** measures the flow of funds for the principal value of investment into a country from abroad and out of a country due to investment by its citizens in foreign assets. This includes investment in real assets as well as purchases of financial securities. When a country runs a current account deficit (imports more than it exports), one way to make up the difference is to borrow from foreign countries, which leads to a capital account surplus.

The **official settlements account** is where changes in official reserves are recorded. **Official reserves** are funds held by a government in foreign currencies. In 1997, the U.S. ran a current account deficit and a smaller surplus in its capital account. As a result, the U.S. ran a surplus in the reserve account to balance the BOP accounts. A surplus in the official reserve account means that the U.S. traded dollars for foreign currency. These reserve balances are used by the Fed to *intervene* in the foreign exchange markets in an attempt to loosely control exchange rates.

The impact of borrowing to finance a deficit in the current account over time depends on whether the country is borrowing to finance investment or borrowing to finance consumption. If the deficit is the result of borrowing primarily to finance consumption, consumption in the future must be reduced to repay the borrowings. If, on the other hand, the borrowing is primarily to finance investment, then future growth in the economy will provide the means to repay the borrowings without an equal decrease in consumption.

SUPPLY AND DEMAND FOR FOREIGN EXCHANGE

LOS 17.b: Explain the law of demand and the law of supply for foreign exchange, and how changes in demand and supply occur.

Consider the demand for U.S. dollars and for euros. The reason there is a demand by foreigners for U.S. dollars is to purchase U.S. goods or to buy U.S. financial assets (securities) or U.S. real assets (e.g. real estate or factories). We can construct a demand curve for U.S. dollars in terms of euros. As shown in Figure 1, the demand for a country's currency is downward sloping, as it is for any good. The price of dollars expressed in euros is an exchange rate. From the graph in Figure 1, we can see that the quantity of dollars demanded is greater at an exchange rate (price) of 0.85 euros per U.S. dollar than the quantity demanded at an exchange rate of 0.90. At a lower exchange rate in terms of euros per dollar, U.S. goods and assets are relatively cheaper to euro-based consumers and investors, and they will demand a greater quantity of both, leading to an increase in the quantity of dollars demanded to fund these purchases.

Two factors are important determinants of the demand for a currency: the interest rate for deposits in that currency, and expected future exchange rates. Changes in these factors can either increase or decrease the demand for currency as illustrated in Figure 1.

Figure 1: Demand for U.S. Dollars

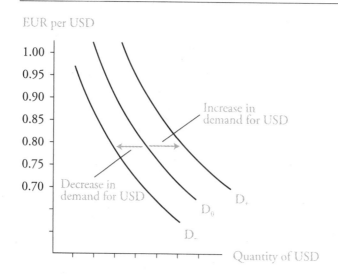

Investors make investment decisions based on interest rate differentials, the difference between what they can earn on investments in their own currency and what they can earn in other currencies. If the euro rate of interest rises relative to the U.S. dollar rate of interest, U.S. dollar-based investors will find euro investments more attractive, and demand for euros will increase. When a country's interest rates fall relative to those of other countries, demand for that country's currency will fall because the demand for investments denominated in that currency will decrease.

When the exchange rate for a country's currency in terms of another currency rises, we say that the country's currency has *appreciated*. If the price of euros in terms of yen rises from 140 yen per euro (140 ¥/€) to 145 ¥/€, we say that the euro has appreciated relative to the yen. Each euro will now purchase more yen and, in that sense, has become more valuable. When the exchange rate falls, from 140¥/€ to 135 ¥/€ for example, we say that the euro has *depreciated* relative to the yen. Notice that the currency of reference is in the denominator.

The second factor that influences demand for a currency is its expected future exchange rate. Other things equal, if a currency is expected to appreciate over time, it is more attractive. Consider a current (spot) exchange rate quote of 0.80 €/$ and an initial expectation that the dollar will appreciate so that the exchange rate in one year will be 0.81 €/$. If the expected future exchange rate rises to 0.83 €/$, the expected appreciation in the dollar has increased, and demand for dollars will increase. From the standpoint of a euro-based investor, an investment in U.S. assets is now more attractive because the expected return in euros is not only the expected U.S. interest, but also additional expected gains when dollar investments are converted back to euros at the end of one year. Rather than receiving 0.81 euros for each dollar, investors now expect to receive 0.83 euros for each dollar, making the expected euro return from an investment in dollars almost 2.5% greater than when the expected exchange rate was 0.81 €/$. So, an increase in the expected future exchange rate for a country's currency will increase demand for that currency, and a decrease in the expected future exchange rate will decrease the demand for the currency.

Supply of Foreign Exchange

Typically in microeconomics, the factors that affect the supply of a good (e.g. input costs) are separate from those that affect demand (e.g. tastes, price of substitute goods). In foreign exchange markets this is not the case. When a U.S. dollar-based investor's demand for euros increases, he wants to buy euros, but this also means selling dollars. For this reason, the supply of a currency in foreign exchange markets is driven by the same factors that affect demand: interest rate differentials and the expected future exchange rate.

If the U.S. dollar/euro exchange rate falls from 1.25 $/€ to 1.23 $/€, the euro has depreciated and the dollar has appreciated. This increase in the value (appreciation) of the dollar makes U.S. goods relatively more expensive. Demand for imports from the U.S. and the demand for dollars to purchase those imports will decrease as we have seen. At the same time, however, the appreciation of the dollar relative to the euro will make imports from the euro zone more attractive to dollar-based consumers. Their demand for euros will increase, which is an increase in the supply of dollars. So an appreciation in a currency (an increase in its exchange rate) will decrease demand for that currency and increase the supply of that currency. For this reason we draw the supply curve for a currency as an upward sloping function of its exchange rate in terms of another currency. We illustrate this in Figure 2, where the supply of dollars is shown as a function of the exchange rate in terms of euros per dollar.

Figure 2: Supply of U.S. Dollars

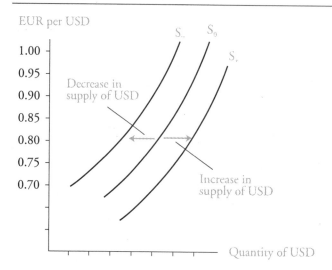

The same factors that cause shifts in the demand for a currency, interest rate differentials and expected future exchange rates, can also increase or decrease the supply of that currency. These shifts are illustrated in Figure 2. However, the effects are opposite to those on demand. An increase in the U.S. dollar interest rate relative to the euro interest rate or an increase in the expected future euro-dollar exchange rate will decrease the supply of dollars. A decrease in the U.S. dollar interest rate relative to the euro interest rate or a decrease in the expected future euro-dollar exchange rate will increase the supply of dollars.

 Professor's Note: These supply and demand effects get a bit confusing sometimes. I think you should focus on understanding the effects of interest rate differentials and expected future exchange rates on demand curves. Then, just remember that the effects are all opposite for supply curves.

DETERMINING THE EQUILIBRIUM EXCHANGE RATE

LOS 17.c: Discuss the influence of supply and demand on the exchange rate, and why exchange rates can be volatile.

In our typical analysis of supply and demand equilibrium, supply and demand are considered independently, as noted previously. Other things equal, an increase (decrease) in demand leads to an increase (decrease) in equilibrium price and an increase (decrease) in equilibrium quantity. An increase or decrease in supply has the opposite effect on equilibrium price and quantity.

Since supply and demand curves for foreign exchange are both affected by the same factors, the adjustment is different. Figure 3 shows the demand and supply for dollars as functions of the euro-dollar exchange rate. Initially, the equilibrium price of a dollar

©2008 Schweser

is 0.80 euros, at the intersection of S_0 and D_0. If the exchange rate is lower than this, there is excess demand for dollars and the exchange rate will rise toward equilibrium. If the exchange rate is greater than 0.80 €/$, then there is an excess supply of dollars, and the exchange rate will fall toward the equilibrium rate.

Figure 3: Demand and Supply Shifts in the Foreign Exchange Market

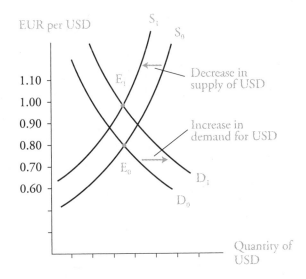

The curves S_1 and D_1 represent the increased demand for and decreased supply of dollars that would result from either an increase in the U.S. dollar interest rate or an increase in the expected future euro-dollar exchange rate. Note that while the new equilibrium euro-dollar exchange rate is higher from both the increase in demand and the decrease in supply, the equilibrium quantity of trading may be very close to the quantity traded prior to the shifts in supply and demand. For this reason, exchange rates may be quite volatile (more so than if supply and demand were independent), even though the quantity of currencies actually exchanged is not.

PURCHASING POWER PARITY VERSUS INTEREST RATE PARITY

LOS 17.d: Distinguish between purchasing power and interest rate parity.

The concept of purchasing power parity is based loosely on the idea that the same goods should cost the same in different countries, once we have factored in the current exchange rate. If a barrel of oil costs $70 in the U.S. and the yen/dollar exchange rate is 125, a barrel of oil should cost ¥8,750 (125 × 70) in Japan. While differences in transportation costs and some other factors may mean that such a relation need not hold exactly, purchasing power parity is based on the idea that changes in the price levels in the two countries should be reflected in changes in the exchange rate. Consider an example where inflation in the U.S. is greater than inflation in Japan. Since U.S. goods have increased more in price than Japanese goods, they are less attractive at the existing exchange rate. Purchasing power parity requires that the exchange rate adjust (dollar depreciate relative to the yen) so that exchange-rate adjusted goods prices return to the same relation that existed before the changes in the

Japanese and U.S. price levels. Another way to state this is that exchange rates will change to reflect differences in inflation between countries. We will have more to say about purchasing power parity later in this study session.

Interest rate parity is the idea that exchange rates must change so that the return on investments with identical risk will be the same in any currency. Another way to say this is that differences in interest rates are equal to differences in expected changes in exchange rates. If the U.S. interest rate is 6% and the U.K. interest rate (on British pounds) is 4%, we might think that all U.K. investors would want to convert their pounds to dollars so that they could earn 2% more. The key here is expected future exchange rates. If the dollar is expected to depreciate 2% relative to the pound over the next year, there is no expected gain from investing in dollars rather than pounds. At the end of one year, a U.K.-based investor could have 6% more dollars, but would have to exchange them for pounds at an exchange rate 2% below the current rate. So, rather than having 6% more pounds at the end of one year, a U.K. investor would have 4% more pounds, just as they would have investing in pounds rather than in dollars. This is the meaning of interest rate parity—changes in exchange rates over time should just offset interest rate differences between countries. We will look at interest rate parity in more detail in the next two topic reviews as well.

LOS 17.e: Discuss how and why intervention by a central bank in the exchange market may be required.

A central bank can intervene in the foreign exchange market by entering the market as a buyer, increasing the demand for its currency, or as a seller, increasing the supply of its currency. To reduce exchange rate volatility, for example, the U.S. Federal Reserve can buy dollars when the value of a dollar falls and sell dollars when the value of a dollar rises. While a central bank cannot do this indefinitely, if exchange rates are fluctuating due to short-term changes in the supply and demand for its currency, intervention can reduce volatility. True shifts in the supply and demand for a currency that lead to a new equilibrium exchange rate, however, will eventually have their expected effect. Central banks have limited power of intervention in markets because their reserves of both domestic and foreign currency, while they may be large, are in fact, limited.

KEY CONCEPTS

1. The balance of payments relation states that
   current account + capital account + official reserve account = 0.
2. The current account includes international payments for goods and services (net exports), the net income from asset ownership, and net gifts.
3. The capital account includes international payments for the purchase and sales of debt and equity securities and real assets.
4. Official reserve accounts consist of the foreign currencies held by governments.
5. The demand for a country's currency is a downward-sloping function of its exchange rate and is increased by increases in the country's interest rate and by increases in the expected future value of the currency.
6. The supply of a country's currency is an upward-sloping function of its exchange rate and is decreased by increases in the country's interest rate and by increases in the expected future value of the currency.
7. Since the same factors shift currency supply and demand curves, exchange rates can be quite volatile even with relatively stable trading volume.
8. Purchasing power parity refers to the relation between differences between countries' inflation rates and changes in the exchange rates for their currencies.
9. Interest rate parity refers to how differences in interest rates for two currencies are related to changes in their exchange rate over time.
10. Central bank intervention in currency markets (buying or selling their country's currency) can reduce short-term exchange rate volatility but cannot prevent real long-term changes in equilibrium exchange rates.

CONCEPT CHECKERS

1. Which of the following is *least likely* a component of the current account?
    A. Unilateral transfers.
    B. Flow of funds for investment.
    C. Payments for goods and services.
    D. Investment income.

2. Which of the following equations is *most accurate*?
    A. Balance of payments = current account + capital account.
    B. Official settlements account = current account + capital account.
    C. Current account = goods and service balance + official reserves.
    D. Current account + capital account + official settlements account = 0.

3. The Fredonian currency (the fredo) is currently valued at 2.50 per U.S. dollar. Fredo deposit rates are 1% above U.S. dollar deposit rates. All other things equal, which of the following scenarios would decrease demand for the fredo on the foreign exchange markets?

	Fredonia interest rate - U.S. interest rate differential	Expected dollar-per-fredo exchange rate in one year
A.	Increases	Decreases
B.	Increases	Increases
C.	Decreases	Decreases
D.	Decreases	Increases

4. Which of these statements is *most accurate*? Exchange rates can be especially volatile because:
    A. the quantities of currencies traded are volatile.
    B. interest rate differentials determine the demand for currencies.
    C. supply and demand for currencies are affected by the same factors.
    D. the supply of a currency is a function of expected future exchange rates.

5. The theory of interest rate parity suggests that:
    A. exchange rates will change to reflect differences in inflation between countries.
    B. changes in the price levels in two countries should be reflected in changes in the exchange rate.
    C. the same combinations of goods should cost the same in different countries, once we have factored in the current exchange rates.
    D. exchange rates will change so that the return on investments with identical risk will be the same in any currency.

6. A central bank's primary goal when intervening in the foreign exchange markets is typically to:
    A. reduce exchange rate volatility.
    B. increase its foreign currency holdings.
    C. prevent long-term currency depreciation.
    D. offset structural shifts in the demand for the domestic currency.

ANSWERS – CONCEPT CHECKERS

1. **B**   The flow of funds for investment in debt and equity is recorded in the capital account. Exchange of investment income, such as interest payments, is a component of the current account, along with goods and services trade and unilateral transfers.

2. **D**   The three balance of payments accounts must sum to zero.

3. **C**   A decrease in fredo interest rates minus U.S. rates and a decrease in the expected future exchange rate would both decrease demand for the fredo. When a country's interest rates fall relative to those of other countries, demand for that country's currency decreases because demand for investments denominated in that currency will decrease. A decrease in the expected future exchange rate also decreases the demand for a currency.

4. **C**   Because shifts in supply and demand are affected by the same factors, exchange rates may be quite volatile even though the quantity of currencies actually exchanged is not.

5. **D**   The other three choices describe the concept of purchasing power parity.

6. **A**   Central banks can reduce exchange rate volatility in the short term through intervention in the foreign exchange market. Longer-term shifts in supply and demand, however, will eventually have their expected effects on exchange rates. Intervention can increase or reduce the central bank's foreign currency holdings, but that would rarely be the central bank's primary objective.

The following is a review of the Economics for Valuation principles designed to address the learning outcome statements set forth by CFA Institute®. This topic is also covered in:

FOREIGN EXCHANGE

EXAM FOCUS

Most of this material was in the Level 1 curriculum last year, but was moved to Level 2 for the 2008 exam season. No fluff here; you need it all. Take it slow and get a good understanding of direct and indirect quotes, spot rates and spreads, forward rates, forward discounts and premiums, currency cross rates, interest rate parity, and covered interest arbitrage. Triangular arbitrage is always a challenging topic for Level 2 candidates. Master the basics now so if you see a triangular arbitrage question on exam day, it won't slow you down. The probability of this material being tested is very high.

WARM UP: EXCHANGE RATES AND THE FOREIGN EXCHANGE MARKET

An **exchange rate** is a ratio that describes how many units of one currency you can buy per unit of another currency. Note that an exchange rate is quoted relative to another currency. You *cannot* quote three exchange rates (three currencies) with one ratio.

> *Professor's Note: As you work through the foreign exchange material, you will notice that the notation for currency rates is not consistent. For example, for the Japanese yen, you may see the currency symbol, such as ¥, or the three-letter notation, JPY. The U.S. dollar may be shown as USD, $, or U.S. dollar. Be prepared to see various notations on the exam.*

For example, if the Australian dollar (AUD) is trading at 0.60 U.S. dollars ($0.60), each AUD will buy 60 U.S. cents. Remember the following: AUD = $0.60 = 0.60 dollars per AUD. Whatever currency in which the *quote* is made (in this case, $U.S.) belongs in the numerator while the denominator is always *one* unit of the currency you are interested in (in this case the AUD). For instance, $/AUD = 0.60.

Exchange rates between countries are the *inverse* of one another. Thus the U.S. dollar quote in terms of AUD is:

U.S. dollar = 1/0.60 = 1.67 AUD per U.S. dollar

Therefore, if you are given dollars per AUD, you can easily get AUD per dollar by taking the inverse of the original quote.

Example: Transactions with exchange rates

Suppose that you want to buy some Australian beer. The Australian distributor tells you the beer sells for 25 AUD per case. How many U.S. dollars will it cost you to buy one case, given that the AUD exchange rate is $0.60?

Answer:

- You know that the beer is quoted in AUD per case. So the numerator is AUD and the denominator is a case (AUD/case).
- You know that your exchange rate has $ in the numerator and AUD in the denominator ($/AUD).
- You want $ in the numerator and cases in the denominator, so multiply the two together:

$$\left(\frac{25\ \text{AUD}}{\text{case}}\right) \times \left(\frac{0.60\ \$}{\text{AUD}}\right) = \frac{\$15}{\text{case}}$$

The AUDs cancel and you are left with $15 in the numerator and case in the denominator, so the beer costs $15 per case.

Example: Exchange rate appreciation and depreciation

If the AUD moves from $0.60 to $0.70, has the AUD depreciated or appreciated?

Answer:

The AUD has *appreciated*—previously each AUD would only buy 60 cents, whereas now each AUD buys 70 cents. What has the U.S. dollar done in this example? To find out, invert each quote so that you get the U.S. dollar moving from 1/$0.6 = AUD1.67 to 1/$0.7 = AUD1.43. The dollar has *depreciated* in value. It used to buy 1.67 AUD but only buys 1.43 AUD today. Again, always remember what is in the *denominator*.

It is important to note that the *appreciation* of a currency makes that country's goods more *expensive* to residents of other countries while *depreciation* makes a country's goods more *attractive* to foreign buyers. In our Australian beer example, if we let the AUD depreciate against the U.S. dollar, the U.S. dollar price of the beer will fall.

You must know how to determine whether a currency has depreciated or appreciated over time. As a straightforward example, if the Swiss franc goes from 1.7799 CHF/USD to 1.8100 CHF/USD, the Swiss franc has depreciated relative to the dollar. Why? It is worth less—it now takes more Swiss francs to buy a dollar. This example could have been worded, "If the CHF to USD exchange rate increases from 1.7799 to 1.8100, the Swiss franc has depreciated relative to the U.S. dollar." Don't be confused by the word "increases"—the CHF still depreciated. Focus on the numbers and the logic.

Foreign Exchange Markets

The trading of currencies takes place in foreign exchange markets, which have the primary function of facilitating international trade and investment. Knowledge of the operation and mechanics of these markets is important for a fundamental understanding of international financial management.

The foreign exchange market permits the transfer of purchasing power denominated in one currency for that of another currency. This market is not a physical place but rather an electronically linked network of banks, foreign exchange brokers, and dealers whose function it is to bring together buyers and sellers of foreign exchange. Transactions occur over the phone, telex, or the SWIFT system (Society for Worldwide Interbank Financial Telecommunications).

Participants in the foreign exchange (interbank) market are large commercial banks, foreign exchange brokers, major multinational corporate customers, and central banks. Most of the trading in the U.S. goes through foreign exchange brokers, who match buyers and sellers for a small commission (1/32 of 1%).

Foreign-exchange brokers provide *information*, participant *anonymity*, and *reduced time and effort* (meaning a bank need only deal with one broker rather than contracting several other banks) in trading.

The typical small client gets foreign exchange from a local bank. The local bank in turn gets the exchange from its major correspondent bank, and the major bank gets the exchange from a foreign exchange broker.

The *interbank market* is the wholesale market where the major banks trade with one another. Most currency transactions occur here. The interbank market is generally referred to as the foreign exchange market and is segmented into three separate markets: (1) the spot market, (2) the forward market, and (3) the currency swap market.

 Professor's Note: The old Level 1 material that is new to Level 2 includes LOS 18.a through 18.g.

DIRECT AND INDIRECT QUOTES

LOS 18.a: Define direct and indirect methods of foreign exchange quotations and convert direct (indirect) foreign exchange quotations into indirect (direct) foreign exchange quotations.

Local *nonbank public customer* quotes can be stated as:

- **Direct quotes** are expressed in domestic currency units per foreign currency unit: DC/FC. For example, a direct quote to a U.S. investor for euros might be 1.21 $/€. This represents an exchange rate of $1.21 per euro.
- **Indirect quotes** are expressed as foreign currency unit per domestic currency unit: FC/DC.

To convert a direct quote to an indirect quote, or vice versa, you simply take the reciprocal of the one that you are given. For example, in Japan, a direct quote of

125 ¥/$ is equivalent to an indirect quote of $\left(\dfrac{1}{125 \text{ ¥/\$}}\right) = 0.0080$ \$/¥. Just use the 1/x

key on your calculator to turn the indirect quote 125 ¥/$ into the direct quote of 0.0080 $/¥.

BID-ASK SPREADS

Banks and other dealers generally do not charge commissions on foreign currency transactions. Instead, they make their profit from the *bid-ask spread*.

- The *bid price* is always listed first. It is the price the *dealer will pay* for FC.
- The *ask price* is always listed second. It is the price at which the *dealer will sell* FC.
- The bid is less than the ask for direct quotes.

Example: Bid-ask spread

Consider the following quotations: The bid of $1.6625 \dfrac{\text{USD}}{\text{GBP}}$ and the ask of

$1.6635 \dfrac{\text{USD}}{\text{GBP}}$ are listed as USD1.6625 – 35. Calculate the bid-ask spread as a direct quote from the perspective of a British banker.

Answer:

Note that this quote is a direct quote in the U.S. To switch the bid-ask spread to a direct quote from the British perspective $\left(\dfrac{\text{GBP}}{\text{USD}}\right)$, which is an indirect quote to a U.S. investor, take the reciprocal of each number.

$$\frac{1}{1.6625 \dfrac{\text{USD}}{\text{GBP}}} = 0.60150 \frac{\text{GBP}}{\text{USD}}$$

$$\frac{1}{1.6635 \dfrac{\text{USD}}{\text{GBP}}} = 0.60114 \frac{\text{GBP}}{\text{USD}}$$

Note that buying Currency 1 in terms of units of Currency 2 is equivalent to selling Currency 2 for units of Currency 1. A bid-ask dealer quote using direct exchange rates can be converted to indirect terms by taking the reciprocals, but the ask and the bid are reversed. A direct Canadian dealer quote of $1.25 - 1.26 \left(\text{CDN}/\text{USD} \right)$ for the U.S dollar is equivalent to an indirect Canadian dealer quote of $\text{USD} \left(\dfrac{1}{1.26} \right)$ bid and $\text{USD} \left(\dfrac{1}{1.25} \right)$ ask or USD0.7937 bid and USD0.8000 ask for Canadian dollars, which will be a direct quote for a U.S. dealer.

Spreads are often expressed as a percentage of the ask. For the direct U.S. quote, we get a percentage spread as:

$$\frac{0.80 - 0.7937}{0.80} = 0.0079 = 0.79\%$$

How Spreads Differ as a Result of Market Conditions, Bank/Dealer Positions, and Trading Volume

Market conditions affect currency spreads because the bid-ask spread on foreign currency quotations increases as exchange rate volatility (uncertainty) increases. Larger spreads compensate dealers for the higher risk of dealing in more volatile currencies.

Bank and currency dealer positions do not directly affect the size of foreign currency spreads. If a dealer wants to reduce her holdings, she will usually adjust the midpoint of the spread rather than the absolute size of the spread. For example, a dealer who changes her bid-ask in U.S. dollars for euros from 1.30 – 1.33 to 1.29 – 1.32 would expect to buy less euros (lower bid) and to sell more euros (lower ask), which would decrease her inventory position in euros.

Greater trading volume leads to narrower spreads (and vice versa), just as with equities trading.

 Professor's Note: The factors that affect the spread on forward foreign currency transaction are discussed in LOS 18.e.

CROSS RATES

LOS 18.c: Calculate and interpret currency cross rates, given two spot exchange quotations involving three currencies.

The **cross rate** is the rate of exchange between two countries, computed from the exchange rates between each of these two countries and a third country. Cross exchange rate calculations are necessary because each currency is quoted against the dollar in the interbank market but currencies are quoted using the direct method against other currencies in local nonbank markets.

As a simple example of calculating a cross rate, consider that spot rates are 0.00833 $/¥ and 148 ¥/€, and we wish to calculate the dollar/euro cross rate. When we multiply $/¥ by 148¥/€, the yen term drops out and we have 0.00833 × 148 = 1.2328 $/€. If the quotes are not given in a form that yields a simple solution for the cross rate to be calculated, the easiest way to proceed is to convert the rates using reciprocals as needed. Consider the following example.

Example: Currency cross rate calculation

If spot rates are 120 ¥/$ and 148 ¥/€, what is the cross rate expressed as €/$?

Answer:

We want our answer expressed as €/$, so we can multiply ¥/$ times €/¥ since

$\frac{¥}{$} \times \frac{€}{¥} = \frac{€}{$}$. We take the reciprocal of 148 ¥/€ and get 0.006757 €/¥. We can then multiply 120 × 0.006757 to get 0.8108 €/$.

Since multiplying by the reciprocal of a fraction is equivalent to dividing by the fraction we could also get our answer by taking 120/148 = 0.8108 €/$. The spot rates given show that one euro is worth more yen (148) than one U.S. dollar (120). This tells us that one euro is worth more than one dollar and that our €/$ quote of less than one is to be expected.

One more example will further illustrate the technique.

Example: 3-currency cross rate calculation

The spot exchange rate between the Swiss franc (CHF) and the USD is 1.7799 CHF/USD, and the spot exchange rate between the New Zealand dollar (NZD) and the U.S. dollar is 2.2529 NZD/USD. Calculate the CHF/NZD spot rate.

Answer:

In Switzerland, the direct exchange rate is:

$$\frac{1.7799\dfrac{CHF}{USD}}{2.2529\dfrac{NZD}{USD}} = 0.79005\frac{CHF}{NZD}$$

If you are a visual learner, another way to do this is to draw a diagram with each of the three currencies in the shape of a triangle, as shown in the following example.

Example: Cross rates without bid-ask spreads

The spot exchange rate between the Swiss franc and the U.S. dollar is 1.4860 Sf per $, and the spot exchange rate between the pound and the U.S. dollar is 1.5600 $ per £. Calculate the Sf-to-£ spot cross exchange rate.

Answer:

First, let's do the algebra. We know that:

$$\frac{Sf}{£} = \left(\frac{\$}{£}\right) \times \left(\frac{Sf}{\$}\right)$$

That means the Sf/£ cross rate is calculated as:

$$\frac{Sf}{£} = (1.5600) \times (1.4860) = \frac{Sf\,2.3182}{£}$$

You can see from the following figure what we're doing here. We can either exchange francs for pounds at 2.3182 Sf per £, or we can exchange francs for dollars and then dollars for pounds. Therefore, by arbitrage, the exchange rates implied by the two different routes around the triangle must be equal.

Cross Rates Without Bid-Ask Spreads

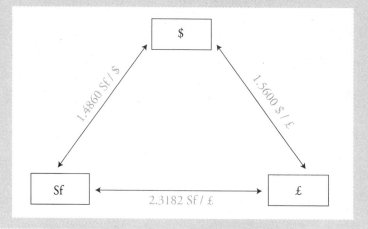

Bid-ask spreads complicate the calculation of cross rates considerably. Basically, it means that there are two exchange rates between each currency, depending on which way we're going around the triangle, so we end up with two cross rates, a bid rate and an ask rate. Once again, the best way to illustrate this is by diving right into an example.

[handwritten: bid]
$$\frac{Sf}{£}$$

Example: Calculating cross rates with bid-ask spreads

We have the following bid-ask quotes on the Sf per $ and the $ per £:

- Sf per $: 1.5000 – 10. *[handwritten: bid = 1.5 Sf/$; ask = 1.5 Sf/$]*
- $ per £: 1.3500 – 10. *[handwritten: bid = 1.35 $/£; ask = 1.351 $/£]*

Calculate the bid and ask rates on the Sf per £. *[handwritten: 1.351 $/£]*

Answer:

Let's first think about what bid and ask rates really mean. A bid rate in Sf per $ is the rate at which the foreign exchange dealer will buy U.S. dollars from us with francs, and the ask rate is the rate at which the FX dealer will sell U.S. dollars to us for francs. Instead of thinking about buying and selling, let's think about it in a different way. The bid rate on Sf per $ is the rate at which we can convert dollars to francs, and the ask rate is the rate at which we can convert francs to dollars. We can fill in the bid-ask table in the next figure using this idea.

Exchange Rate	Bid	Ask
Sf per $	Convert $ to Sf 1.5000	Convert Sf to $ 1.5010
$ per £	Convert £ to $ 1.3500	Convert $ to £ 1.3510
Sf per £	Convert £ to Sf ?.????	Convert Sf to £ ?.????

An easy way to remember which way the arrows go around the triangle is to remember the phrase "up the bid and down the ask." The bid rate is always the rate at which the investor can convert the currency in the denominator of the quote into the currency in the numerator. In other words, the bid goes "up" from the denominator to the numerator. For example, if the quotes are in $/€, the bid rate is the rate at which the investor can convert € (in the denominator) into $ (in the numerator). The ask rate is the rate for converting the numerator currency into the denominator currency. This relationship is illustrated in the following figure.

The "Up the Bid and Down the Ask" Rule

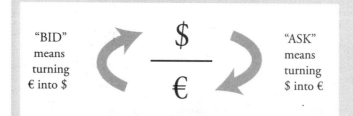

"BID" means turning € into $

"ASK" means turning $ into €

Now we can convert this information into our familiar triangle with the arrows going in the direction that we are converting, shown in the next figure.

Cross Rates with Bid-Ask Spreads

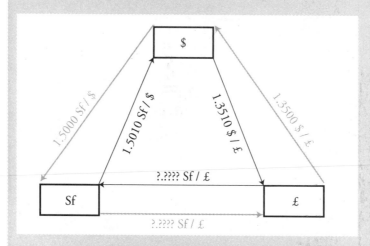

The bid rate on Sf per £ is the rate that converts pounds to francs. We can get there by going around the triangle through 1.3500 $ per £ and then through 1.5000 Sf per $ into Sf per £:

$$\frac{Sf}{£} = \left(\frac{\$}{£}\right) \times \left(\frac{Sf}{\$}\right)$$

That means the Sf per £ cross **bid** rate is calculated as:

$$\frac{Sf}{£} = (1.3500) \times (1.5000) = \frac{Sf\,2.0250}{£}$$

The cross **ask** rate (converting francs to pounds) goes in the opposite direction around the triangle:

$$\frac{Sf}{£} = (1.5010) \times (1.3510) = \frac{Sf\,2.0279}{£}$$

Therefore, our bid-ask quote is Sf 2.0250 – 79.

We will use this approach to calculate the profits from triangular arbitrage in LOS 18.h.

SPOT AND FORWARD MARKETS

LOS 18.d: Distinguish between the spot and forward markets for foreign exchange.

Spot markets refer to transactions that call for immediate delivery of the currency. In practice, the settlement period is two business days after the trade date.

Forward markets are for an exchange of currencies that will occur in the future. Both parties to the transaction agree to exchange one currency for another at a specific future date. Forward contracts are typically for transactions 30, 60, or 90 days in the future, although the contracts can be written for any period. There is no option involved in the contract; both parties to a forward currency contract are obligated to execute the specified transaction in the future.

A firm that has a foreign-currency-denominated obligation in 60 days can remove any uncertainty about the cost of the obligation in its home currency by entering into a forward contract to buy the required amount of foreign currency 60 days from now (at the 60-day forward rate). The forward exchange rate in the contract will reflect the expected movement of exchange rates over the next 60 days so that the forward rate may be greater than or less than the current spot rate. Note that the current spot rate is not locked in by entering a forward contract, unless the expectation is that the exchange rate will be the same 60 days from now so that the forward and spot rates are the same.

> **Example: Foreign currency forward transactions**
>
> A U.S. firm is obligated to make a future payment of CHF100,000 in 60 days. To manage its exchange rate risk, the firm contracts to buy the Swiss franc 60 days in the future at 1.7530 CHF/USD. The current exchange rate is 1.7799 CHF/USD. (Note this is the indirect method of quoting exchange rates.)
>
> **Part 1:** How much would the U.S. firm gain or lose on its commitment if, at the time of payment, the exchange rate fell below the 1.7530 Swiss francs to the dollar forward rate to 1.6556 Swiss francs to the dollar? What is the net impact on the firm?

Answer:

Without the forward contract, the firm *would have lost* (100,000 / 1.7530) – (100,000 / 1.6556) = – USD3,356.00 on its commitment. Fortunately, the firm gets to buy the Swiss franc at 1.7530 CHF/USD rather than at the 1.6556 rate in effect at the time the payment must be made. The actual loss on the commitment is exactly offset by the gain on the forward contract. The forward contract has locked in the price (in $) that the firm will pay for CHF in the future. Fluctuations in the actual spot rate in 60 days do not affect the (net) cost of CHF at contract expiration.

Part 2: Keeping in mind the information from Part 1 of this example, how much would the U.S. firm gain or lose on its commitment if at the time of payment the exchange rate had risen to 1.8250 CHF, and what is the net impact on the firm?

Answer:

Without the forward contract, the firm *would have gained* (100,000 / 1.7530 – 100,000 / 1.8250) = +USD2,250.55 by being able to pay off its commitment with cheap Swiss francs. Unfortunately, the firm must buy the Swiss francs at 1.7530 CHF/USD. Thus the gain on the commitment is exactly offset by the loss on the forward contract.

You should learn three things from this example:

1. The gain or loss on the forward contract is unrelated to the current spot rate, 1.7799 CHF/USD.
2. The gain or loss on the forward contract exactly offsets the loss or gain on the dollar cost of the original commitment. Note that gains and losses are measured *relative to the forward contract rate*, not the initial spot rate.
3. The forward contract is not an option contract. Both parties (the firm and the bank) must perform on the agreed contract.

SPREADS IN THE FORWARD MARKET

LOS 18.e: Calculate and interpret the spread on a forward foreign currency quotation and explain how spreads on forward foreign currency quotations can differ as a result of market conditions, bank/dealer positions, trading volume, and maturity/length of contract.

Consider a 6-month forward exchange rate quote from a U.S. currency dealer of 1.63843 – 1.64073 USD/GBP. This means that the dealer will commit today to buy pounds for 1.63843 dollars in six months or sell pounds in six months for 1.64073 dollars.

As with spot rates, the forward foreign currency spread is the difference between the bid and the ask quotes.

Example: Forward bid-ask spread

Assume that the USD/GBP 6-month forward rate is quoted at a bid of 1.63843 and an ask of 1.64073. From a U.S. dealer's perspective, calculate the bid-ask spread.

Answer:

In this case, the spread is simply 0.0023 USD/GBP = 1.64073 – 1.63843.

Forward Spreads and Market Conditions, Bank/Dealer Positions, Trading Volume, and Maturity/Length of Contract

Just as with spot market foreign currency spreads, spreads in the forward foreign currency market increase with greater exchange rate volatility and decrease when trading volume is higher. Spreads tend to increase with the term of the forward contract, and forward currency spreads are typically greater than spot currency spreads.

FORWARD PREMIUM/DISCOUNT

LOS 18.f: Calculate and interpret a forward discount or premium and express it as an annualized rate.

LOS 18.i: Distinguish between spot and forward transactions, and calculate the annualized forward premium/discount for a given currency and infer whether the currency is "strong" or "weak."

 Professor's Note: Your life will be a lot easier on the exam if you make sure all of your quotes are in domestic currency over foreign currency (DC/FC) when using these formulas. If you work in FC/DC, a premium is a negative number, and your confusion factor will rise significantly!

A foreign currency is at a **forward discount** if the forward rate *expressed in domestic currency units* is less than the spot rate. Foreign currency units will be *cheaper* in the future.

forward discount = forward rate – spot rate = negative number

A foreign currency is at a **forward premium** if the forward rate *expressed in domestic currency units* is greater than the spot rate. Foreign currency units will be more expensive in the future.

forward premium = forward rate – spot rate = positive number

The **forward premium or discount** is frequently stated as an annualized percentage using the following formula:

$$\left(\begin{array}{c} \text{forward premium} \\ \text{or discount} \end{array} \right) = \left(\frac{\text{forward rate} - \text{spot rate}}{\text{spot rate}} \right) \left(\frac{360}{\text{number of forward contract days}} \right)$$

The forward and spot rates in this equation are direct quotes, DC/FC.

There are three things to note here:

1. If you are given bid-ask spot and forward quotes, use the bid-ask midpoints to calculate the forward premium/discount, unless you're specifically instructed to do something else.

2. The forward premium or discount is always on the currency in the denominator of the quote. For example, if the quote is U.S. dollars per euro, the forward premium/ discount calculated using the formula is on the euro.

3. If one currency is trading at a forward premium relative to a second currency, the second currency is trading at a forward discount relative to the first currency.

A currency selling at a forward premium is considered "strong" relative to the second currency, while a currency selling at a forward discount is considered "weak."

Example: Annualized forward rate premium and discount

Assume the 90-day forward rate for the NZD is USD0.4439 and the spot rate is USD0.4315. Determine if the NZD is trading at a premium or discount to the USD. Calculate the annualized premium or discount and determine whether the NZD is strong or weak.

Answer:

Since it takes more dollars to buy the NZD in the forward market relative to the spot, the NZD is trading at a *premium* to the dollar.

$$\left(\text{forward premium} \right) = \left(\frac{0.4439 - 0.4315}{0.4315} \right)\left(\frac{360}{90} \right) = 0.1149 \text{ or } 11.49\%$$

The NZD is selling at a forward premium to the USD, so the NZD is considered "strong."

Example: Calculating the forward premium/discount

Given the following quotes in yen per U.S. dollar, calculate the forward premium/discount on the U.S. dollar relative to the Japanese yen and indicate whether the U.S. dollar is strong or weak:

> Spot bid rate: 124.500
> Spot ask rate: 125.500
> Spot rate midpoint: 125.00
> 90-day forward bid rate: 125.75
> 90-day forward ask rate: 126.75
> 90-day forward midpoint: 126.25

Answer:

$$\text{forward premium on } \$ = \left(\frac{126.25 - 125.00}{125.00} \right) \left(\frac{360}{90} \right) = 0.04 = 4.0\%$$

The USD is selling at a forward premium, so it is considered strong.

INTEREST RATE PARITY AND COVERED INTEREST ARBITRAGE

LOS 18.g: Explain interest rate parity and illustrate covered interest arbitrage.

Interest Rate Parity

The only difference between exchanging currencies in the spot market and exchanging currencies in the forward market is the timing of the transaction, where time is represented by interest rates. Covered interest rate parity, or simply **interest rate parity** (IRP), shows that there is a relationship between the spot and forward exchange rates and the domestic (r_{DC}) and foreign (r_{FC}) interest rates in the countries represented. Covered interest rate parity holds because investors will take advantage of interest rate differentials to move funds between countries where spot and forward exchange rates are not in balance. Covered means that the currency exposure in the foreign investment is hedged or "covered" by a forward contract.

IRP is approximated by equating the difference between the domestic interest rate and the foreign interest rate to the forward premium or discount. That is:

> interest differential ≈ forward differential

Restating this relationship in more familiar terms gives:

$$\left(r_{DC} - r_{FC} \right) \approx \left(\frac{\text{forward exchange rate} - \text{spot exchange rate}}{\text{spot exchange rate}} \right)$$

where the forward and spot exchange rates are expressed as DC/FC.

When the above condition prevails, equilibrium exists in the international money markets.

You should also know that the exact IRP equation using direct quotes is:

$$\frac{DC}{FC} \times \frac{FC}{DC} \qquad \frac{\text{forward}}{\text{spot}} = \left(\frac{1 + r_{DC}}{1 + r_{FC}}\right) \qquad \frac{F}{Spot} = \frac{1 + r_{FC}}{1 + r_{DC}}$$

> *Professor's Note: If this equality does not hold, an arbitrage opportunity exists. To remember this formula, note that when the forward and spot rates are expressed as direct quotes (DC/FC), right-hand side of the equation also has the domestic (interest rate) in the numerator and the foreign (interest rate) in the denominator. If we expressed the forward and spot rates as indirect quotes (FC/DC), then the right-hand side of the equation would have the foreign (interest rate) in the numerator and the domestic (interest rate) in the denominator. So it's either domestic over foreign for everything, or foreign over domestic for everything. We'll call this the "numerator/denominator" rule in the next topic review.*

IRP ensures that the return on a hedged (covered) foreign investment will just equal the domestic interest rate of investments of identical risk. When this happens, there are no arbitrage possibilities, and the difference between the domestic interest rate and the hedged foreign rate (called the covered interest differential) is zero.

Example: Covered interest rate parity

Suppose you can invest in NZD at 5.127%, or you can invest in Swiss francs at 5.5%. You are a resident of New Zealand, and the current spot rate is 0.79005 NZD/CHF. Calculate the 1-year forward rate expressed in NZD/CHF.

Answer:

$$\text{forward (DC/FC)} = \text{spot (DC/FC)}\left(\frac{1 + r_{DC}}{1 + r_{FC}}\right) = 0.79005\left(\frac{1.05127}{1.05500}\right) = 0.78726$$

Covered Interest Arbitrage

Covered interest arbitrage is a trading strategy that exploits currency positions when the interest rate parity equation is not satisfied. You can check for an arbitrage opportunity by using the *covered interest differential*. The covered interest differential says that the domestic interest rate should be the same as the hedged foreign interest rate. More specifically, the difference between the domestic interest rate and the hedged foreign rate should be *zero*. The covered interest differential can be viewed by rewriting IRP in the following way:

$$1 + r_{DC} = \frac{(1 + r_{FC})(\text{forward rate})}{\text{spot rate}}$$

The left-hand side of the equation is the domestic interest rate, while the right-hand side is the hedged foreign rate (the foreign rate expressed in domestic terms). Arbitrage will prevent this relationship from getting out of line. To preclude arbitrage, the left-hand side minus the right-hand side should equal zero. Hence, the *covered interest differential* can be written as:

$$\left(1 + r_{DC}\right) - \left(\frac{(1 + r_{FC})(\text{forward rate})}{\text{spot rate}}\right) = \text{covered interest differential}$$

For example, if the domestic interest rate is less than the hedged foreign interest rate, an arbitrageur will borrow in the domestic cash market, buy foreign currency at the spot rate, and enter into a forward contract, granting him the ability to convert the foreign funds back to domestic funds at some future date. The foreign funds are invested at the foreign interest rate until the forward contract expires, at which time the arbitrageur will convert the proceeds from the foreign investment back into the domestic currency via the forward contract. This results in an arbitrage (riskless) profit with no net investment.

> *Professor's Note: This parity relationship can seem complex but you must learn it; this important concept will come up in other contexts at Level 2 and Level 3. Consider an extreme example: the U.S. interest rate is 5% and the Mexican interest rate is 25%. Why can't a U.S. investor make a 25% return by investing in pesos at the Mexican risk-free rate?*
>
> *The intuition here is that he can't because the Mexican peso will depreciate; he can have 25% more pesos at the end of one year but (if interest rate parity holds) he will be able to exchange these pesos for only 5% more dollars than he started with. The peso must depreciate. The exact calculation is:*
>
> $$\frac{1 + r_{DC}}{1 + r_{FC}} - 1 = \frac{1.05}{1.25} - 1 = -16\%$$

> *For interest rate parity to hold, the forward exchange rate for the peso (quoted in USD/peso) must be 16% less than the spot exchange rate. The peso is expected to depreciate 16% relative to the dollar over the next year. If a dollar currently buys 10 pesos (1 peso = 0.10 USD), he has 12.5 pesos at the end of the year. The peso value in USD falls to 0.10 × 0.84 = 0.084 (a depreciation of 16%), the ending value is 12.5 × 0.084 = 1.05 USD, the same ending result as if he had invested the $1 at the U.S. interest rate of 5%. The parity relation is:*
>
> $$\frac{1.05}{1.25} = \frac{0.084}{0.10}$$

> *If the forward peso rate is greater than 0.084 USD, a dollar-based investor can earn more than 5% by investing in pesos; if the forward peso rate is less than 0.084 USD, a peso-based investor can earn more than 25% by investing in dollars. When you can create an example like this with different numbers and work through it, you have mastered interest rate parity and covered interest arbitrage.*

Example: Identifying covered interest arbitrage opportunities

Assume you are a New Zealand investor and have 1,000 NZD. You can invest in NZD at 5.127%, or invest in Swiss francs at 5.5%. The current spot rate is 0.79005 NZD/CHF, and the forward rate is 0.78726 NZD/CHF.

Determine if there are any arbitrage opportunities.

Answer:

Let's insert the numbers and see if interest rate parity holds.

$$\frac{0.78726}{0.79005} = \frac{1.05127}{1.05500}$$

No arbitrage is available.

To verify this, work through the following steps:

- Convert your 1,000 NZD to Swiss francs at the spot rate.

$$\left(\frac{1{,}000 \text{ NZD}}{0.79005 \frac{\text{NZD}}{\text{CHF}}} \right) = 1{,}265.74 \text{ CHF}$$

- Invest your Swiss francs at 5.5% in Switzerland. At year-end you will have:

$$1{,}265.74 \text{ CHF} \times 1.055 = 1{,}335.36 \text{ CHF}$$

- Simultaneously enter into a 1-year forward contract to convert Swiss francs back to NZD at the forward rate of 0.78726 NZD/CHF.
- When the Swiss franc investment matures, collect the interest and principal (1,335.36 CHF) and convert it back to NZD:

$$1{,}335.36 \text{ CHF} \times \left(0.78726 \frac{\text{NZD}}{\text{CHF}} \right) = 1{,}051.28 \text{ NZD}$$

- If you had invested the NZD directly in New Zealand, you would have at year-end:

$$1{,}000 \text{ NZD} \times 1.05127 = 1{,}051.27 \text{ NZD}$$

- While there is a modest rounding error, there is no arbitrage opportunity here.

Example: Covered interest arbitrage opportunities

The forward rate between GBP and U.S. dollars is 0.7327 GBP/USD, and the current spot rate is 0.7045 GBP/USD. The U.K. interest rate is 6.056%, and the U.S. rate is 5.95%. Assume you can borrow GBP1,000 or the equivalent in USD and that you live in the U.K. Is there an arbitrage opportunity? If so, how would you take advantage of it?

Answer:

First check to see if arbitrage is possible.

$$\frac{0.7327}{0.7045} > \frac{1.06056}{1.0595}$$

So an arbitrage opportunity exists because the interest rate parity condition is not met.

Second, determine whether to borrow domestically or in the foreign market.

Since the left-hand side is "too high," we know that the forward exchange rate is greater than the forward exchange rate for parity. This means the forward price of USD is too high in GBP. We know from this that we do not want to hold GBP and buy (overpriced) USD in the future. The profitable arbitrage must be based on holding USD.

To arbitrage:

- Borrow GBP1,000 at 6.056%. At year-end you must pay back:

  $$1,000\,GBP \times 1.06056 = GBP1,060.56$$

- Convert the borrowed pounds to dollars:

  $$\left(\frac{1,000\,GBP}{0.7045\,\dfrac{GBP}{USD}}\right) = 1,419.45\,USD$$

- Lend out the USD1,419.45 in the U.S. at 5.95%. At year-end you will have:

  $$1,419.45\,USD \times 1.0595 = 1,503.91\,USD$$

- Simultaneously, enter into a 1-year forward contract to convert USD back to GBP at the forward rate of 0.7327 GBP/USD.

- When the USD investment matures, collect the interest and principal (1,503.91 USD) and convert it back to GBP:

$$1,503.91 \text{ USD} \times \left(0.7327 \frac{\text{GBP}}{\text{USD}} \right) = 1,101.91 \text{ GBP}$$

- After you pay off your GBP1,000 loan and interest for GBP1,060.56, you will have GBP41.35 left over.

So it is profitable to borrow money in the U.K. and make a hedged loan in the U.S. You will continue to do this until the money markets (interest rates) and exchange rates adjust and interest rate parity holds.

Example (continued): Another perspective on covered interest arbitrage

Let's do this example again, looking at things from a slightly different perspective. Recall that the purpose of interest rate parity is to keep the hedged foreign interest rate (the foreign rate expressed in domestic terms) equal to the domestic interest rate. Since this *must* be the case, recall that we rewrote IRP by setting the domestic rate equal to the hedged foreign rate:

$$1,503.91 \text{ USD} \times \left(0.7327 \frac{\text{GBP}}{\text{USD}} \right) = 1,101.91 \text{ GBP}$$

If we put the data from the previous example into this relationship, we get the following:

$$1.06056 \neq 1.0595\text{USD} \left(\frac{0.7327\text{GBP}}{0.7045\text{USD}} \right) = 1.1019\text{GBP}$$

We find that the domestic rate is 6.056%, whereas the hedged foreign rate is 10.19% (multiplying the foreign interest rate by F/S serves to *lock-in* the foreign rate in domestic terms). Your goal here is to *borrow at the low rate* and *lend at the high rate*. Hence, your arbitrage procedure is to borrow pounds, convert these pounds into dollars at today's spot rate, lend these dollars in the U.S., and simultaneously enter into a forward contract to sell dollars for pounds. Through this procedure, you will have an arbitrage profit.

 Professor's Note: Here's where the old Level 2 material left over from 2007 starts.

TRIANGULAR ARBITRAGE

LOS 18.h: Calculate the profit on a triangular arbitrage opportunity, given the bid-ask quotations for the currencies of three countries involved in the arbitrage.

To calculate the profits from triangular arbitrage we start in the home currency (whatever that is) and go around the triangle by exchanging the home currency for the first foreign currency, then exchanging the first foreign currency for the second foreign currency, and then exchanging the second foreign currency back into the home currency. If we end up with more money than we started with, we've earned an arbitrage profit. If not, we go the other way around the triangle (buy the second currency, then trade it for the first), and see if arbitrage profits are available that way. The tricky part is that the rates at which we trade the currencies depend on which way we're going around the triangle. The bid-ask spread forces us to buy a currency at a higher rate going one way than we can sell it for going the other way.

Professor's Note: There is no way to know which direction around, if either, will result in an arbitrage profit. The only way to do it is by brute force: first, go one way around the triangle and if no arbitrage profit results, then try the other way. Note that you might not generate an arbitrage profit in either direction.

Example: Triangular arbitrage with bid-ask spreads

Given the following bid-ask quotes, calculate the potential arbitrage profits from an initial position of $1 million.

- Swiss franc (Sf) per U.S. dollar ($): 1.2500 – 10
- U.S. dollar ($) per British pound (£): 1.8000 – 10
- Swiss franc (Sf) per British pound(£): 2.3000 – 10

Answer:

The following figure shows what the triangle looks like with the bid-ask spreads filled in.

Cross Rates with Bid-Ask Spreads

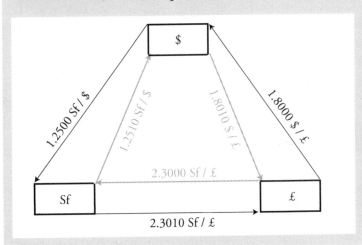

If we start with $1 million and move clockwise around the triangle ($ to £ to Sf to $) we first convert $1 million into pounds:

$$\frac{\$1,000,000}{\$1.8010/\pounds} = \pounds555,247$$

Then we convert the pounds into francs:

$$\pounds555,247 \times \left(Sf2.300/\pounds\right) = Sf1,277,068$$

Finally, we convert the francs back into dollars:

$$\frac{Sf1,277,068}{Sf1.2510/\$} = \$1,020,838$$

We've turned $1 million into $1,020,838, which is an arbitrage profit of $20,838. If we go the other way around the triangle ($ to Sf to £ to $), we end up with $977,836 (you can check this on your own). Therefore, arbitrage profits are not available going the other way around the triangle.

KEY CONCEPTS

1. Direct foreign exchange quotations are in domestic currency per unit (or 100 units) of foreign currency and indirect quotations are in the foreign currency per unit of the domestic currency.

2. The difference between the bid and ask prices for foreign currency is the spread, sometimes expressed as a percentage of the ask price.

3. Foreign currency spreads increase with exchange rate volatility and decrease with increased trading volume, but the size of the spread is not dependent on dealer positions in the market.

4. The reciprocals of the bid and ask as a direct quote are an indirect quote, but viewed from the foreign country the bid and ask are reversed.

5. The exchange rates of two countries with a third can be used to obtain a cross rate (of exchange) between the two countries.

6. Forward foreign exchange rates are for currency to be exchanged at a future date while spot rates are for immediate delivery.

7. Forward foreign exchange rates have a bid-ask spread calculated as for spot rates.

8. The forward contract price is said to be at a forward premium (discount) for a currency if the direct quote of the forward rate is higher (lower) than the spot rate.

9. A forward premium or discount is often stated as an annualized percentage of the spot rate as: $\left(\dfrac{\text{forward rate}}{\text{spot rate}} - 1\right)\left(\dfrac{360}{\text{term in days}}\right)$.

10. A currency selling at a forward premium is considered "strong" relative to the second currency, while a currency selling at a forward discount is considered "weak."

11. Interest rate parity equates forward premiums or discounts to interest rate differentials between countries by the relation: $\dfrac{\text{forward}\left(\dfrac{DC}{FC}\right)}{\text{spot}\left(\dfrac{DC}{FC}\right)} = \dfrac{1 + r_{DC}}{1 + r_{FC}}$.

12. When interest rate parity does not hold, there is a profitable arbitrage either from lending a currency that has a forward rate above the parity value or borrowing a currency that has a forward rate below the parity value.

13. To calculate the profits from triangular arbitrage, start in the home currency and go both ways around the triangle by exchanging the home currency for the first foreign currency, then exchanging the first foreign currency for the second foreign currency, and then exchanging the second foreign currency back into the home currency. If we end up with more money than we started with, we've earned an arbitrage profit. The bid-ask spread forces us to buy a currency at a higher rate going one way than we can sell it for going the other way. In constructing the triangle, think "up the bid and down the ask."

CONCEPT CHECKERS

1. Suppose that the quote for British pounds (GBP) in New York is 1.3110 USD/GBP. What is the quote for U.S. dollars (USD) in London (GBP/USD)?
    A. 1.3110.
    B. 0.3110.
    C. 0.7628.
    D. 0.2372.

2. The interest rates in the U.S. (USD) and Sweden (SEK) are 4% and 7% per year, respectively. If the current spot rate is 9.5238 SEK/USD, then the 1-year forward rate in SEK/USD from the perspective of a U.S. investor is:
    A. 9.2568 SEK/USD.
    B. 10.2884 SEK/USD.
    C. 10.1905 SEK/USD.
    D. 9.7985 SEK/USD.

3. The nominal risk-free interest rate is 10% in the U.S. and 4% in Switzerland (CHF), respectively, and the 1-year forward rate is USD0.80/CHF. If interest rate parity holds, today's spot rate:
    A. cannot be determined using the above information.
    B. must be 0.8462 USD/CHF.
    C. must be 0.7564 USD/CHF.
    D. must be 0.8888 USD/CHF.

4. The spot rate on the New Zealand dollar (NZD) is 1.4286 NZD/USD, and the 180-day forward rate is 1.3889 NZD/USD. This difference means:
    A. interest rates must be lower in the U.S. than in New Zealand.
    B. interest rates must be higher in the U.S. than in New Zealand.
    C. the NZD is expected to depreciate.
    D. the dollar is expected to appreciate.

5. Today's spot rate for the Indonesian rupiah (IDR) is 2,400 IDR/USD, and the New Zealand dollar trades at 1.60 NZD/USD. The NZD/IDR cross rate is:
    A. 0.00067 NZD/IDR.
    B. 1,492.53 NZD/IDR.
    C. 3,840 NZD/IDR.
    D. 0.00015 NZD/IDR.

6. Today's spot USD/NZD ask exchange rate is 0.6010, and the bid is 0.6000. The percentage spread on the USD is:
    A. 0.6600%.
    B. 0.1664%.
    C. 6.0010%.
    D. 1.5151%.

7. The NZD is trading at 0.3500 USD/NZD and the SEK is trading at 0.3100 NZD/SEK. The USD/SEK exchange rate is:
   A. 0.1129 USD/SEK.
   B. 9.2166 USD/SEK.
   C. 0.1085 USD/SEK.
   D. 0.1050 USD/SEK.

8. Suppose that the quote for GBP in New York is 1.7574 – 84 USD/GBP. The equivalent quote for U.S. dollars in London would be:
   A. 0.5687 – 90 GBP/USD.
   B. 0.5690 – 87 GBP/USD.
   C. 1.7574 + 09 GBP/USD.
   D. 1.7584 – 09 GBP/USD.

9. Assuming no transaction costs, if a U.S. investor can make risk-free profits by borrowing the Japanese yen, then:
   A. the hedged Japanese interest rate is low relative to the U.S. interest rate.

   B. $1 + r_{DC} < \dfrac{(1 + r_{FC})(\text{forward rate})}{\text{spot rate}}$.

   C. the U.S. interest rate is low relative to the hedged Japanese interest rate.
   D. the interest rate differential is approximately equal to the forward premium.

10. Assume the Philippine peso is at a 1-year forward discount of 1.25% to the Thai baht and that Thailand's 1-year interest rate is at 3.00%. If a Thai investor has no arbitrage opportunities, the Philippine interest rate is *closest* to:
    A. 3.10%.
    B. 4.25%.
    C. 1.76%.
    D. 1.25%.

11. The bid-ask quote for yen (JPY) in London (£/JPY) is 0.0050 – 0.00504. In New York, the bid-ask quote for British pounds ($/£) is 1.671 – 1.678. What is the $/JPY ask as a cross rate?
    A. 0.008390.
    B. 0.008457.
    C. 0.008422.
    D. 0.008355.

Use the following information to answer Questions 12 and 13.

$/Sf spot rate = 0.8000 – 0.8100
$/Sf 180-day forward rate = 0.8400 – 0.8500

£/$ spot rate = 0.5500 – 0.5600
£/$ 180-day forward rate = 0.5300 – 0.5400

12. Relative to the Swiss franc, the dollar is *closest* to trading at a 6-month annualized forward:
    A. premium of 10.38%.
    B. premium of 9.47%.
    C. discount of 9.47%.
    D. discount of 10.38%.

13. What is the *most appropriate* characterization of the strength of the U.S. dollar versus the Swiss franc and the pound?

	U.S. dollar vs. Swiss franc	U.S. dollar vs. pound
A.	Strong	Strong
B.	Strong	Weak
C.	Weak	Strong
D.	Weak	Weak

CHALLENGE PROBLEMS

14. Suppose that the spot rate for the dollar is 0.7102 USD/CHF. Swiss and U.S. interest rates are 7.6% and 5.2%, respectively. If the 1-year forward rate is 0.7200 USD/CHF, a U.S. investor could earn an arbitrage profit per dollar invested of:
    A. USD0.0000.
    B. USD0.7200.
    C. USD1.0908.
    D. USD0.0388.

15. The bid-ask quotes for the U.S. dollar, British pound, and Swiss franc are:
    • Swiss franc (Sf) per U.S. dollar ($): 1.6500 – 10
    • U.S. dollar ($) per British pound (£): 1.2000 – 10
    • Swiss franc (Sf) per British pound (£): 2.0000 – 10

    The potential arbitrage profits (not losses) from an initial position of $1 million are *closest* to:
    A. $0.
    B. $8,649.
    C. $10,495.
    D. $20,098.

ANSWERS – CONCEPT CHECKERS

1. **C** $0.7628 = 1/1.311$

2. **D** The formula is as follows: $\text{forward (DC/FC)} = \text{spot (DC/FC)} \left(\dfrac{1 + r_{DC}}{1 + r_{FC}} \right)$.

   Since our quotes are in foreign/domestic instead of domestic over foreign, it may be easier for us to express interest rate parity in FC/DC terms as follows:

   $$\text{forward (FC/DC)} = \text{spot (FC/DC)} \left(\frac{1 + r_{FC}}{1 + r_{DC}} \right)$$

   Hence, the forward rate in SEK/USD is $9.7985 = 9.5238 \left(\dfrac{1.07}{1.04} \right)$. Since it takes more SEK to buy a USD in the forward market, the forward SEK is depreciating relative to the USD. The forward SEK must be depreciating because the Swedish interest rate exceeds the U.S. rate, and the purpose of interest rate parity is to keep the hedged foreign rate equal to the domestic rate. You can either invest in the U.S. at 4% or in Sweden at 7%. When you lock in your Swedish lendings by selling SEK forward, you *must* face a loss of 3% on this forward currency trade.

3. **C** We can solve interest rate parity for the spot rate as follows:

   $$\text{spot (DC/FC)} = \text{forward (DC/FC)} \left(\frac{1 + r_{FC}}{1 + r_{DC}} \right)$$

   Hence, spot is $0.7564 = 0.80 \left(\dfrac{1.04}{1.10} \right)$. Since the interest rate is higher in the U.S., it should take fewer USD to buy CHF in the spot market. In other words, the forward USD must be depreciating relative to the spot.

4. **B** Interest rates are higher in the U.S. than in New Zealand. It takes fewer NZD to buy one USD in the forward market than in the spot market, so the USD is expected to depreciate (is at a forward discount).

5. **A** (1.60 NZD/USD) / (2,400 IDR/USD) = 0.00067 NZD/IDR

6. **B** The USD percent spread = $\dfrac{0.6010 - 0.6000}{0.6010} (100) = 0.1664\%$.

7. **C** 0.3500 USD/NZD × 0.3100 NZD/SEK = 0.1085 USD/SEK. Notice that the NZD cancels in the multiplication.

8. **A** Invert the quotes: 1/1.7574 = 0.5690 and 1/1.7584 = 0.5687. Remember, when you invert a quote, the ask becomes the bid for the other currency and vice versa. So the quote is 0.5687–90 GBP/USD in London.

9. **A** Stating that an investor can make risk-free profits is just another way of saying that arbitrage opportunities exist. This choice is equivalent to saying that the domestic (U.S.) rate is high relative to the hedged foreign rate, or:

$$1 + r_{DC} > \frac{(1 + r_{FC})(\text{forward rate})}{\text{spot rate}}$$

The other statements are false (note that choices B and C are the same). If the U.S. interest rate is low relative to the Japanese hedged interest rate, a U.S. investor could earn risk-free profits by borrowing domestic. When the interest rate differential is approximately equal to the forward premium, interest rate parity holds, and there are *no* arbitrage profits.

10. **B** If there are no arbitrage opportunities, IRP holds, and the interest rate differential is equal to the forward differential, or:

$$r_{DC} - r_{FC} = -0.0125, \ 0.030 - r_{FC} = -0.0125, \ r_{FC} = 0.0425 = 4.25\%$$

11. **B** Multiplying the asks yields $0.00504 \times 1.678 = 0.008457$ \$/JPY.

12. **C**
$$\text{spot midpoint in Sf per \$} = \frac{1}{0.805} = 1.2422$$
$$\text{forward midpoint in Sf per \$} = \frac{1}{0.845} = 1.1834$$

$$\text{forward discount on \$} = \left(\frac{1.1834 - 1.2422}{1.2422}\right)\left(\frac{360}{180}\right) = -0.0947 = -9.47\%$$

13. **D** The dollar is selling at a discount relative to the Swiss franc (as we determined in Question 12); therefore, it is weak relative to the Swiss franc. The pound/U.S. dollar rates are quoted in £/\$, and the spot rate midpoint (0.555) is greater than the forward rate midpoint (0.535), so the dollar is also selling at a forward discount relative to the pound; therefore, the dollar is also weak relative to the pound.

ANSWERS – CHALLENGE PROBLEMS

14. **D** To determine any arbitrage opportunities, you should first examine the interest rate parity relationship:

$$(1 + r_{DC}) < \frac{(1 + r_{FC})(\text{forward rate})}{\text{spot rate}}$$

$$1.052 < \frac{(1.076)(0.72)}{0.7102} = 1.0908$$

By viewing this relation, we find that the investor will want to borrow in the U.S. and lend in Switzerland.

Today:
- Borrow USD1 at 5.2%. (You will owe $1 \times 1.052 = \$1.052$ at the end of the year.)
- Exchange $1 borrowed and buy CHF = $1/0.7102 = 1.408$ CHF at spot rate.
- Lend the purchased CHF at the Swiss rate (you will receive 1.408 CHF × 1.076 = 1.5150 in one year).
- Purchase a forward contract to sell the 1.5150 CHF and buy 1.098 USD (1.5150 CHF × 0.7200 USD/CHF = 1.0908 USD) to pay off the loan.

In one year:
- Close the Swiss savings account. Proceeds: (1.408)(1.076) = 1.5150 CHF.
- Use the proceeds of the savings account to purchase USD1.0908 at the prespecified forward rate (1.515 CHF × 0.72 USD/CHF).
- Pay off the loan. Money needed = USD1 × 1.052 = USD1.052.
- Riskless profit = USD1.0908 – USD1.052 = USD0.0388.

15. **B**   Here's what the triangle looks like with the bid-ask spreads filled in:

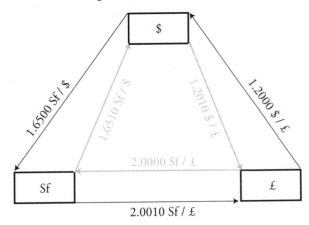

If we start with $1 million and move clockwise around the triangle ($ to £ to Sf to $), we first convert $1 million into pounds:

$$\frac{\$1,000,000}{\$1.2010/£} = £832,639$$

Then we convert the pounds into francs: $£832,639 \times \left(\frac{Sf2.0000}{£}\right) = Sf1,665,279$

Finally, we convert the francs back into dollars: $\frac{Sf1,665,279}{Sf1.6510/\$} = \$1,008,649$

Arbitrage profits are $1,008,649 – $1,000,000 = $8,649.

The following is a review of the Economics for Valuation principles designed to address the learning outcome statements set forth by CFA Institute®. This topic is also covered in:

FOREIGN EXCHANGE PARITY RELATIONS

EXAM FOCUS

Some of this material was in the Level 1 curriculum last year but was moved to Level 2 for the 2008 exam season. The topic review deals with five international parity relationships that help us understand the theoretical framework for explaining the interrelationships between exchange rates, interest rates, and inflation rates. This material is considered to be core body of knowledge material at Level 2 and is often tested. There is a lot of detail and many calculations. For those not regularly involved with the foreign exchange markets, the concepts may be very challenging and require considerable time to digest. Your primary areas of focus should be purchasing power parity, international Fisher relation, interest rate parity, uncovered interest rate parity, foreign exchange expectations, and the theory of exchange rate determination. However, you should also spend some time on the balance-of-payments accounts and the factors that influence exchange rates between countries. Finally, try to grasp the analytical arguments about how monetary and fiscal policy affect the balance-of-payments accounts through their effects on inflation, incomes, and real interest rates.

 Professor's Note: LOS 19.a through 19.f were part of the Level 1 curriculum last year but were moved to Level 2 for the 2008 exam.

EXCHANGE RATE DETERMINATION

LOS 19.a: Explain how exchange rates are determined in a flexible or floating exchange rate system.

Exchange rates are determined by supply and demand in a flexible exchange rate system (also called a floating exchange rate system). If there is an excess demand for U.S. dollars by Australians at the current exchange rate, they will sell AUD and buy U.S. dollars. This will cause the U.S. dollar to appreciate relative to the AUD. Intuitively, when might this happen? Australians would create an excess demand for U.S. dollars if they desired to increase their *imports* of U.S. goods. In order to buy U.S. goods, Australians need U.S. dollars. Hence, the value of the U.S. dollar rises relative to the AUD.

BALANCE OF PAYMENTS ACCOUNTS

LOS 19.b: Explain the role of each component of the balance-of-payments accounts.

Professor's Note: The balance-of-payments accounts were also discussed in LOS 17.a in this study session.

Balance-of-payments (BOP) accounting is a method used to keep track of transactions between a country and its international trading partners. It includes government transactions, consumer transactions, and business transactions. The balance-of-payments accounts reflect all payments and liabilities to foreigners and all payments and obligations received from foreigners. The BOP equation is:

current account + financial account + official reserve account = 0

The **current account** measures the exchange of merchandise goods, the exchange of services, the exchange of investment income, and unilateral transfers (gifts to and from other nations). The *balance on current account* summarizes the balance on goods and services, the exchange of investment income, and unilateral transfers. All other factors constant, a deficit balance on a country's current account implies that there is an excess supply of its currency in foreign exchange markets. Hence, its currency should depreciate (decline in value).

The **financial (capital) account** measures the flow of funds for debt and equity investment into and out of the country. All other factors constant, a surplus balance in a country's financial account implies that there is an excess demand for assets denominated in its currency. Hence, its currency should appreciate.

Official reserve account transactions are funds held at the *International Monetary Fund* (IMF) in the form of gold, other foreign currencies, and special drawing rights at the IMF. In 1997, the U.S. ran a current account deficit and a smaller surplus in its capital account. As a result, the U.S. ran a surplus in the reserve account to balance the BOP account. These reserve balances are used by the Fed to *intervene* in the foreign-exchange markets in an attempt to loosely control exchange rates.

Professor's Note: For the exam, assume that the official reserve account is equal to zero (or fixed). Then, if you are given (or you determine) a change in the current account, say a decrease, you know that the financial account must change in the opposite direction, or increase. The current account measures exports minus imports, while the financial account measures the flow of capital transactions. If a country imports more than it exports, the difference must be made up by foreign investment (i.e., an increase in the financial account).

LOS 19.c: Explain how current account deficits or surpluses and financial account deficits or surpluses affect an economy.

Is a nation's current account balance a good measure of its economic health? No, there is no law, economic or political, which states that the current account must be positive to indicate economic health. Unlike running a *budget deficit* in which a person or institution spends more than it makes, running a deficit in the current account balance simply means a country imports more than it exports, and a country can do this for a long time. Also, countries that run current account deficits tend to run financial account surpluses so that they offset each other. Is an inflow of capital bad? No, if the capital is being invested in such a way as to enhance the productive capacity of the country. Is a current account surplus and financial account deficit an indication of economic strength? No, particularly if this occurs because there are few good investment opportunities in the country to attract investment and there are more attractive investment opportunities abroad.

FACTORS AFFECTING CURRENCY APPRECIATION AND DEPRECIATION

LOS 19.d: Describe the factors that cause a nation's currency to appreciate or depreciate.

There are *three major factors* that cause a country's currency to appreciate or depreciate relative to another's.

- **Differences in income growth** among nations will cause nations with the highest income growth to demand more imported goods. The heightened demand for imports will increase demand for foreign currencies, appreciating the foreign currencies relative to the domestic currency.
- **Differences in inflation rates** will cause the residents of the country with the highest inflation rate to demand more imported (cheaper) goods. For example, if prices in the U.S. are rising twice as fast as in Australia, U.S. citizens will increase their demand for Australian goods (because Australian goods are now cheaper relative to domestic goods). If a country's inflation rate is higher than its trading partners', the demand for the country's currency will be low, and the currency will depreciate.
- **Differences in real interest rates** will cause a flow of capital into those countries with the highest available *real* rates of interest. Therefore, there will be an increased demand for those currencies, and they will appreciate relative to the currencies of countries whose available real rate of return is low.

Figure 1 summarizes the factors that cause a nation's currency to appreciate or depreciate.

Figure 1: Factors That Affect Currency Movements

Factors*	Lower	Higher
Income growth rate	Appreciation	Depreciation
Inflation rate	Appreciation	Depreciation
Domestic real interest rate	Depreciation	Appreciation

* Relative to trading partners.

EFFECTS OF MONETARY AND FISCAL POLICY

LOS 19.e: Explain how monetary and fiscal policies affect the exchange rate and balance-of-payments components.

Exchange rate effects. Since monetary and fiscal policies affect income growth, inflation, and real interest rates, they will also influence exchange rates. The monetary and fiscal policy effects on exchange rates discussed below are only relevant in a system of flexible (floating) exchange rates.

An unanticipated shift to an expansionary monetary policy will lead to more rapid economic growth, an accelerated inflation rate, and lower real interest rates. The rapid economic growth stimulates imports, the higher inflation rate makes domestic products more expensive, which reduces exports, and the low real interest rate reduces foreign investment. Each of these factors increases the demand for foreign currencies relative to the domestic currency, causing the domestic currency to *depreciate*. Given an unanticipated shift to a restrictive monetary policy, the opposite occurs.

An unanticipated shift to a more restrictive fiscal policy will result in budget surpluses. The reduced aggregate demand causes an economic slowdown and lower inflation. These factors discourage imports and encourage exports, resulting in appreciation of the domestic currency. However, budget surpluses suggest that government borrowing declines, which reduces real rates and causes investment funds to flow out of the country. As a result, the domestic currency tends to depreciate. Thus, the results are conflicting. However, since financial capital is mobile, the effect of the interest rate change generally dominates in the short run, leading to short-run depreciation. Given an unanticipated shift to an expansionary fiscal policy, appreciation occurs.

BOP component effects. Monetary and fiscal policy can also affect the current and financial accounts through their impact on income, inflation, and real interest rates.

An unanticipated shift to an expansionary monetary policy will lead to higher income, an accelerated inflation rate, and lower real interest rates. The higher income and higher domestic prices stimulate imports and discourage exports, causing the current account balance to move toward deficit. The lower real interest rate discourages foreign and domestic investment at home, moving the financial account toward deficit. At the same time, the value of the domestic currency declines because of the earlier shift to imports. Now, however, the depreciation in the domestic currency encourages exports and discourages imports. This more than offsets the movement toward deficit in the current account. Thus, the impact of an unanticipated shift to an expansionary monetary policy will be a shift toward a deficit in the financial account and a shift toward surplus in the current account. An unanticipated shift to a more restrictive monetary policy produces opposite effects.

An expansionary change in fiscal policy (to a larger budget deficit) will cause an increase in aggregate demand and an increase in domestic interest rates (due to crowding out). The increased aggregate demand encourages imports, which moves the current account toward deficit. Meanwhile, the higher interest rates attract foreign investment and discourage domestic investment from leaving the country. Thus, the financial account will move toward surplus. An unanticipated shift to a budget surplus would produce opposite results.

Figure 2 summarizes the impacts of expansionary monetary and fiscal policy on currency rates, the current account, and the financial account. The impacts of restrictive policy are the reverse.

Figure 2: Impacts of Expansionary Monetary and Fiscal Policy

Policy	Currency	Current Account	Financial Account
Monetary policy	Depreciation	Surplus	Deficit
Fiscal policy	Appreciation	Deficit	Surplus

 Professor's Note: Here's where the "trick" about assuming that the BOP official reserve account is fixed comes in handy. As long as you know the impact on the current account, you know the impact on the financial account is the opposite.

FIXED AND PEGGED EXCHANGE RATE SYSTEMS

LOS 19.f: Describe a fixed exchange rate and a pegged exchange rate system.

Up until now, we have been dealing with flexible exchange rate systems. There are two other exchange rate systems that may also occur: a fixed exchange rate system and a pegged exchange rate system.

A **fixed exchange rate system** has a set rate of exchange and is supported by giving up discretion in monetary policy. Some countries fix their exchange rates to other currencies, such as the U.S. dollar, and sacrifice independent monetary policy. For example, Panama, Hong Kong, and the U.S. have a unified currency. The non-U.S. countries accomplish this through the use of a *currency board*, which has the power to create domestic currency only in exchange for a specific quantity of U.S. dollars they hold in bonds and other liquid assets. The currency board promises to redeem the domestic currency at the fixed exchange rate into dollars.

The EU has a similar system with the 11 countries that have joined the system using the euro as the unified currency. The distinguishing characteristic of a fixed-rate, unified currency system is the existence of only one central bank that can increase or decrease the money supply. A country that imports more than it exports under this system will find a net decrease in the money supply, which should lead to downward pressure on prices. Lower prices should reverse the export-import relationship until the country's exports begin to exceed its imports.

A **pegged exchange rate system** involves a commitment of a country to use fiscal and monetary policy to maintain the country's exchange rate within a narrow band relative to another (stronger) currency or to a bundle of currencies. This type of system requires a country to use its monetary policy to maintain the desired exchange rate.

 Professor's Note: The old Level 2 material from 2007 starts here.

INTERNATIONAL PARITY RELATIONS

Purchasing Power Parity

LOS 19.g: Discuss absolute purchasing power parity and relative purchasing power parity, and calculate the end-of-period exchange rate implied by purchasing power parity, given the beginning-of-period exchange rate and the inflation rates.

The **law of one price** states that identical goods should have the same price in all locations. For instance, a pair of designer jeans should cost the same in New York and London after adjusting for the exchange rate. The potential for arbitrage profits is the basis for the law of one price. If widgets cost less in New York than in Paris, an enterprising individual will buy widgets in New York and sell them in Paris until the price differential disappears. The law of one price does not hold in practice due to the effects of tariffs and transportation costs.

Instead of focusing on individual products, **absolute purchasing power parity** (absolute PPP) compares the average price of goods between countries. Absolute PPP only requires that the law of one price is correct *on average*.

So, according to absolute PPP, the ratio of the weighted average of the prices of all goods in two economies should equal the exchange rate. In practice, such weighted averages are never calculated and, even if the law of one price held for every good in the two economies, absolute PPP might not hold. This could be the case, since the weights of the various goods in the two economies may not be the same. Absolute PPP is not used in practice to predict exchange rate movements, and the weighted-average price of all goods in an economy is not calculated in any event.

Relative Purchasing Power Parity

The practical measure of the change in a country's price level is a price index, such as the CPI or the GDP deflator. Either can be used to calculate the inflation rate based on a particular "basket" of goods and services. **Relative purchasing power parity** (relative PPP) is based on a relation between exchange rate movements and differences in inflation rates between two countries. Simply put, if (over a 1-year period) Country A has a 6% inflation rate and Country B has a 4% inflation rate, then Country A's currency should *depreciate* by approximately 2% relative to Country B's currency over the period. Relative PPP states that changes in exchange rates should exactly offset any inflation differential between the two countries.

The equation for relative PPP is as follows:

$$\frac{E(S_1)}{S_0} = \frac{1 + E(i_{FC})}{1 + E(i_{DC})}$$

where:
S_0 = spot exchange rate at the start of the period (in FC per unit of DC)
$E(S_1)$ = expected spot exchange rate at the end of the period (in FC per unit of DC)
$E(i_{FC})$ = expected inflation rate for the foreign country
$E(i_{DC})$ = expected inflation rate for the domestic currency

We have to make a slight adjustment to the relative PPP equation if the problem involves multiple years or fractions of years:

$$\frac{E(S_t)}{S_0} = \frac{\left[1 + E\left(i_{FC}\right)\right]^t}{\left[1 + E\left(i_{DC}\right)\right]^t}$$

Professor's Note: One of the most confusing things about using relative PPP is deciding which inflation rate to put in the numerator and which to put in the denominator. If you mix them up in a multiple choice question, your answer will be wrong, but it will almost certainly be included among the choices. The key is to pay attention to how the exchange rates are quoted. You can see from the formula that the spot rate is quoted in FC per unit of DC, the FC inflation rate is in the numerator, and the DC inflation rate is in the denominator. So whichever rate is on the top in the spot quote is also on the top in the inflation ratio. For example, if the spot rate is quoted as U.S. dollars ($) per Japanese yen (¥), the U.S. inflation rate should be in the numerator and the Japanese inflation rate should be in the denominator.

We can restate relative PPP in order to solve for the end-of-period exchange rate implied by relative PPP:

$$E(S_1) = S_0 \times \left(\frac{1 + E\left(i_{FC}\right)}{1 + E\left(i_{DC}\right)}\right)$$

Relative PPP is a theory, and while it tends to hold in the long run, violations of the relative PPP relation in the short run are common in real markets. With covered interest rate parity, we noted that arbitrage will move forward exchange rates to levels consistent with our parity relation. There is no arbitrage available to force the PPP relation to hold; the question is whether the relation can be used to predict future exchange rate movements (how well the relation predicts future spot rates).

The following example illustrates using the relative PPP relation to calculate the expected spot exchange rate more than one period in the future.

Example: Calculating the exchange rate predicted by relative PPP

Suppose that the current spot quote for the Australian dollar is 0.20 USD/AUD. Also, annual Australian inflation is expected to be 10%, while annual U.S. inflation is expected to be 5%. Calculate the expected future spot rate in two years under relative PPP.

Answer:

$$E(S_2) = 0.20 \left[\frac{1.05}{1.10} \right]^2 = 0.1822 \text{ USD}/\text{AUD}$$

This example illustrates that to keep the relative cost of goods and services the same across borders, countries with higher rates of expected inflation should see their currencies depreciate. This is precisely what has happened in this example. Today it takes USD0.20 to buy each AUD. However, since prices are expected to rise faster in Australia relative to the U.S., it should only take USD0.1822 to buy each AUD two years from now. In a relative PPP world, the relative cost of Australian widgets to a U.S. purchaser will be constant after adjusting for exchange rates.

Here are two more examples to illustrate the use of relative PPP.

Example: Relative PPP

Suppose the indirect exchange rate quote is 8.385 South African rand (ZAR) for one euro, and inflation rates are 8.0% in the European Economic Community (EEC) and 10.0% in South Africa. Calculate the end-of-period exchange rate implied by relative PPP.

Answer:

In this example, the rand is the foreign currency and the euro is the domestic currency because the spot quote is rand per euro and we've defined the spot rate in FC per unit of DC.

$$E(S_1) = \text{ZAR8.3850} \times \left(\frac{1+0.10}{1+0.08} \right) = \text{ZAR8.3850} \times \left(\frac{1.10}{1.08} \right) = \text{ZAR8.5403}$$

In this example, the higher South African inflation rate means that the rand depreciates against the euro from ZAR8.3850 to ZAR8.5403 (i.e., it takes more rand to buy one euro).

Example: Relative PPP for multiple periods

Suppose the indirect exchange rate quote is 8.385 South African rand for one euro and annual inflation rates are 8.0% in the European Economic Community (EEC) and 10.0% in South Africa. Calculate the exchange rate at the end of four years implied by relative PPP.

Answer:

In this example, the rand is the foreign currency and the euro is the domestic currency.

$$E(S_4) = ZAR8.3850 \times \frac{1.10^4}{1.08^4} = ZAR9.0236$$

The rand depreciates even more over the four years because of the higher inflation rate in South Africa.

INTERNATIONAL FISHER RELATION

LOS 19.h: Discuss the international Fisher relation and calculate and interpret 1) interest rates exactly and by linear approximation, given expected inflation rates and the assumption that the international Fisher relation holds, 2) the real interest rate, given interest rates and inflation rates and the assumption that the international Fisher relation holds, and 3) the international Fisher relation, and its linear approximation, between interest rates and expected inflation rates.

The **international Fisher relation** specifies that the interest rate differential between two countries should be equal to the expected inflation differential. That means countries with higher expected inflation will have higher nominal interest rates. The condition assumes that real interest rates are stable over time and equal across international boundaries. We could argue that this should be the case because differences in real interest rates between countries would encourage capital flows to take advantage of the differentials, ultimately equalizing real rates across countries.

In order to construct the formula, let's first work with the domestic relationship. The nominal interest rate, r, is the compounded sum of the real interest rate, *real r*, and the expected rate of inflation, $E(i)$, over an estimation horizon. We can state the domestic version of the Fisher relation without the DC subscripts as:

Exact methodology: $(1+r) = (1+\text{real } r)\big[1+E(i)\big]$

Linear approximation: $r \approx \text{real } r + E(i)$

where:
r   = nominal interest rate
real r = real interest rate
E(i) = expected inflation

Now, if we move to a 2-country scenario, we have to introduce domestic and foreign currency nominal interest rates and expected inflation rates over the estimation horizon. If the real rates for both countries are assumed to be equal, they drop out of the equation, and we are left with the international Fisher relation in both its exact formulation and as a linear approximation:

Exact methodology: $\dfrac{1+r_{FC}}{1+r_{DC}} = \dfrac{1+E\left(i_{FC}\right)}{1+E\left(i_{DC}\right)}$

Linear approximation: $r_{FC} - r_{DC} \approx E\left(i_{FC}\right) - E\left(i_{DC}\right)$

Example: Calculating the nominal interest rate

Suppose the real South African interest rate is 4.3% and the expected inflation rate is 3.5%. Calculate the South African nominal interest rate.

Answer:

Exact methodology: $\left(1+r_{ZAR}\right) = \left(1.043\right)\left(1.035\right) \Rightarrow r_{ZAR} = 0.080 = 8.0\%$

Linear approximation: $r_{ZAR} \approx 0.043 + 0.035 = 0.078 = 7.8\%$

Example: Calculating a nominal interest rate using the international Fisher relation

Suppose the interest rate in Brazil is 9.0% and the expected inflation rate is 7.2%. If the expected inflation rate in Costa Rica is 12%, calculate the interest rate in Costa Rica using the international Fisher relation.

Answer:

Exact methodology: $\dfrac{1+r_{CR}}{1.090} = \dfrac{1.120}{1.072} \Rightarrow r_{CR} = 0.139 = 13.9\%$

Linear approximation: $r_{CR} - 0.09 \approx \left(0.12 - 0.072\right) \Rightarrow r_{CR} = 0.138 = 13.8\%$

Example: Calculating the approximate interest rate differential using the international Fisher relation

The expected inflation rate is 4.0% in the Eurozone and 2.7% in the U.S. Calculate the approximate interest rate differential assuming the international Fisher relation holds.

Answer:

Linear approximation: $r_{\text{€}} - r_{\$} = 0.040 - 0.027 \approx 0.013$, or 1.3%

If real rates in Europe and the U.S. are equal, the 1.3% inflation differential should reflect a 1.3% interest rate differential.

Example: Calculating the real interest rate

Suppose the nominal South African interest rate is 9.0% and the expected inflation rate is 3.5%. Calculate the real interest rate.

Answer:

Exact methodology:
$$(1.090) = (1 + \text{real } r_{ZAR})(1.035) \Rightarrow \text{real } r_{ZAR} = 0.053 = 5.3\%$$

Linear approximation:
$$0.090 \approx \text{real } r_{ZAR} + 0.035 \Rightarrow \text{real } r_{ZAR} \approx 0.090 - 0.035 = 0.055, \text{ or } 5.5\%$$

Example: Calculating the international Fisher relation

Suppose the spot exchange rate between the euro and the South African rand is €0.119 per rand. In addition, the Eurozone expected annual inflation rate is 9.0% and the expected South African inflation rate is 13.0%. The interest rates are 10.09% in the Eurozone and 14.13% in South Africa. Calculate the international Fisher relation, and its linear approximation, between interest rates and expected inflation rates. Also calculate the real interest rate for both countries.

Answer:

In this example, with the spot quote in euro per rand, we'll treat the euro as the foreign currency and the rand as the domestic currency.

Exact methodology:

$$\frac{1 + r_{\epsilon}}{1 + r_{ZAR}} = \frac{1 + E(i_{\epsilon})}{1 + E(i_{ZAR})}$$

$$\frac{1.1009}{1.1413} = \frac{1.09}{1.13}$$

$$0.9646 = 0.9646$$

Linear approximation:

$$0.1009 - 0.1413 \approx 0.0900 - 0.1300$$

$$-0.0404 \approx -0.0400$$

The international Fisher relation holds in the example, which means that the real rates are equal:

$$(1.1009) = (1 + \text{real } r_{\epsilon})(1.0900) \Rightarrow \text{real } r_{\epsilon} = 0.0100 = 1.0\%$$

and

$$(1.1413) = (1 + \text{real } r_{ZAR})(1.1300) \Rightarrow \text{real } r_{ZAR} = 0.0100 = 1.0\%$$

UNCOVERED INTEREST RATE PARITY

LOS 19.i: Discuss the theory of uncovered interest parity, and explain the theory's relationship to other exchange rate parity theories and calculate and interpret the expected change in the exchange rate, given interest rates and the assumption that uncovered interest rate parity holds.

If we combine PPP and the international Fisher relation, we get the **theory of uncovered interest rate parity**, which links spot exchange rates, expected spot exchange rates, and nominal interest rates:

Exact methodology:

$$\frac{E(S_1)}{S_0} = \frac{1 + r_{FC}}{1 + r_{DC}}$$

or

$$\frac{E(S_1) - S_0}{S_0} = \%\Delta S = \left(\frac{1 + r_{FC}}{1 + r_{DC}}\right) - 1 = \frac{r_{FC} - r_{DC}}{1 + r_{DC}}$$

where :
$E(S_1)$ = expected spot rate in one period, quoted in FC per unit of DC
S_0 = spot rate today, quoted in FC per unit of DC
r_{FC} = interest rate on the FC
r_{DC} = interest rate on the DC
$\%\Delta S$ = percentage change in the spot rate

Linear approximation:

$$\frac{E(S_1) - S_0}{S_0} = \%\Delta S \approx r_{FC} - r_{DC}, \quad \text{or } E(S_1) = S_0\left[1 + (r_{FC} - r_{DC})\right]$$

Professor's Note: Use the same guideline for uncovered interest rate parity as we did for relative PPP—if the spot rate is quoted as FC/DC, put the FC interest rate in the numerator and the DC interest rate in the denominator. For example, if the spot rate is quoted as Canadian dollar per Australian dollar, put the Canadian interest rate in the numerator and the Australian interest rate in the denominator.

In other words, nominal interest rates reflect expected changes in exchange rates and vice versa. Unlike interest rate parity, whose relationship must hold by arbitrage because we know today what the forward rate at some future point is, the empirical validity of uncovered interest rate parity is less certain. This is because the expected future spot rate is uncertain. The point is, while covered interest rate parity must hold exactly, uncovered interest rate parity is only an approximation of the relationship between changes in spot exchange rates and interest rate differentials.

The best we can say is that countries with high nominal interest rates should experience a depreciation of their currency in the long run. Here's the economic intuition: if the U.S. has a higher interest rate than Japan and we assume real rates are equal, then, according to the international Fisher relation, the U.S. must be expecting higher inflation. Higher inflation in the U.S. will translate into an expected decline in the value of the U.S. dollar relative to the Japanese yen.

However, we can use uncovered interest rate parity to *forecast* future spot exchange rates using market interest rates.

Example: Forecasting spot rates with uncovered interest rate parity

Suppose the spot exchange rate quote is ZAR8.385 per euro. The 1-year nominal rate in the Eurozone is 10.0% and the 1-year nominal rate in South Africa is 8.0%. Calculate the exact expected spot rate and the expected change in the exchange rate using uncovered interest rate parity.

Answer:

In this example, the rand is the foreign currency, and the euro is the domestic currency.

Exact methodology:

$$\%\Delta S = \frac{0.08 - 0.10}{1.10} = \frac{-0.02}{1.10} = -0.0182 = -1.82\%$$

$$E(S_1) = ZAR8.3850 \times (1 - 0.0182) = ZAR8.2324$$

Linear approximation:

$$\%\Delta S \approx 0.08 - 0.10 = -0.02 = -2.00\%$$

$$E(S_1) \approx ZAR8.3850 \times (1 - 0.020) = ZAR8.2173$$

The rand interest rate is lower than the euro rate, so uncovered interest rate parity predicts that the value of the rand will rise (it will take fewer rand to buy one euro) because of higher inflation expectations in the Eurozone.

FOREIGN EXCHANGE EXPECTATION RELATION

LOS 19.j: Discuss the foreign exchange expectation relation between the forward exchange rate and the expected spot exchange rate, and calculate and interpret the expected change in the exchange rate, given the forward exchange rate discount or premium, and discuss the implications of a foreign currency risk premium.

The **foreign exchange expectation relation** says that the forward rate is an unbiased predictor of the expected future spot rate:

$$F = E(S_1)$$

We can also say that the forward discount or premium is an unbiased predictor of the expected change in the spot exchange rate:

$$\frac{F - S_0}{S_0} = E\left(\%\Delta S\right)$$

Example: Forecasting spot rates with the foreign exchange expectation relation

The spot exchange rate between the Canadian dollar (C\$) and the U.S. dollar (\$) is 1.40 C\$ per \$. The 6-month forward rate is 1.45 C\$ per \$. Calculate the expected change in the spot exchange rate over the next six months.

Answer:

In this example, the C\$ is the foreign currency and the \$ is the domestic currency. The forward premium on the \$ is:

$$\frac{F - S_0}{S_0} = \frac{1.45 - 1.40}{1.40} = 0.036 = 3.6\%$$

The foreign exchange parity relation indicates that the expected change in the spot rate over the next six months is also 3.6%:

$$E\left(\%\Delta S\right) = \frac{F - S_0}{S_0} = 3.6\%$$

If it turns out that the forward rate *is* an unbiased predictor of the expected future spot rate, then there is no reward for bearing foreign currency exposure. In other words, there's no advantage to locking in the known forward rate with a forward contract versus waiting and transacting at the future spot rate, because on average the spot rate will equal the forward rate.

If this relationship doesn't hold, then there is a foreign currency risk premium. For example, some investors with foreign currency assets may be willing to pay more than the expected spot rate to hedge the uncertainty of holding foreign currency assets by taking a short position in the foreign currency. Others will demand more than the expected spot rate to sell the foreign currency forward and bear the uncertainty of the spot rate. That extra amount is the risk premium; think of it as a "cost" of hedging foreign currency-denominated assets with forward contracts. If there were no risk premium, hedging with forward contracts would be costless.

 Professor's Note: The empirical evidence seems to suggest that the forward rate is not an unbiased predictor of the expected future spot rate and, therefore, there is a premium for bearing foreign exchange risk. In the topic review of international asset pricing in Study Session 18, we deal with the existence of this risk premium.

INTEREST RATE PARITY

LOS 19.k: Calculate the forward exchange rate, given the spot exchange rate and risk-free interest rates, using 1) interest rate parity, and 2) its linear approximation.

 Professor's Note: Interest rate parity was discussed in detail in LOS 18.g in the previous topic review.

Interest rate parity (IRP) is a no-arbitrage relationship that describes the relationship that must exist between the current spot rate of exchange and today's forward rate of exchange. IRP must hold exactly (within transaction cost bounds) because investors will take advantage of interest rate differentials to move funds between countries whose spot and forward exchange rates are not in balance and earn arbitrage profits.

The exact and approximate formulations of interest rate parity are:

Exact methodology:

$$\frac{F}{S_0} = \frac{1 + r_{FC}}{1 + r_{DC}}$$

$$\text{forward premium or discount} = \frac{F - S_0}{S_0} = \left(\frac{1 + r_{FC}}{1 + r_{DC}}\right) - 1 = \frac{r_{FC} - r_{DC}}{1 + r_{DC}}$$

Linear approximation:

$$\text{forward premium or discount} = \frac{F - S_0}{S_0} \approx r_{FC} - r_{DC}$$

where S and F are quoted in FC per unit of DC

 Professor's Note: Once again, our numerator/denominator rule applies—if the spot and forward quotes are in FC/DC, the FC interest rate should be on top and the DC interest rate should be on the bottom. For example, if S and F are in euros per Swiss franc, put the European interest rate on the top and the Swiss interest rate on the bottom.

Example: Covered interest rate parity

Suppose the spot exchange rate between the South African rand and the euro is 8.385 rand per euro. The 1-year risk-free rate in the Eurozone is 10% and the 1-year risk-free rate in South Africa is 8%. Calculate the exact forward rate and the approximate forward rate.

Answer:

Exact methodology:

$$F = S_0 \times \left(\frac{1 + r_{FC}}{1 + r_{DC}}\right) = ZAR8.3850 \times \left(\frac{1.08}{1.10}\right) = ZAR8.2325$$

Using the linear approximation method, first calculate the approximate forward premium or discount, and then compute the approximate forward rate given the spot rate and the forward premium or discount:

$$\text{forward premium or discount} = \frac{F - S_0}{S_0} \approx r_{FC} - r_{DC} \approx 0.08 - 0.10 \approx -0.02$$

$$F = ZAR8.3850 \times (1 - 0.02) = ZAR8.2173$$

LOS 19.1: Discuss the implication of the parity relationships combined.

The international parity relationships explain the foundational relationships among interest rates, spot and forward exchange rates, and inflation rates, as shown in Figure 3.

Figure 3: The International Parity Relationships Combined

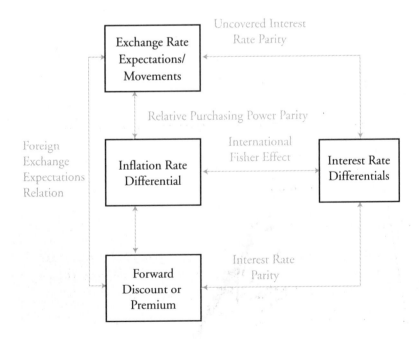

Combining all parity relationships indicates that the expected return on risk-free securities should be the same in all countries and that exchange rate risk is really just inflation risk. There are five practical implications from this framework:

1. The real risk-free return will be the same in all countries.
2. Investing in countries with high nominal interest rates will not generate excess returns because the high nominal interest rates will be accompanied by local currency depreciation.
3. All investors will earn the same expected real return in their own currency on any investment denominated in a foreign currency.
4. Exchange rate risk is simply inflation risk, so investors interested in real returns will not face exchange rate risk.
5. Foreign currency risk can be hedged without cost because there is no foreign currency risk premium.

EXCHANGE RATE DETERMINATION

LOS 19.m: Explain the roles of absolute purchasing power parity and relative purchasing power parity in exchange rate determination.

Empirical evidence tends to suggest that purchasing power parity does not hold, at least in the short run. That means exchange rates tend to change by amounts different than that implied by the inflation differentials. For example, suppose annual inflation for 2007 is 4% in the U.S. and 1% in Japan. Relative PPP would predict that the U.S. dollar (USD) should have *depreciated* by 3% during the year. However, suppose that the USD actually *appreciates* by 2%. We would conclude that the USD is overvalued in relation to relative PPP. In other words, the USD is above its "fundamental" value.

Empirical evidence also suggests that relative PPP *does* tend to hold more closely over the longer term. Currencies that become overvalued or undervalued in relation to PPP over time tend to eventually revert back to the long-term level predicted by relative PPP. That means *relative PPP is somewhat useful in exchange rate determination in the short run* because currencies that are overvalued relative to their PPP-determined fundamental value will tend to depreciate, while undervalued currencies will tend to appreciate. However, the adjustment period can sometimes be quite long (i.e., several years).

> *Professor's Note: It appears that we've made two contradictory statements—relative PPP doesn't hold in the short run, but it is useful in exchange rate determination. The key to understanding this LOS is to recognize that because relative PPP holds in the long run, exchange rates that deviate from fundamental value in the short run tend to revert back to the level predicted by relative PPP in the long run. We can use this fact to make short run predictions: overvalued currencies will depreciate over time, while undervalued currencies will appreciate.*

Absolute purchasing power parity is of little use in determining exchange rates. In order to directly compare the prices of goods and services between two countries, we would need to have identical individual goods and services to establish the validity of the law of one price. However, goods are rarely identical between various countries. In reality, differences in taxes, transportation and labor costs, rents, and government controls (e.g., tariffs) between countries provide complexities that prevent direct comparison. Therefore, it's difficult (if not impossible) to confirm whether exchange rates are under- or overvalued according to absolute PPP.

LOS 19.n: Discuss the elements of balance of payments and their role in exchange rate determination.

As discussed in LOS 19.b, the **balance of payments** is a summary of a country's international transactions. The traditional approach to foreign exchange rate determination suggests that exchange rate adjustments are required to restore balance of payments equilibrium. This is a difficult model to implement, though, because an analysis of these potential adjustments requires an estimate of trade flow elasticity in response to movements in exchange rates. Further, the model must be dynamic and complex enough to handle the impact of capital flows and the effect on the balance of payment components.

Ultimately, however, small changes in current account flows cannot substantiate the dramatic volatility in the exchange rate markets. That means an analysis of the elements of *the balance of payments is not useful in explaining how exchange rates are determined*. Therefore, additional models, such as the asset market approach, may provide more insight and be more useful.

ASSET MARKETS APPROACH

LOS 19.o: Discuss the asset markets approach to pricing exchange rate expectations.

The **asset market approach** views exchange rates as financial prices traded in efficient markets. Under this approach, the price of a currency, expressed as an exchange rate, is determined by investors' expectations about the future, not by trade flows and the balance of payments. Essentially, exchange rates represent the supply and demand for currency based on the market's forecasts of inflation and real interest rates. As a result, only news concerning inflation expectations and real interest rates will affect exchange rates. The asset market approach is used to estimate the change in exchange rates based on some disturbance in the fundamental value of a currency. For example, a sudden change in monetary policy will change inflation expectations and exchange rates.

The asset market approach assumes the international parity relationships apply in the long run. As we mentioned before, market imperfections prevent PPP from holding in the short run. Since the asset market approach assumes that exchange rates are financial prices, they reflect long-run equilibrium values. The pricing of exchange rate expectations by the asset market approach requires two steps.

Step 1:   Identify the long-run expected exchange rate value $[E(S_1)]$ based on PPP.

$$E(S_1) = S_0 \times \frac{1 + E(i_{FC})}{1 + E(i_{DC})}$$

Step 2:   Infer the short-run value of the exchange rate, S_0, assuming uncovered interest rate parity holds. Remember that uncovered interest parity is a relationship between the spot rate, the expected spot rate, and the interest rate differential:

$$\frac{E(S_1)}{S_0} = \frac{1 + r_{FC}}{1 + r_{DC}}$$

If we assume this relationship holds, then we can solve for the value of the spot rate today, given our long-run expected value and current interest rates:

$$S_0 = E(S_1) \times \frac{1 + r_{DC}}{1 + r_{FC}}$$

If the price adjustment occurs over a longer time period, say t periods, then:

$$S_0 = E(S_t) \times \frac{(1 + r_{DC})^t}{(1 + r_{FC})^t}$$

 Professor's Note: Once again, pay attention to which currency is used in the numerator of the formulas in this topic review. Up to this point, the formulas had $(1 + r_{FC})$ in the numerator. Solving for S_0 here places $(1 + r_{DC})$ in the numerator.

EFFECTS OF UNEXPECTED INCREASE IN MONEY SUPPLY

LOS 19.p: Calculate the short-term and the long-run exchange rate effects of a sudden and unexpected increase in the money supply.

Based on the asset market approach, a sudden and unexpected increase in money supply will cause the domestic currency to depreciate in the short run. This short-run effect is caused by an increase in expected inflation (equal to the percentage increase in the money supply) and a drop in real domestic interest rates. In the long run, the exchange rate will appreciate to the long run, PPP-determined equilibrium level.

Example: Exchange rate effects of an increase in the money supply

Suppose the spot exchange rate on 12/31/2006 is 0.66 U.S. dollars ($) per Australian dollar (A$). Suppose that the United States unexpectedly increases its money supply by 3.0%, and U.S. interest rates immediately drop from 4.0% to 3.0%. Assume that it will take three years for the increase in money supply to translate into higher price levels in the U.S. Assume both price indices are currently equal to 100. The interest rate in Australia is 4.0%. Calculate the short- and long-run effects on the exchange rate.

Answer:

The 3% increase in the money supply will translate into a 3% increase in the price level from 100 to 103 by the end of the third year (i.e., approximately 1% inflation per year, not 3% per year). The expected spot rate at the end of the third year is therefore equal to:

$$E\left(S_3\right) = \$0.6600 \times \frac{103}{100} = \$0.6798 \text{ per A\$}$$

Notice that the *wrong* calculation is $\$0.6600 \times \dfrac{1.03^3}{1.00^3}$ because prices rise by 3% in total over the three years, *not* by 3% per year.

The U.S. dollar will therefore immediately depreciate to:

$$S_0 = \$0.6798 \times \left(\frac{1.04^3}{1.03^3}\right) = \$0.6998 \text{ per A\$}$$

 Professor's Note: The time horizon is three years and, therefore, the interest rate differential is raised to the third power.

The result of the 3% increase in the U.S. money supply is an immediate increase in the exchange rate (a depreciation of the U.S. $) from $0.6600 to $0.6998. Then, over the next three years, the rate will fall back to $0.6798 as the U.S. dollar appreciates back to the long-run PPP fundamental value. The exchange rate "overshoots" its long-run equilibrium level initially and then falls back to it as interest rates adjust, as shown in the following figure.

Effect of Increase in Money Supply

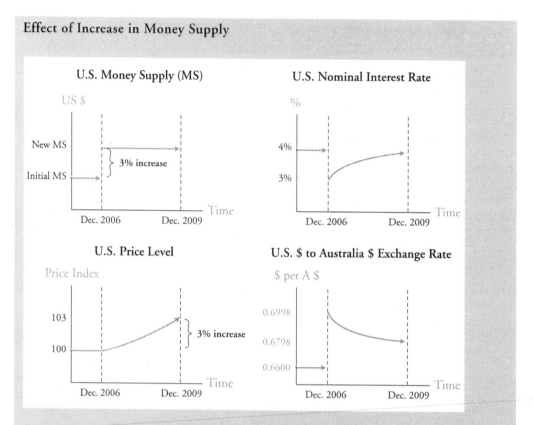

Notice that before the money supply change the nominal interest rate is 4% and expected inflation is zero, so the real rate is 4%. After the money supply shock, the nominal rate has fallen to 3% and inflation is approximately 1% per year, so the real rate has fallen to 2% (3% − 1%). It is this drop in the real rate that causes the exchange rate to overshoot.

KEY CONCEPTS

1. Supply and demand determine the exchange rates in flexible (or floating) exchange rate systems; there is supply of and demand for every currency in the foreign exchange market.

2. The balance of payments is given by the equation:
   current account balance + financial account balance + official reserve account balance = 0.
   The current account includes the exchange of goods, services, and investment income, while the financial account includes payments for securities, direct investment, and bank deposits.

3. A current account deficit simply means that a country imports more than it exports and if offset by a surplus in the financial account, a deficit in the current account can continue for a long period with no apparent problem.

4. Three major factors cause a country's currency to appreciate or depreciate:
   - The growth rate of income relative to trading partners (high growth → depreciation).
   - The rate of inflation relative to trading partners (high inflation → depreciation).
   - Domestic real interest rates relative to those of other countries (high real rates → appreciation).

5. An unanticipated shift to an expansionary monetary policy causes higher income, accelerated inflation, and lower real interest rates, leading to currency depreciation, a current account surplus, and a financial account deficit, while restrictive monetary policy has the opposite effect.

6. An unanticipated shift to expansionary fiscal policy (a larger budget deficit) causes currency appreciation, a current account deficit, and a financial account surplus, while restrictive fiscal policy has the opposite effect.

7. A fixed exchange rate system exists when a country fixes its exchange rate to the currency of another country; a pegged exchange rate system involves a commitment to use fiscal and monetary policy to maintain the country's exchange rate within a narrow band relative to another currency.

8. Under absolute PPP, the average price of all goods should be the same across borders after adjustment has been made for exchange rates.

9. Absolute PPP compares the price of a basket of similar goods between two countries. Under absolute PPP, price levels should be the same across borders after adjustment has been made for the exchange rate.

10. Relative PPP depends on the ratio of the growth rates of prices in two countries [S is defined in foreign currency (FC) per unit of domestic currency (DC)]:

$$\frac{E(S_1)}{S_0} = \frac{1 + E(i_{FC})}{1 + E(i_{DC})}$$

11. Countries with higher relative inflation rates should see their currencies depreciate through time, all else equal.

12. The international Fisher relation specifies that the interest rate differential between two countries should be equal to the expected inflation differential:

Exact methodology: $\dfrac{1+r_{FC}}{1+r_{DC}} = \dfrac{1+E(i_{FC})}{1+E(i_{DC})}$

Linear approximation: $r_{FC} - r_{DC} \approx E(i_{FC}) - E(i_{DC})$

13. Uncovered interest rate parity combines both the purchasing power parity and the international Fisher relation, where the expected currency depreciation should be offset by interest rate differentials between two countries:

Exact methodology: $\dfrac{E(S_1)}{S_0} = \dfrac{1+r_{FC}}{1+r_{DC}}$ or

$$\frac{E(S_1) - S_0}{S_0} = \%\Delta S = \left(\frac{1+r_{FC}}{1+r_{DC}}\right) - 1 = \frac{r_{FC} - r_{DC}}{1+r_{DC}}$$

Linear approximation: $\dfrac{E(S_1) - S_0}{S_0} = \%\Delta S \approx r_{FC} - r_{DC}$ or

$$E(S_1) = S_0\left[1 + (r_{FC} - r_{DC})\right]$$

14. The foreign exchange expectation relation states that the forward exchange rate quoted today for delivery at some time in the future is equivalent to the expected value of the spot exchange rate at some time in the future:

$$F = E(S_1), \text{ or } \frac{F - S_0}{S_0} = E(\%\Delta S)$$

15. If it turns out that the forward rate is an unbiased predictor of the expected future spot rate, then there is no reward for bearing foreign currency exposure. In other words, there's no advantage to locking in the known forward rate with a forward contract versus waiting and transacting at the future spot rate, because on average the spot rate will equal the forward rate. If this relationship doesn't hold, then there is a foreign currency risk premium.

16. Interest-rate parity is a no-arbitrage condition:

Exact methodology: $\dfrac{F}{S_0} = \dfrac{1+r_{FC}}{1+r_{DC}}$

forward premium/discount $= \dfrac{F - S_0}{S_0} = \dfrac{r_{FC} - r_{DC}}{1+r_{DC}}$

Linear approximation: Forward premium/discount $= \dfrac{F - S_0}{S_0} \approx r_{FC} - r_{DC}$

17. Combining all parity relationships indicates that the expected return on risk-free securities should be the same in all countries and exchange rate risk is reduced to inflation uncertainty.

18. Relative PPP is somewhat useful in exchange rate determination in the short run because currencies that are overvalued relative to their PPP-determined fundamental value will tend to depreciate, while undervalued currencies will tend to appreciate.

19. Small changes in current account flows cannot substantiate the dramatic volatility in the exchange rate markets. An analysis of the elements of the balance of payments is not useful in explaining how exchange rates are determined.

20. The asset market approach indicates that expectations regarding exchange rates are based on investor's expectations about expected inflation rates and interest rates.

21. A sudden and unexpected increase in money supply, all else equal, will cause the domestic currency to depreciate in the short run. This short-run effect is caused by an increase in expected inflation (equal to the percentage increase in the money supply) and a drop in domestic real interest rates. In the long run, the domestic currency will appreciate to the long-run, PPP-determined equilibrium level.

CONCEPT CHECKERS

1. If the U.S. dollar was quoted at AUD1.73 yesterday and today the U.S. dollar is trading at AUD1.80, the U.S. dollar has:
   A. appreciated, and will purchase less Australian goods.
   B. depreciated, and will purchase less Australian goods.
   C. appreciated, and will purchase more Australian goods.
   D. depreciated, and will purchase more Australian goods.

2. A country's currency will *depreciate* if its:
   A. income is growing slowly relative to the rest of the world.
   B. inflation rate is lower than that of its trading partners.
   C. real interest rate is lower than real rates in other countries.
   D. monetary policy becomes more restrictive.

3. If there were an unexpected decline in the growth rate of the money supply:
   A. real interest rates, output, and prices would fall, causing the dollar to depreciate.
   B. real interest rates would rise, causing an appreciation of the dollar.
   C. nothing would happen to exchange rates in the short run.
   D. real interest rates, output, and prices would rise, causing the dollar to appreciate.

4. If the current account is in surplus, the *sum* of the financial account and official reserve transactions must be:
   A. in deficit.
   B. in surplus.
   C. equal to zero.
   D. non-negative.

5. In a flexible exchange rate system, the value of a currency is determined by the:
   A. amount of gold held in reserve.
   B. country's currency board.
   C. supply and demand for the country's currency in the foreign exchange markets.
   D. World Bank at its weekly executive-committee meeting.

6. Which of the following would be the *most likely* negative consequence for a country that ran a current account deficit for ten consecutive years?
   A. Hyperinflation.
   B. Rapid economic growth.
   C. High real interest rates.
   D. There would be no negative consequences.

7. Relative purchasing power parity:
   A. does not hold in the short run or the long run.
   B. tends to hold in both the short run and long run.
   C. tends to hold in the short run but not the long run.
   D. tends to hold in the long run but not the short run.

8. Assume that the current spot rate of exchange between the U.S. dollar and the euro is €1.2500 per $. If the U.S inflation rate is expected to be 5% and the inflation rate in Europe is expected to be 4%, the expected spot rate of exchange three years from today is *closest* to:
    A. €1.0000.
    B. €1.2146.
    C. €1.2381.
    D. €1.2864.

9. Suppose the exchange rate quote is $1.15 per euro, and expected inflation rates are 10% in the European Economic Community (EEC) and 8% in the United States. The end-of period exchange rate implied by PPP is *closest* to:
    A. $1.1291.
    B. $1.1270.
    C. $1.1710.
    D. $1.1730.

10. The balance of payments approach to exchange rate determination is a:
    A. simple model to implement, and useful in explaining exchange rate movements.
    B. simple model to implement, but not useful in explaining exchange rate movements.
    C. difficult model to implement, but useful in explaining exchange rate movements.
    D. difficult model to implement, and not useful in explaining exchange rate movements.

11. The asset market approach to pricing exchange rate expectations:
    A. is determined by trade flows and the balance of payments.
    B. views exchange rates as financial prices traded in efficient markets.
    C. ignores news concerning inflation expectations and real interest rates.
    D. assumes the international parity relationships apply in the short run.

12. Suppose the spot exchange rate quote is 0.7132 Canadian dollars (C$) per U.S. dollar. The 1-year nominal interest rate in Canada is 7.0% and the 1-year nominal interest rate in the United States is 5.0%. The expected exchange rate using the linear approximation of uncovered interest rate parity is *closest* to:
    A. C$0.6896.
    B. C$0.6989.
    C. C$0.7275.
    D. C$0.7572.

13. The spot exchange rate between the domestic currency, the Danish kroner (DK), and the foreign currency, the U.S. dollar, is 6.812 DK per $. The 6-month forward rate is 6.953 DK per $. The expected change in the U.S. dollar over the next six months is *closest* to:
    A. −2.1%.
    B. −1.4%.
    C. 1.4%.
    D. 2.1%.

14. The five international parity relationships indicate that the expected return on risk-free securities should be the same in all countries and exchange rate risk is really just inflation risk. Which of the following is *least likely* to be considered a practical implication from this framework?
    A. Investors will earn the same real rate of return on investments once their own currency impact is accounted for.
    B. Exchange rates adjust over the long term to eliminate inflation uncertainty. Consequently, purchasing power will be similar whether importing or exporting goods.
    C. Interest rate differentials reflect currency expectations. As a result, covered interest arbitrage will provide a return in any foreign currency that is equal to the domestic return.
    D. There are significant rewards for bearing foreign exchange risk.

CHALLENGE PROBLEMS

Use the information below to answer Questions 15 through 20.

Sally Franklin, CFA, is a financial advisor to Jamie Curtess, a U.S. citizen interested in learning more about how her investments will be affected by exchange rates and differences in interest rates internationally. Franklin has gathered the following information based on Curtess's investment interests.

The current spot rate: $1 = €0.74.

	Europe	U.S.
Nominal 1-year interest rate:	0.04	?
Expected annual inflation:	0.02	0.01

15. According to international parity relations, the 1-year interest rate in the United States is *closest* to:
    A. 2.98%.
    B. 4.34%.
    C. 6.24%.
    D. 7.11%.

16. The expected exchange rate (in $ per €) in one year is *closest* to:
    A. $0.7335 per €.
    B. $0.7463 per €.
    C. $1.1650 per €.
    D. $1.3381 per €.

17. Use the answer from Question 15 to answer this question. According to interest rate parity, the 1-year forward rate (in $ per €) is *closest* to:
    A. $0.6772 per €.
    B. $0.7463 per €.
    C. $1.1650 per €.
    D. $1.3381 per €.

③ Asset Based approach

18. Assume for this question only that the expected inflation in each country is equal to zero. Curtess asks Franklin, "What would happen to the spot rate if the United States unexpectedly increases its money supply by 3.0% and the nominal U.S. interest rate immediately drops to 2.0%?" Assuming that currently both price indices are equal to one prior to the money supply increase and that it will take four years for the increase in money supply to translate into higher price levels in the U.S., the spot rate immediately after the money supply announcement is *closest* to:
    A. €0.8238 per $.
    B. €0.3919 per $.
    C. €0.7622 per $.
    D. €0.6648 per $.

Franklin also gathers the following information.

	Switzerland	South Africa
Nominal 1-year interest rate:	0.05	0.07
Expected annual inflation:	0.03	0.05

19. Curtess wonders how spot rates are expected to change in the future and asks the following question: "What are the implications for the South African rand relative to the Swiss franc for uncovered interest rate parity, and the implications for the euro relative to the U.S. dollar for purchasing power parity?" Franklin responds by making two statements:

Statement 1: I expect the South African rand to depreciate relative to the Swiss franc.

Statement 2: I expect the euro to depreciate relative to the U.S. dollar.

Are Franklin's expectations in Statements 1 and 2 accurate?

	Statement 1	Statement 2
A.	Yes	No
B.	Yes	Yes
C.	No	No
D.	No	Yes

20. For this question only, assume the nominal interest rate in the United States is 3%. Real interest rates using the linear approximation are *most likely* to be:
    A. greater in the United States than in Europe.
    B. lower in Europe than in South Africa.
    C. equal across all four countries.
    D. greater in Switzerland than in South Africa.

Answers – Concept Checkers

1. **C** If it took AUD1.73 to buy one U.S. dollar yesterday and today it takes AUD1.80 to buy one U.S. dollar, the dollar has appreciated and will purchase more Australian goods.

2. **C** A country's currency will depreciate when the real interest rate is lower than real rates in other countries. With a lower real interest rate, foreign investors will not buy the country's currency to invest.

3. **B** If there were an unexpected decline in the growth rate of the money supply, real interest rates would rise, causing an appreciation of the dollar.

4. **A** The balance-of-payments equation is:

    current account + financial account + official reserve account = 0

    So, if the current account balance is in surplus, the sum of the other two accounts must reflect a deficit in order for the sum of all three to be zero.

5. **C** In a flexible exchange rate system, currency value is determined by the supply of and demand for the country's currency. Anything that affects the supply of or demand for the country's currency will affect the exchange rate.

6. **D** A current account deficit simply means that a country imports more than it exports. There is no reason that this should have a negative effect on the country's economy. If it persists, it is an indication that the country's financial assets have been willingly purchased to maintain the balance of payments.

7. **D** PPP is a poor predictor of short-run exchange rate movements. However, PPP tends to converge to parity and hold over the long run. Reasons why PPP does not hold in the short term:
    *   The measurement of inflation varies across countries. A homogeneous basket of goods does not exist.
    *   Transaction, labor, taxes, and tariffs prevent arbitrage.
    *   Factors of production are not completely mobile in the short term.
    *   Since physical goods arbitrage is constrained in the short run, other variables can have a major impact on the short-term exchange rates. Factors such as political risk and supply and demand imbalances also create disequilibria pressures.

8. **B** $S_3 = €1.2500 \times \dfrac{1.04^3}{1.05^3} = €1.2146$

    The higher expected rate of inflation in the U.S. should force the $ to depreciate over the 3-year period. The purpose of the expected depreciation is to ensure that the relative cost of goods and services between the U.S. and Europe remains constant after adjusting for inflation.

9. **A** $S_1 = \$1.15 \times \dfrac{1.08}{1.10} = \$1.1291$

10. **D** The balance of payments approach to exchange rate determination is a difficult model to implement and not useful in explaining exchange rate movements. An analysis of these potential adjustments requires an estimate of trade flow elasticity in response to movements in exchange rates. Further, the model must be dynamic and complex enough to handle the impact of capital flows and the effect on the balance of payment components. Ultimately, however, small changes in current account flows cannot substantiate the dramatic volatility in the exchange rate markets.

11. **B** The asset market approach is not determined by trade flows and the balance of payments but, rather, views exchange rates as financial prices traded in efficient markets. The model assumes that exchange rates represent the supply and demand for currency based on the market's forecasts of inflation and interest rates and assumes the international parity relationships apply in the long run.

12. **C** The higher interest rates in Canada suggest that the C$ will depreciate (the U.S. $ will appreciate) by 2% to C$0.7275, according to uncovered interest rate parity:

$$\frac{E(S_1) - S_0}{S_0} = \%\Delta S \approx r_{C\$} - r_{U.S.\$} = 0.07 - 0.05 = 0.02 = 2.0\%$$

$$E(S_1) = C\$0.7132 \times (1.02) = C\$0.7275$$

13. **D** According to the forward foreign exchange relation:

$$E(\%\Delta S) = \frac{F - S_0}{S_0} = \frac{6.9530 - 6.8120}{6.8120} = 0.021 = 2.1\%$$

14. **D** Combining all parity relationships indicates that the expected return on risk-free securities should be the same in all countries and exchange rate risk is really just inflation risk. There are five practical implications from this framework:

1. The real, risk-free return will be the same in all countries.

2. Investing in countries with high nominal interest rates will not generate excess returns because the high nominal interest rates will be accompanied by local currency depreciation.

3. All investors will earn the same expected return in their own currency on any investment denominated in a foreign currency.

4. Exchange rate risk is simply inflation risk, so investors interested in real returns will not face exchange rate risk.

5. Foreign currency risk can be hedged without cost because there is no foreign currency risk premium. There is no reward for bearing foreign currency risk.

ANSWERS – CHALLENGE PROBLEMS

15. **A**   According to the international Fisher relation:

$$\frac{1+r_\$}{1+r_€} = \frac{1+E\left(i_\$\right)}{1+E\left(i_€\right)}$$

$$1+r_\$ = \frac{1+E\left(i_\$\right)}{1+E\left(i_€\right)} \times \left(1+r_€\right) = \frac{1.01}{1.02} \times 1.04 = 1.0298$$

$$r_\$ = 0.0298 = 2.98\%$$

16. **D**   According to relative purchasing power parity, the expected spot rate in one year (in $ per €) is calculated as follows:

$$€0.74 \text{ per } \$ = \$\left(\frac{1}{0.74}\right) \text{ per } €$$

$$E(S_1) = S_0 \times \left(\frac{1+i_\$}{1+i_€}\right) = \left(\frac{1}{0.74}\right) \times \left(\frac{1.01}{1.02}\right) = \$1.3381 \text{ per } €$$

Notice that you would get the same answer by using the uncovered interest rate parity relation and the U.S. interest rate of 2.98% calculated from Question 15:

$$€0.74 \text{ per } \$ = \$\left(\frac{1}{0.74}\right) \text{ per } €$$

$$E(S_1) = S_0 \times \left(\frac{1+r_\$}{1+r_€}\right) = \left(\frac{1}{0.74}\right) \times \left(\frac{1.0298}{1.04}\right) = \$1.3381 \text{ per } €$$

17. **D**   According to interest rate parity, the forward rate in one year (in $ per €) is calculated as follows:

$$€0.74 \text{ per } \$ = \$\left(\frac{1}{0.74}\right) \text{ per } €$$

$$F = S_0 \times \left(\frac{1+r_\$}{1+r_€}\right) = \left(\frac{1}{0.74}\right) \times \left(\frac{1.0298}{1.04}\right) = \$1.3381 \text{ per } €$$

Note that this is the same as the expected spot exchange rate in one year from Question 16, which means the forward exchange expectation relation also holds.

©2008 Schweser

18. **D**   The exchange rate effect of a sudden and unexpected increase in the money supply is an immediate depreciation of the $ from 0.7400 to 0.6648. After the money supply announcement, the expected spot rate in four years changes to:

$$E(S_4) = \frac{1}{0.7400} \times \left(\frac{1.03}{1.00} \right) = \$1.3919 \text{ per } €$$

Note that the *wrong* calculation is $\frac{1}{0.7400} \times \left(\frac{1.03^4}{1.00^4} \right)$ because prices are expected to rise by 3% in total over the four years, not 3% per year.

Using uncovered interest rate parity, solve for the spot rate today (S_0):

$$\frac{E(S_4)}{S_0} = \frac{\left(1 + r_\$ \right)^4}{\left(1 + r_€ \right)^4} \Rightarrow S_0 = E(S_4) \times \frac{\left(1 + r_€ \right)^4}{\left(1 + r_\$ \right)^4} = 1.3919 \times \frac{1.04^4}{1.02^4}$$

$$= \$1.5043 \text{ per } €, \text{ or } €0.6648 \text{ per } \$$$

19. **B**   Purchasing power parity predicts that countries with higher relative expected inflation will experience a depreciation of their currencies. South Africa's inflation rate (5%) is higher than the inflation rate in Switzerland (3%). The inflation rate in Europe (2%) is higher than the inflation rate in the United States (1%). According to purchasing power parity, the rand should depreciate relative to the franc, and the euro should depreciate relative to the U.S. dollar.

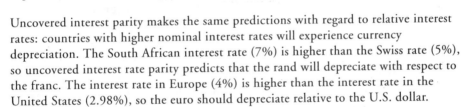

Uncovered interest parity makes the same predictions with regard to relative interest rates: countries with higher nominal interest rates will experience currency depreciation. The South African interest rate (7%) is higher than the Swiss rate (5%), so uncovered interest rate parity predicts that the rand will depreciate with respect to the franc. The interest rate in Europe (4%) is higher than the interest rate in the United States (2.98%), so the euro should depreciate relative to the U.S. dollar.

Franklin is correct with respect to both of his statements: the rand should depreciate relative to the franc and the euro should depreciate relative to the dollar.

20. **C**   The real interest rate is equal to the nominal interest rate minus the expected inflation rate. The real interest rate in each of the four countries is 2%.

The following is a review of the Economics for Valuation principles designed to address the learning outcome statements set forth by CFA Institute®. This topic is also covered in:

MEASURING ECONOMIC ACTIVITY

EXAM FOCUS

We've talked a lot about economic growth in the topic review of Reading 14, but until now we haven't addressed the issue of how to measure economic activity and growth in economic activity. In this topic review the various measures of economic activity are discussed. Remember that GDP is the preferred measure of economic activity, and understand how the GDP inflator is used as a measure of inflation.

MEASURES OF ECONOMIC ACTIVITY

LOS 20.a: Distinguish between the different measures of economic activity and their components.

The three most widely utilized measures of economic activity are **gross domestic product** (GDP), **gross national income** (GNI), and **net national income** (NNI).

- *GDP* is the total market value of all final goods and services produced in a country over a stated period of time, typically one year. To accurately reflect a country's productivity, the value of goods and services at their intermediate stages of production are not included in the calculation. Also, financial transactions and transfers of income are not included because they do not involve current production but are, economically speaking, a reclassification of assets. GDP only counts those goods and services produced within the geographic boundaries of the country. Thus, the output of a U.S.-owned company that manufactures products in factories in Mexico would not count toward the GDP of the United States. Conversely, the income earned in the United States by non-U.S. citizens would count toward U.S. GDP.

- *GNI* (formerly referred to as gross national product or GNP) is a measure of the total goods and services produced by the citizens of a country. It differs from GDP in that it includes the incomes (rent, interest, profits, and dividends) earned by all of the residents of the country, regardless of where the assets are located. Therefore, the GNI of the United States would include income earned by a U.S.-owned company that manufactures products in Mexico. GNI would not include the income earned in the United States by non-U.S. citizens.

- *NNI* is equal to GNI less depreciation. Depreciation (which is also called capital consumption) attempts to quantify the amount of resources utilized or worn out by the production process throughout the year. In practice, it is difficult to measure by actual usage. Therefore, it is measured by various accounting conventions.

Estimates of depreciation are based upon the expected life of the asset and may vary greatly from the actual usage of the asset.

GDP, GNI, and NNI are related as follows:

GDP
<u>+ net property income from abroad</u>
GNI
<u>– depreciation</u>
NNI

Although NNI is theoretically more accurate, the measure is not widely used because of the difficulty in quantifying the actual economic cost of depreciation. In most instances, there is very little difference between GDP and GNI. GDP is considered to be the preferred method of productivity measurement among industrialized nations; however, the GDP measure has several shortcomings. First, data for the GDP calculation is collected primarily through surveys, which is time-consuming to process and may contain inaccuracies. Second, GDP understates a country's productivity because of the presence of shadow or underground economies.

A country's GDP can be measured in one of three different ways: output, expenditure, and income.

- *Output* is measured as the net value added (total production less total cost) of all business in a country. Output data are presented as an index, with a designated base year's output set equal to 100, and data for subsequent years are expressed as a percentage of the base year.
- *Expenditure* is broadly defined as all spending within a country over a given year. Specifically, Total Final Expenditure (TFE) is calculated by adding the total value of three components: all consumption (e.g., spending on consumer items), investment (e.g., capital spending) and export of goods and services (e.g., spending by foreigners).
- *Income* includes all earnings of both employees and self-employed workers, trading profits of corporate and governmental endeavors, and rental income.

In a perfect world, output = expenditure = income. Because of date inaccuracies and timing issues, there may be discrepancies among the three. Typically, output is considered to be the most reliable measure, while income is regarded as the least reliable.

The specific calculations for each measure of GDP are shown in Figure 1.

Figure 1: Methods of Measuring GDP

Output	*Expenditure*	*Income*
Value of production <u>– Cost of inputs</u> GDP	Consumption <u>+ Investment</u> *Total domestic expenditure* <u>+ Exports of goods and services</u> *Total final expenditure* <u>– Imports of goods and services</u> GDP	Wages and salaries + Self-employment income + Company trading profits + Government and enterprise trading surpluses <u>+ Rental income</u> GDP

GDP AT MARKET PRICES VS. GDP AT FACTOR PRICES

LOS 20.b: Distinguish between GDP at market prices and GDP at factor cost, and explain the adjustments made.

The expenditure component of GDP is composed of market prices, which for certain transactions may include taxes and/or subsidies. Examples include sales taxes levied by various governmental entities or state-subsidized medical care. However, the output and income components of GDP are stated at their factor prices, which are net of taxes and subsidies. Therefore, an adjustment must be made to compare all GDP components in a consistent manner at either all market prices or all factor prices.

The factor cost adjustment can be utilized to convert GDP at market price to GDP at factor price and vice versa. This adjustment facilitates a more consistent measure, as well as identifies the economic impact of governmental involvement. Beginning with GDP at market prices, subtract indirect taxes and add back subsidies to arrive at GDP at factor cost. The reverse adjustment can be made to convert GDP at factor cost to GDP at market price:

> GDP at market prices
> – indirect taxes
> <u>+ subsidies</u>
> GDP at factor prices

Note that both GDP at market prices and at factor prices are accepted conventions, and it is important to clarify which method a country is using to measure its productivity. The U.S. economy is measured at market prices, while Great Britain reports its productivity both ways.

CURRENT PRICES, CONSTANT PRICES, AND THE GDP DEFLATOR

LOS 20.c: Discuss the difference between current and constant prices, and the GDP deflator.

As for the effect of inflation on productivity, various components of GDP are reported in different ways, either in current prices or constant prices that have been indexed for inflation. The three measures of GDP, output, expenditure, and income, are each collected and then reported differently.

- Output data is collected in both current and constant prices. Current prices are then converted to equivalent prices from a designated base year. For example, a country may select 1995 as its "base" year, and then convert all current market output to the equivalent amount in 1995 currency.
- Expenditure data is measured in current prices and then adjusted in a manner similar to the one used with output data. Both the current and constant

expenditure data is utilized to calculate a price index, also known as the implicit price deflator or **GDP deflator.**
- Income data is gathered in current prices and converted into constant prices using the price index.

The GDP deflator is also commonly used as an estimator of inflation trends, but is not accurate in a volatile economic environment. It is also affected by the composition of GDP.

KEY CONCEPTS

1. Gross domestic product (GDP) is the total market value of all final goods and services produced in a country over a period of time, typically one year. Gross national income (GNI) is a measure of the total goods and services produced by the citizens of a country. Net national income (NNI) is GNI less depreciation. GDP is the most widely used measure of productivity.

2. The expenditure component of GDP is composed of market prices, including taxes and/or subsidies, while the output and income components are stated at their factor prices, which are net of taxes and subsidies. A factor cost adjustment can be utilized to convert GDP at market price to GDP at factor price and vice versa.

3. The components of GDP may be reported in either current prices or constant prices that have been adjusted for inflation. The GDP deflator can be derived and used as a general measure of inflation trends.

CONCEPT CHECKERS

1. GDP is *best* described as the measure of total goods and services produced:
    A. by the citizens of a country.
    B. in a country.
    C. by the citizens of a country, net of depreciation.
    D. in a country, net of depreciation.

2. Which of the following statements regarding GDP and GNI is *least accurate*?
    A. GDP and GNI are used interchangeably by the major industrialized countries as their main measure of economic productivity.
    B. There is typically very little difference between the GDP and GNI measures for most countries in any given year.
    C. Neither GDP or GNI are adjusted for depreciation.
    D. GDP and GNI tend to understate productivity, in part because of the existence of shadow economies.

3. The *most* significant difference between GDP at market prices and GDP at factor prices is an adjustment for:
    A. tax avoidance or evasion.
    B. black market activity.
    C. indirect taxes and subsidies.
    D. inflation.

4. A factor cost adjustment to GDP is necessary for consistent comparison among its components because the:
    A. income measure of GDP is reported at market prices, while expenditure and outcome measures are recorded at factor cost.
    B. expenditure measure of GDP is reported at market prices, while income and output measures are recorded at factor cost.
    C. output measure of GDP is reported at market prices, while income and expenditure measures are recorded at factor cost.
    D. income and expenditure measures are reported at market prices, while the output measure is recorded at factor cost.

5. The GDP deflator, or price index, is calculated from the:
    A. expenditure component of GDP, using both current and constant prices.
    B. output component of GDP, using current prices.
    C. income component of GDP, using constant prices.
    D. output component of GDP, using both current and constant prices.

6. Which of the following statements regarding the GDP deflator is *least accurate*?
    A. Governments typically measure GDP figures in both current and constant prices.
    B. The GDP deflator is an effective tool for assessing economy-wide inflationary trends.
    C. The accuracy of the GDP deflator may be affected by changes in the composition of the GDP measure.
    D. Utilizing the GDP deflator to adjust for the effects of inflation is most reliable when prices are changing rapidly.

ANSWERS – CONCEPT CHECKERS

1. **B** GDP is the total market value of all final goods and services produced in a country over a stated period of time, typically one year. GNI is a measure of the total goods and services produced by the citizens of a country. It differs from GDP in that it includes the incomes (rent, interest, profits, and dividends) earned by all of the residents of the country, regardless of where the assets are located. NNI is GNI net of depreciation.

2. **A** All major industrialized countries now use GDP as their primary measure of productivity.

3. **C** The factor cost adjustment begins with GDP at market prices, subtracts indirect taxes and adds back subsidies, resulting in GDP at factor cost.

4. **B** The expenditure measure of GDP is stated at market prices, which include taxes and subsidies. The income and output measures are stated at factor cost, which excludes taxes and subsidies.

5. **A** Expenditure data is collected in current prices. It is converted into constant prices by deflating each component by an estimated price indicator, which is derived from data from a given base year. The current and constant prices are then used to calculate a deflator or price index, which is used with the income measure of GDP.

6. **D** Making the adjustment for inflation with the GDP deflator is least accurate when prices are changing rapidly, because small inaccuracies in measuring current prices can result in large inaccuracies when calculating constant prices.

Use the following information to answer Questions 1 through 6.

Teresa Young, CFA, is the head of the research department manager for a large financial services corporation based in New York City. The company's clients include pension funds, endowments, and large foundations. Young manages the group that produces research for use within the company as well as for its clients. Members of the research department include economists that perform short- and long-range forecasting, as well as analysts that follow industry trends and the various individual companies within the industry.

Many of the firm's clients have globally diversified portfolios, and one of Young's group's responsibilities is to provide appropriate support to the firm's portfolio managers. One of the European equities managers has come to Young for some assistance in handling a longtime client who is based in Dallas. The client's existing portfolio is well-diversified, with approximately 60% domestic securities and the remaining 40% in global investments, primarily in Europe and Asia. The client is unhappy with the portfolio's recent performance and is convinced that there is too much exchange rate exposure because of the large foreign allocation. The manager would like to provide evidence to the contrary to the client, and believes the client is lacking a fundamental understanding of foreign exchange parity relations.

Young pulls together some basic information regarding the theoretical relationships between exchange rates, interest rates, and inflation rates. She also obtains information on some of the client's key non-U.S. holdings. She observes that the client currently has a large position in Banyo, a Japanese manufacturer and distributor of consumer electronics with a dominant position in markets worldwide. The client also has a substantial investment in Seine Industries, a French producer of paper products whose primary market is Western Europe.

Current bid-ask spot rates:

- Euro (€) per U.S. dollar ($): 1.3200.
- U.S. Dollar ($) per Japanese Yen (¥): 1.2000.

Expected inflation rates:

- United States: 4.00%.
- France: 6.50%.
- Japan: 8.00%.

1. The major difference between the law of one price (LOP) and absolute purchasing power parity (absolute PPP) is the LOP:
    A. reflects the relative rate of change in price for a good in two countries, while absolute PPP is adjusted for absolute changes in price.
    B. does not consider the effects of differences in inflation rates between countries, while absolute PPP makes adjustments for any differences.
    C. focuses on the price of a single good, while absolute PPP is concerned with a weighted average price of a representative basket of goods.
    D. assumes that competitive markets exist without transportation costs or tariffs, while absolute PPP takes into consideration all transaction costs.

2. Utilizing the spot exchange rate and the inflation rate information given above, calculate the exchange rate predicted by relative purchasing power parity (relative PPP).
   A. $1.1556.
   B. $1.2462.
   C. $1.2480.
   D. $1.2960.

3. In her explanation of the International Fisher Relation, Young explains that real interest rates are stable over time and equal across international boundaries because:
   A. increased market efficiency will prevent any potential for arbitrage opportunities.
   B. forward rates already reflect any difference in expected real interest rates between countries.
   C. any expected inflation differential between countries will be brought back to equilibrium by consumers' demands for the least expensive goods and services.
   D. any difference in real interest rates between countries would encourage capital flows to take advantage of the disparity, ultimately bringing rates back to equilibrium.

4. Assume that the 1-year nominal interest rate for the European Economic Community (EEC) is 7.25% and for the United States is 6.50%. The expected exchange rate using the linear approximation of uncovered interest rate parity is *closest* to:
   A. €1.3101.
   B. €1.3299.
   C. €1.4058.
   D. €1.4157.

5. Assume that the 6-month forward rate is €1.35/$. Utilizing the foreign exchange expectation relation, the expected change in the spot exchange rate over the next six months is *closest* to:
   A. 2.27%.
   B. –2.27%.
   C. 5.34%.
   D. –5.34%.

6. Which of the following statements regarding the elements of the balance of payments and their role in exchange rate determination is *least accurate*?
   A. The financial account excludes transactions made by the country's central bank.
   B. Of the four accounts, the capital account generally has the greatest impact on the balance of payments.
   C. The current account is composed of the merchandise trade balance, balance of services, net income from investments, and current transfers of wealth.
   D. The official account represents the net change in a government's international reserves, and includes foreign currency holdings and loans to foreign governments.

SELF-TEST ANSWERS: ECONOMICS

1. **C** The law of one price (LOP) states that any one good or service should have the identical real price in all countries. Absolute PPP is an average version of the law of one price and is based upon a weighted average price level of a representative basket of goods and services.

2. **A** The equation for relative PPP is: $E(S_1) = S_0 \times [(1 + E(i_{FC})) / (1 + E(i_{DC}))]$. Since the rate is quoted as $ per ¥, the $ is considered to be the "foreign currency" and the U.S. inflation rate is placed in the numerator. Therefore, $1.200 \times [(1 + 0.04) / (1 + 0.08)]$ = 1.20×0.9630 = $1.1556.

3. **D** The International Fisher Relation states that the interest rate differential between two countries should be equal to the expected inflation differential. Countries with higher expected inflation will have higher nominal interest rates, but real interest rates are stable over time.

4. **B** The higher interest rates in the EEC imply that the euro will depreciate relative to the U.S. dollar.
$[E(S_1) - S_0] / S_0 = \%\Delta S \approx r_€ - r_\$ = 7.25\% - 6.50\% = 0.75\%$
$E(S_1) = €1.3200 \times (1.0075) = €1.3299$

5. **A** The foreign exchange expectation relation states that the forward rate is an unbiased predictor of the expected future spot rate. Additionally, the forward discount or premium is an unbiased predictor of the expected change in the spot exchange rate. Therefore: $E(\%\Delta S) = (F - S_0) / S_0 = (1.35 - 1.32) / 1.32 = 0.0227 = 2.27\%$.

6. **B** The capital account is comprised of unilateral transfers, such as debt forgiveness or investment capital given without future repayment, and generally has very little impact on the balance of payments.

The following is a review of the Financial Statement Analysis principles designed to address the learning outcome statements set forth by CFA Institute®. This topic is also covered in:

ANALYSIS OF INTERCORPORATE INVESTMENTS

EXAM FOCUS

There are no shortcuts here. Spend the time necessary to learn how and when to use each method of accounting for intercorporate investments because the probability of this material being tested is high. Know how to determine the effects of each method on financial statements to calculate financial ratios under each method. Pay particular attention to the examples illustrating the difference between the equity method and the consolidation method. You should be able to calculate and determine the effects of marking-to-market securities held for investment.

WARM-UP: ACCOUNTING METHODS FOR INVESTMENT SECURITIES

There are three accounting methods used for reporting the holdings of investments in securities of other entities. In each case, the investee must recognize dividends and interest in the year they are earned. However, carrying values are different under the three accounting treatments when the market values of the securities change.

1. The *cost method* recognizes changes in the market values upon sale of securities.

2. The *market method* recognizes changes in the market values in the period in which they occur.

3. The *lower of cost or market method* recognizes declines in market value in the period in which they occur. Gains are only recognized at recovery (if there was a previous decline) or when securities are sold. In other words, the carrying value of the securities can never exceed the purchase price.

CLASSIFICATION OF DEBT AND EQUITY SECURITIES

LOS 21.a: Distinguish whether a debt security or equity security should be classified as held-to-maturity, available-for-sale, or as a trading security.

SFAS 115, "Accounting for Certain Investments in Debt and Equity Securities," requires a hybrid of these three methods, depending on the security classification. The accounting treatment for securities that have a public market or a readily estimated fair value is determined based upon management's designation of the purpose of the security holdings. In the United States, the cost method must be used for securities that have no public market or readily determined fair value. SFAS 115 requires a company to classify its securities into categories based upon the company's *intent* relative to the eventual disposition of the securities. The classification will determine the accounting method used. SFAS 115 establishes three categories of securities classification:

Debt securities held-to-maturity are securities that a company has the positive *intent and ability* to hold to maturity. These securities are carried at amortized cost and cannot be sold prior to maturity except under unusual circumstances. This classification applies only to debt securities; it does not apply to equity investments.

Debt and equity securities available-for-sale may be sold to address liquidity and other needs of a company. Debt and equity securities classified as available-for-sale are carried at fair market value on the balance sheet. All interest income, dividends, and realized gains or losses are reported on the income statement. Unrealized gains and losses are excluded from income but reported (net of deferred income tax) as a separate component of shareholders' equity.

Debt and equity trading securities are securities acquired for the purpose of selling them in the near term. These securities are measured at fair market value and are listed as current assets on the balance sheet. Unrealized and realized gains and losses as well as interest income and dividends are reported in income.

SECURITY CLASSIFICATION: EFFECT ON RATIOS

LOS 21.b: Calculate and analyze the effect of marketable securities classification on the financial statements and financial ratios under SFAS 115.

A convenient way to keep track of the accounting methods applied to each security classification is as follows:

- Debt securities held-to-maturity use the cost method.
- Available-for-sale securities use the cost method on the income statement and the market method on the balance sheet.
- Trading securities use the market method.

The classification of the securities will affect the financial statements of the firm. Important financial statement effects are summarized in Figure 1.

Figure 1: Financial Statement Effects of Investment Security Classification

	Security Classification:		
	Trading	*Available-for-Sale*	*Held-to-Maturity***
Balance sheet or carrying value:	Fair market value	Fair market value with unrealized G/L* in comprehensive income	Amortized cost
Recognized as income:	Dividends Interest Realized G/L Unrealized G/L	Dividends Interest Realized G/L	Interest Realized G/L

* G/L stands for gains/losses.

**In the extended example that follows, we treat an equity security as held-to-maturity in order to compare the effect of the three different methods on the same set of facts. However, in practice, equities cannot be classified as held-to-maturity, so dividends cannot be recognized as income for held-to-maturity securities.

Management determines the appropriate classification of its investment securities at the time of purchase, reevaluates such determination at each balance sheet date, and transfers securities from one category to another.

SFAS 115 identifies the following rules related to transfers between portfolios:

- Securities transferred from either held-to-maturity or available-for-sale to trading are transferred at fair market value, and any unrealized gains or losses are included in income.
- Debt securities held-to-maturity transferred to available-for-sale are transferred at fair market value, and any unrealized gains or losses are recorded directly to equity.
- Available-for-sale debt securities transferred to held-to-maturity are transferred at fair market value, and any unrealized gains or losses remain in equity but are subsequently amortized over the remaining life of the security.

Securities listed in the available-for-sale and trading securities classifications are measured at fair market value, so a portfolio of investment securities can have a value *above* original cost at the balance sheet date.

Extended Example: Demonstrating Ratio Impact of Security Classification

The following example illustrates the application of the trading, available-for-sale, and held-to-maturity accounting methods and their respective impacts on financial statements and financial ratios. Focus your attention on how the financial statements are affected by the classification of the securities. Don't worry too much about the calculations.

Figure 2 contains transactions for nonoperating investments executed by Genco, together with associated market data and year-end values.

Figure 2: Market and Trading Data for Genco

	2004	2005	2006
Shares bought (sold)	1,000	(300)	500
Total shares: year-end	1,000	700	1,200
Purchase price	$50.00		$50.00
Sale price		$30.00	
Year-end market price	60.00	40.00	60.00
Year-end holdings at cost	50,000	35,000	60,000
Year-end holdings at market	60,000	28,000	72,000

Figure 3 contains annual income and realized and unrealized gains and losses on the trades.

Figure 3: Genco Portfolio Income Data

Income Source	2004	2005	2006
Total dividends	$1,000	$700	$1,200
Realized gains/losses	0	(6,000)	0
Unrealized gains/losses	10,000	(17,000)	19,000

Professor's Note: As you'll see in the next LOS, unrealized losses are most easily calculated as the change in the market valuation adjustment (MVA), which is the difference between the market value and the cost of the portfolio. The following table shows how the unrealized gains/losses for each year were derived.

	2004	2005	2006
Market value	60,000	28,000	72,000
Original cost	50,000	35,000	60,000
MVA	10,000	(7,000)	12,000
Δ in MVA = unrealized gain / loss	10,000	(17,000)	19,000

Figure 4 contains the pre-tax income statement effects of the three reporting methods. Recall that the three methods are virtually identical except that unrealized gains and losses related to securities held for trading are included in current period income. Unrealized gains and losses are not included for the two other categories, which results in the same reported income for those methods.

Professor's Note: For illustration purposes, we are treating equity investments as held-to-maturity securities, although in practice only debt securities can be classified as held-to-maturity.

Figure 4: Reported Income for Genco Portfolio

Classification	2004	2005	2006	Explanation
Trading	$11,000	($22,300)	$20,200	(divs + all G/L)
Available-for-sale	1,000	(5,300)	1,200	(divs + realized G/L)
Held-to-maturity	1,000	(5,300)	1,200	(divs + realized G/L)

The resulting reported income for trading securities is more volatile than it is for income associated with available-for-sale and held-to-maturity securities.

Figure 5 contains the reported figures found on the balance sheet under the three categories.

Figure 5: Balance Sheet Carrying Values for Genco Portfolio

Classification	2004	2005	2006	Explanation
Trading	$60,000	$28,000	$72,000	(Market value)
Available-for-sale	60,000	28,000	72,000	(Market value)
Held-to-maturity	50,000	35,000	60,000	(Amortized cost)

For the trading and the available-for-sale securities, the carrying value on the balance sheet is adjusted to reflect changes in the market value of the securities. Unrealized gains and losses on available-for-sale securities are reported net of deferred income tax as a separate component of other comprehensive income. For held-to-maturity securities there are no adjustments to the carrying value on the balance sheet or to comprehensive income.

The impact on financial ratios is varied. To begin an illustration of some of the effects, let's consider the rates of return on the carrying value (reported income divided by beginning carrying value) of the portfolio found in Figure 6.

Figure 6: Book Rate of Return for Genco Portfolio

Classification	2005	2006
Trading	−37.2%	72.1%
Available-for-sale	−8.8%	4.3%
Held-to-maturity	−10.6%	3.4%

In general, including realized and unrealized gains and losses from trading securities in the income statement and on the balance sheet will result in the most extreme outcomes. For example, any ratio involving net income will be larger (smaller) when unrealized gains (losses) are experienced. Although the pre-tax income for available-for-sale and held-to-maturity securities is the same, the book rate of return varies because unrealized gains and losses are included in the carrying value of the securities under the available-for-sale method, while the cost of the securities is used under the held-to-maturity method. The best approach to address exam questions on this topic is to follow the impact of the unrealized gains and losses under each accounting method and determine the marginal effect on financial ratios.

Effect of Security Classification on Financial Statements

The most significant effect of security classification on the firm's reported financial performance that you have to worry about on the exam is the result of management's ability to manipulate reported earnings and financial performance by reclassifying securities from one category to another.

For example, reclassifying securities that have appreciated in value from available-for-sale to trading results in reporting the unrealized gain in income. Because management classifies investments individually, it is possible for management to move securities with unrealized gains to the trading classification and recognize the gains while leaving securities with unrealized losses in the available-for-sale classification where the income statement is not affected.

There is another more subtle effect on the firm's investment and financing decisions. Under SFAS 115, firms are restricted from selling held-to-maturity securities prior to maturity, except in unusual circumstances. If the firm does sell a held-to-maturity security, it is required by SFAS 115 to carry its remaining held-to-maturity securities at market value instead of cost, which increases the volatility of assets reported on the balance sheet. Therefore, the firm's investing and financing decisions (e.g., whether to sell marketable securities to pay down debt) will be influenced by the anticipated accounting effects on the financial statements.

MARK-TO-MARKET INVESTMENT RETURN

LOS 21.c: Calculate and analyze the mark-to-market investment return on a marketable securities portfolio under SFAS 115.

 Professor's Note: In this reading, MVA is the acronym for market valuation adjustment. Elsewhere in Level 2 curriculum, MVA refers to market value added.

By now you know that dividends, interest, and realized gains and losses are recognized and recorded in the period they occur. The computation of mark-to-market investment return requires the inclusion of unrealized gains and losses.

mark-to-market return = dividends + interest + realized gains (losses) +
unrealized gains (losses)

Unrealized gains and losses are usually tracked through the use of a **market valuation adjustment**. The MVA is simply the difference between the fair market value of the investment portfolio and its cost on a given balance sheet date. Unrealized gains and losses are reflected in changes in the MVA:

unrealized holding gains (losses) = increase (decrease) in MVA

Example: Calculating mark-to-market investment return

Universal Insurance Co. reported the following book values (cost), market values (MV), and market valuation adjustments (MVA) for their investment portfolio for 2005 and 2006.

Universal Insurance's Reported Portfolio Balances and MVA

Classification	2005			2006		
	Cost	MV	MVA	Cost	MV	MVA
Held-to-maturity	$356	$391	$35	$377	$426	$49
Available-for-sale	323	301	(22)	298	308	10
Trading securities	155	172	17	214	237	23

In addition, Universal provided the following reported (realized) returns for 2006:

Universal's Reported Investment Income

Income Source	Held-to-Maturity	Available-for-sale	Trading Securities	Total
Dividend and interest income	$39	$33	$12	$84
Realized gains or losses	5	(11)	14	8
Reported income	$44	$22	$26	$92

Calculate Universal's mark-to-market return in total and for each security classification.

Answer:

Income Source	Held-to-Maturity	Available-for-sale	Trading Securities	Total
Reported income	$44	$22	$26	$92
Change in MVA	14	32	6	52
Mark-to-market return	$58	$54	$32	$144

The reported realized return to Universal's portfolio is $92. The mark-to-market return is $144. The difference is due to the unrealized gains that each investment sub-category experienced during 2006. If these portfolios had experienced losses, the mark-to-market return would have been less than the realized return.

To analyze the relative performance of a company's marketable securities portfolio, the analyst should compare the mark-to-market returns to a comparable risk portfolio over one complete business cycle. The analyst should also separate operating results from investment results by assessing the trend in pre-tax income after removing investment income. See Challenge Problem 19 for an example.

ACCOUNTING FOR INTERCORPORATE INVESTMENTS

LOS 21.d: Distinguish, given various ownership and/or control levels and relevant accounting standards, whether the cost method, equity method, proportionate consolidation method, or consolidation method should be used, and analyze and contrast the earnings effects of using the cost method, equity method, consolidation method, and proportionate consolidation method on a company's financial statements and financial ratios.

U.S. GAAP

Percentage of ownership (or voting control) is typically used as a practical guide to determine influence or control for financial reporting purposes. Figure 7 contains the guidelines used to determine which reporting method is required for intercorporate investments. Note that these are only *guidelines*. Nevertheless, the conceptual distinction for determining reporting methods centers on the degree to which the investee (affiliate) is an integral part of the investor (parent).

Figure 7: FASB Guidelines for Accounting for Investments

Ownership	Criterion (degree of influence)	Method
Less than 20%	No significant influence	Cost or market
20%–50%	Significant influence	Equity
Greater than 50%	Control	Consolidation

Cost or market. Ownership of less than 20% is typically viewed as a noncontrolling interest, and the two firms are treated as separate entities. The cost or market methods described in the previous discussion are used for financial reporting purposes in these instances.

Equity method. The equity method is used when the investor has a noncontrolling interest but may significantly influence the decisions of the firm whose stock is owned. The critical test for using the equity method involves the issue of **significant influence**. FASB defines this to mean at least 20% ownership and/or significant influence over the management, operations, investing, and financing decisions of the investee (e.g., it may be possible to have significant influence with only 10% ownership).

The use of the equity method is not allowed, even if the ownership level is more than 20%, if *any one* of the following conditions applies:

- The investor cannot exercise influence over the investee because of pending litigation between the two entities.
- The investor is unable to vote its shares or otherwise influence management of the investee because of restrictions such as a standstill agreement.
- A majority shareholder controls the investee's operations.
- There are other factors that indicate lack of influence on the part of the investor, such as a lack of seats on the board of directors.

Under the equity method, the proportionate share of the investee's income is included in the parent's income. The parent's reported income is not affected by changes in the market value of the investee unless the value decline is considered permanent or realized losses are incurred upon sale of the investment. The equity method of reporting must be used if significant influence is present but ownership is less than 20%.

Consolidated method. Under SFAS 94, direct or indirect ownership of more than 50% of the voting shares requires the parent to use consolidated reporting. Consolidated reporting results in two firms being presented as one economic entity, even though the firms may be separate legal entities. All income of the affiliate (less any minority interest) is reported on the parent's income statement. There are two exceptions under SFAS 94: (1) if control is temporary or (2) if barriers to control exist such as governmental intervention, bankruptcy, civil disorder, or if a nonconvertible currency is involved. These exceptions exist to accommodate situations where the parent cannot use the subsidiaries' assets or control its actions.

Professor's Note: The LOS says "given... relevant accounting standards." Our discussion to this point has focused on U.S. GAAP standards. Country standards vary considerably, but you are not expected to know the specific standards in each non-U.S. country. However, expect a question on the exam in which you are given a set of hypothetical standards for a fictitious country and asked to analyze the effects of using those standards on the reported financial performance.

EFFECT OF CHOICE OF METHOD ON FINANCIAL STATEMENTS

Professor's Note: We now turn our discussion to the effects of the different reporting methods on financial statements and financial ratios. The financial statement and financial ratio effects of the cost method were discussed in previous sections.

The Equity Method

The equity method allows the investing firm to include a proportionate share of the investee's income in its earnings, regardless of whether the earnings are actually received (i.e., whether or not the investee pays out earnings as dividends). The investor also reports a proportionate share of the investee's net assets.

Under the equity method, market values are ignored, but for purposes of analysis, market values can be compared with the carrying amount under the equity method. Clearly, market values are a better indicator of value.

Example: Implementing the equity method

Assume the following:

- December 31, 2004, Company P (i.e., the parent company) invests $1,000 in Company S (the subsidiary) and receives 30% of the shares of Company S.
- During 2005, Company S earns $400 and pays dividends of $100.
- During 2006, Company S earns $600 and pays dividends of $150.

Calculate the investment in Company S reported by Company P on the balance sheet, the reported income, and cash flow.

Answer:

Using the equity method for 2005, Company P will:

- Recognize $120 = ($400 × 0.3) on its income statement as equity in the net income of Company S.
- Increase the investment in the Company S account on the balance sheet by $120 to $1,120, reflecting its share of the net assets of Company S.
- Receive $30 = ($100 × 0.3) in cash dividends from Company S and reduce its investment in Company S by that amount to reflect the decline in the net assets of Company S due to the dividend payment.

At the end of 2005, the carrying value of Company S on Company P's balance sheet will be $1,000 original investment + $120 proportional share of Company S earnings – $30 dividend received = $1,090.

For 2006, Company P will recognize income of $180 = ($600 × 0.3) and increase the investment by $180. Also, P will receive dividends of $45 ($150 × 0.3) and lower the investment account by $45. Hence, at the end of 2006, the carrying value of Company S on Company P's balance sheet will be $1,225 ($1,090 for the carryover balance from 2005 + $180 proportional share of Company S earnings – $45 dividend received).

Equity Method vs. Cost Method: Effect on Ratios

To summarize, under the equity method Company P will report income and cash flow as shown in Figure 8.

Figure 8: Equity Method Accounting

Year	Investment in Company S	Income Reported	Cash Flow
2004	$1,000		
2005	1,090	$120	$30
2006	1,225	180	45

For comparison purposes, observe what would happen if the cost method had been used by Company P. The investment is carried at the original book value of $1,000, and dividends received are reported as income. The results are shown in Figure 9.

Figure 9: Cost Method Accounting

Year	Investment in Company S	Income Reported	Cash Flow
2004	$1,000		
2005	1,000	$30	$30
2006	1,000	45	45

The point here is that under the equity method, Company P reports higher income, as long as the subsidiary has positive earnings and pays out less than 100% of its earnings as dividends, but cash flows will be the same. Hence, interest coverage ratios and return on investment will be higher using the equity method. The parent's leverage ratios will improve because assets and equity increase, but debt is not affected. If Company S reported losses, Company P would have to write down the investment account (but not below zero) and recognize its share of the loss in net income.

Hence, the possibility of earnings management—a firm that acquires stock in an unprofitable firm may try to keep proportional ownership just below 20% (so it doesn't have to recognize the loss). There is some evidence that firms straddle the 20% line to get the desired accounting treatment. Using the equity method makes sense when the investee's undistributed income is increasing.

The use of the equity method results in an assumption that the undistributed earnings of the investee (income less dividends) will eventually accrue to the investing firm. In cases when this assumption is questionable, analysts should adjust equity earnings to a cost basis by including only actual dividends received.

The Consolidation Method

In a consolidated set of financial statements, each account consists of the sum of the corresponding accounts from each of the individual firms, less any intercompany transactions. When firms are consolidated, it is assumed that each subsidiaries' assets and liabilities are now also held by the parent company.

Let's do an example using the consolidation method.

Figure 10: Consolidated Method Accounting

Pre-acquisition Balance Sheets December 31, 2005	Company P	Company S
Current assets	$48,000	$16,000
Other assets	32,000	8,000
Total	$80,000	$24,000
Current liabilities	$40,000	$14,000
Common stock	28,000	6,000
Retained earnings	12,000	4,000
Total	$80,000	$24,000

Assume that on December 31, 2005, Company P acquires 80% of the common stock of Company S by paying $8,000 *in cash* to the shareholders of Company S. The following two balance sheets compare the consolidation method and the equity method of accounting for this transaction.

Figure 11: Consolidation vs. Equity Method

Post-acquisition Balance Sheet for Company P *December 31, 2005*	Consolidated	Equity Method
Current assets	$56,000	$40,000
Investment in S		8,000
Other assets	40,000	32,000
Total	**$96,000**	**$80,000**
Current liabilities	$54,000	$40,000
Minority interest	2,000	
Common stock	28,000	28,000
Retained earnings	12,000	12,000
Total	**$96,000**	**$80,000**

Note that under both methods the current assets will be the original values less the cash used in the investment. Under consolidation the cash balance equals $48,000 + $16,000 – $8,000 = $56,000. Under the equity method the cash balance is $48,000 – $8,000 = $40,000.

The most important thing to recognize is that just about all of the balance sheet accounts are different between the two methods, except common stock and retained earnings. Most balance sheet accounts will be larger under the consolidation method, including total assets and liabilities.

Although under consolidation all of the asset and liability accounts of the subsidiary are added to the parent's accounts, the parent does not "own" all of these assets and liabilities—the parent "owns" only 80%, and the remaining 20% are owned by other investors. This difference is accounted for as a liability by use of the **minority interest** account and is computed as (1 – parent's ownership) times the subsidiary's net worth. In our example, this is:

minority interest = (1 – 0.80) × ($24,000 – $14,000) = $2,000

Now, assume we have the following information about the individual income of P and S for 2006.

Figure 12: Company P and S Income Data

	Company P	Company S
Revenue	$60,000	$20,000
Expenses	40,000	16,000
Net income	**$20,000**	**$4,000**
Dividends		$1,000

The following two income statements compare consolidation with the equity method for the parent.

Figure 13: Income Statements Under the Consolidated and Equity Methods

	Consolidated	Equity Method
Revenue	$80,000	$60,000
Expenses	56,000	40,000
Operating income	$24,000	$20,000
Equity in income of S		3,200
Minority interest	(800)	
Net income	$23,200	$23,200

Once again, notice that every income statement item is different between the two methods, except net income. In particular, sales is larger under the consolidated method. Note also that the minority interest account in the consolidated income statement reflects the fact that although the parent included all the income of the subsidiary in the consolidated statement, minority interests have a claim to 20% of that amount: $(1 - 0.8) \times \$4,000 = \$800$.

Professor's Note: This example assumes that the parent company acquired its interest in the subsidiary by paying the proportionate share of the subsidiary's book value. If the parent pays more than its proportionate share of book value, the excess is allocated to tangible and intangible assets. See LOS 22.c for how this situation affects the calculations.

Consolidation Method vs. Equity Method: Effect on Ratios

Consolidation and the equity method both *result in the same net income and the same equity but differ in two important ways*:

1. *Consolidation* results in all of the assets, liabilities, revenues, expenses, and cash flows of the subsidiary being added to those of the investor. Minority interest is subtracted out. The subsidiary's operating, investing, and financing activities affect virtually every account in the consolidated statements. Parent company cash flows exclude those between parent and investee but include all others.

2. The *equity method* reports only the parent's share of net income and assets, including it as equity in the earnings of the subsidiary and investment in the subsidiary. Hence, only the investment account and net income are affected by investee results. Moreover, under the equity method, only capital flows between parent and investee (such as dividends) are included in cash flows of the parent.

Figure 14 shows the differences in a few key ratios between the equity and consolidation methods, using the data from the example.

Figure 14: Ratio Comparison of Consolidation vs. Equity Methods

Ratio	Consolidation Method	Equity Method
Return on equity	58%	58%
Return on assets	24%	29%
Net profit margin	29%	39%
Debt to equity	1.4	1.0

ROE will be the same because net income and equity are the same under both methods. In general, however, if the parent's consolidated net income is positive, the equity method reports better results than the consolidation method.

- ROA will be greater with the equity method because reported assets are lower than with the consolidation method.
- Net profit margin will also be higher because sales are lower with the equity method.
- Leverage ratios will be lower with the equity method because, with consolidation, equity is the same but assets and liabilities are larger.

The Proportionate Consolidation Method (Joint Ventures)

Joint ventures may take place for many reasons and may take various legal, operating, and accounting forms. In many cases, financial statements need adjustment to better reflect the economic substance of the joint venture.

Some joint ventures are only contractual arrangements and do not require the issuance of new equity. Each party reports its own assets, liabilities, revenues, and expenses separately, so there are no new accounting or analytical problems. Other joint ventures result in common ownership of assets but do not start a separate entity. Each party recognizes its share of the common assets, liabilities, revenues, expenses, and income of the joint operations in its own statements. Again, there are no new accounting or analytical problems.

However, in many cases the joint venture is a separate entity created by the contribution of capital from two or more parties. In these cases, the joint venture prepares its own financial statements, and the investors account for their interest in the joint venture using the equity method. If the equity method is used to account for a joint venture, the investor will report only a proportionate share of the net income and net assets in the joint venture. The point is that the equity method results in less than complete information about the total assets, liabilities, revenues, and expenses of a joint venture, which may be as much an integral part of the parent as any wholly owned subsidiary.

Proportionate consolidation accounting for joint ventures provides better information to users of financial statements. When reporting using the proportionate consolidation method, the parent company's share of each asset and liability of the joint venture is included. Only stockholder's equity will be the same under the proportionate consolidation and equity methods. The parent will also include its share of the joint venture's revenues and expenses in its income statement. Net income will not be affected, *but many financial ratios will change.*

A proportionate consolidation is not a provision of U.S. GAAP, although it has been adopted for use under International Accounting Standards (IAS). Analysts may employ proportionate consolidation on a firm that is currently accounted for using the equity method if the analysts believe that a stronger link exists between the two firms than is implied by the ownership percentage.

A joint venture is a typical example in which you would most likely apply a proportionate consolidation. A proportionate consolidation will lead to the same results as a normal consolidation *except* there are no minority interest computations. You simply add the parent's proportionate share of all accounts net of intercorporate transfers. Once again, do not add the equity accounts together.

For example, assume Company P owns 30% of a joint venture (JV), and the companies each report the financial information shown in Figure 15 (note that the statements for Company P already include the joint venture and have been prepared using the equity method).

Figure 15: Parent and Joint Venture Financial Information

Income Statements	Company P (Consolidated)	JV
Revenues	**$5,000**	**$800**
Equity in JV*	12	
Cost of goods sold	2,000	560
Selling and admin. expense	400	104
Interest expense	100	68
Earnings before tax	**$2,512**	**$68**
Tax (40% of $2,500)	1,000	27
Net income	**$1,512**	**$41**

Balance Sheets	Company P	JV
Cash	$500	$80
Inventory	1,000	200
Accounts receivable	1,500	200
Property, plant, & equipment	1,400	720
Investment in JV**	60	
Total	**$4,460**	**$1,200**
Accounts payable	$1,000	$320
Long-term debt	1,000	680
Equity	2,460	200
Total	**$4,460**	**$1,200**

* Equity in JV = $12 = 0.3 × $41 = (ownership share) × (JV's net income).
** Investment in JV = $60 = 0.3 × $200 = (ownership share) × (JV's equity).

In order to adjust the statements for Company P to the proportionate consolidation method, we further assume that the parent purchases 40% of the output of the JV, and the JV has an account receivable from Company P for $40 at year-end.

Figure 16: Proportionate Consolidation

Income Statement—Company P		Calculations
Revenues	$5,144	$= \$5,000 + (0.3 \times \$800) - (0.3 \times 0.4 \times \$800)$[1]
Cost of goods sold	2,072	$= \$2,000 + (0.3 \times \$560) - (0.3 \times 0.4 \times \$800)$
Selling and admin. expense	431	$= \$400 + (0.3 \times \$104)$
Interest expense	120	$= \$100 + (0.3 \times \$68)$
Earnings before tax	$2,521	
Tax	1,008	$= \$1,000 + (0.3 \times \$27)$
Net income	$1,513	(slight rounding error)[2]

Balance Sheet—Company P		Calculations
Cash	$524	$= \$500 + (0.3 \times \$80)$
Inventory	1,060	$= \$1,000 + (0.3 \times \$200)$
Accounts receivable	1,548	$= \$1,500 + [0.3 \times (\$200 - 40)]$
Property, plant, & equipment	1,616	$= \$1,400 + (0.3 \times \$720)$
Total	$4,748	
Accounts payable	$1,084	$= \$1,000 + [0.3 \times (\$320 - \$40)]$
Long-term debt	1,204	$= \$1,000 + (0.3 \times \$680)$
Equity	2,460[2]	
Total	$4,748	

1. Note the way the intercompany transactions are eliminated. In particular, revenues and cost of goods sold (COGS) are both lowered by the proportionate value of the intercompany transactions (a good way to think of this is that the revenue for one company is the COGS for the other), and the accounts receivable and accounts payable are adjusted by the proportionate value of the intercompany transaction.

2. Note that using the proportionate consolidation method results in the same net income and equity as the equity method.

The effect on ratios between the proportionate consolidation and equity methods is similar to that of consolidation and equity. Net income and total equity are the same, which means ROE is the same. However, if the parent's consolidated net income is positive, the equity method will report more favorable results for net profit margin, ROA, and debt to equity.

ANALYZING A REPORTABLE SEGMENT

LOS 21.e: Analyze a reportable segment under SFAS 131, and evaluate the uses and limitations of segment data.

Reportable Segments

Companies with multiple businesses present challenges for financial analysts. Aggregation of units with different financial structures, operations, risk, and performance profiles obscures the characteristics of each segment. SFAS 131, *Disclosures About Segments of an Enterprise and Related Information*, seeks to overcome some of these problems.

A "segment" is not strictly defined under U.S. GAAP. However, a **reportable segment**, as defined in SFAS 131, is a component of an enterprise that has at least 10% of one of the following:

- Revenues.
- Operating profit or loss.
- Combined identifiable assets of the enterprise as a whole.

Companies are required to disclose the following two items for all reportable segments:

1. Some measure of profitability, typically operating profit.

2. Identifiable assets.

Companies are also required to disclose the following seven items if they were also reported internally to the chief operating decision maker:

1. Intersegment sales and sales to unaffiliated customers.

2. Interest income and expense.

3. Expenses related to depreciation, amortization, or depletion.

4. Unusual or extraordinary items.

5. Income tax expense.

6. Capital expenditures.

7. Income from, and investments in, equity income investees.

In addition, geographical disclosures include revenues from external customers and long-term assets for the firm's home country and all foreign countries, including identification of any material information from a single foreign country. Companies must also report sales of more than 10% to any one customer. They are also required to disclose if 10% of sales comes from any domestic government agency or foreign government.

Uses of Segment Data

The secret to segment reporting is the determination of the segments of the business. Segments can be determined by the profit center concept or by similarities in product, production processes, markets, or marketing methods.

One of the best uses of segment data is to compute trends. As long as the computations are consistent from period to period, trends can be compared with results of other companies in the same business and with similar segments in other businesses to provide useful information about relative performance.

Segment data allows an analyst to better understand a company's operations and, hence, improve estimates in sales and earnings. Recent empirical evidence indicates that forecast accuracy has improved since the introduction of SFAS 131. Segment reporting on a geographical basis provides more limited information, but trends are still important when combined with economic projections for specific regions. The information from geographical segments can also be used to examine the effects of foreign exchange rate changes.

In practice, most analysts make their forecasts using segment data, especially if the firm operates in different industries. The segment data provides information about the source of sales and earnings growth and helps to assess future performance.

Limitations of Segment Data

Weaknesses related to segment reporting requirements include:

- The lack of detailed information on liabilities under U.S. GAAP makes it difficult to calculate some ratios. Operating income is calculated before interest payments, which may distort profitability ratios.
- The computation of segment profit may be affected by intercompany transfers and transfer pricing.
- The lack of segment cash flow data can hamper the analysis. Resource allocation to various segments is poorly calculated by changes in assets.
- The effects of exchange rates, cyclicality, and extraordinary items can distort segment data and increase the difficulty of segment data analysis.

ANALYZING SEGMENT DATA DISCLOSURES

LOS 21.f: Calculate financial ratios for the reportable segments of a company, and interpret the level and trend of each ratio.

 Professor's Note: This comprehensive example illustrates the analysis of 3M Company's segment data from 1998 to 2002. While you won't find anything this lengthy on the actual exam, all of the key concepts in business segment analysis are covered here.

Analysis of Business Segment Data

Figure 17 contains the business segment information reported by 3M Company for the periods 1998 through 2002[1].

---

1. United States Securities and Exchange Commission, n.d., <http://www.sec.gov/Archives/edgar/data/66740/000006674003000005/0000066740-03-000005-index.htm> (September 2007).

Figure 17: 3M Business Segment Information (in millions of $)

Business Segment Information	Year	Net Sales	Operating Income	Assets	Depreciation and Amortization	Capital Expenditures
Industrial	2002	$3,225	$563	$2,155	$154	$144
	2001	3,199	518	2,134	185	191
	2000	3,525	641	2,392	213	214
	1999	3,409	612	2,357	220	202
	1998	3,372	561	2,394	199	281
Transportation, Graphics, and Safety	2002	3,840	915	3,526	212	161
	2001	3,526	695	2,621	238	208
	2000	3,518	783	2,741	186	239
	1999	3,234	675	2,673	140	199
	1998	3,025	532	2,652	170	336
Health Care	2002	3,560	900	2,409	171	183
	2001	3,301	753	2,190	187	171
	2000	3,007	675	2,025	188	189
	1999	3,138	680	2,076	203	189
	1998	3,102	571	2,168	161	225
Consumer and Office	2002	2,792	514	1,519	118	100
	2001	2,817	454	1,588	127	114
	2000	2,951	434	1,711	101	134
	1999	2,705	401	1,589	118	123
	1998	2,624	398	1,614	136	182
Electro and Communication	2002	1,914	265	1,670	139	80
	2001	2,171	218	1,807	157	132
	2000	2,467	404	1,961	158	208
	1999	2,017	402	1,359	130	194
	1998	1,743	263	1,177	111	225
Specialty Materials	2002	953	136	1,221	94	87
	2001	1,022	141	1,208	97	136
	2000	1,197	57	1,230	144	131
	1999	1,194	185	1,323	79	143
	1998	1,133	194	1,112	66	188
Corporate and Unallocated	2002	48	(247)	2,829	66	8
	2001	18	(506)	3,058	98	28
	2000	34	64	2,462	35	0
	1999	51	1	2,519	10	0
	1998	95	(480)	3,036	23	16
Total Company	2002	16,332	3,046	15,329	954	763
	2001	16,054	2,273	14,606	1,089	980
	2000	16,699	3,058	14,522	1,025	1,115
	1999	15,748	2,956	13,896	900	1,050
	1998	15,094	2,039	14,153	866	1,453

Figure 18 contains the trends in the data from 1998 to 2002 for each reporting segment. The last two columns contain ratios calculated from the data provided by 3M.

Figure 18: Five-Year Trend Analysis of 3M Business Segment Data

Business Segment	Net Sales	Oper. Inc.	Assets	Dep. and Amort.	Cap. Ex.	Operating Margin	Return on Assets
Industrial	Down	Flat	Dow	Down	Down	Up	Up
Transportation	Up	Up	Up	Up	Down	Up	Flat
Health Care	Up	Up	Up	Up	Down	Up	Up
Consumer and Office	Up	Up	Dow	Down	Down	Up	Up
Electro and	Up	Flat	Up	Up	Down	Down	Down
Specialty Materials	Down	Down	Up	Up	Down	Down	Down
Total Company	Up	Up	Up	Up	Down	Up	Flat

The preceding trend analysis indicates that 3M, as a whole, experienced increasing sales (average annual growth = 2.0%), operating income (average annual growth = 10.6%), and operating margins (from 13.5% in 1998 to 18.7% in 2002). While four of 3M's segments contributed to these gains, the Industrial and Specialty Materials segment experienced declining sales and negative trends in its operating income. The Industrial segment was able to maintain its operating income on declining sales (average annual rate = −1.1%), which resulted in an increase in its operating margin (from 16.6% to 17.5%). The Specialty Materials segment's operating margin was down significantly (from 17.1% to 14.3%) because of declining sales (average annual growth rate = −4.2%) and operating income (average annual growth rate = −8.5%), which was deteriorating more rapidly than sales.

Some of 3M's investment patterns were also evident in the data. Overall, the firm's assets grew from $14,153 million in 1998 to $15,329 million in 2002, or an average of 2.0% per year over the period. This growth was due in part to net capital expenditures of $527 million (cumulative capital expenditures less cumulative depreciation). The remaining $649 million in asset growth was most likely attributable to acquisitions. Using similar analysis, we can see that the Transportation, Health Care, and Electro and Communications segments were all net acquirers. The Industrial, Consumer and Office, and Specialty Materials segments were all net sellers.

The expansion seemed to work for the Transportation segment. Over the period its operating margins improved from 17.6% to 23.8% while its asset turnover was mostly flat (from 1.14 to 1.09). This was also true for the Health Care segment, as operating margins improved from 18.4% to 25.3% over the period. Its asset turnover was also relatively flat (1.43 to 1.48). The Electro and Communications segment appeared to be struggling to make its expansion work. Its operating margin has declined from 15.1% to 13.8% over the period, as did its asset turnover (1.48 to 1.15).

Diverting within the Industrial group seemed to be working. Its operating margin and asset turnover improved from 16.6% to 17.5% and 1.41 to 1.50, respectively. The Consumer and Office group enjoyed a similar experience. Its operating margins and asset turnover improved from 15.2% to 18.4% and 1.63 and 1.84, respectively. The Specialty Materials segment seemed to be struggling. Its operating margin and asset turnover were down over the period from 17.1% to 14.3%, and 1.02 to 0.78, respectively.

It appears that two of 3M's segments, Transportation and Health Care, were enjoying healthy growth in sales and robust profit margins. It seemed reasonable for them to pursue their internal and external growth strategies. The repositioning and divesting of the Industrial and Consumer and Office segments also seemed to be working. The Electro and Communications segment appeared to be an acquirer until 2000. Its operating margin and asset turnover peaked in 1999 at 19.9% and 1.48, respectively. It began divesting in 2001 but hadn't been able to reverse its misfortunes as of 2002. The Specialty Materials segment seemed to be under pressure but was still maintaining double-digit operating margins at 14.3%.

KEY CONCEPTS

1. Debt securities held-to-maturity are securities the company has a positive intent and ability to hold to maturity. Available-for-sale securities may be sold to address the company's liquidity needs. Trading securities are acquired for the purpose of selling them in the short term.

2. The unrealized gains and losses of trading securities are reported on the income statement. The unrealized gains and losses of available-for-sale securities are reported as a component of equity on the balance sheet.

3. The MVA is the difference between the fair market value and the book value of the marketable securities portfolio. Unrealized gains (losses) are equal to the change in the MVA.

4. To use the equity method, an investor must exert significant influence over the investee's operations and management (the investor usually owns between 20% and 50% of the outstanding shares of the investee).

5. Under the equity method, the investment is listed at cost on the balance sheet. Dividends that are paid by the investee increase cash and decrease the investment account on the assets side of the balance sheet. In addition, the investor's pro rata share of the investee's net income increases the asset account and is listed as income on the investor's income statement.

6. The equity method differs from the cost method in that when the dividend payout is not 100% and the income of the investee is positive, the reported net income under the equity method will exceed the net income reported under the cost method (all else the same). Under these same circumstances, the reported amount in the investment account will be greater for the equity method than for the cost method. The reported cash flow will not differ between the two methodologies.

7. To use consolidation, the parent must control a subsidiary (the investor usually owns more than 50% of the subsidiary).

8. The mechanics of a consolidation are as follows: add together all asset and liability accounts net of intercorporate transfers; do not adjust the equity accounts of the parent; list the minority interest account on the liabilities and equity side of the parent's balance sheet. Minority interest is equal to the proportion of the subsidiary that the parent does not own times the net equity of the subsidiary.

9. On the consolidated income statement, add the revenues and expenses of the parent and the subsidiary together. Subtract the minority shareholders' stake in the subsidiary's net income from this amount. The minority interest balance on the income statement equals the proportion of the subsidiary that the parent does not own times the net income of the subsidiary.

10. A consolidation will differ from financial statements generated using the equity method in the following ways. First, the consolidated assets and liabilities will exceed those listed under the equity method in most cases. Also, consolidated revenues, expenses, and operating income will exceed those reported under the equity method. Reported equity and net income will be the same under both methods.

11. In general, if the subsidiary is profitable, the equity method reports better results than the consolidation method: ROA and net profit margin will be greater, and leverage ratios will be lower under the equity method.

12. A proportionate consolidation is not a provision of U.S. GAAP, although it has been adopted for use under IAS. Analysts may employ proportionate consolidation on a firm that is currently accounted for using the equity method if the analysts believe that a stronger link exists between the two firms than is implied by the ownership percentage. A joint venture is a typical example in which you would most likely apply a proportionate consolidation.

13. A proportionate consolidation will lead to the same results as a normal consolidation except there are no minority interest computations in a proportionate consolidation. You simply add the parent's proportionate share of all accounts net of intercorporate transfers. Do not add the equity accounts together.

14. A reportable segment under U.S. GAAP is a component of an enterprise that has at least 10% of revenues, operating profit or loss, or combined identifiable assets of the enterprise as a whole.

15. Reportable segments disclose sales and intersegment sales, operating profit, assets, depreciation, depletion and amortization expenses, and capital expenditures. Segment data allows an analyst to better understand a company's operations and track trends.

CONCEPT CHECKERS

1. If a company uses the equity method to account for an investment in another company:
    A. income is combined to the extent of ownership.
    B. income to the company is actual dividends, interest, or capital gains.
    C. all income of the affiliate is included except intercompany transfers.
    D. earnings of the affiliate are included but reduced by any dividends paid to the company.

Use the following data to answer Questions 2 through 7.

Kirk Company acquired shares in the equity of both Company A and Company B. We have the following information from the public market about Company A and Company B's investment value at the time of purchase and at two subsequent dates:

Security	Cost	$t = 1$	$t = 2$
A	$950	$850	$900
B	250	180	350

2. Kirk Company will report the initial value of its Marketable Equity Securities (MES) account as:
    A. $250.
    B. $600.
    C. $1,100.
    D. $1,200.

3. At t = 1, Kirk will:
    A. no longer use the cost method.
    B. carry the MES portfolio at cost.
    C. write down the MES portfolio to $1,030 and recognize a realized loss of $170.
    D. write down the MES portfolio to $1,030 and recognize an unrealized loss of $170.

4. At t = 2, Kirk will report the carrying value of its MES account as:
    A. $1,030.
    B. $1,150.
    C. $1,200.
    D. $1,250.

5. Based on the information provided, which of the following statements is *most accurate*?
    A. Classifying the shares as trading securities would result in greater reported earnings volatility for Kirk.
    B. Classifying the shares as available-for-sale securities would result in a $220 realized gain for Kirk between t = 1 and t = 2.
    C   It is optimal for Kirk to classify its shares in Company A and Company B as available-for-sale securities since it results in a net $50 gain recognized on the income statement at t = 2.
    D. It is optimal for Kirk to classify its shares in Company A and Company B as trading securities because, of the two methods, the trading securities classification results in the highest reported market value of $1,250 at t = 2.

6. Assume for this question only that at t = 3, Kirk sells all of the Company A shares for $975 and sells all of the Company B shares for $275. At t = 3, there will *most likely* be a:
    A. $75 unrealized gain for Company A shares.
    B. $75 unrealized loss for Company B shares.
    C. $50 realized gain and a $25 unrealized gain for Company A shares.
    D. $100 unrealized loss and a $25 realized gain for Company B shares.

7. Assume for this question only that Security A and Security B are both debt securities held-to-maturity. At t = 2, Kirk will report the carrying value of its MES account as:
    A. $1,030.
    B. $1,150.
    C. $1,200.
    D. $1,250.

Use the following data to answer Questions 8 through 10.

Assume Company P acquired 40% of the shares of Company A for $1.5 million on January 1, 2005. During the year, Company A earned $500,000 and paid dividends of $125,000. Assume the use of the equity method.

8. At the end of 2005, Company P reported investment in Company A as:
    A. $1.5 million.
    B. $1.65 million.
    C. $1.7 million.
    D. $1.875 million.

9. Company P reported investment income of:
    A. $50,000.
    B. $150,000.
    C. $200,000.
    D. $500,000.

10. Company P received cash flow from the investee of:
    A. $50,000.
    B. $150,000.
    C. $200,000.
    D. $500,000.

Use the following data to answer Questions 11 though 13.

Assume Company P acquires 80% of the common stock of Company S on December 31, 2005 by paying $120,000 cash to the shareholders of Company S. The two firms' pre-acquisition balance sheets as of December 31, 2005 and income statements for the year ending December 31, 2006 follow:

Balance Sheets	Company P	Company S
Current assets	$720,000	$240,000
Other assets	480,000	120,000
Total Assets	**$1,200,000**	**$360,000**
Current liabilities	$600,000	$210,000
Common stock	420,000	90,000
Retained earnings	180,000	60,000
Total Liabilities & Equity	**$1,200,000**	**$360,000**

Income Statements	Company P	Company S
Revenue	$900,000	$300,000
Expenses	600,000	240,000
Net income	**$300,000**	**$60,000**
Dividends		$15,000

11.   Company P will use consolidation and report the following values on the consolidated balance sheet:

	Current assets	Total assets	Investment in S
A.	$960,000 ✓	$1,560,000	$120,000
B.	$840,000	$1,440,000	N/A
C.	$792,000	$1,440,000	N/A
D.	$720,000	$1,200,000	$120,000

12.   For the year ended December 31, 2006, Company P's income statement will show "minority income interest" and "consolidated net income" of:

	Minority income interest	Consolidated net income
A.	$3,000	$300,000
B.	$3,000	$348,000
C.	$12,000	$348,000
D.	$12,000	$360,000

13.   The year-end 2006 balance sheet account "minority interest" will show:
    A. $30,000.
    B. $39,000.
    C. $42,000.
    D. $45,000.

Use the following data to answer Questions 14 and 15.

Company M acquired 20% of Company N for $6 million on January 1, 2005. Company N reports the following values for fiscal years 2005 and 2006, and M has significant influence over N:

Year	Net income (loss)	Dividends
2005	($450,000)	$600,000
2006	$1,500,000	$750,000

14. If the shares of Company N are publicly traded, what is the value of the investment in Company N stock that *likely* will be reported on Company M's balance sheet in:

	2005?	2006?
A.	$5,790,000	$5,940,000
B.	$5,790,000	$6,300,000
C.	$6,000,000	$6,000,000
D.	$6,000,000	$6,300,000

15. If the shares of Company N are publicly traded, what is the *likely* effect on the net income reported on the income statement of Company M from its investment in Company N in:

	2005?	2006?
A.	$90,000 decrease	$300,000 increase
B.	$90,000 decrease	$150,000 increase
C.	$600,000 decrease	$300,000 increase
D.	$600,000 decrease	$175,000 increase

Use the following data to answer Questions 16 and 17.

Company C owns a 25% interest in a joint venture, JVC, and accounts for it using the equity method. They have each reported the following 2006 financial results.

Balance Sheets	Company C	JVC
Cash	$1,750	$300
Accounts receivable	3,500	700
Inventory	3,000	800
Fixed assets	5,000	2,600
Investment in JVC	200	
Total Assets	**$13,450**	**$4,400**
Accounts payable	$3,500	$1,200
Long-term debt	4,000	2,400
Equity	5,950	800
Total Liabilities & Equity	**$13,450**	**$4,400**

Income Statements	Company C	JVC
Revenues	$17,500	$2,800
Equity in JVC earnings	50	
Cost of goods sold	7,000	2,000
Other expenses	9,000	467
Income before tax	$1,550	$333
Tax	620	133
Net income	$930	$200

During 2006, Company C purchased 35% of the output of JVC. Additionally, JVC has an account receivable from Company C of $150 at the end of 2006.

16. Using proportionate consolidation, the accounts receivable of Company C reported on the balance sheet are *closest* to:
    A. $3,500.00.
    B. $3,637.50.
    C. $3,560.00.
    D. $4,050.00.

17. Using proportionate consolidation, the Company C's cost of goods on its 2006 income statement is *closest* to:
    A. $6,020.
    B. $6,520.
    C. $7,000.
    D. $7,255.

Use the following data to answer Question 18.

Ridgeview Corporation (in $):	2006	2005
Dividends	$400	$350
Interest	660	250
Realized gains (losses)	(1,040)	750
Investment in securities (at cost)	52,700	24,900
Investment in securities (at FMV)	55,300	23,900

18. The mark-to-market investment return for Ridgeview Corporation for 2006 is *closest* to:
    A. $1,620.
    B. $2,620.
    C. $3,620.
    D. $4,970.

CHALLENGE PROBLEMS

19. Selected operating results for Lowdown Inc. in 2005 and 2006 are shown in the following table.

Lowdown Inc.	2005	2006
Sales and operating revenues	$1,000	$1,140
Investment income	$45	$160
Total revenues	1,045	1,300
Operating costs	500	640
Pre-tax operating income	545	660

Martha Patterson, an analyst with Cauldron Associates, has been assigned the task of separating Lowdown's operating and investment results. She intends to do this by removing the effects of the returns on Lowdown's marketable securities portfolio and forecasting operating income for 2007. Patterson assumes that growth trend in operating income from 2005 to 2006 will continue in 2007.

The appropriate forecast of Lowdown's operating income in 2007 based on Patterson's analysis is *closest* to:
A. $500.
B. $650.
C. $700.
D. $800.

20. Lowdown Inc. uses the consolidation method to report the results of its investment in Highbrow Company because it controls 51% of the voting shares. Highbrow has reported positive net income in each of the last five years. Martha Patterson, an analyst with Cauldron Associates, determines that the equity method more appropriately captures the economics of the relationship between Lowdown and Highbrow and adjusts consolidated statements of Lowdown to reflect the equity method. Don Reilly, her supervisor, disagrees with her analysis; he argues that the consolidation method is appropriate in this case because the equity method will overstate Lowdown's operating performance and financial condition; in particular, he argues that return on equity and return on assets will be overstated.

Is Reilly correct in his assessment of the effect of Patterson's adjustments on:

	Return on equity?	Return on assets?
A.	Yes	Yes
B.	No	Yes
C.	Yes	No
D.	No	No

ANSWERS – CONCEPT CHECKERS

1. **A** With the equity method, the proportional share of the affiliate's income (% ownership × affiliate earnings) is reported on the investor's income statement.

2. **D** Initially, the carrying value of all security investments is cost.

    initial cost = $950 + 250 = $1,200

3. **D** Both the available-for-sale and trading securities are carried at market value on the balance sheet. Also, both classifications call for recognition of unrealized losses and gains. Market value at t = 1 is $850 + $180 = $1,030. Unrealized loss is ($850 – $950) + ($180 – $250) = –$170. Note that the recognition differs. With available-for-sale securities, the recognition is only on the balance sheet. With trading securities, the recognition impacts the income statement.

4. **D** The increase in value requires that investment securities be written up to $900 + $350 = $1,250.

5. **A** Classifying the shares as trading requires both realized and unrealized gains and losses to be recognized on the income statement. As a result, this would have the effect of greater reported earnings volatility. There is actually a $220 *unrealized* gain between t = 1 and t = 2; the gain is unrealized because the shares were not actually sold. The net gain of $50 between the acquisition date and t = 2 is unrealized; therefore, by classifying as available-for-sale, the gain is not recognized on the income statement (it goes directly to equity). Classification as either trading or available-for-sale securities results in the same fair market value of $1,250 reported on the balance sheet at t = 2.

6. **D** The sale of Company A's shares results in a net $25 realized gain ($975 selling price less $950 cost). The sale of Company B's shares also results in a net $25 realized gain ($275 selling price less $250 cost).

    You can calculate the unrealized loss on both securities as the change in the MVA. Because the company will sell the shares in year 3, the marketable securities balance will be zero at the end of year 3.

	Security A		Security B	
	t = 2	*t = 3*	*t = 2*	*t = 3*
Market value	$900	$0	$350	$0
Cost	$950	$0	$250	$0
MVA	($50)	$0	$100	$0
Change in MVA = unrealized gain/loss		$50		($100)

7. **C** Debt securities held-to-maturity are securities that a company has the positive intent and ability to hold to maturity. They are carried at amortized cost ($1,200), and no unrealized or realized gains or losses are recognized until disposition.

8. **B** $1,500,000 + 0.4($500,000 – $125,000) = $1,650,000

9. **C** $500,000 × 0.4 = $200,000; dividends are not included in income under the equity method.

10. **A** $125,000 × 0.4 = $50,000; the dividend is cash flow = $50,000.

11. **B** current assets = $720,000 + $240,000 – $120,000 = $840,000

    total assets = $1,200,000 + $360,000 – $120,000 = $1,440,000

    Investment in Company S is not relevant with the consolidation method.

12. **C** minority interest income = $60,000 (0.2) = $12,000

    consolidated net income (after minority interest income is subtracted) = $300,000 + $60,000 – $12,000 = $348,000

13. **B** Ending balance sheet minority interest = $30,000 + income statement minority interest of $12,000 – minority interest dividend share of $3,000 = $39,000.

    beginning balance sheet minority interest = (1 – 0.8)(60,000 + 90,000) = $30,000

14. **A** 2005: $6,000,000 + 0.2 (–$450,000) – 0.2 ($600,000) = $5,790,000

    2006: $5,790,000 + 0.2($1,500,000) – 0.2 ($750,000) = $5,940,000

15. **A** 2005: 0.2 (–$450,000) = –$90,000

    2006: 0.2 ($1,500,000) = $300,000

16. **B** $3,500 + 0.25(700 – 150) = $3,637.50

17. **D** $7,000 + (0.25 × $2,000) – (0.25 × 0.35 × $2,800) = $7,255

    The combined cost of goods sold for both entities (100% of Company C and 25% of JVC) must be reduced by the proportionate share of sales from JVC to Company C.

18. **C** $23,900 – $24,900 = –$1,000 is 2005's MVA; $55,300 – $52,700 = $2,600 is 2006's MVA; the increase in MVA from 2005 to 2006 is $2,600 – (–$1,000) = $3,600. The mark-to-market return is the change in MVA plus 2006 dividends, interest, and realized gains/losses = $3,600 + $400 + $660 – $1,040 = $3,620.

ANSWERS – CHALLENGE PROBLEMS

19. **A** After removing the investment gains in 2005 and 2006, operating income remained unchanged at $500. Based on a growth trend of 0% the appropriate operating income forecast for 2007 is also $500.

	2005	2006
Sales and operating revenues	$1,000	$1,140
Operating costs	500	640
Adjusted operating income	500	500

20. **B**   Reilly is incorrect in his assessment of the effect of the application of the equity method on return on equity. There is no difference in return on equity under the equity and consolidation methods because net income and equity are the same under both methods.

Reilly is correct in his assessment of the effect on return on assets. Assuming that Highbrow is profitable, return on assets is higher under the equity method because reported assets are lower but net income is the same.

MERGERS, ACQUISITIONS, AND OTHER INTERCORPORATE INVESTMENTS

Study Session 5

EXAM FOCUS

Historically, two procedures were used to account for the surviving entity in a merger or acquisition—the purchase method and the pooling method. Although only the purchase method is now permitted under U.S. GAAP and international accounting standards, you need to have a working knowledge of both methods because the transactions accounted for as a pooling of interests prior to the change in accounting standards may still affect the financial statements of the company. Therefore, your focus in this topic review should be on understanding the differences in the impact of the purchase versus the pooling method on reported financial results. Intercorporate investments, material that is covered in much more detail in the first topic review in Study Session 5, is also covered here. Therefore, in this topic review we only provide a brief review of the basic issues and some discussion of a few additional concepts that were not addressed in the previous topic review.

ACCOUNTING FOR MERGERS AND ACQUISITIONS

LOS 22.a: Compare and contrast U.S. and international accounting for mergers, acquisitions, and other intercorporate investments.

Historically, two accounting methods have been used for mergers and acquisitions: (1) the purchase method and (2) the pooling method. U.S. GAAP and international accounting standards (IAS) rules for reporting of acquisitions were changed in 2001 and 2003, respectively, to require the use of the purchase method and eliminate the use of the pooling method. For our purposes, there are basically no longer any differences between U.S. GAAP and IAS merger accounting rules.

Professor's Note: You need to know the basic features of both methods for the exam, however, because these accounting changes were not made retroactively. The financial statement effects of pooling transactions conducted prior to the change in standards are still apparent and require your careful attention.

The key attributes of the **purchase method** include the following:

- The transaction is structured so that the liabilities and assets of one company are assumed by another company.
- If the fair market value of the tangible assets of the target company minus the fair market value of its liabilities is less than the purchase price, then the excess purchase price is attributed to separately identifiable intangible assets (e.g. patents, licenses, and in-process R&D). The tangible assets are then depreciated, and the intangible assets are amortized, over their estimated remaining life, which reduces reported net income.
- Any remaining excess value is allocated to goodwill, which is an intangible asset but not "separately identifiable." Goodwill is not amortized under either U.S. or international standards. Instead it is tested annually for impairment and written down only if the company determines that the fair value of the goodwill is less than its carrying value.
- The operating results of the acquired company are included in the income statement of the purchaser from the date of acquisition onward. Operating results occurring before the acquisition are not restated, resulting in pre- and post-acquisition income and cash flow statements that are not comparable.

The **pooling of interests method** (which was called the **uniting of interests method** under IAS) combines the ownership interests of two companies, and views the participants as equals—neither firm acquires the other (intuitively, you can think of the purchase method as an acquisition and the pooling method as a merger). Assets and liabilities of the two firms are combined (and any intercompany accounts are eliminated). Major attributes of the pooling method include the following:

- The two companies are combined using accounting book values.
- Operating results for prior periods are restated as though the two firms were always combined.
- Ownership interests continue, and former accounting bases are maintained.

Note that fair market values play no role in accounting for a business combination using the pooling method—the actual price paid is suppressed from the balance sheets and income statements.

PURCHASE VS. POOLING

LOS 22.b: Evaluate the impact of the purchase versus pooling methods on reported financial results.

The reported financial results of the combined entity after the merger or acquisition depend on whether the combination was accounted for using the purchase or the pooling method, even if all of the underlying cash flows and economics of the transaction remain the same. In the discussion that follows, we assume that the merger was an all-equity transaction because transactions not made entirely with stock were not allowed to use the pooling method under U.S. GAAP or IAS. We also assume that under the purchase method the tangible assets are written up (not down) to market value, resulting in higher depreciation after the merger.

Three primary effects drive the differences in reported financial results from the application of the purchase versus pooling methods:

1. *Effect on assets.* Under the purchase method, assets are typically written up to market value so that assets reported on the balance sheet after the merger are higher than they would be under the pooling method.
2. *Effect on net income.* There is an incremental increase in depreciation subsequent to the merger under the purchase method, assuming the tangible assets were written up, which reduces reported net income relative to the pooling method.
3. *Effect on equity.* Equity after the acquisition is higher under the purchase method because the book value of equity in the acquired company is replaced by the amount of the purchase price.

These effects result in performance measures that are less favorable under the purchase method versus the pooling method, assuming the fair value of the assets acquired exceeds the book value of those assets prior to the merger, and both companies are profitable:

- *Profit margin* is lower under the purchase method because net income is lower but sales are the same.
- *Return on assets* (ROA) is lower under the purchase method because net income is lower and assets are higher.
- *Return on equity* (ROE) is lower under the purchase method because net income is lower and equity is higher.

These results are summarized in Figure 1.

Figure 1: Impact of Purchase vs. Pooling Method on Reported Financial Results*

Financial Statement Item / Ratio	Purchase Method	Pooling Method
Assets	Higher	Lower
Equity	Higher	Lower
Net income	Lower	Higher
Profit margin	Lower	Higher
ROA	Lower	Higher
ROE	Lower	Higher

*Assuming the fair value of the assets acquired exceeds the book value, and both companies are profitable.

The following example illustrates these effects.

Suppose Acquirer Inc. purchases 100% of the common stock of Target Inc. for a purchase price of $3,800 by issuing new shares. The balance sheets of both companies prior to the acquisition and the market value of the Target's assets and liabilities are shown in Figure 2.

Figure 2: Pre-Acquisition Balance Sheets

	Acquirer Book Value	Target Book Value	Target Market Value
Assets	$10,000	$4,000	$7,000
Liabilities	$6,000	$3,200	$3,200
Paid in capital	$1,000	$200	
Retained earnings	$3,000	$600	
Equity	$4,000	$800	$3,800

Also assume the following:

- Under the purchase method, the incremental $3,000 in fair value of Target's assets in excess of book value will be depreciated using the straight-line method over three years. The incremental depreciation each year is $1,000.
- The net income of the combined company after the acquisition prior to the incremental depreciation is $2,500 per year for each of the next three years.
- The company does not pay dividends, so each year retained earnings is increased by the amount of net income.
- Sales in each of the next three years is $25,000.

The income statement for the combined company over each of the next three years after the acquisition under both methods is shown in Figure 3. We assume that the acquisition takes place on the first day of the fiscal year, so the two entities are combined for the entire first year.

Figure 3: Post Acquisition Income Statement for Next Three Years

Income Statement Item	Purchase Method	Pooling Method
Income before incremental depreciation	$2,500	$2,500
Incremental depreciation	$1,000	
Net income	$1,500	$2,500

The balance sheet at acquisition and at the end of each of the next three years under the purchase method is shown in Figure 4 and under the pooling method in Figure 5. Notice that assets, retained earnings, and equity increase each year by the amount of net income ($1,500 for the purchase method and $2,500 for the pooling method).

Figure 4: Post Acquisition Balance Sheet (Purchase Method)

	At Acquisition	End of Year 1	End of Year 2	End of Year 3
Assets	$17,000	$18,500	$20,000	$21,500
Liabilities	$9,200	$9,200	$9,200	$9,200
Paid in capital	$4,800	$4,800	$4,800	$4,800
Retained earnings	$3,000	$4,500	$6,000	$7,500
Equity	$7,800	$9,300	$10,800	$12,300

Figure 5: Post Acquisition Balance Sheet (Pooling Method)

	At Acquisition	End of Year 1	End of Year 2	End of Year 3
Assets	$14,000	$16,500	$19,000	$21,500
Liabilities	$9,200	$9,200	$9,200	$9,200
Paid in capital	$1,200	$1,200	$1,200	$1,200
Retained earnings	$3,600	$6,100	$8,600	$11,100
Equity	$4,800	$7,300	$9,800	$12,300

At end of the third year, the book value of assets, liabilities, and equity are the same under both methods, but the pooling method reported additional earnings over the three years of $3,000.

We can also confirm using this example that the pooling method reports better operating results than the purchase method during each of the three years, as shown in Figure 6.

Figure 6: Operating Results (Purchase and Pooling Methods)*

	Year 1		Year 2		Year 3	
	Purchase	Pooling	Purchase	Pooling	Purchase	Pooling
Net margin	6.0%	10.0%	6.0%	10.0%	6.0%	10.0%
ROA*	8.8%	17.8%	8.1%	15.2%	7.5%	13.2%
ROE*	19.2%	52.1%	16.1%	34.2%	13.9%	25.5%

*ROA and ROE are calculated using beginning-of-period balance sheet numbers.

ACCOUNTING FOR INTERCORPORATE INVESTMENTS

LOS 22.c: Distinguish between cost investments, equity investments, proportionately consolidated investments, and consolidated investments.

The equity, consolidation and proportionate consolidate methods were covered in detail in the first topic review in this study session, so we won't repeat the basic concepts. However, in this LOS we are going to provide an example for a situation not addressed in the previous material: How do you apply the three methods when the investment in the subsidiary is purchased for more than the proportionate share of the subsidiary's book value?

We will use the data in the example from LOS 22.b on Acquirer Inc. and Target Inc. to illustrate how the calculations change in this situation. Let's suppose Acquirer purchases a 50% interest in Target for $1,900, which is greater than 50% of Target's book value equity: 50% of $800 is only $400. Assume the $1,500 difference is assigned to depreciable assets with a remaining useful life of three years. Using the straight line method, the additional annual depreciation on the assets that were written up is $500.

Income statements for the two companies for each of the next three years (before any effects resulting from Acquirer's investment of Target) are shown in Figure 7.

Figure 7: Income Statements for Acquirer Inc. and Target Inc.

	Acquirer	Target	Combined
Revenues	$18,000	$7,000	$25,000
Expenses	17,000	5,500	22,500
Net income	$1,000	$1,500	$2,500

Equity Method

Using the equity method, in each of the three years Acquirer would recognize the 50% of Target's income (0.5 × $1,500 = $750), adjusted for the additional depreciation on the assets that were revalued, on its income statement:

Percentage of Target's earnings	$750
Adjustment for depreciation	(500)
Income from equity investee	$250

Acquirer's income statement after reflecting the investment is shown in Figure 8.

Figure 8: Income Statement for Acquirer Inc. Using Equity Method

	Acquirer
Revenues	$18,000
Expenses	(17,000)
Income from equity investee	$250
Net income	$1,250

Proportionate Consolidation Method

Under proportionate consolidation, Acquirer would report 100% of its revenues and expenses, 50% of Target's revenues and expenses, and the additional depreciation of $500 per year, as shown in Figure 9.

Figure 9: Income Statement for Acquirer Inc. Using Proportionate Consolidation

	Acquirer	*Calculation*
Revenues	$21,500	$18,000 + 0.5($7,000)
Expenses	(20,250)	$17,000 + 0.5($5,500) + $500
Net income	$1,250	

Consolidation Method

Under the consolidation method Acquirer reports 100% of its revenues and expenses, 100% of Target's revenues and expenses, and the $500 adjustment. In addition, the minority share of consolidated income in Target is subtracted. The results are shown in Figure 10.

Figure 10: Income Statement for Acquirer Inc. Using Consolidation

	Acquirer	*Calculation*
Revenues	$25,000	$18,000 + $7,000
Expenses	(23,000)	$17,000 + $5,500 + $500
Less: Minority share of consolidated income	(750)	$1,500 × 0.50
Net income	$1,250	

Notice that net income is the same in each case: $1,250.

DETERMINATION OF PROPER METHOD

LOS 22.f: Identify situations when companies should apply the equity and consolidation methods of accounting for investments.

The accounting for intercorporate investments in which one company does not merge with or acquire all of the outstanding shares of another company was covered in detail in the first topic review in Study Session 5. Recall that the accounting treatment depends on the degree of control and the percentage ownership, as shown in Figure 11.

Figure 11: Accounting Standards for Intercorporate Investments

Ownership	Degree of Influence/Control	U.S. GAAP Method	IAS Method
Less than 20%	Passive investment with no significant influence	Cost or market	Same as U.S. GAAP
20% to 50%	Significant influence	Equity method	Same as U.S. GAAP
Each party owns 50%	Shared control	Equity method	Choice of equity method or proportionate consolidation
More than 50%	Control	Consolidation	Same as U.S. GAAP

Furthermore, the accounting treatment for marketable securities (i.e., those that trade in a secondary market) in which the company has a passive investment depends on management's intent regarding the securities. These standards are summarized in Figure 12.

Figure 12: Accounting Treatment for Passive Investments Under U.S. GAAP and IAS

Classification	Management Intent	U.S. GAAP Balance Sheet Treatment	U.S. GAAP Income Statement Treatment	Difference Between U.S. GAAP and IAS
Trading securities	Acquired for the purpose of selling in the near-term.	Reported at fair market value.	Interest, dividends, realized and unrealized gains and losses reported.	No difference between U.S. GAAP and IAS.
Available-for-sale securities	May be sold to address liquidity needs.	Reported at fair market value with unrealized gains and losses in comprehensive income in shareholders' equity.	Interest, dividends, and realized gains and losses reported.	Company can elect to report unrealized gains and losses as comprehensive income in stockholders' equity or on the income statement.
Held-to-maturity debt securities	Management has positive intent and ability to hold to maturity.	Reported at historical cost.	Interest and any realized gains and losses reported.	No difference between U.S. GAAP and IAS.

RECOGNIZING INCOME USING THE COST METHOD

LOS 22.d: Determine when income should be recognized on investments that are accounted for using the cost method.

Passive investments in other companies that are not publicly traded in a liquid secondary market are accounted for using the cost method. The key points of the cost method include the following:

- The investment is recorded at the original cost (which is the fair market value on the date it was purchased).
- Dividends are recognized as income in the period in which they are declared.
- Impairments are recognized immediately and reported as a loss on the income statement (see LOS 22.e).
- A realized gain or loss is reported on the income statement when the security is sold.

REPORTING MARKET VALUE INCREASES

LOS 22.e: Describe the reporting of market value increases and decreases in the financial statements for cost-method investments.

A security is considered **impaired** when its fair value is less than the carrying value reported on the balance sheet, and the decline in market value is "other than temporary." U.S. and international accounting standards require that impaired assets be written down to fair value on the balance sheet, with the accompanying loss reported on the income statement as a charge against net income.

The concept of "other than temporary" is applied to determining impairment of securities accounted for using the cost method, and for available-for-sale securities and debt securities held to maturity. Other than temporary is not the same thing as a permanent decline; accounting standards require the asset be impaired if it is likely (but not for certain) that the company will be unable to recover the entire amount of its investment in the security.

Subsequent increases in market value of cost-based investments and investments held to maturity, however, are not reflected on the balance sheet as increases in reported value, and no unrealized gain is reported on the income statement. The treatment is slightly different for available-for-sale securities: subsequent market value increases are reflected on the balance sheet (because available-for-sale securities are reported at market value), but the resulting unrealized gain is required to be reported in comprehensive income in shareholders' equity under U.S. GAAP and may be reported that way under IAS.

EFFECT OF METHOD ON FINANCIAL PERFORMANCE

LOS 22.g: Explain the implications of proportionate consolidation methods for the evaluation of leverage, profitability, and return on assets (ROA).

The effect of the choice of methods on reported financial results is covered extensively in the first topic review in Study Session 5, so we won't repeat that analysis here. Instead, we'll simply review the effect of the proportionate consolidation method versus the equity method or consolidation on leverage, profitability (as measured by net profit margin and ROE), and ROA.

There are four important effects on certain balance sheet and income statement items of the choice of accounting method (in most situations):

1. All three methods report the same net income.
2. All three methods report the same equity.
3. Assets and liabilities are highest under consolidation and lowest under the equity method; proportionate consolidation is somewhere in between those two.
4. Sales are highest under consolidation and lowest under the equity method; proportionate consolidation is somewhere in between.

These effects generally result in the equity method reporting the most favorable results, consolidation the least favorable, with proportionate consolidation somewhere in between, as shown in Figure 13.

Figure 13: Differences in Reported Financial Results from Choice of Method

	Equity Method	Proportionate Consolidation	Consolidation
Leverage	Lower (more favorable) because liabilities are lower and equity is the same	In between	Higher
Net profit margin	Higher because sales are lower and net income is the same	In between	Lower
ROE	Same because net income and equity are the same	Same	Same
ROA	Higher because net income is the same and assets are lower	In between	Lower

KEY CONCEPTS

1. U.S. GAAP and international accounting standards (IAS) rules for reporting of acquisitions require the use of the purchase method. The option of using of the pooling method has been eliminated.

2. Under the purchase method, the assets and liabilities of the acquired company are written up to fair value, any identifiable intangible assets are recorded, and the excess of the purchase price over the fair value of net tangible and identifiable intangible assets is recorded as goodwill. Goodwill is not amortized, but is subject to an annual impairment test. Prior operating results are not restated.

3. Under the pooling method, the two companies are combined using book values, and prior operating results are restated.

4. The pooling method generally results in more favorable results than the purchase method; net income, net profit margin, ROA, and ROE are higher under pooling versus purchase.

5. Under both U.S. GAAP and IAS: (1) passive investments with less than 20% ownership are accounted for using the cost or market method, (2) investments with significant influence (20% to 50%) are accounted for using the equity method, and (3) investments in which the parent controls (more than 50% ownership) are consolidated. The only difference between U.S. GAAP and IAS is for joint ventures under shared control: U.S. GAAP requires the equity method while IAS allows the choice of either the equity method or proportionate consolidation.

6. Under the cost method, dividends are recognized as income in the period in which they are received, impairments are recognized immediately and reported as a loss, and realized gains and losses are reported when the security is sold.

7. An asset is considered impaired when its fair value is less than the book value reported on the balance sheet, and the decline in market value is "other than temporary." Accounting standards require that impaired assets be written down to fair value on the balance sheet, with the accompanying loss reported on the income statement as a charge against net income.

8. Subsequent increases in market value of cost-based investments and investments held to maturity, however, are not reflected on the balance sheet as increases in reported value, and no unrealized gain is reported on the income statement.

9. The equity method generally reports the most favorable financial results, consolidation the least favorable, with proportionate consolidation somewhere in between the two. However, ROE is the same under all three methods.

CONCEPT CHECKERS

1. Which of the following statements about the pooling and purchase methods is *most accurate*?
    A. In the pooling method, the balance sheets and income statements of the two firms are added together.
    B. In the pooling method, the balance sheets and income statements are added together after adjusting the target firm's statements to reflect the fair market values of the acquired firm.
    C. In the purchase method, prior period statements are never restated to reflect the results of the acquired firm's assets and liabilities.
    D. In the purchase method, the statement is structured so that all the liabilities and assets of both companies are combined together.

2. Adam Corporation acquired Hardy Corporation recently using the purchase method. Adam is preparing to report its year-end results to include Hardy according to IAS. Which of the following statements regarding goodwill is *most accurate*?
    A. Adam would amortize its goodwill over no more than 20 years.
    B. Adam would test its goodwill annually to ensure the carrying value is not greater than the fair value.
    C. Adam would test its goodwill annually to ensure the fair value is no greater than the carrying value.
    D. Hardy would test its goodwill for impairments annually.

3. Assuming a company issues new equity to acquire a target company and the market value of the target's assets is greater than book value, which of the two methods, purchase or pooling, will *likely* produce the higher balance for (1) total assets and (2) net earnings in the year following the transaction?

	Total assets	Net earnings
A.	Purchase	Purchase
B.	Purchase	Pooling
C.	Pooling	Purchase
D.	Pooling	Pooling

4. Is the pooling method of accounting for mergers and acquisitions permitted according to:

	U.S. GAAP?	International Accounting Standards (IAS)?
A.	Yes	Yes
B.	Yes	No
C.	No	Yes
D.	No	No

5. Are the equity method and proportionate consolidation allowed under International Accounting Standards (IAS) for joint ventures when each party controls 50% of the shares?

	Equity method	Proportionate consolidation
A.	Yes	Yes
B.	Yes	No
C.	No	Yes
D.	No	No

6. A company accounts for its investment in a subsidiary using the equity method. The reported net profit margin is 14%. An analyst adjusts the financials to reflect consolidation and determines that the adjusted net profit margin is 8%. The net profit margin based on proportionate consolidation is *most likely* to be:
    A. less than 8%.
    B. equal to 8%.
    C. between 8% and 14%.
    D. greater than 14%.

7. A company accounts for its investment in a subsidiary using the equity method. The reported return on equity (ROE) is 21% and return on assets (ROA) is 14%. An analyst adjusts the financials to reflect proportionate consolidation. ROE based on proportionate consolidation is *most likely* to be:
    A. less than 14%.
    B. between 14% and 21%.
    C. equal to 21%.
    D. greater than 21%.

CHALLENGE PROBLEMS

8. Under which accounting method, purchase or pooling, are net profit margin and return on equity (ROE) *likely* to be lower?

	Net profit margin	ROE
A.	Purchase	Purchase
B.	Purchase	Pooling
C.	Pooling	Purchase
D.	Pooling	Pooling

9. Use the financial information for the Acquirer Inc./Target Inc. example in the topic review to answer this question. Assume beginning-of-period balance sheet figures are used to calculate the ratios. Under which accounting method, purchase or pooling, are total asset turnover and assets-to-equity *likely* to be higher in year 1?

	Total asset turnover	Assets-to-equity
A.	Purchase	Purchase
B.	Purchase	Pooling
C.	Pooling	Purchase
D.	Pooling	Pooling

10. According to U.S. GAAP, is the loss associated with the impairment of an available-for-sale-security, and any subsequent gains that result from increases in the value of that same security, charged against net income or comprehensive income?

	Impairment loss	Subsequent gains
A.	Net income	Net income
B.	Net income	Comprehensive income
C.	Comprehensive income	Net income
D.	Comprehensive income	Comprehensive income

ANSWERS – CONCEPT CHECKERS

1. **C** Pooling allows the balance sheets and income statements to be added together but only after adjusting for interfirm transactions (if any). Fair market value is not considered in pooling. Pooling restates past financial statements, but purchase doesn't. Purchase combines results from the effective date forward. In the purchase method, the transaction is structured so that all of the liabilities and assets of one company are assumed by another.

2. **B** Adam is required to perform an annual impairment test. The carrying value cannot exceed the fair value; if it does, then an impairment has taken place and the goodwill must be written down.

3. **B** Total assets after the acquisition will be higher for both methods, though the purchase method involves revaluing to fair market values (FMV). For the pooling method, book values are used. Therefore, total assets will most likely be higher under the purchase method versus pooling. Earnings are also likely to increase after the acquisition for both methods, since the earnings from both entities are combined. However, the purchase method would usually include higher depreciation charges as a result of the FMV revaluation, and therefore would show somewhat lower earnings than under the pooling method.

4. **D** The pooling method (also called uniting-of-interests method under IAS) is no longer permitted under U.S. GAAP or IAS.

5. **A** Under IAS, companies have the choice of accounting for investments in joint ventures in which they own 50% of the shares using either the equity method or proportionate consolidation.

6. **C** The equity method typically yields the highest measure of net profit margin and consolidation the lowest. Proportionate consolidation is most likely to result in a net profit margin somewhere between the two.

7. **C** All three methods (equity, consolidation, proportionate consolidation) report the same net income and equity, so ROE is the same under all three methods.

ANSWERS – CHALLENGE PROBLEMS

8. **A** Assuming the fair value of the assets acquired exceeds the book value, and both companies are profitable, profit margin is lower under the purchase method because net income is lower but sales are the same. ROE is lower under the purchase method because net income is lower and equity is higher.

9. **D** Pooling reports a higher asset turnover ratio and a higher assets-to-equity ratio.
   Purchase: total asset turnover = $25,000/$17,000 = 1.47
               assets-to-equity = $17,000/$7,800 = 2.18
   Pooling: total asset turnover = $25,000/$14,000 = 1.79
               assets-to-equity = $14,000/$4,800 = 2.92

10. **B** U.S. GAAP require that impaired assets be written down to fair value on the balance sheet, with the accompanying loss reported on the income statement as a charge against net income. For available-for-sale securities, subsequent market value increases are reflected on the balance sheet (because available-for-sale securities are reported at market value), but the resulting unrealized gain is reported in comprehensive income in shareholders' equity.

VARIABLE INTEREST ENTITIES, INTERCOMPANY DEBT, CONSOLIDATED CASH FLOWS, AND OTHER ISSUES

Study Session 5

EXAM FOCUS

Although this is a new topic review for 2008, the subject of variable interest entities (VIE) has been part of the Level 2 curriculum for many years. The focus of the LOS in this review is on the form of, rationale for, and consolidation of VIEs. Understand the form and characteristics of VIEs and know under what conditions a VIE must be consolidated. Also know how to identify the VIE's primary beneficiary.

WARM-UP: SEPARATE ENTITIES

 Professor's Note: Although intercompany debt, consolidated cash flows and other issues are mentioned in the title of this review, these topics are not covered in either the LOS or the CFA Program Curriculum.

A **special purpose entity** (SPE), also known as a special purchase vehicle or off-balance sheet entity, is a legal structure created to isolate certain assets and obligations of the sponsor. SPEs are usually formed to serve a specific purpose, so they are limited in scope. The typical motivation is to obtain low-cost financing.

For example, SPEs have been created to purchase assets, fund research and development, lease assets, hedge transactions, and enhance the balance sheet. Of course, there have been some abuses, such as in the case of Enron and instances where transactions were not arms-length. These abuses led to calls for revised accounting standards. This topic review provides a brief discussion of FASB Interpretation No. 46(R), *"Consolidation of Variable Interest Entities,"* which has stricter consolidation requirements than existed previously.

The Financial Accounting Standards Board (FASB) coined the name **variable interest entity** (VIE) to identify an SPE that meets certain conditions set forth in FASB Interpretation No. 46(R), *"Consolidation of Variable Interest Entities"* (FIN 46R). If an entity is considered a VIE under FIN 46(R), it must be consolidated by the primary beneficiary.

Prior to the issuance of FIN 46(R), firms applied ARB No. 51, *"Consolidated Financial Statements,"* which based the consolidation decision on a firm's controlling financial interest. Under ARB No. 51, consolidation was generally based on voting control. In contrast, FIN 46(R) necessitates the use of a risk/reward approach; that is, the firm that absorbs the majority of the risks or receives the majority of the rewards is required to consolidate the VIE. This firm is known as the **primary beneficiary**.

Professor's Note: Not all SPEs are covered by FIN 46(R). For example, employee benefit plans and qualifying special purpose entities covered by FASB Statement No. 140, "Accounting for Transfers and Servicing of Financial Assets and Extinguishments of Liabilities," are exempted from consolidation. Therefore not all SPEs are considered VIEs. An SPE that is not a VIE does not need to be consolidated.

VARIABLE INTEREST ENTITIES

LOS 23.a: Describe the form of, characteristics of, and rationale for establishing VIEs.

There are a number of legitimate business reasons to create an SPE. The structure is often used to lower the cost of capital since the assets of the SPE are protected in the event the sponsor experiences financial difficulties. By isolating assets from other creditors, the lender has less risk because it is easier for the lender to gain control of the collateral in the event that the firm experiences financial distress. Of course, less risk results in lower financing cost to the company that creates the SPE.

An SPE can take the form of a corporation, partnership, joint venture, or trust, although the entity does not necessarily have separate management or even employees. The entity's activities are specifically detailed in governing documents, thereby further protecting the lender from unauthorized transactions, and reducing the financing costs.

Like most firms, SPEs are usually financed with a combination of debt and equity, although the equity component is typically quite small. Unlike normal shareholders, the equity investors have limited risk and, thus, usually receive a small fixed rate of return.

Because of the small equity investment, lenders are hesitant to provide low-cost debt financing to an SPE without additional support or assurances. This support is usually provided by the sponsor, or some other firm, in the form of additional collateral or guarantees. In return for providing the support, the firm may receive pro-rata profits or other residual interests in the project. Thus, the sponsor, or other firm, has a *variable interest* since the risks and rewards are based on the success of the created entity. The structure of the SPE transfers the risks and rewards from the equity investors to the other variable interest owners.

According to FIN 46(R), a variable interest is a contractual, ownership, or other pecuniary interest in an entity that changes as a result of the fair value of the entity's net assets. The variable interest will absorb portions of the SPE's potential losses and receive portions of the potential residual returns. The potential losses and residual returns can include the variability of net income and the variability of an asset's fair value.

Following are some examples of common variable interests and the potential risks and residual rewards:

- *At-risk equity investment.* The investor receives the residual benefits but also absorbs the potential losses.
- *Debt guarantee.* In the event of default, the guarantor will experience a loss.
- *Subordinated debt.* Since senior debt is repaid before subordinated debt, the subordinated debtholders absorb the loss in the event the senior debtholders cannot be repaid.
- *Lease residual guarantee.* The lessee guarantees the fair value of the asset at the end of the lease. If the fair value is less than the guaranteed amount, the lessee experiences a loss.
- *Participation rights.* The holder receives a predetermined share of the profit.
- *Asset purchase option.* The holder benefits from an increase in the fair value of the asset.

VIE CONSOLIDATION REQUIREMENTS

LOS 23.b: Describe the conditions under which a VIE must be consolidated.

As discussed in the topic review on intercorporate investments, consolidation is usually required when a parent has a controlling interest in another firm. This controlling interest is usually based on the parent's voting control as evidenced by its percentage of ownership. By creating an SPE, a firm could avoid consolidation by maneuvering around the issue of voting control.

With the issuance of FIN 46(R), firms must now use factors other than voting control to determine whether an entity should be consolidated. Accordingly, if an entity is considered a VIE, it must be consolidated by the primary beneficiary.

According to FIN 46(R), an entity is considered a VIE if *any* of the following conditions are met:

1. *Insufficient at-risk equity investment.* The total at-risk equity is not sufficient to finance the entity's activities without additional subordinated financial support. Although not an absolute rule, at-risk equity of less than 10% of total assets is considered insufficient.

    Professor's Note: In some cases, more than 10% at-risk equity may still be insufficient.

2. *Shareholders lack decision-making rights.* This relates to the shareholders' inability to make decisions about the entity's activities either directly or indirectly. This usually occurs when the SPE shareholders are issued nonvoting stock.

3. *Shareholders do not absorb the expected losses.* This occurs when the losses are redistributed from the SPE shareholders to the other variable interest owners. For example, the sponsor might agree to reimburse the equity investors for any accrued losses.

4. *Shareholders do not receive the expected residual returns.* This occurs when the residual returns are redistributed from the SPE shareholders to the other variable interest owners. For example, the equity investors might only receive a small, fixed rate, return.

Figure 1 summarizes the conditions that identify a VIE.

Figure 1: Is an Entity a VIE?

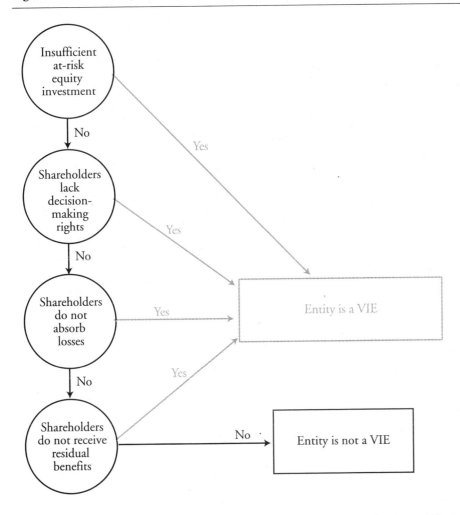

Once it is determined that an entity is a VIE, the entity must be consolidated. The firm that must consolidate the VIE is known as the **primary beneficiary**. The primary beneficiary is the entity that is exposed to the majority of the loss risks or receives the majority of the residual benefits, or both. Voting control is inconsequential at this point.

Example: Identifying a VIE and the primary beneficiary

Southeast Airlines is growing and is in need of a new airplane. Southeast creates a separate entity, Global Aircraft Corporation, to purchase the airplane from the manufacturer using a combination of debt and equity.

Southeast Airlines will lease the airplane from Global Aircraft, and the lease will be structured as an operating lease with a 10-year term. At any point before expiration, Southeast can extend the lease for up to five more years. Once the lease expires, Southeast can purchase the airplane for its then fair value.

The First National Bank has agreed to loan Global Aircraft 90% of the airplane's purchase price. The loan will be secured by the airplane and the lease agreement. In addition, Southeast Airlines must guarantee the bank loan. Global Aircraft was unable to locate any lender that would waive the guaranty requirement.

An independent investor will provide 10% of the purchase price in the form of equity capital in exchange for 100% of Global Aircraft's nonvoting stock. The independent investor will receive a fixed rate of return of 6% paid annually.

Once the lease expires, Global Aircraft will be liquidated. Southeast Airlines will guarantee any deficiency in the event the liquidation proceeds are not sufficient to redeem the investor's stock at par value.

Should Southeast Airlines consolidate Global Aircraft in accordance with FIN 46(R)?

Answer:

We need to consider two separate issues in order to answer the question. First, is Global Aircraft considered a VIE? Second, if Global Aircraft is a VIE, which firm is the primary beneficiary? Recall that if *any* of the following conditions are met, an entity is considered a VIE under FIN 46(R):

1. Insufficient at-risk equity investment.
2. Shareholders lack decision making rights.
3. Shareholders do not absorb losses.
4. Shareholders do not receive residual returns.

The first condition is met since the total at-risk equity investment made by the independent investor is not sufficient to finance Global Aircraft's activities without additional support. Although the independent investor contributed 10% of the total capital needed to purchase the airplane, the bank would not finance the transaction without the support of Southeast Airlines' guarantee. This condition alone makes Global Aircraft a VIE.

The second condition is also met because the stock issued to the at-risk equity investor is nonvoting. Therefore, the independent investor lacks decision making rights. This condition alone makes Global Aircraft a VIE.

Finally, the third and fourth conditions are met since the at-risk equity investor does not absorb the losses or receive the residual returns of a normal stockholder. The independent investor receives a fixed rate of return. Also, at the end of the lease, the investor's stock is liquidated and any deficiency is guaranteed by Southeast Airlines. Therefore, the risks and rewards have been transferred away from the independent investor. Either one of these conditions makes Global Aircraft a VIE.

Since it has been determined that Global Aircraft is a VIE, we now turn our attention to identifying the primary beneficiary. Since Southeast Airlines is exposed to the majority of the risks and rewards associated with the VIE, they are considered the primary beneficiary. As such, Southeast Airlines must consolidate Global Aircraft in its financial statements.

KEY CONCEPTS

1. An SPE is a legal structure created to isolate certain assets and liabilities from the sponsor.
2. The structure lowers the cost of capital since the assets of the SPE are protected in the event the sponsor experiences financial difficulties.
3. A VIE is an entity whereby any of the following conditions are met:
   - Insufficient at-risk equity investment.
   - Shareholders lack decision-making rights.
   - Shareholders do not absorb losses.
   - Shareholders do not receive residual benefits.
4. At-risk equity of less than 10% is usually consistent with a VIE.
5. A VIE is consolidated by the primary beneficiary.
6. The primary beneficiary is the firm that is exposed to the majority of the risks and rewards associated with the VIE.

CONCEPT CHECKERS

1. Are debt guarantees and asset purchase options examples of variable interests?

	Debt guarantees	Asset purchase options
A.	Yes	Yes
B.	Yes	No
C.	No	Yes
D.	No	No

2. Which of the following statements about a variable interest entity (VIE) is *most accurate*?
    A. The legal form of a VIE must be a corporation or a partnership; no other forms are allowed.
    B. A VIE is nothing more than a shell; that is, there are no assets or liabilities.
    C. The business activities of a VIE are typically governed by the independent shareholders.
    D. The risks and rewards of a VIE are not distributed on the basis of stock ownership.

3. According to FASB Interpretation No. 46(R), would an entity qualify as a VIE if the equity investors had no voting rights or the entity has sufficient at-risk equity to finance its operations?

	No voting rights	Sufficient at-risk equity
A.	Yes	Yes
B.	Yes	No
C.	No	No
D.	No	Yes

4. The First National Bank sells automobile loans to a separate entity known as Auto Finance Partners (AFP). AFP is financed with 90% debt and 10% equity issued to an independent investor. First National Bank's risk is virtually nonexistent.

    Triple A Company wants to build a new manufacturing plant and creates a separate entity known as Property Finance Incorporated (PFI). PFI borrows 90% of the construction cost. In order to entice the construction lender to fund the project, Triple A had to agree to pledge its common stock as additional collateral.

    Are Auto Finance Partners and Property Finance Incorporated considered variable interest entities?

	Auto Finance Partners	Property Finance Incorporated
A.	Yes	No
B.	Yes	Yes
C.	No	No
D.	No	Yes

5. Which of the following statements about the primary beneficiary is *most accurate*?
    A. A firm cannot be the primary beneficiary unless it owns a voting interest in the VIE.
    B. The primary beneficiary will usually consolidate an entity when the independent investors' at-risk equity ownership is greater than 10% of total assets.
    C. The primary beneficiary absorbs the majority of the VIE's expected losses or receives the majority of the VIE's expected residual returns, or both.
    D. The primary beneficiary is the entity that owns more than 50% of the outstanding stock of the VIE.

ANSWERS – CONCEPT CHECKERS

1. **A** Both are examples of variable interests. Honoring a debt guarantee would result in a loss. The holder of an asset purchase option would benefit if the asset's value increases.

2. **D** The risk and rewards of ownership are not distributed based on stock ownership. Rather the risks and rewards are distributed based on other variable interests.

    The other choices are incorrect. A VIE can take a variety of structures besides a corporation or a partnership, including joint ventures or trusts. The independent shareholders typically exercise little or no control over the VIE's day-to-day operations. Finally, the VIE is structured specifically so that it can hold and incur liabilities (such as issuing debt).

3. **B** No voting rights would indicate that equity investors lack decision-making authority. Thus, the entity is considered a VIE. An entity would not be considered a VIE if it has sufficient at-risk equity capital to finance its operations unless the entity meets any of the other conditions.

4. **D** Auto Finance Partners is not a VIE since it appears to be adequately capitalized and FNB's risk is nonexistent. Property Finance Incorporated is a VIE since it is unable to finance the project without additional collateral provided by the sponsor.

5. **C** The primary beneficiary absorbs the majority of the VIE's expected losses or receives the majority of the VIE's expected residual returns, or both, even if it has no voting interest or at-risk ownership of less than 10%. It is not necessary for the primary beneficiary to own stock in the VIE in order to consolidate.

UNDERSTANDING RETIREMENT BENEFITS ACCOUNTING AND DISCLOSURES FOR FINANCIAL ANALYSIS

Study Session 6

EXAM FOCUS

This is a complicated topic, but don't be intimidated. The economics of pension plan accounting are not too difficult to grasp, but the accounting for pension plans under U.S. GAAP is extremely complex. Please note that the U.S. pension accounting standards changed in December 2006, and you are now required to know those changes for the 2008 exam. Focus your attention on the economic intuition behind the accounting numbers: (1) the PBO is a measure of the firm's pension liability, and the difference between the PBO and the fair value of the plan assets determines whether the plan is over- or underfunded; (2) pension expense represents the present value of the pension benefits earned by the firm's employees during the year. Make sure you know how to adjust financial statements prepared under the old Standards so that they are consistent with the new Standards. You should be able to explain how reported results are affected by management's assumptions regarding the discount rate, the rate of compensation increase, and the expected rate of return on plan assets. You should also be able to adjust the reported financial results for economic reality by calculating adjusted pension expense, and be able to analyze the effects of these adjustments on key financial ratios.

Professor's Note: As noted in the Exam Focus, U.S. GAAP pension standards have changed for firms with fiscal-year end after December 2006. For the exam, you need to know both the old standards in effect prior to December 2006 and the new standards.

DEFINED CONTRIBUTION AND DEFINED-BENEFIT PENSION PLANS

LOS 24.a: Explain the types of post-employment benefit plans and the implications for financial reports.

A **defined contribution plan** is a retirement plan (e.g., cash balance plan, 401(k) plan, profit sharing plan) into which the employee makes contributions and the employer may promise to make periodic contributions (through matching programs) to the retirement accounts of eligible employees. The firm makes no promise to the employee

Study Session 6

Cross-Reference to CFA Institute Assigned Reading #24 – Understanding Retirement Benefits Accounting and Disclosures ...

regarding the amount of funds that will accumulate in the plan over time. Investment decisions for the funds are left to the employees, who bear all of the shortfall risk at retirement.

The financial reporting implications for defined contribution plans are straightforward. During the reporting period, the employer accrues a liability until the firm makes its contributions to the employees' accounts. Once the contributions are made, the contribution amount is recorded as pension expense on the firm's income statement and the liability is removed from the balance sheet. The pension cost for the period is equal to the required contribution.

In a **defined-benefit plan**, the company promises to make periodic payments to the employee after retirement. The employer invests funds to meet the future obligation and the employer, not the employee, assumes the risks and rewards associated with the plan assets and liabilities. Defined-benefit plans can be categorized as pay-related or non-pay-related:

- In *pay-related plans*, pension benefits are based on the employee's future compensation. They may be based on an employee's salary at or near retirement, or on an employee's average compensation over her career. For example, the employer might promise the employee an annual pension payment equal to 2% per year of service, applied to the employee's annual salary at the time of retirement. Under this plan, an employee who worked for the company for 20 years and earned $100,000 in the year she retired is promised $40,000 per year after retirement.
- In *non-pay-related plans*, pension benefits are set as a fixed amount for each year of service or derived in some other way that is unrelated to the employee's salary level. The benefits are not related to the employee's present or expected future compensation. For example, the employer could promise the employee $240 a month after retirement for every year of service, so an employee who worked for the company for 20 years is promised $4,800 per month after retirement.

The financial reporting implications for defined-benefit pension plans are much more complicated than for defined contribution plans because the employer must estimate the value today of the future obligations (i.e., promises) made to its employees. To estimate the value of this liability today, the company must make assumptions concerning the discount rate to use to calculate the present value of the future obligations, the expected increase in employee compensation (for pay-related plans in which the pension payment depends on the employee's salary at retirement), how long employees will work before they retire, how many will quit or be fired and move on to other jobs (i.e., employee turnover) and how long they will live (and receive pension benefits) after they retire. The rest of this topic review addresses the issue of analyzing companies with defined-benefit plans.

A company with a defined-benefit plan also funds a pension fund, which is a portfolio of financial securities managed to generate the income and principal growth necessary to fund the pension obligations as they come due. The amount the company reports on its balance sheet is a net amount: the difference between the value of the assets (the pension fund) and the value of the pension liability.

MEASURING THE PENSION OBLIGATION

LOS 24.c: Explain the measures of a defined-benefit pension plan's liabilities, including the projected benefit obligation, accumulated benefit obligation, and vested benefit obligation.

The first step in accounting for defined-benefit plans is to measure the obligation (i.e., the liability). There are three different measures of the pension obligation you should be aware of:

1. The **projected benefit obligation** (PBO) is the actuarial present value (at the assumed discount rate) of all future pension benefits earned to date, *based on expected future salary increases*. It measures the value of the obligation assuming the firm is a going concern and that the employees will continue to work for the firm until they retire.

2. The **accumulated benefit obligation** (ABO) is the actuarial present value of all future pension benefits earned to date based on current salary levels, *ignoring future salary increases*. It is an estimate of the pension liability on a current basis, which is relevant if the company expects to liquidate and settle (i.e. pay off) its pension obligation. The ABO is used to determine whether a minimum liability allowance must be reported (See LOS 24.e). Note that for a non-pay-related plan, the ABO will equal the PBO.

3. The **vested benefit obligation** (VBO) is the amount of the ABO to which the employees are entitled based on the company's vesting schedule. Most companies require that employees work for the company for a specified period of time before they are entitled to full pension benefits. For example, a company may use a 4-year vesting schedule, under which the employees earn the right to receive 25% of benefits under the pension plan each year. After working for the company for four years, an employee is fully vested, which means the employee is entitled to all pension benefits accrued to date.

Professor's Note: The best way to "explain the measures" of the PBO, ABO, and VBO (as required by the LOS) is to walk through a very simple pension example. You are not required to perform the calculations outlined in the example that follows, however, as part of the LOS.

A SIMPLE EXAMPLE OF A DEFINED-BENEFIT PENSION PLAN

John McElwain was hired on January 1, 2005 as the only employee of Transfer Trucking, Inc. and is eligible to participate in the company's defined-benefit pension plan. Under the plan, he is promised an annual payment of 2% of his annual salary (based on his salary when he retires) for each year of service, to be paid at the end of the year. The vesting schedule stipulates that McElwain will be entitled to 25% of the ABO for each year of service until he becomes fully vested in four years. McElwain is starting at a salary of $50,000 per year for 2005.

Study Session 6

Cross-Reference to CFA Institute Assigned Reading #24 – Understanding Retirement Benefits Accounting and Disclosures ...

Calculating the PBO for 2005

Remember that the PBO is the present value of the benefits McElwain is expected to receive in retirement. In order to calculate the PBO at the end of the first year, the company needs to make a number of assumptions:

- The **discount rate** is 8%.
- McElwain's salary will increase by 4% per year (this is called the **rate of compensation increase**).
- McElwain will work for 25 years and retire on December 31, 2029.
- McElwain will live for 15 years after retirement and receive 15 annual pension benefit payments.

The company is only required to disclose the first two assumptions (the discount rate and the rate of compensation increase) in the footnotes to the financial statements. They are discussed in more detail in the next LOS.

Based on a starting salary of $50,000 in 2005 and 4% annual increases over 24 years, McElwain's salary in the year he retires, 2029, will be $128,165.21. Remember that if he works for 25 years he will receive 24 pay increases.

 Professor's Note: We're going to assume that you know how to do basic time value of money calculations like this, so we won't clutter up the presentation by continually showing you the formulas or calculator key strokes necessary to arrive at these numbers. You may also encounter some very minor rounding error.

If McElwain is earning $128,165.21 in his last year of employment (2029), he will be entitled to an annual pension payment equal to 2% of his final salary for each year of service. With one year of service so far, this promised pension payment is $128,165.21 × 0.02 × 1 = $2,563.30. Assuming he lives for 15 years and receives 15 payments at the end of each of the next 15 years, the present value of those payments at 8% on the day he retires in 2029 is $21,940.55. At the end of his first year of employment (24 years earlier at the end of 2005), the present value of this amount is $3,460.01.

Therefore the PBO at the end of 2005 (McElwain's first year of employment) is $3,460.01. A table outlining these cash flows is shown in Figure 1.

Figure 1: Calculation of the PBO at the End of 2005

Year	Years of Service	Projected Salary	Years in Retirement	Benefit Payment (end of year)	Present Value (end of year)
2005	1	$50,000.00			PBO = $3,460.01
2006	2	$52,000.00			
2007	3	$54,080.00			
2027	23	$118,495.94			
2028	24	$123,235.78			
2029	25	$128,165.21			$21,940.55
2030			1	$2,563.30	
2031			2	$2,563.30	
2032			3	$2,563.30	
2043			14	$2,563.30	
2044			15	$2,563.30	

Calculating the ABO for 2005

The ABO represents the company's pension obligation assuming no increase in employee compensation, so the pension payment is based on today's salary. Therefore, the pension payments will be $50,000 × 0.02 × 1 = $1,000, and the ABO (the present value of those payments at 8% at the end of year 1) will be $1,349.82. These cash flows are shown in Figure 2.

Study Session 6

Cross-Reference to CFA Institute Assigned Reading #24 – Understanding Retirement Benefits Accounting and Disclosures ...

Figure 2: Calculation of the ABO at the End of 2005

Year	Years of Service	Projected Salary	Years in Retirement	Benefit Payment (end of year)	Present Value (end of year)
2005	1	$50,000.00			ABO = $1,349.82
2006	2	$50,000.00			
2007	3	$50,000.00			
2027	23	$50,000.00			
2028	24	$50,000.00			
2029	25	$50,000.00			$8,559.48
2030			1	$1,000.00	
2031			2	$1,000.00	
2032			3	$1,000.00	
2043			14	$1,000.00	
2044			15	$1,000.00	

Calculating the VBO for 2005

Based on the company's vesting schedule, after his first year of service, the VBO is 25% of the ABO, or $337.46. This is the amount McElwain would be entitled to if he was to leave the company after one year of service.

Calculating the Net Pension Liability for 2005

Assume that the company does not make any contributions to fund the pension liability at the end of 2005. Therefore, the net pension liability that is reported on the balance sheet is the PBO of $3,460.01.

Calculating Pension Expense for 2005

The pension expense in 2005 is the present value of the projected benefits earned by McElwain during the year, which is the amount of the increase in the PBO, or $3,460.01. This component of pension expense is called the **service cost**. The service cost and the other cost components of pension expense are discussed in more detail later in LOS 24.b.

Calculating the PBO, ABO, and VBO for 2006

If McElwain is earning $128,165.21 in his last year of employment (2029), he will be entitled to an annual pension payment equal to 2% of his final salary for each year of service. After two years, this promised pension payment is $128,165.21 × 0.02 × 2 = $5,126.61. The present value of these 15 payments at 8% on the day he retires in 2029 is \$43,881.09. At the end of his second year of employment (23 years earlier at the end of 2006) the present value is \$7,473.62.

Therefore, the PBO at the end of 2006 (McElwain's second year of employment) is \$7,473.62. A table outlining these cash flows is shown in Figure 3.

Figure 3: Calculation of the PBO at the End of 2006

Year	Years of Service	Projected Salary	Years in Retirement	Benefit Payment (end of year)	Present Value (end of year)
2005	1	\$50,000.00			
2006	2	\$52,000.00			PBO = \$7,473.62
2007	3	\$54,080.00			
2027	23	\$118,495.94			
2028	24	\$123,235.78			
2029	25	\$128,165.21			\$43,881.09
2030			1	\$5,126.61	
2031			2	\$5,126.61	
2032			3	\$5,126.61	
2043			14	\$5,126.61	
2044			15	\$5,126.61	

The ABO at the end of 2006 is \$3,032.24 (based on a salary of \$52,000) and the VBO is \$1,516.12 (50% of the ABO because he's vested for two years).

Calculating the Net Pension Liability for 2006

Suppose that the company decides to begin funding its pension obligation by contributing \$5,000 to the pension plan at the end of 2006. The plan invests the \$5,000 in a portfolio of equity and debt securities. The net pension liability for 2006 after the contribution is the difference between the value of the plan assets and the PBO, or \$2,473.62. As we'll discuss later on in this topic review, this amount is called the **funded status**.

Calculating Pension Expense for 2006

Pension expense for 2006 is equal to the increase in the PBO during the year. The increase in the PBO during the year is the result of (1) the **service cost**, which is equal to the present value of the benefits earned by McElwain during the year because his pension payments are larger by \$5,126.61 – \$2,563.30 = \$2,563.31 (they are now based on two years of service); and (2) the **interest cost** on the PBO balance from the beginning of the year:

2005 PBO	$3,460.01
+ Service cost	$3,736.81 (PV (end 2006) of 15 extra payments of $2,563.31)
+ Interest cost	$276.80 ($3,460.01 × 0.08)
2006 PBO	$7,473.62

Notice that this reconciles to the PBO reported in Figure 3. Pension expense is equal to service cost plus interest cost:

Service cost	$3,736.81
+ Interest cost	$276.80
2006 pension expense	$4,013.61

Calculating the PBO, ABO, and VBO for 2007

If McElwain is earning $128,165.21 in his last year of employment (2029), he will be entitled to an annual pension payment equal to 2% of his final salary for each year of service. After three years, this promised pension payment is $128,165.21 × 0.02 × 3 = $7,689.91. The present value of these 15 payments at 8% on the day he retires in 2029 is $65,821.62. At the end of his third year of employment (22 years earlier at the end of 2007) the present value is $12,107.26.

Therefore, the PBO at the end of 2007 (McElwain's third year of employment) is $12,107.26. The ABO is $5,108.73 and the VBO (based on three years of vested service) is 75% of the ABO, or $3,831.55.

Calculating the Net Pension Liability for 2007

Suppose that the pension fund assets earned a return of 20% on the original $5,000 contribution. Therefore, the **actual return on assets** is $1,000, and the value of the plan assets at the end of 2007 is $6,000. The net pension liability of the plan (i.e., the funded status) for 2007 after the contribution is the difference between the value of the plan assets and the PBO, or $6,107.26.

 Professor's Note: In LOS 24.d, we'll clarify the distinction between actual and expected return on assets.

Calculating Pension Expense for 2007

The company has funded the pension obligation by contributing to a pension fund, and the returns on the fund reduce pension expense for the year. Service cost and interest cost are computed the same way as before:

2006 PBO	$7,473.62
+ Service cost	$4,035.75 (PV (end 2007) of 15 extra payments of $2,563.31)
+ Interest cost	$597.89 ($7,473.62 × 0.08)
2007 PBO	$12,107.26

Pension expense for 2007 is equal to service cost plus interest cost minus the actual return on assets:

Service cost	$4,035.75
+ Interest cost	$597.89
– Actual return on assets	$1,000.00
2007 pension expense	$3,633.64

CALCULATING PENSION EXPENSE

LOS 24.b: Describe the components of a company's defined-benefit pension expense and explain the impact of plan assumptions on that pension expense.

Professor's Note: Everything covered in this LOS is consistent with the pre-2006 and post-2006 U.S. GAAP pension accounting standards.

Reported **pension expense** under U.S. GAAP is calculated as follows:

Actual Events
Service cost
+ Interest cost
                  Smoothed Events
– Expected return on plan assets
± Amortization of unrecognized prior service costs
± Amortization of transition asset or liability
± Amortization of and deferral of actuarial gains and losses
= Reported pension expense (income) on income statement

Each of these six components of pension expense is discussed next.

Service cost. Service cost is equal to the pension benefits earned during the year. Service cost reflects the increase in the PBO that results from the employee working another year.

Interest cost. Interest cost is the increase in the PBO resulting from interest owed on the current benefit obligation.

Expected return on plan assets. As part of the computation of pension expense, the company must estimate an expected long-term rate of return on plan assets. The expected return on plan assets serves to reduce the amount reported as pension expense. Rather than use the actual return on plan assets from year to year, the company uses its assumption of the average long-term annual rate of return to smooth out the volatility in pension expense that would be caused by fluctuating market returns. Any difference between the actual return on plan assets and the expected return is deferred and accumulated. This issue is addressed in more detail in LOS 24.d.

Amortization of unrecognized prior service cost. The prior service cost reflects the change in the PBO that results from an amendment to the pension plan. Amortizing the prior service cost smooths reported pension expense.

Let's illustrate the accounting of prior service costs with the Transfer Trucking example. Suppose Transfer Trucking changes its promise to McElwain and instead of offering a payment based on 2% of his ending salary times his years of service, the company suddenly increases that to 3%. This **plan amendment** results in an immediate increase in the PBO, because the company has promised him higher pension payments when he retires and the present value of that obligation increases.

However, under U.S. GAAP, pension expense doesn't immediately increase by the entire amount; instead, the unrecognized loss is held "off the financial statements" as **unrecognized prior service cost** and amortized over time as an increase in pension expense. U.S. GAAP requires that the unrecognized prior service cost be amortized over the expected remaining service life of the employees affected by the amendment.

Amortization and deferral of gains or losses. Amortization of gains (or losses) that occur from changing actuarial assumptions (i.e., changes in the discount rate) directly reduce (or increase) pension expense.

Amortization of the transition liability or asset. SFAS 87: Employer's Accounting for Pensions was enacted in 1985. Employers that had a pension plan in place prior to 1985 were required to transition to SFAS 87 requirements and the resulting amount was amortized over the expected remaining service life of the affected employees. Since this item is more than 20 years old, many companies have already amortized most of their transition gain or loss, making it a less important component of pension expense.

EFFECT OF CHANGES IN ACTUARIAL ASSUMPTIONS

The company must make and disclose three actuarial assumptions in the pension footnotes:

1. The **discount rate** is the interest rate used to compute the present value of the pension obligations. This is the interest rate at which the company could settle its pension obligation. For example, the company could purchase an annuity to fund the promised pension payments as they come due. The interest rate that makes the present value of the promised pension payments equal to the amount the company would have to pay for the annuity is the discount rate necessary to settle the pension liability. Notice that this is not the risk-free rate.

2. The **rate of compensation increase** is the average annual rate that employee compensation is expected to increase over time.

3. The **expected return on plan assets** is the long-term assumed rate of return on the investments in the plan. Using an expected long-run return assumption rather than actual returns serves to smooth the net pension expense calculation. This issue is discussed in more detail in LOS 24.d.

Assumptions of high discount rates, low compensation growth rates, and high expected rates of return on plan assets will decrease pension expense, increase earnings, and reduce the pension liability. The more aggressive these assumptions are, the lower the earnings quality of the firm.

The use of a *higher discount rate* will improve reported results because it will:

- Result in lower present values and, hence, lower pension liabilities (i.e., lower PBO).
- Almost always result in lower pension expense. Service cost will decrease because it is a present value calculation: as the discount rate increases, the present value of the benefits earned during that year decreases. Interest cost (PBO times the discount rate) will usually decrease, although there are two offsetting effects. A higher discount rate will decrease the PBO, but the product of the *lower* PBO and the *higher* discount rate will usually result in a lower interest cost. In very mature plans with high interest cost relative to service cost, interest cost may actually increase when the discount rate increases because the PBO declines only slightly. This occurs because the product of the *slightly* lower PBO and the higher discount rate now results in a higher interest cost. In fact, the increase in the interest cost may be large enough, in rare cases, to completely offset the lower service cost and actually increase pension expense.

The use of a *lower rate of compensation increase* will improve reported results because it will result in:

- Lower future pension payments and, hence, a lower PBO.
- Lower service cost and a lower interest cost; thus, pension expense will decrease.

The assumption of a *higher return on plan assets* will improve reported results because it will:

- Not affect the calculated PBO.
- Result in lower pension expense.

Figure 4 summarizes the effects of changes in these assumptions on the PBO, the ABO, the VBO.

Figure 4: Effect of Changes in Assumptions on Pension Liability

Effect on...	Increase Discount Rate	Decrease Rate of Compensation Increase	Increase Expected Rate of Return
PBO	Decrease	Decrease	No effect
ABO	Decrease	No effect	No effect
VBO	Decrease	No effect	No effect

Study Session 6

Cross-Reference to CFA Institute Assigned Reading #24 – Understanding Retirement Benefits Accounting and Disclosures ...

Figure 5 summarizes the effect of changes in these assumptions on pension expense.

Figure 5: Effect of Changes in Assumptions on Pension Expense

Effect on...	Increase Discount Rate	Decrease Rate of Compensation Increase	Increase Expected Rate of Return
Service cost	Decrease	Decrease	No effect
Interest cost	Decrease*	Decrease	No effect
Expected return	No effect	No effect	Increase
Pension expense	Decrease*	Decrease	Decrease

* For mature plans, a higher discount rate might increase interest costs. In rare cases, interest cost will increase by enough to offset the decrease in the service cost, and pension expense will increase.

Note that only these three assumptions are required to be disclosed by management; the other assumptions that are necessary to estimate the pension obligation (e.g., how long employees will work for the company and how long they will live after they retire) are not required to be disclosed.

U.S. GAAP PENSION ACCOUNTING STANDARDS BEFORE DECEMBER 2006

LOS 24.d: Explain the impact on financial statements of U.S. generally accepted accounting principles (U.S. GAAP) and international financial reporting standards (IFRS) for pension and other post-employment benefits that permit some items to be reported in the footnotes rather than being reflected in the financial statements themselves.

Professor's Note: We address the pre-2006 U.S. GAAP standards in this LOS and leave the post-2006 U.S. GAAP and IFRS until later on. You need to know the old standards for the exam because companies are not required to retroactively adjust previous years' results to reflect the new standards, and because IFRS still reflects the pre-2006 U.S. standards.

Now we move from the relatively easy part of pension accounting (the economics of the pension assets and liabilities illustrated in the example in the previous section) to the complicated part: the accounting standards applied to pension accounting according to U.S. GAAP. In this LOS we will discuss the application of U.S. GAAP pension accounting standards before December of 2006. The changes to the U.S. standards are discussed later on in this topic review.

Delayed Recognition of Certain Events

It would make sense if U.S. GAAP pension accounting was applied as in the example, so that the net pension liability reported on the balance sheet would actually be equal to the funded status. Recall that the funded status is equal to the difference between the fair value of the plan assets (which is relatively easy to value) and the PBO (which is not easy to calculate, but which does provide a reasonably good estimate of the company's true pension obligation).

However, U.S. GAAP allows for the delayed recognition of certain events that affect the value of the plan assets and the pension obligation. The effects of these events on the net pension liability are not reflected immediately in the financial statements; instead, they are deferred off of the financial statements and amortized over time into the reported financial statements. The result is that under the old standards there were "unrecognized" amounts that were disclosed in the footnotes but not reflected in the balance sheet. Under the new standards, the unrecognized items are now recognized immediately in the balance sheet, as discussed later in this topic review.

Professor's Note: This is probably the part of pension accounting that is most difficult for candidates to grasp. Under the old standards, there were "unrecognized" amounts that were not included in the balance sheet yet, but would eventually be recognized.

The treatment of prior service costs resulting from plan amendments is an example of the delayed recognition of certain events.

Netting of Assets and Liabilities

There are two ways in which the pension assets and the associated pension obligation could be reported on the firm's financial statements: (1) by reporting the value of the pension fund assets on the company's balance sheet as an asset, and reporting the value of its pension obligation as a liability on the balance sheet; or (2) reporting only the net asset or liability amount (the difference between the value of the fund assets and the fund liabilities) on the balance sheet.

Companies are required under both the old and new U.S. GAAP standards to use the second method, so pension assets and liabilities are netted against each other and only the net amount is reported on the balance sheet. If the fund assets are greater than the liabilities, a net asset is reported; if liabilities are greater than assets, a net liability is reported. There are two reasons for netting pension assets and liabilities in this way under U.S. GAAP:

1. The employer largely controls both the pension fund assets and the liabilities and therefore bears the risks and potential rewards.

2. The company's decisions regarding funding and accounting for the pension plan are more likely to be affected by the net pension obligation, not the gross amounts, because the plan assets can only be used for paying pension benefits to its employees.

This unique netting procedure affects certain ratios because the firm's total assets and total liabilities are lower than they would be if the firm was required to report the gross amounts. For example, return on assets (ROA) would likely be higher using the netting procedure, while leverage ratios would also potentially be affected. If a net pension liability is reported, reporting the gross amounts instead would increase liabilities and leverage.

The fact that the pension assets and liabilities are netted is the reason why an analysis of the effect of changes in pension assumptions on reported results is very important. Any changes in assumptions that might only cause a small change in the total pension obligation itself can still have a large impact on the net pension amount.

Reporting Net Pension Expense

The same is true with pension expense; because it is a net amount (service and interest cost net of return on assets), relatively minor changes in the assumptions can have a major impact on reported pension expense.

EXPECTED RETURN ON ASSETS AND THE MARKET-RELATED PLAN VALUE

Pension plan expense is a measure of the present value of the cost of providing the promised future benefits. This involves the accrual of costs that may differ from the actual funding of the plan. The net pension cost on the income statement is a smoothed expense. The smoothing is the result of the use of expected return on plan assets in lieu of actual returns. Also, the amortization of gains/losses and prior service costs smooths pension costs by spreading these items out over the remaining service life of employees.

As part of the computation of pension expense, under both the old and new standards, the company must estimate an expected long-term rate of return on plan assets. The expected return on plan assets is then included as a part of pension expense and serves to reduce the amount reported as pension expense. Any difference between the actual return on plan assets and the expected return is deferred and accumulated. In addition, any liability gains and losses from changes in actuarial assumptions or the life expectancy of plan participants that increase or decrease the PBO are also deferred and accumulated.

This net amount is deferred to future years and amounts in excess of 10% of the greater of the PBO or the market related value are amortized. The amortization is made over the average remaining service life of the employees. Note, however, that if the unamortized deferred and accumulated amount falls below the corridor amount, the amortization stops until the corridor amount is exceeded in a future year.

In addition, the expected (dollar) return on plan assets is not a function of the actual fair market value of the plan assets, but what is called the **market-related value** of the plan assets. Think of the market-related value as an "average" asset value that we get by amortizing the differences between actual and expected return over a period of five years.

The idea is to reduce ("smooth") the variability of reported pension expense by reducing the volatility of the asset base on which the expected (dollar) return on plan assets is calculated. The market-related value is calculated as:

Beginning market-related value
+ Expected return on plan assets
+ Employer contributions
+ Participant contributions
− Benefits paid
 ± 20% of deferred asset gains/losses over past 5 years
= Ending market-related value

ACTUAL VS. EXPECTED RETURN ON PLAN ASSETS

Expected return on plan assets (measured in $) is calculated as:

beginning market-related value × expected return (%) on assets

Notice that expected return (in $) and actual return (in $) are calculated differently:

expected return on assets ($) = beginning market-related value
× expected return on assets (%)

actual return on assets ($) = beginning fair value of plan assets
× actual return on assets (%)

Therefore, *expected* return on plan assets (which affects reported pension expense) can differ from the *actual* return (both measured in $) because (1) the market-related value does not necessarily equal the fair value of plan assets, and (2) the long-term assumption of expected percentage return does not necessarily equal the actual percentage return in any given year.

We can draw two conclusions about the effects of these two measures on pension expense:

1. *Expected* return on plan assets (a number assumed and disclosed by management) *directly affects* pension expense: increasing the expected return assumption reduces pension expense.

2. Actual return on plan assets only affects pension expense indirectly because differences between actual and expected returns affect the market-related value, which affects pension expense. However, the effect will be small if over the long term the average actual return is approximately equal to the expected return assumption. Notice, however, that actual returns directly affect that fair value of plan assets and the funded status.

ECONOMIC LIABILITY (FUNDED STATUS) OF THE PENSION PLAN

LOS 24.e: Calculate the underlying economic liability (or asset) of a company based upon pension and other post-employment benefit disclosures.

Reconciliation of Beginning and Ending PBO

Under both the old and new U.S. standards, companies are required to disclose a reconciliation of beginning and ending balances of the PBO. The disclosure includes the following:

PBO at the beginning of the year
    Cost Components
+ Service cost
+ Interest cost
± Actuarial gains and losses
± Prior service cost from plan amendments
− Benefits paid
= **PBO at the end of the year**

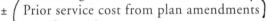

Fair Value of Plan Assets

The fair value of the pension plan's assets must also be disclosed in the footnotes under both standards. Recall that the plan assets are a portfolio of securities (stocks and bonds) managed with the goal of generating sufficient cash to pay the benefits owed to the plan beneficiaries. The fair value of the plan assets is increased by the actual return on the plan assets (dividends and interest), as well as contributions made by the employer. Recall that the balance is decreased by benefits paid to the plan beneficiaries. Companies are also required to disclose a reconciliation of the beginning and ending balances of the fair value of the plan assets.

Fair value of plan assets at the beginning of the year
+ Actual return on assets
+ Employer contributions
− Benefits paid
= **Fair value of plan assets at the end of the year**

Pension Plan Funded Status

As we discussed earlier, the **funded status of the plan** is the difference between the assets (the fair value of the plan assets) and the liability (the PBO):

funded status = fair value of plan assets − PBO

The plan is "overfunded" if the funded status is positive; it is "underfunded" if the funded status is negative.

Reconciliation of Funded Status to Net Pension Liability

Professor's Note: This is where the new standards are different from the old standards. Under the old standards, the pension liability or asset reported on the balance sheet reflected the funded status adjusted for unrecognized items. Under the new standards, the pension liability or asset is equal to the funded status, which is not adjusted for unrecognized items.

The funded status of the plan is the true economic position of the plan: the fair market value of the assets minus the liabilities. However, under the old standards, these amounts were "off-balance sheet" items; they were disclosed only in the footnotes. The pension liability (or asset) reported on the balance sheet under the old standards was not the funded status of the plan, and usually bore no resemblance to the true economic position of the plan.

If the company had actually recorded the funded status of the plan on its financial statements, the amount recorded would have fluctuated dramatically, mainly due to the volatility of the actual return caused by volatility in the financial markets. For the reported pension liability (or asset), the old standards required various adjustments that smoothed out this volatility, which created opportunities for earnings management.

Under the old standard, U.S. GAAP required the reconciliation of the funded status (which is the true economic pension liability or asset) to the reported (accounting) liability or asset. This involved adjusting the funded status for the unrecognized gains or losses resulting from the transition asset or liability, unrecognized prior service costs, and unrecognized actuarial gains and losses. Unrecognized costs, losses, and liabilities were added back to the funded status to arrive at the reported pension asset or liability. Unrecognized gains and assets were subtracted from the funded status to arrive at the reported pension asset or liability. The following reconciliation was required to be disclosed in the footnotes.

> **Funded status (Fair value of plan assets minus the PBO)**
> +   Unrecognized actuarial losses
>   or
> −   Unrecognized actuarial gains
> +   Unrecognized prior service cost
> +   Unrecognized prior transition obligation
>   or
> −   Unrecognized prior transition asset
> =   **Net pension asset (liability) recorded on balance sheet**

This amount was reported as an asset or liability on the balance sheet. Note that different plans may be reported separately, so the company could have both a pension asset and a pension liability on its balance sheet.

Under the new standards, which we will discuss later in this topic review, companies are required going forward to recognize the funded status on the balance sheet, so all the previously unrecognized items must now be recognized.

Study Session 6

Cross-Reference to CFA Institute Assigned Reading #24 – Understanding Retirement Benefits Accounting and Disclosures ...

The transition liability is the amount that was created when FAS 87 was first applied. This is not a very important component of the pension liability or pension expense because it has been almost completely extinguished for most companies.

PBO = 120

(10)

 Professor's Note: You are probably asking yourself, "Why do we add back losses and subtract out gains under the old standard?" Here's a simple example to illustrate the point. Suppose that the FMV of plan assets is $100, PBO is $110, and there are no unrecognized deferrals, so the funded status equals the pension asset (liability), which equals ($10). Now instead suppose that there is a loss of $10 because the forecasted life expectancy of the employees is increased (which is a change in an actuarial assumption). The FMV of assets is $100, the PBO increases to $120 because of the higher liability, and the funded status is now ($20). However, the loss was not recognized, but rather deferred and amortized over time as an increase in pension expense. Therefore, the pension liability remained at ($10). Then you had to add back the loss to reconcile the funded status to the liability: ($20) + $10 = ($10).

$10 liability

(20)

120

10

10/10

120

Minimum Liability Allowance

Pension accounting allows for built-in smoothing of pension expense reporting for the purpose of reducing the volatility of pension expense. This is accomplished by allowing delayed recognition of the effect of plan amendments and losses and allowing pension expense to be computed based on an expected rate of return rather than on the actual rate of return. In order to partially compensate for this smoothing, both the old and new U.S. GAAP standards require that if the ABO exceeds the fair value of plan assets, at least that difference must show on the balance sheet as a liability. If necessary, the existing pension asset or liability balance must be adjusted to this liability value by recording an additional pension liability called the **minimum liability allowance** (or the **additional liability**). This allowance is partially offset by an intangible asset with the remainder included in comprehensive income as a charge to equity.

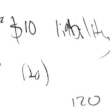 *Professor's Note: On the exam, you're likely to be asked to determine whether the company is required to report an additional liability, and you may be asked to calculate the additional amount, as in the following example.*

Example: Calculating the minimum liability allowance

General Mechanics, Inc. has a defined-benefit pension plan with an ABO of $522 million. General Mechanics' pension plan assets have a fair value of $488 million. On its balance sheet, the company shows a net pension liability of $12 million. Calculate the minimum liability allowance.

Answer:

General Mechanics is required to record $22 million as "additional pension liability" on its balance sheet, with a corresponding entry on the asset side to an intangible asset or on the equity side as a contra-equity account.

($522 million – $488 million) – $12 million = $22 million

OTHER POSTRETIREMENT BENEFITS

The most important employee benefit accounting issue at Level 2 is pension benefit accounting, but many U.S. companies also provide health care benefits to retirees. These **non-pension postretirement benefits** are generally accounted for in the same manner as pension benefits, with a few minor differences (which are noted in italics in the following discussion).

- The company is required to estimate an **accumulated postretirement benefit obligation (APBO)** that is analogous to the PBO in pension accounting. The APBO is the actuarial present value of the expected postretirement benefits earned up to that point. The discount rate used to estimate the APBO is usually different than the discount rate used to estimate the PBO.

  Difference: Estimate the APBO using the unique discount rate for postretirement benefit plan.

- Estimation of the APBO requires a number of assumptions, including the **health care cost trend rate** (i.e., the health care inflation rate), per-capita claims costs, Medicare reimbursement rates (for U.S. companies), required employer contributions (which is referred to as cost sharing), and cost caps. The discount rate, the expected return on plan assets, and the health care cost trend rate must be disclosed. Because these are not pay-related plans, a forecast of the rate of compensation increase is not required.

  Difference: An estimate of the APBO requires a forecast of the health care cost trend rate, which must be disclosed. The company must also disclose the impact of a 1% increase and a 1% decrease in the health care cost trend rate on the APBO and the recurring benefit costs (service cost plus interest cost).

- **Net postretirement benefit cost** is calculated the same way as pension cost, using the same components: service cost, interest cost, expected return on plan assets, amortization of gains and losses, amortization of prior service costs, amortization of transition asset or liability, and curtailments and settlements.

- The **funded status** of the postretirement plan is the difference between the APBO and the fair value of the postretirement benefits plan assets. Under the old standards, the company was required to disclose the reconciliation between the funded status and the balance sheet asset or liability, as was the case with pension accounting. The difference between the two reflected unrecognized prior service costs, unrecognized net gains or losses, and an unrecognized transition obligation. Under the new standards, the company recognizes the funded status.

  Difference: There is no minimum liability adjustment.

  Difference: Many postretirement plans are "unfunded," which means that there are no plan assets, employer contributions equal benefits paid each year, and the funded status equals the APBO.

- The balance sheet adjustment necessary to reflect the new standard (as discussed in the next section) is also the same: report the funded status on the balance sheet by removing the unrecognized components.

Study Session 6

Cross-Reference to CFA Institute Assigned Reading #24 – Understanding Retirement Benefits Accounting and Disclosures ...

- The effects of changes in the discount rate assumption and (if the firm funds the plan) the expected return on assets assumption on reported financial results are the same: a higher discount rate and a higher expected return on assets are aggressive assumptions that reduce post-retirement benefit expense and increase reported earnings.

Difference: The analyst should also analyze the health care cost trend rate. A lower rate assumption is an aggressive assumption which decreases the APBO, decreases reported postretirement benefit expense, and increases reported earnings.

NEW U.S. STANDARDS AFTER DECEMBER 2006

What changed? U.S. GAAP pension accounting standards for public companies changed in December 2006. **The funded status (the difference between the PBO and the fair value of plan assets) must now be reported on the balance sheet.** Under the old standard, the liability on the balance sheet reflected the funded status *adjusted for unrecognized items.*

As we discussed previously, under the old standard, companies were required to provide a reconciliation between the funded status and the net pension liability. Suppose, for example, that Payroll Professionals had provided the following information in the footnotes to its financial statements:

Reconciliation of Funded Status to Pension Asset (Liability)	
Fair value of plan assets	$1,100
PBO	(2,250)
Funded status	**($1,150)**
Unrecognized prior service cost	920
Unrecognized actuarial losses	160
Net pension asset (liability) on balance sheet	**($70)**

Under the old standard, this company would have reported a net pension liability of only $70. However, under the new standard, the company is required to report a net pension liability of $1,150.

What didn't change? The calculation of pension expense remains the same: it still includes service cost and interest cost plus the effects of smoothing and amortized items (expected return on plan assets, amortization of prior service cost, and amortization of actuarial gains or losses.)

What are the adjustments necessary to implement the new standards? The pension asset or liability must be adjusted to reflect the funded status. The offsetting entries are to shareholders' equity (as part of comprehensive income) and deferred tax liabilities.

- An *increase in a pension liability* (or decrease in a pension asset) to reflect the funded status results in *offsetting decreases* in deferred tax liabilities and shareholders' equity.

- A *decrease in a pension liability* (or increase in a pension asset) to reflect the funded status results in *offsetting increases* in deferred tax liabilities and shareholders' equity.

What will be the likely effect on reported financial results? For most companies, the pension liability and financial leverage will increase as a result of applying the new standard. Notice also that under the new standard pension items are not accounted for the same way on the balance sheet and the income statement. Deferred and unrecognized items are recognized on the income statement, but not on the balance sheet. Therefore the balance sheet now reflects the true economic position of the pension plan, but the income statement still does not necessarily reflect a true measure of economic pension expense.

Why do you need to know the old standard? Companies have the choice of applying the standard retroactively to prior years' results under U.S. GAAP, but they aren't required to. **Therefore, on exam day you need to know how the old standard was applied and the adjustments necessary to convert the results to the new standard.** You also need to know the pre-2006 U.S. GAAP standards because IFRS didn't change, so it is still consistent with the old U.S. standards.

Example: Applying the new pension accounting standard

Under the old pension accounting standards, Payroll Professionals reported the following information in the footnotes to its financial statements:

Reconciliation of Funded Status to Pension Asset (Liability)	
Fair value of plan assets	$1,100
PBO	(2,250)
Funded status	($1,150)
Unrecognized prior service cost	920
Unrecognized actuarial losses	160
Net pension asset (liability) on balance sheet	($70)

The liability and shareholders' equity portion of the balance sheet was reported as follows:

Liabilities and Shareholders' Equity	
Current liabilities	$200
Liabilities for pension benefits	70
Deferred income taxes	500
Other long-term liabilities	1,600
Total liabilities	$2,370
Common stock	100
Retained earnings	1,400
Accumulated other comprehensive income	730
Total shareholders' equity	2,230
Total liabilities and shareholders' equity	$4,600

The marginal tax rate is 40%. Determine the effect on the balance sheet and the financial leverage ratio (total assets divided by total equity) of converting to the new standard.

Answer:

The appropriate adjustments are to increase the pension liability to the funded status with offsetting declines in deferred income taxes and accumulated other comprehensive income.

- Liabilities for pension benefits will increase by $1,080 from $70 to $1,150.
- Deferred income taxes will decrease by $1,080 × 0.40 = $432.
- Accumulated other comprehensive income will decrease by $1,080 − $432 = $648.

The effect of these adjustments on the balance sheet is shown in the following figure. The financial leverage ratio increases from 2.1 to 2.9 because liabilities increase and equity decreases.

Adjusted Liabilities and Shareholders' Equity			
	Old Standard	*Adjustment*	*New Standard*
Current liabilities	$200		$200
Liabilities for pension benefits	70	+1,080	1,150
Deferred income taxes	500	(432)	68
Other long-term liabilities	1,600		1,600
Total liabilities	$2,370		$3,018
Common stock	100		100
Retained earnings	1,400		1,400
Accumulated other comprehensive income	730	(648)	82
Total shareholders' equity	2,230		1,582
Total liabilities and shareholders' equity	$4,600		$4,600
Financial leverage ratio	2.1		2.9

INTERNATIONAL FINANCIAL REPORTING STANDARDS (IFRS) FOR PENSION PLANS

In general, IFRS pension rules are similar to U.S. standards, with a few notable differences.

- The most important difference is that IFRS treatment of the pension liability is still the same as the old U.S. standard: the liability on the balance sheet still reflects the funded status *adjusted for unrecognized items*. Therefore, the amount of the pension liability reported on the balance sheet can be significantly different depending on the standards according to which the financial statements were prepared.

     Professor's Note: We think this will be a key source of pension accounting questions on the Level 2 exam. You are likely to be asked to analyze the differences in the balance sheet and leverage resulting from the application of the new U.S. standard versus IFRS to the same set of facts. Remember that the difference is that U.S. standards will recognize the funded status as a liability on the balance sheet, while the liability from IFRS will reflect the funded status adjusted for the unrecognized items. This will typically (but not always!) result in higher leverage under U.S. standards.

- Defined-benefit and defined-contribution plans are defined differently under IFRS.

Study Session 6

Cross-Reference to CFA Institute Assigned Reading #24 – Understanding Retirement Benefits Accounting and Disclosures ...

- IFRS requires that actuarial gains and losses be amortized over the employee's service life, rather than over the employee's life expectancy, as is the case under U.S. GAAP. The difference is most apparent in plans in which most of the participants are retired.
- IFRS requires that prior service costs for retired participants and current employees vested in the plan be expensed in the period incurred rather than deferred and amortized.
- IFRS does not require that a minimum liability be recognized when the ABO is larger than fair value of plan assets.

UNDERLYING ECONOMIC PENSION EXPENSE

LOS 24.f: Calculate the underlying economic pension and other post-employment expense (income) based upon disclosures after removing the effect of amortized items and smoothing mechanisms.

Adjustments to the Income Statement

A common method for adjusting the income statement is to calculate **adjusted pension expense**, which is calculated without reflecting the amortization of the unrecognized items and smoothing mechanisms included in pension expense and using actual instead of expected return on assets:

adjusted pension expense = service cost + interest cost − actual return on plan assets

Adjusted pension expense is a better measure of the firm's true economic pension cost than reported pension expense.

Example: Calculating adjusted pension expense

Payroll Professionals reported the following information in the footnotes to its financial statements:

Reconciliation of Beginning and Ending PBO	
Beginning PBO	1,250
+ Service cost	580
+ Interest cost	70
− Benefits paid	(90)
± Plan amendments	440
= Ending PBO	2,250

Changes in Plan Assets	
Fair value of plan assets - beginning of year	1,000
± Actual return on plan assets	(150)
+ Employer contribution	340
– Benefits paid	(90)
= Fair value of plan assets - end of year	1,100

Pension Expense	
Service cost	580
+ Interest cost	70
– Expected return on plan assets	(80)
± Amortization of prior service cost	10
± Recognized actuarial (gain) loss	30
= Net periodic benefit (income) expense	610

Calculate pension expense adjusted for unrecognized items and smoothing mechanisms.

Answer:

adjusted pension expense = service cost + interest cost – actual return on plan assets
= 580 + 70 – (–150) = $800

Adjusted pension expense was significantly higher than reported pension expense ($800 versus $610) because actual return on assets was negative for the year. Instead of reducing adjusted pension expense (as it would if actual return on plan assets was positive), the negative return on plan assets actually increased adjusted pension expense.

Study Session 6

Cross-Reference to CFA Institute Assigned Reading #24 – Understanding Retirement Benefits Accounting and Disclosures ...

EXTENDED EXAMPLE USING UPS FINANCIAL DATA

This example demonstrates the process of converting statements prepared prior to December 2006 to the new standard. The following pension plan data was reported by United Parcel Service, Inc. (UPS) in its 2004 10-K[1].

Figure 6: UPS Pension Plan Rate Assumptions

	Pension Benefits		
	2004	2003	2002
Discount rate	6.25%	6.75%	7.50%
Rate of compensation increase	4.00%	4.00%	4.00%
Expected return on plan assets	8.96%	9.21%	9.42%

Figure 7: Reported Components of UPS Change in PBO Calculation

	Pension Benefits	
Change in benefit obligations ($millions)	2004	2003
Benefit obligation at beginning of year	$8,092	$6,670
Service cost	332	282
Interest cost	521	465
Plan amendments	3	3
Actuarial (gain) loss	290	876
Gross benefits paid	(201)	(204)
Net benefit obligation	$9,037	$8,092

Figure 8: Reported Components of UPS Change in Plan Assets and Funded Status Calculation

	Pension Benefits	
Change in plan assets ($millions)	2004	2003
Fair value of plan assets at beginning of year	$7,823	6,494
Actual return on plan assets	1,140	1,143
Employer contributions	1,200	390
Benefits paid	(201)	(204)
Fair value of plan assets	9,962	7,823
Funded status	925	(269)
Unrecognized net actuarial loss	1,918	2,085
Unrecognized prior service cost	297	331
Unrecognized transition obligation	18	23
Other	2	752
Net amount recognized	$3,160	2,922

---

1. United States Securities and Exchange Commission, nd, <http://www.sec.gov/Archives/edgar/data/1090727/000119312505049642/d10k.htm> (September, 2007).

Figure 9: Reported Components of UPS Pension Expense Calculation

	Pension Benefits		
Net periodic benefit cost ($millions)	2004	2003	2002
Service cost	$332	$282	$217
Interest cost	521	465	413
Expected return on plan assets	(800)	(669)	(654)
Amortization of:			
Transition obligation	6	8	8
Prior service cost	37	37	30
Actuarial (gain) loss	119	28	4
Net expense	$215	$151	$18

Figure 10: Funded Status vs. Reported Pension Asset

	Pension Benefits ($ millions)	
	2004	2003
Fair value of plan assets, current year	$9,962	$7,823
Benefit obligation, current year	9,037	8,092
Funded status	925	(269)
Unrecognized net actuarial loss	1,918	2,085
Unrecognized prior service cost	297	331
Unrecognized transition obligation	18	23
Other	2	752
Net amount recognized	$3,160	$2,922
Prepaid pension cost	$3,227	$2,970
Accrued benefit cost	(188)	(153)
Intangible asset related to minimum liability allowance	4	5
Accumulated other comprehensive income	117	100
Net amount recognized	$3,160	$2,922

From Figure 10 we can determine that in 2004, UPS had a pension asset on the balance sheet of $3,227 (it's called "prepaid pension cost") and a pension liability of $188 ("accrued benefit cost"). The net pension asset on the balance sheet is $3,227 – $188 = $3,039 and the funded status is $925.

 Professor's Note: UPS reports both a pension asset and a pension liability on its balance sheet because it has multiple plans, some of which are overfunded and others that are underfunded. These are net amounts, as discussed in LOS 24.d. Do not interpret the pension asset on UPS's balance sheet as the fair value of the plan assets and the liability as the gross pension liability.

Therefore, the necessary adjustment to reflect the new U.S. standards is to reduce the *net* pension asset of $3,039 by $2,114 to $925, with an offsetting decrease to equity and deferred taxes totaling $2,114. Assuming a 40% marginal tax rate, the following adjustments should be made to reflect the new standard:

- Increase the $188 pension liability by $2,114.
- Reduce deferred taxes by $2,114 × 0.40 = $846.
- Reduce equity by $2,114 – 846 = $1,268.

We can also calculate UPS's adjusted pension expense.

2004 adjusted pension expense
= 2004 service cost + 2004 interest cost – 2004 actual return on plan assets

= $332 + $521 – $1,140 = –$287

Notice that the large actual return on assets completely offsets service cost and interest cost and results in a "negative adjusted pension expense" (i.e., an economic gain from pension activities).

KEY CONCEPTS

1. Defined contribution pension plans are those in which the employee makes contributions and the company may promise to contribute a specified amount of funds for each employee for each period through a matching program. Employees bear the shortfall risk. In defined-benefit plans, the company promises to pay a certain amount at retirement, and the firm bears the shortfall risk. The accounting for defined-benefit plans is much more complicated than for defined contribution pension plans. In pay-related defined-benefit plans, pension benefits are based on the employee's future compensation.

2. There are three different measures of the obligation you should be aware of:
   - The projected benefit obligation (PBO) is the actuarial present value (at the assumed discount rate) of all future pension benefits earned to date, based on expected future salary increases. It measures the value of the obligation assuming the firm is a going concern and that the employees will continue to work for the firm until they retire.
   - The accumulated benefit obligation (ABO) is the actuarial present value of all future pension benefits earned to date based on current salary levels, ignoring future salary increases.
   - The vested benefit obligation (VBO) is the amount of the ABO to which the employee is entitled based on the company's vesting schedule.

3. Assumptions of high discount rates, low compensation growth rates, and high expected rates of return on plan assets will decrease pension expense, increase earnings, and reduce the pension liability. The more aggressive these assumptions are, the lower the earnings quality of the firm.

4. U.S. GAAP allows for the delayed recognition of certain events that affect the value of the plan assets and the pension obligation. Under the old standards, the effects of these events on the net pension liability were not reflected immediately in the financial statements; instead, they were deferred off the financial statements and amortized over time into the reported financial statements. The result is that there were "unrecognized" amounts that were disclosed in the footnotes but not reflected in the balance sheet.

5. Companies are required under U.S. GAAP to net pension assets and liabilities against each other and only report the net amount on the balance sheet. If the fund assets are greater than the liabilities, a net asset is reported; if liabilities are greater than assets, a net liability is reported.

6. Any changes in assumptions that might have only a small change in the total pension obligation itself can still have a large impact on the net pension liability. The same is true with pension expense; because it is a net amount (service and interest cost net of expected return on plan assets), relatively minor changes in the assumptions can have a major impact on reported pension expense.

Study Session 6

Cross-Reference to CFA Institute Assigned Reading #24 – Understanding Retirement Benefits Accounting and Disclosures ...

7. Pension expense components include:
   - Service cost—increase in the PBO reflecting the pension benefits earned during the year.
   - Interest cost—increase in PBO resulting from interest owed on the current benefit obligation.
   - Expected return on plan assets—assumed long-run rate of return on plan assets used to smooth the volatility that would be caused by using actual returns.
   - Amortization of unrecognized prior service cost—amortized costs for changes in the PBO that result from amendments to the plan.
   - Amortization and deferral of gains or losses—amortization of gains and losses caused by changes in actuarial assumptions.
   - Amortization of transition liability or asset—amortized amount caused by switching to SFAS 87 in 1985.

8. Expected return on plan assets can differ from the actual return because (1) the market-related value does not necessarily equal the fair value of plan assets, and (2) the long-term assumption of expected return does not necessarily equal the actual return in any given year. Changes in the assumed expected rate of return directly affect reported pension expense; actual returns only indirectly affect reported pension expense to the extent that these changes are reflected in the market-related value of the plan.

9. Under the old U.S. GAAP pension accounting standards, the net pension liability and pension expense don't immediately increase by the entire amount of the increase in the PBO that results from a plan amendment. Instead, the unrecognized loss is held "off the financial statements" as unrecognized prior service cost and amortized over time as an increase in pension expense.

10. If the ABO exceeds the fair value of plan assets, at least that difference must be reported on the balance sheet as a liability. If necessary, the existing pension asset or liability must be adjusted to this liability value by recording an additional pension liability called the minimum liability allowance or the additional liability.

11. Accounting for non-pension postretirement benefits is very similar to accounting for pension benefits, with the following differences:
    - The APBO is the actuarial present value of the expected postretirement benefits. It is estimated using the unique discount rate applied specifically to those benefits.
    - The health care cost trend rate, which is used to estimate the APBO, must be disclosed.
    - There is no minimum liability adjustment.
    - Many postretirement benefit plans are unfunded, which means there are no plan assets, employer contributions equal benefits paid, and the funded status equals the APBO.
    - A lower health care cost trend rate decreases the APBO and postretirement benefit expense.

12. U.S. GAAP pension accounting standards for public companies changed in December 2006. The funded status (the difference between the PBO and the fair value of plan assets) must now be reported on the balance sheet. The offsetting entries are to shareholders' equity (as part of comprehensive income) and deferred tax liabilities.

13. Adjusted pension expense is equal to service cost plus interest cost minus actual return on plan assets.

14. IFRS rules are similar to the new U.S. standards, with a few notable differences.
    - The pension liability on the balance sheet for financials prepared according to IFRS will reflect the funded status adjusted for the unrecognized items. U.S. standards now recognize only the funded status.
    - IFRS requires that actuarial gains and losses be amortized over the employee's service life, rather than over the employee's life expectancy, as is the case under U.S. GAAP.
    - IFRS requires that prior service costs for retired participants and current employees vested in the plan be expensed in the period incurred rather than deferred and amortized.
    - IFRS does not require that a minimum liability be recognized when the ABO is larger than fair value of plan assets.

CONCEPT CHECKERS

1. Pyramid Consulting Group is considering starting either a defined-benefit or defined contribution plan for its employees. Lynne Woods, an accounting intern for Pyramid, is asked to draft a report comparing defined contribution with defined-benefit plans. Woods makes the following statements in her report:

    Statement 1: In a defined contribution plan, pension expense is recorded directly on the income statement and is calculated as the difference between the required contribution amount and the actual return on plan assets.

    Statement 2: The amount recorded on the balance sheet for a defined-benefit plan under the pre-U.S. GAAP standards is the plan's funded status.

    Are Statements 1 and 2 accurate?

	Statement 1	Statement 2
A.	Yes	Yes
B.	No	No
C.	Yes	No
D.	No	Yes

2. Which of the following components of the projected benefit obligation is *most likely* to increase every year as a direct result of the employee working another year for the company?
    A. Service cost.
    B. Interest cost.
    C. Benefits paid.
    D. SFAS 87 transition loss.

Use the following data to answer Questions 3 through 5.

The financial statements of Tanner, Inc. for the year ended December 31, 2004, include the following (in $ millions):

PBO at January 1, 2004	$435
Service cost	63
Interest cost	29
Benefits paid	– 44
PBO at December 31, 2004	$483
Fair value of plan assets at January 1, 2004	$522
Actual return on plan assets	77
Employer contributions	48
Benefits paid	– 44
Fair value of plan assets at December 31, 2004	$603
Average remaining years of service for employees	10
Expected return on plan assets: 12 months ended 12/31/04	$32

There were no deferred or amortized amounts as of January 1, 2004.

3. The amount Tanner, Inc., reported as pension expense (in millions) on its income statement for the year ended December 31, 2004, is *closest* to:
    A. –$33.
    B. –$14.
    C. $31.
    D. $60.

4. The funded status of the Tanner pension plan (in millions) as of December 31, 2004, is *closest* to:
    A. underfunded by $212.
    B. underfunded by $120.
    C. overfunded by $120.
    D. overfunded by $212.

5. Adjusted pension expense (in millions) for the Tanner pension plan for 2004 is *closest* to:
    A. $0.
    B. $15.
    C. $41.
    D. $60.

6. Suppose management changes its assumption related to mortality rates of its employees, which results in an increase in the projected benefit obligation (PBO) of $40 million. The increase in the PBO is *most likely* to be reported as:
    A. an increase in service cost of $40 million.
    B. an actuarial loss of $40 million.
    C. prior service costs of $40 million.
    D. an actuarial gain of $40 million.

7. NICEE Company's pension plan on December 31, 2005 is underfunded by $85 million. Unrecognized actuarial gains total $12 million, and unrecognized prior service cost is equal to $27 million. There is no prior transition asset or liability. What is the amount of the pension liability on NICEE's balance sheet on December 31, 2005, assuming the financials were prepared according to U.S. GAAP under the:

	Old pension standards?	New pension standards?
A.	$70	$70
B.	$70	$85
C.	$100	$70
D.	$100	$85

8. Best Taste Marketing reports a ($33) million accrued pension cost liability on its fiscal year 2004 balance sheet. In the footnotes to the financial statements, the company discloses a projected benefit obligation (PBO) of $106 million, and a fair value of pension plan assets of $81 million. Assume the marginal tax rate is zero. The *most appropriate* adjustment to the financial statements to reflect the new pension accounting standards is:
    A. decrease liabilities by $8 million and increase equity by $8 million.
    B. decrease liabilities by $30 million and increase equity by $30 million.
    C. increase assets by $3 million and increase liabilities by $3 million.
    D. increase assets by $30 million and increase equity by $30 million.

9. All else equal, an *increase* in the discount rate will *most likely* have what impact on future pension expense and PBO?

	Pension expense	PBO
A.	Increase	Increase
B.	Increase	Decrease
C.	Decrease	Increase
D.	Decrease	Decrease

10. All else equal, an *increase* in the expected return on plan assets will *most likely* have what impact on current pension expense and PBO?

	Pension expense	PBO
A.	No effect	Increase
B.	No effect	No effect
C.	Decrease	Increase
D.	Decrease	No effect

Use the following information to answer Questions 11 through 14.

You have just been hired as the controller at Vincent, Inc. Vincent has a defined-benefit retirement plan for its employees. The firm has a relatively young workforce, with a low percentage of retirees. Your first task is to analyze the effects of changing assumptions on different variables used to calculate certain pension amounts.

11. All else equal, an *increase* in the rate of compensation increase will *most likely* have what impact on future pension expense and the ABO?

	Pension expense	ABO
A.	Increase	Increase
B.	Increase	No effect
C.	Decrease	Increase
D.	Decrease	No effect

12. All else equal, a *decrease* in the discount rate will *most likely* have what impact on the fair market value of plan assets and the ABO?

	FMV of plan assets	ABO
A.	No effect	No effect
B.	No effect	Increase
C.	Increase	No effect
D.	Increase	Increase

13. All else equal, a *decrease* in the rate of compensation increase will *most likely* have what impact on the funded status and VBO?

	Funded status	VBO
A.	Favorable	No effect
B.	Favorable	Increase
C.	Unfavorable	No effect
D.	Unfavorable	Increase

14.   All else equal, a *decrease* in the expected return on plan assets will *most likely* have what effect on the service cost and funded status?

	Service cost	Funded status
A.	No effect	No effect
B.	No effect	Decrease
C.	Increase	No effect
D.	Increase	Decrease

15.   Company Z has a defined-benefit plan. The projected benefit obligation for its plan is $60 million, the accumulated benefit obligation is $50 million, and the vested benefit obligation is $40 million. The fair value of the plan's assets is $40 million. If Company Z currently reports a pension liability of $6 million, the minimum liability allowance is *closest* to:

A. –$4 million.

B. $0.

C. $4 million.

D. $14 million.

CHALLENGE PROBLEMS

16.   Jacklyn King has been asked to do some accounting for Alexeeff Corp.'s pension plan. At the beginning of the period, the PBO was $12 million, and the fair market value of plan assets totaled $8 million. The discount rate is 9%, expected return on plan assets is $0.96 million, and the anticipated compensation growth rate is 4%. At the end of the period, it was determined that the actual return on assets was 14%, plan assets equaled $9 million, and the service cost for the year was $0.9 million. Ignore amortization of unrecognized prior service costs and deferred gains and losses. Pension expense for the year is *closest* to:

A. $0.72 million.

B. $0.86 million.

C. $0.90 million.

D. $1.02 million.

17.   The net amount of the cost components of Heritage Bakery's projected benefit obligation for 2004 is $38 million. Cost components include service cost, interest cost, actuarial gains and losses, and prior service costs. The fair market value of plan assets on January 1, 2004 is $159 million. The projected benefit obligation (PBO) on January 1, 2004 is $193 million, and the PBO on December 31, 2004 is $220 million. There are no effects of foreign currency exchange rate changes, business combinations, divestitures, curtailments, settlements, special terminations, or contributions by the employer or plan participants. Actual return on assets in 2004 was $32 million. The expected return on plan assets for 2004 was 10%. The fair value of plan assets on December 31, 2004 is *closest* to:

A. $148 million.

B. $164 million.

C. $180 million.

D. $191 million.

Study Session 6

Cross-Reference to CFA Institute Assigned Reading #24 – Understanding Retirement Benefits Accounting and Disclosures ...

The following disclosures related to postretirement medical benefits are from UPS's 2004 annual report. They were prepared according to the U.S. GAAP pension standards in effect prior to December 2006. Use this information to answer Questions 18 through 21.

Benefit Obligations

	Postretirement Medical Benefits (millions of $)	
	2004	2003
Net benefit obligation, prior year	$2,592	$2,149
Service cost	91	79
Interest cost	164	148
Plan participants' contributions	9	6
Plan amendments	(115)	(22)
Acquired businesses	46	–
Actuarial (gain) loss	36	337
Gross benefits paid	(129)	(105)
Net benefit obligation, current year	$2,694	$2,592

Plan Assets

	Postretirement Medical Benefits (millions of $)	
	2004	2003
Fair value of plan assets, prior year	$409	$337
Actual return on plan assets	51	47
Employer contributions	115	124
Plan participants' contributions	9	6
Gross benefits paid	(129)	(105)
Fair value of plan assets, current year	✓$455	$409

Funded Status

	Postretirement Medical Benefits (millions of $)	
	2004	2003
Fair value of plan assets, current year	$455	$409
Benefit obligation, current year	(2,694)	(2,592)
Funded status, current year	(2,239)	(2,183)
Amounts not yet recognized:		
Unrecognized net actuarial loss	810	820
Unrecognized prior service cost	(104)	11
Unrecognized net transition obligation	–	–
Other	17	17
Net asset (liability) recorded at year end	($1,516)	($1,335)

Net Periodic Benefit Cost

	Postretirement Medical Benefits (millions of $)		
	2004	2003	2002
Service cost	$91	$79	$63
Interest cost	164	148	134
Expected return on assets	(34)	(29)	(33)
Amortization of:			
Transition obligation	–	–	–
Prior service cost	–	1	(1)
Actuarial (gain) loss	30	15	4
Net periodic benefit cost (benefit)	$251	$214	$167

Weighted-average assumptions used to determine net costs			
Discount rate	6.25%	6.75%	7.50%
Rate of compensation increase	N/A	N/A	N/A
Expected return on plan assets	9.00%	9.25%	9.50%

Study Session 6

Cross-Reference to CFA Institute Assigned Reading #24 – Understanding Retirement Benefits Accounting and Disclosures ...

The notes also include the following disclosure:

"Future postretirement medical benefit costs were forecasted assuming an initial annual increase of 9.0%, decreasing to 5.0% by the year 2009 and with consistent annual increases at those ultimate levels thereafter."

18. The UPS postretirement benefit plan is somewhat unique because it is funded, as opposed to most postretirement plans, which are unfunded. If the UPS plan were to be unfunded, fair market value of plan assets and the funded status in 2004 would be *closest* to:

	Fair value of plan assets	Funded status
A.	$0	$2,239
B.	$0	$2,694
C.	$455	$2,239
D.	$455	$2,694

19. What are the *likely* effects on the accumulated postretirement benefit obligation (APBO) and reported earnings of assuming that future postretirement medical benefit costs will increase at an annual rate of 9% indefinitely, instead of the assumption disclosed in the footnotes?

	APBO	Reported earnings
A.	Increase	Decrease
B.	Decrease	Increase
C.	Decrease	Decrease
D.	Increase	Increase

20. Assume for this question that the marginal tax rate is 40%. What is the *most appropriate* balance sheet adjustment necessary to reflect the postretirement benefit liability in 2004 according to the new U.S. GAAP pension accounting standards?
   A. Increase liabilities by $848 and decrease equity by $848.
   B. Decrease assets by $848 and increase liabilities by $848.
   C. Decrease liabilities by $723 million and increase equity by $723 million.
   D. Increase liabilities by $723 million and decrease equity by $434.

21. What were the *likely* effects of the changes in the discount rate and the expected return on assets assumptions on net periodic benefit cost from 2002 to 2004?

	Discount rate assumptions	Expected ROA assumption
A.	Increase benefit cost ✓	Increase benefit cost ✓
B.	Decrease benefit cost	Increase benefit cost
C.	Increase benefit cost ✓	Decrease benefit cost
D.	Decrease benefit cost	Decrease benefit cost

ANSWERS – CONCEPT CHECKERS

1. **B** Both of Woods' statements are incorrect. For a defined contribution plan, the total employer contribution is recorded as an expense directly on the income statement. The contribution amount is usually calculated based on a matching percentage of the employee contribution. For defined contribution plans, the employee bears all investment risk, so there are no plan assets, and no actual return on plan assets. For a defined-benefit plan, the amount recorded on the balance sheet is a smoothed figure that may bear little resemblance to a plan's funded status. The difference between the funded status and the balance sheet asset or liability reflects unrecognized actuarial gains/losses, unrecognized prior service costs, and the unrecognized prior transition asset or obligation.

2. **A** The service cost is the present value of new benefits earned by the employee working another year. It is an expense that increases the PBO. Note that the interest cost increases every year whether or not the employee works another year.

3. **D** Where there are no amortizations, pension expense is calculated by subtracting expected return from the sum of interest cost and service cost ($63 + $29 − $32 = $60).

4. **C** A plan is overfunded when the fair value of plan assets exceeds PBO. This plan is ($603 − $483) = $120 overfunded.

5. **B** Adjusted pension expense = service cost + interest cost − actual investment return ($63 + $29 − $77 = $15). No figures for actuarial losses and plan amendments were given, so we assume they are zero.

6. **B** An actuarial loss resulting from changes in actuarial assumptions (such as mortality rates) leads to an increase in the PBO. Prior service costs reflect increases in the PBO that result from amendments to the pension plan. Service cost is the present value of the pension benefits earned during the year.

7. **B** The plan is underfunded, which means the funded status is negative. Under the new standards, the liability is equal to the funded status of $85. To reconcile the funded status to the balance sheet amount under the old standard, subtract unrecognized actuarial gains and add unrecognized prior service cost: ($85) − $12 + $27 = ($70). This amount is negative, so a $70 million liability appears on the balance sheet under the old standard. See the Professor's Note in LOS 24.e for an explanation of why you subtract the unrecognized gain.

8. **A** The funded status of the plan is the difference between the PBO ($106 million) and the fair value of plan assets ($81), which is a liability of $25 million. The actual pension liability on the balance sheet is $33 million. Therefore, the pension liability should be decreased by $8 million to $25 million, with an offsetting increase in equity. There is no adjustment to deferred taxes because the marginal tax rate is zero. There is no pension asset, so the net pension liability would be $0 − $25 = −$25, which is equal to the funded status.

9. **D** The use of a higher discount rate will result in lower present values and, hence, lower PBO. In most cases, both the service cost and the interest cost will decrease, so higher discount rates almost always result in lower pension expense. Note that the question asks for the *most likely* impact.

10. **D**   The expected return on assets does not affect the calculation of the PBO. Pension expense is decreased by the expected return on assets. If the expected return assumption is increased, then pension expense will fall.

11. **B**   The use of a higher compensation growth rate will increase the PBO, but the ABO will not be affected. It will also result in a higher service cost and a higher interest cost, and thus increase pension expense.

12. **B**   The decrease in the discount rate does not affect the FMV of plan assets. However, the use of a lower discount rate results in higher present values and, hence, higher pension liabilities (i.e., higher ABO).

13. **A**   funded status = fair value of plan assets – PBO

   VBO is the amount of the ABO to which the employee is entitled based on the company vesting schedule. A decrease in the rate of compensation increase will decrease the PBO, thereby improving the funded status (i.e., making it more favorable). The rate of compensation increase only affects PBO; it has no effect on either ABO or VBO.

14. **A**   The decrease in expected return on plan assets has no effect on service cost and no effect on the funded status. Service cost is the change in the PBO attributed to employee efforts during the year. Although expected return and service cost are components of pension expense, there is no clear relationship between expected return and service cost, and therefore no effect on service cost or funded status.

15. **C**   The minimum liability allowance is the amount of the adjustment required so the ABO less the fair value of plan assets is equal to the liability shown on the books. $50 million – 40 million = $10 million; minimum liability allowance = $10 million – 6 million = $4 million.

ANSWERS – CHALLENGE PROBLEMS

16. **D**   pension expense = service cost + interest cost – expected return on assets
   service cost = $0.90 million (given)
   interest cost = PBO at the beginning of the period × discount rate = $12 million × 0.09 = $1.08 million
   expected return on plan assets = $0.96 million (given)
   total pension expense = $0.90 million + $1.08 million – $0.96 million = $1.02 million

17. **C**   The first step is to solve for benefits paid. The beginning PBO balance plus the cost components minus benefits paid is equal to the ending PBO balance: $193 + $38 – benefits paid = $220 million, which implies benefits paid are equal to $11 million. The ending fair value of plan assets is equal to beginning value plus actual return on assets less benefits paid: $159 + $32 – $11 = $180 million.

18. **B**   If the plan was unfunded, there are no plan assets, and UPS would make annual contributions equal to the benefits paid each year. The fair market value of plan assets would be zero and the funded status would equal the accumulated postretirement benefit obligation (APBO), which is $2,694 in 2004.

19. **A**   UPS has assumed that the annual increase in medical benefit costs will increase by 9% in 2005, but the rate of increase will fall to 5% by 2009. The effect of making the more conservative assumption that costs will continue to increase at 9% indefinitely would be to increase the APBO, increase benefit cost, and decrease reported earnings.

20. **D**   The funded status of the plan is a liability of $2,239, but the balance sheet liability is only $1,516. The balance sheet liability should be increased by $723 to $2,239, with offsetting decreases to deferred taxes of $289 ($723 × 0.4) and equity of $434 ($723 − $289).

21. **A**   The discount rate assumption has fallen from 6.75% to 6.25% over the last three years, which will most likely increase net periodic benefit cost as both the service cost and the interest cost are likely to increase. The expected rate of return on assets has fallen from 9.50% to 9.00% over the last three years, which will decrease expected return on assets and increase period benefit cost.

FAS 123(B)—ACCOUNTING FOR STOCK-BASED COMPENSATION: HAPPY ANNIVERSARY?

Study Session 6

EXAM FOCUS

This new reading for 2008 provides a brief discussion of the key features of the latest standard on accounting for stock-based compensation plans. The key result is that firms must now report compensation expense related to stock option plans on the income statement at the time the options are granted. This significantly decreases reported earnings for companies with large compensation plans. Pay attention to the key features of stock option accounting and be prepared to identify the differences between accounting for stock options in the United States and under international standards.

WARM UP: STOCK COMPENSATION PLANS

Stock compensation plans come in many forms. Basically, the plans provide employees the opportunity to receive stock that is tied to the performance of the firm. Performance is typically measured by increases in earnings per share, revenues, stock price, or market share. Our discussion will focus mostly on stock option compensation.

 Professor's Note: This is a lengthy warm-up section and, at times, the material is quite detailed. Focus on the "big picture" here and spend most of your time on the material that appears after each LOS.

Intrinsic Value Method

Prior to 1995, stock option compensation plans were covered by APB No. 25, *"Accounting for Stock Issued to Employees."* Under APB No. 25, compensation expense was recognized in the income statement if the option had intrinsic value on the grant date. Recall from Level 1 that the intrinsic value of the option is equal to the difference between the market price and exercise price, or zero, whichever is greater. Since most options do not have intrinsic value on the date granted because the exercise price is set at a level greater than the current market price, compensation expense was rarely recognized.

Fair Value Method

In 1995, the Financial Accounting Standards Board (FASB) issued SFAS No. 123, *"Accounting for Stock-Based Compensation."* Under SFAS No. 123, firms were encouraged, but not required, to recognize compensation expense based on the fair value of the option as of the grant date. The fair value is estimated using an option-pricing model based on the number of options expected to vest over the **service (vesting) period.**

> *Professor's Note: "To vest" means to earn rights to. Many stock option plans have a vesting schedule, whereby the employee does not have the right to a benefit until they have been employed for a certain amount of time. Employees can be immediately vested, be 100% vested after a certain number of years, or may earn a certain percentage each year up to 100% at the end of a certain number of years. When vested, an employee's award is no longer contingent on remaining service to the firm.*

An option with no intrinsic value still has time value remaining until the option expires. It is this time value that is recognized as compensation expense over the service (vesting) period.

Under SFAS No. 123, firms that did not wish to use the fair value method could continue to use the intrinsic value method. Since the fair value method would usually result in higher compensation expense, most firms continued to use the intrinsic value method.

Stock-Based Compensation Today

In 2004, the FASB issued SFAS No. 123(R), "*Share-Based Payment.*" Under SFAS 123(R), firms are now required to use the fair value method. As discussed earlier, compensation expense is based on the fair value of the options, expected to vest, on the grant date. The fair value is allocated to compensation expense over the service (vesting) period.

Let's look at an example of the fair value method.

On January 1, 2006, the shareholders of Park Glen Corporation granted 500 stock options to its CEO. The CEO can exercise the options over the next five years at a price of $60 per share and vest 20% each year until he's fully vested in five years. On the grant date, the price of Park Glen's stock was $55 per share. Using an option-pricing model, Park Glen determines that the value of the options on the grant date was $1,000. At the end of the first year, the CEO exercised 100 options when the stock price was $67 per share.

Under the intrinsic value method, no compensation expense is recognized since the options are "out-of-the-money" on the grant date. Under the fair value method, Park Glen recognizes compensation expense over the 5-year service (vesting) period. Accordingly, Park Glen recognizes $200 of compensation expense [$1,000/five years] each year. The offset to compensation expense is an increase in paid-in-capital, a stockholders' equity account.

When the CEO exercised 100 options, Park Glen's cash increased $6,000 ($60 exercise price × 100 options). Note that compensation expense is not affected when the options are exercised. Ignoring the actual journal entries, the offset to cash is an increase in stockholders' equity.

Study Session 6

Cross-Reference to CFA Institute Assigned Reading #25 – FAS 123(B)—Accounting for Stock-Based Compensation: Happy Anniversary?

If the CEO fails to exercise the remaining stock options before they expire, no adjustment is made to compensation expense. However, if the CEO fails to satisfy the service requirement (e.g., leaves after four years), the firm will adjust compensation expense in the current period as a change in accounting estimates.

Income Tax Benefits

Compensation expense from stock options is not immediately deductible for income tax purposes; thus, a deferred tax asset is created. This deferred tax asset is equal to the compensation expense (a temporary difference) multiplied by the firm's tax rate.

For nonqualified stock options, the issuing firm receives an income tax benefit when the options are exercised. The tax benefit is equal to the employee's profit (the difference between the market price and the exercise price) multiplied by the firm's tax rate. Since a deferred tax asset is reported when the compensation expense is recognized, excess tax benefits are created.

 Professor's Note: A nonqualified stock option is one that does not meet specific requirements in the Internal Revenue Code for special tax treatment.

The excess tax benefits are reported as an increase in additional paid-in-capital, a stockholders' equity account in the balance sheet. The excess tax benefits have no net effect in the income statement.

The tax benefit related to the compensation expense is reported as an operating activity in the cash flow statement. The excess tax benefits are reported as financing activities.

Returning to the earlier example, when Park Glen recognizes compensation expense of $200, an entry is also made to account for the deferred taxes. Assuming a tax rate of 40%, Park Glen increases a deferred tax asset by $80 ($200 temporary difference × 40%). The offset is an increase in deferred tax benefits (reduction of deferred tax expense).

When 100 of the options were exercised at the end of the first year, Park Glen received $6,000. The cash is reported as an inflow from financing activities in the cash flow statement. In addition, the temporary difference also reverses and Park Glen recognizes the actual income tax benefits of $280 [($67 market price – $60 exercise price) × 100 options × 40% tax rate]. Since $80 has already been recognized as deferred taxes related to the compensation expense, the difference of $200 is considered excess tax benefits. Consequently, Park Glen will report an $80 inflow of cash from operating activities and a $200 inflow of cash from financing activities.

 Professor's Note: This relatively complex calculation is not specifically required by the LOS. We have provided it here as background because the issue of the tax treatment of income benefits from stock options is also addressed in LOS 27.a in Study Session 7.

Restricted Stock

With a **restricted stock plan**, the firm transfers shares of stock to the employee with an agreement that the stock cannot be sold, transferred, or pledged until vesting has occurred.

The accounting for restricted stock is similar to stock option compensation plans; that is, the firm determines the fair value of the stock at the grant date and expenses the cost over the service period. Subsequent changes in market value are ignored; however, if vesting is not met, the firm reverses the compensation expense for the portion not vested.

Stock Appreciation Rights

A **stock appreciation award** gives the employee the right to receive compensation based on the increase in the price of the firm's stock over a predetermined amount. The firm might pay the appreciation in cash, equity, or a combination of both.

KEY FEATURES OF U.S. STOCK OPTION ACCOUNTING

LOS 25.a: Explain the key features of stock option accounting in the United States.

Professor's Note: There is a whole lot of accounting in this LOS that can intimidate the average Level 2 candidate. As you read through this material, keep focused on the overall effect of these new standards on financial reporting. Under the old standards, companies didn't have to report stock-based compensation provided to their employees as an expense on the income statement. The result was to significantly boost earnings for companies with large stock compensation plans.

Under the new standards, companies must now report stock-based compensation expense on the income statement, which will significantly reduce reported earnings. The value of the option is estimated using option pricing models that we will discuss in Study Session 17.

Option-Pricing Models and Assumptions

According to SFAS No. 123(R), the fair value of the option is based on the observable market price of a similar option if one is available. Absent a market-based instrument, the firm is required to use an option-pricing model such as the Black-Scholes, the binomial model, or Monte Carlo simulation. There is no preference by either the FASB or the Securities and Exchange Commission (SEC) as to which model to use.

Professor's Note: The Black-Scholes model and the binomial model are discussed in LOS 64.b and 64.c, respectively, in Study Session 17. A version of Monte Carlo simulation is discussed in 61.b in Study Session 15.

Study Session 6

Cross-Reference to CFA Institute Assigned Reading #25 – FAS 123(B)—Accounting for Stock-Based Compensation: Happy Anniversary?

All of the option-pricing models incorporate the following six assumptions:

1. Exercise price.
2. Stock price at the grant date.
3. Expected term.
4. Expected volatility.
5. Expected dividends.
6. Risk-free rate.

In order to project the expected term, the firm must consider past exercise patterns and then estimate the likelihood and timing of exercise. The SEC, in its Staff Accounting Bulletin (SAB) No. 107, allows firms with plain vanilla options granted before January 1, 2008, a simple method to estimate the expected term. Under the simple method, the expected term is equal to the average of the vesting period and the original contractual term. For example, the expected term assumption of an option with a 3-year vesting schedule and a 7-year contractual term is five years $[(3 + 7)/2]$.

SAB No. 107 also provides guidance on the volatility assumption, including both historical and implied volatility. SFAS No. 123(R) allows nonpublic firms without reliable company-specific volatility information to estimate a "calculated value" using an appropriate industry index.

Employee Stock Purchase Plans

With an **employee stock purchase plan**, employees can usually purchase stock at a discounted price over a specific period of time. If the plan is considered compensatory, compensation expense is recognized over the remaining service life of the employees. No compensation expense is recognized if the plan is noncompensatory.

A number of criteria must be met in order for an employee stock purchase plan to be considered noncompensatory (no compensation expense recognized). One of the criteria relates to the size of the discount. Accordingly, the discount cannot exceed the per share transaction cost of a public offering. A discount of 5% or less is considered a safe harbor to avoid recognition of compensation expense.

Performance-Based Awards

Service-based awards are compensation to the employee based on the number of years of service. **Performance-based awards** include stock compensation that links vesting or the number of shares earned to a financial performance measures like return on equity (ROE), earnings per share (EPS), or stock price.

Service-based vesting awards and performance-based vesting awards are treated similarly under the new rules. Both require fair value recognition.

With a service-based award, fair value is measured on the grant date and there is an adjustment ("true-up") to compensation expense at the end of the vesting period for awards that did not vest. In this case, compensation expense would be adjusted downward. There is no adjustment if the award simply expires.

With a performance-based award that is related to a nonstock price goal, such as ROE or EPS, compensation expense is calculated just like a service-based award; that is, there is an adjustment to compensation expense if the nonstock price goal is not met.

With a performance-based award that is "market-based," that is, it is related to the price of the stock, no adjustment is made if the performance goal is missed. However, the probability of meeting the goal is considered when computing the fair value of the option at the grant date.

Expense Recognition Period

Firms that offer *stock-based compensation plans* recognize the cost over the requisite service period.

For *service-based awards*, the requisite service period is the same as the vesting period.

For *performance-based awards*, the requisite service period is more difficult to determine. This is because the firm must estimate when the performance conditions are expected to be met. When there are two or more performance conditions that must be satisfied, the requisite service period does not end until all conditions are met. The requisite service period ends at the earliest vesting date if the award contains "either/or" conditions.

If the award vests automatically when the employee retires, the requisite service period ends when the employee is eligible to retire, whether or not he chooses to do so.

Graded Vesting

Graded vesting only applies to service-based awards. With graded vesting, an employee's benefits increase on a percentage basis until 100% vesting is achieved. Firms that use a graded vesting schedule can use either a front-loaded or straight-line attribution method. In addition, the firm can also choose to value options as a single award or as a series of awards with each vesting segment valued separately.

Grant Date

The **grant date** is the date an award is approved by the board of directors or compensation committee, as long as the key terms and conditions of the award are communicated to the employee within a short time period.

Grouping Awards

The firm is required to combine awards into homogeneous groups based on expected exercise patterns. Exercise behavior may differ because of employees' ages, location, and their position within the firm. For example, senior management tends to wait longer to exercise their options as compared to other employees within the firm. In this case, the senior management awards would be grouped together and valued separately.

Modifying Existing Options

When a firm modifies an existing option, such as repricing an option that is underwater (out-of-the-money) by reducing the exercise price, the additional

Study Session 6

Cross-Reference to CFA Institute Assigned Reading #25 – FAS 123(B)—Accounting for Stock-Based Compensation: Happy Anniversary?

incremental value must be recognized as compensation expense. The incremental value is equal to the difference in the fair value of the award immediately before and immediately after the modification, including any unrecognized cost from the original grant.

Income Tax Benefits

As discussed earlier in the warm up section of this topic review, compensation expense from stock options is not immediately deductible for income tax purposes; thus, a deferred tax asset is created. For tax purposes, the actual tax deduction is based on the employee's profit when the option is exercised. Since a deferred tax asset is reported when the compensation expense is recognized, excess tax benefits are created when the option is actually exercised.

If there is a tax benefit shortfall, that is, the actual income tax deduction is less than the amount recognized for financial reporting purposes, additional-paid-capital is reduced to the extent there is a remaining balance from excess tax benefits from other option grants. If no benefits remain, a tax benefit shortfall is recognized as an expense in the income statement.

Effective Date

For public companies that are not considered small business issuers, SFAS No. 123(R) became effective for fiscal years beginning after June 15, 2005. For small business issuers and nonpublic companies, the effective date began for fiscal years after December 15, 2005.

Transition

When SFAS No. 123(R) became effective, restatement of prior periods was not required unless the firm chose to do so.

Public firms are required to use the "modified prospective" method of transition. Accordingly, SFAS No. 123(R) is used for awards granted, modified, repurchased, or cancelled beginning after the effective date. For granted awards that are still unvested as of the effective date, SFAS No. 123 continues to apply.

Nonpublic firms that followed SFAS No. 123 use the same transition rules as public companies.

For nonpublic firms that do not follow SFAS No. 123, the "prospective" method of transition is used. With the prospective method, no expense is recognized for grants prior to the effective date; only awards granted, modified, repurchased, or cancelled after the effective date are recognized as expense.

CONSEQUENCES OF THE NEW STANDARD

Since SFAS No. 123(R) was issued, many firms have made changes to their compensation plans. Also, firms have had to address numerous implementation issues. A brief discussion of the consequences of SFAS No. 123(R) follows.

Choice of valuation models. It is necessary to forecast extensive data in order to use the binomial model. Many firms base their decision about which valuation model to use by determining the potential impact of the alternative assumptions. Firms with limited resources, particularly newer firms, are finding that Black-Scholes provides a reasonable and practical valuation approach.

Expanded use of restricted stock. Although the accounting for restricted stock is similar to other forms of stock-based compensation, there are some advantages of restricted stock plans:

1. Fewer shares are usually involved, which results in less dilution to existing shareholders.

2. Unlike options, restricted stock does not expire, so it never becomes completely worthless.

3. Better alignment of employee incentives with the firm's long-term objectives is achieved.

Employee stock purchase plans (ESPPs). Many traditional ESPPs were based on a "look-back" provision, whereby employees could purchase stock at 85% of the lowest price during the period. Under the new standard, such a plan would be considered compensatory; thus, the firm would recognize compensation expense. Some firms have eliminated the look-back provision. Now that the safe harbor only allows a 5% discount, many firms have chosen to eliminate their ESPPs entirely.

Performance plans. Firms are exploring new, more complex, performance measures to meet their objectives and to reward employees. Accounting for these complex reward measures is less straight-forward.

Employee choice plans. Some firms provide employees the ability to choose the combination of the equity instruments (options, restricted stock, and stock appreciation rights) that best meets the employees' own financial and risk profiles. The result is higher communication and administrative costs to the firm.

Share-based equity awards (stock appreciation rights). The difference in a share-based equity award and an option is the form of payment. In a share-based equity award, the employee receives shares in an amount equal to the appreciation of the stock over a predetermined amount. Share-based equity awards also provide some income tax advantages to the employee. The accounting for share-based equity awards is similar to other stock compensation plans.

DIFFERENCES BETWEEN U.S. 123(R) AND IFRS 2

LOS 25.b: Describe the differences between the U.S. and international standards of accounting for stock options.

Accounting for stock-based compensation under SFAS No. 123(R) is similar to International Financial Reporting Standard (IFRS) No. 2, "Share Based Payment."

Study Session 6

Cross-Reference to CFA Institute Assigned Reading #25 – FAS 123(B)—Accounting for Stock-Based Compensation: Happy Anniversary?

However, there are a few significant differences. Generally, SFAS 123(R) is more flexible in the following areas:

- *Valuing awards with graded vesting* – Each segment must be valued separately under IFRS, whereas in the U.S., firms can also choose to value options as a single award.
- *Employee stock purchase plans* – There is no "capital-raising transaction" exception under IFRS, whereas in the U.S., a discount can be offered to employees as long as it does not exceed the cost of issuing securities in the public market.
- *Income tax benefits* – All tax benefit shortfalls must be recognized in earnings under IFRS, whereas in the U.S., shortfalls are first used to reduce additional paid-in-capital from other tax benefits, then any remainder is reported in earnings. The calculation of estimated tax benefits also differs under IFRS.

©2008 Schweser

Page 233

KEY CONCEPTS

1. According to SFAS No. 123(R), firms are required to recognize compensation expense based on the fair value of stock-based awards as of the grant date.
2. The fair value is estimated using an option pricing model based on the number of options expected to vest.
3. In estimating fair value, the firm must consider past exercise patterns.
4. There is no adjustment to compensation expense if an option simply expires.
5. For service-based options, the requisite service period is the same as the vesting date.
6. When two or more performance conditions must be satisfied, the requisite service period does not end until all conditions are met.
7. The grant date is the date the award is approved by the board of directors or compensation committee.
8. Compensation expense is recognized if an option is modified.
9. The effective date of the new standard is June 15, 2005 for public firms, and December 15, 2005 for nonpublic firms and small business issuers.
10. Differences between U.S. and international standards for accounting for stock options include:
    - Valuing awards with graded vesting, where U.S. standards are more flexible.
    - Employee stock purchase plans, where U.S. standards are more flexible.
    - Income tax benefits, where U.S. standards allow offset of tax benefits and shortfalls.

Study Session 6

Cross-Reference to CFA Institute Assigned Reading #25 – FAS 123(B)—Accounting for Stock-Based Compensation: Happy Anniversary?

CONCEPT CHECKERS

1. Are the exercise price of a stock option and the actual stock price one year after the grant date inputs that are necessary to compute compensation expense under SFAS No. 123(R)?

	Exercise price	Stock price one year after the grant date
A.	Yes	Yes
B.	Yes	No
C.	No	Yes
D.	No	No

2. The effective date of SFAS No. 123(R) for public companies and nonpublic companies is for fiscal year beginning after:

	Public companies	Nonpublic companies
A.	June 15, 2005	December 15, 2005
B.	June 15, 2005	December 15, 2007
C.	June 15, 2007	December 15, 2005
D.	June 15, 2007	December 15, 2007

3. When recognizing stock-compensation expense under SFAS No. 123(R), which of the following statements about the requisite service period is *most accurate*?
    A. If the award vests automatically when the employee retires, the requisite service period ends when the employee actually retires. ✓
    B. The requisite service period for most service-based awards is the actual life of the employee. ✗
    C. When two or more performance conditions must be satisfied, the requisite service period ends once the first condition is met. ✗
    D. If only one of two different performance conditions must be met, the requisite service period ends at the earliest vesting date.

4. Is it necessary to "true-up" compensation expense at the end of the vesting period for service-based option awards and performance-based option awards if the options are not exercised?

	Service-based award	Performance-based award
A.	Yes	Yes
B.	Yes	No
C.	No	Yes
D.	No	No

5. Is IFRS No. 2 more flexible than SFAS No. 123(R) in valuing awards with graded vesting and determining whether an employee stock purchase plan (ESPP) is noncompensatory?

	Graded vesting	ESPP
A.	Yes	Yes
B.	Yes	No
C.	No	Yes
D.	No	No

ANSWERS – CONCEPT CHECKERS

1. **B** The exercise price is a necessary input to compute the fair value of the option. The actual stock price one year after the grant date has no effect on the value of the option when granted.

2. **A** For public companies that are not considered small business issuers, SFAS No. 123(R) became effective for fiscal years beginning after June 15, 2005. For nonpublic companies, the effective date began for fiscal years after December 15, 2005.

3. **D** The requisite service period ends at the earliest vesting date if the award contains "either/or" conditions. The other choices are incorrect. For awards that vest automatically when the employee retires, the requisite service period ends when the employee is eligible to retire, not when the employee actually retires. For service-based awards, the requisite service period is the same as the vesting period, not the actual life of the employee. Finally, when two or more performance conditions must be satisfied, the service period ends when all conditions have been met, not just the first condition.

4. **D** Compensation expense is not adjusted (trued-up) if an option simply expires for either service-based or performance-based awards.

5. **D** SFAS No. 123(R) is more flexible in terms of valuing awards with graded vesting and Employee Stock Purchase Plans. For valuing awards with graded vesting, each segment must be valued separately under IFRS, whereas in the U.S., firms can also choose to value options as a single award. For employee stock purchase plans, there is no "capital-raising transaction" exception under IFRS, whereas in the U.S., a discount can be offered to employees as long as it does not exceed the cost of issuing securities in the public market.

ANALYSIS OF MULTINATIONAL OPERATIONS

Study Session 6

EXAM FOCUS

This topic review is a detailed illustration related to accounting for the operating results of foreign subsidiaries and operations. The issue addressed is how to reflect the results of foreign operating units in the consolidated financial statements of the multinational parent. You have several significant tasks to master. First, you need to become familiar with the terminology of translation. Second, you need to be able to distinguish between and implement the two methods of accounting for foreign operations (i.e., remeasurement via the temporal method or translation via the all-current method). Third, you need to be able to analyze the impact of these two methods on reported earnings, cash flows, and financial ratios for both the subsidiary and the parent. This reading is important and challenging. Begin by concentrating on the examples of each method, and then move on to the analysis section.

FOREIGN CURRENCY FLOW AND HOLDING EFFECTS

LOS 26.a: Distinguish between the impact of changes in local currency sales and changes in exchange rates on the translated sales of the subsidiary and parent company.

Exchange rates can impact the reporting firm's financial statements in two ways: (1) flow effects and (2) holding gain/loss effects. **Flow effects** are the impact of changes in the exchange rate on income statement items such as revenue. **Holding gain/loss effects** are the impact of changes in the exchange rate on assets and liabilities on the balance sheet, such as cash balances. The best way to illustrate these effects is with an example.

> **Example: The flow effect**
>
> A U.S. firm owns a subsidiary located in a foreign country with a local currency LC. In 2005, the subsidiary generated revenue of LC1,000. In 2006, revenue increased by 20% to LC1,200. The average exchange rates in 2005 and 2006 were, respectively, LC1 = $1.00 and LC1 = $1.50. Calculate the translated revenue of the subsidiary in U.S. dollars in 2005 and 2006, the total for both years, and the change from 2005 to 2006 in absolute and percentage terms. Determine which portion of the dollar increase in revenue is attributable to the flow effect (the effect of the change in the exchange rate) and which portion is due to the 20% revenue growth of the subsidiary.

Answer:

Illustration of the Flow Effect

	2005	2006	Total	Change in LC or $ (%)
Exchange rate	LC1 = $1.00	LC1 = $1.50		
Revenues (LC)	LC1,000	LC1,200	LC2,200	LC200 (20%)
Revenues ($)	$1,000	$1,800	$2,800	$800 (80%)

The $800 increase in revenue is attributable to two components:

1. The $200 (LC200 × $1.00/LC) increase in local currency revenue. In other words, revenue from the subsidiary would have increased by $200 if the exchange rate had not changed.

2. The **flow effect** of $600 (LC1,200 × $0.5 change in the exchange rate).

Example: The holding effect

Let's continue with the previous example and assume that the subsidiary keeps all of the revenue on its balance sheet as cash. Calculate the cash balance in dollars on the consolidated balance sheet at the end of 2005 and 2006. Determine the holding gain/loss effect on the cash balance resulting from the change in the exchange rate.

Answer:

Illustration of the Holding Effect

	2005	2006
Exchange rate	LC1 = $1.00	LC1 = $1.50
Cash (LC)	LC1,000	LC2,200
Cash ($)	$1,000	$3,300

There are two ways to calculate the holding gain/loss effect:

- Total revenue in dollars was $2,800 (from the first table in this example), but the cumulative cash balance at the end of 2006 was $3,300, so the holding effect was a gain of $500 ($3,300 – $2,800).
- The LC1,000 in cash on the balance sheet at the end of 2005 increased in value by $500 (LC1,000 × ($1.50/LC – $1.00/LC)) at the end of 2006.

Let's summarize the analysis. If the exchange rate had remained constant at LC1 = $1.00, the parent would have reported cash on the consolidated balance sheet from the subsidiary at the end of 2006 of $2,200 (LC2,200 × $1.00/LC); the actual amount was $3,300. This $1,100 ($3,300 – $2,200) currency gain is attributable to a:

- Flow effect of $600.
- Holding gain effect of $500.

CURRENCY DEFINITIONS

LOS 26.b: Distinguish among the local currency, the functional currency, and the reporting currency.

- The **local currency** is the currency of the country in which the foreign subsidiary is located.
- The **functional currency** is defined as the currency of the primary economic environment in which the foreign subsidiary generates and expends cash. The choice reflects management's judgment. It can be the currency in which the subsidiary conducts operations or some other currency.
- The **reporting currency** is the currency in which the multinational firm prepares its final, consolidated financial statements.

The following definitions are also necessary to understand accounting for multinational operations and will be used in subsequent sections.

- The **current rate** is the exchange rate as of the balance sheet date.
- The **average rate** is the average exchange rate over the reporting period.
- The **historical rate** is the rate that existed when a particular transaction was conducted. For example, if you bought a widget machine on January 2, 2007, the historical rate for that transaction at every balance sheet date in the future would be the exchange rate on January 2, 2007.
- **Remeasurement** is the translation of local currency transactions into the functional currency.
- **Translation** is the conversion of the functional currency of a subsidiary into the reporting currency.

> *Professor's Note: The term "translation" is used in two different ways in this review. First, translation refers to a specific method of converting account and transaction balances to another currency. Second, translation is used to describe the general process of converting account and transaction balances from one currency to another, without identifying a specific methodology. Thus, both the remeasurement methodology and the translation methodology result in the "translation," or the conversion of account and transaction balances to another currency. The ensuing discussion should make this distinction clear.*

ALL-CURRENT VS. TEMPORAL METHOD

LOS 26.c: Compare and contrast the all-current (translation) method and the temporal (remeasurement) method.

SFAS 52, Foreign Currency Translation, prescribes how financial statements of foreign operations are translated. SFAS 52 uses the provisions of both the temporal method and the current rate method, depending on the definition of the functional currency. Note that remeasurement is the process of converting the local currency into the functional currency using the temporal method, with gains and losses flowing to the income statement. The all-current method, or translation, is the process of converting the functional currency into the reporting currency, with gains and losses flowing to the balance sheet as an adjustment to equity.

Temporal Method

The **temporal method** was the underlying translation method of SFAS 8 under U.S. GAAP. Note that although SFAS 52 has replaced SFAS 8, we still need to know about the temporal method because most of its components are still employed under the new standard. The intent of SFAS 52 is to (1) provide financial information that is reasonably compatible with changes in cash flow and equity due to exchange rate effects and (2) ensure that information is consolidated on the parent's financial reports in conformity with U.S. GAAP.

The provisions of the temporal method state that:

- Cash, accounts receivable, accounts payable, short-term debt, and long-term debt (defined as **monetary assets and liabilities**) are translated using the current rate.
- All other assets and liabilities (**nonmonetary assets and liabilities**) are translated at the historical rate. Hence, a major drawback of the temporal method is that you need to keep track of many different historical exchange rates—one for the building that you purchased two years ago and another for the inventory you purchased last week. On the exam, the only two nonmonetary items you're likely to encounter are inventory and fixed assets. The CFA curriculum does not provide any examples of nonmonetary liabilities.
- Revenues and expenses are translated at the average rate.
- Purchases of inventory and fixed assets are remeasured at the historical rate as of the date of purchase. Therefore, remeasurement of cost of goods sold (COGS) and depreciation is based on historical rates prevailing at the time of purchase.
- The translation gain or loss is shown on the income statement. This was seen as another major drawback to the temporal method under SFAS 8 because exchange rate volatility was reflected in the net income of the firm. This forced managers to decide between hedging the economic effects and the accounting effects of foreign exchange volatility.

Translating Inventory and COGS Under the Temporal Method

Before moving on we will go through an illustration of the calculations of COGS and ending inventory balances to help make more transparent the compound effects related to changing foreign exchange rates and inventory accounting methods on COGS and inventory.

Figure 1 contains information related to the purchases and sales of a foreign subsidiary of a U.S. corporation. For simplicity, we assume that each unit purchased costs one Local Currency (LC) unit. Units purchased equals 150 for both 2005 and 2006. Units sold equals 160 for both 2005 and 2006. At the beginning of 2005, the rate is LC = $1.00. Inventory was acquired at LC1.10 = $1.00 and LC0.95 = $1.00 in 2005 and 2006, respectively.

The calculations for COGS and ending inventory balances in LC are straightforward using the inventory accounting relationship:

COGS = beginning inventory + purchases − ending inventory

©2008 Schweser

Under FIFO, we assume that the units in inventory at the beginning of the year are sold off during the year and that the ending balance consists of units purchased during the year. Under FIFO, these units are valued at the exchange rate at which the purchases were made. Under LIFO, the units sold during the year are the ones purchased during the year, and the ending inventory balance is valued at the historical rate.

Figure 1: FIFO/LIFO and Exchange Rate Effects

		FIFO		LIFO	
2005	LC	Rate	$	Rate	$
Beginning balance	100	1.00	100	1.00	100
Purchases	150	1.10	136	1.10	136
Units sold	160				
Ending balance	90	1.10	82	1.00	90
COGS	160		154		146

		FIFO		LIFO	
2006	LC	Rate	$	Rate	$
Beginning balance	90	1.10	82	1.00	90
Purchases	150	0.95	158	0.95	158
Units sold	160				
Ending balance	80	0.95	84	1.00	80
COGS	160		156		168

These calculations and their interpretations are complicated when the values are translated into U.S. dollars because of a depreciating LC in 2005, an appreciating LC in 2006, and the choice between FIFO and LIFO inventory accounting methodologies.

In 2005, FIFO COGS and ending inventory in U.S. dollars are:

$$\text{ending balance}_{2005} = \frac{90}{1.10} = \$82 \, (\text{rounded})$$

$$COGS_{2005} = \text{beginning inventory} + \text{purchases} - \text{ending inventory}$$
$$= 100 + 136 - 82 = \$154$$

In 2006, FIFO COGS and ending inventory are:

$$\text{ending balance}_{2006} = \frac{80}{0.95} = \$84 \, (\text{rounded})$$

$$COGS_{2006} = \text{beginning inventory} + \text{purchases} - \text{ending inventory}$$
$$= 82 + 158 - 84 = \$156$$

In 2005, LIFO COGS and ending inventory in U.S. dollars are:

$$\text{ending balance}_{2005} = \frac{90}{1.00} = \$90$$

$$COGS_{2005} = \text{beginning inventory} + \text{purchases} - \text{ending inventory}$$
$$= 100 + 136 - 90 = \$146$$

In 2006, LIFO COGS and ending inventory are:

$$\text{ending balance}_{2006} = \frac{80}{1.00} = \$80$$

$$COGS_{2006} = \text{beginning inventory} + \text{purchases} - \text{ending inventory}$$
$$= 90 + 158 - 80 = \$168$$

Figure 2 provides some general intuition on the compound effects of changing exchange rates and the choice of FIFO versus LIFO accounting methods on the translated COGS and ending inventory measures.

Figure 2: Translated COGS and Ending Inventory under FIFO and LIFO

	FIFO	*LIFO*
Depreciating local currency (2005)	Higher COGS	Lower COGS
	Lower ending inventory	Higher ending inventory
Appreciating local currency (2006)	Lower COGS	Higher COGS
	Higher ending inventory	Lower ending inventory

All-Current Method

The **all-current method** is much easier to apply than the temporal method because:

- All income statement accounts are translated at the average rate.
- All balance sheet accounts are translated at the current rate *except for common stock*, which is translated at the appropriate historical rate that applied when the equity was issued.
- Dividends are translated at the rate that applied when they were paid.
- The cumulative translation adjustment is included on the balance sheet as part of equity.

EFFECTS OF METHODS ON PARENT FINANCIALS

LOS 26.d: Analyze and evaluate the effects of the all-current and temporal methods on the parent company's balance sheet and income statement.

The middle column of Figure 3 summarizes the exchange rate used to translate the results of foreign subsidiaries under the temporal method. The last column of Figure 3 summarizes the exchange rate used to translate the results of foreign subsidiaries under the all-current method.

Figure 3: Exchange Rate Usage under the Temporal and All-Current Methods

	Rate used to translate account using the...	
Account	Temporal Method	All-Current Method
Monetary assets and liabilities	current rate	current rate
Nonmonetary assets/liabilities	historical rate	current rate
Common stock	historical rate	historical rate
Equity (taken as a whole)	mixed*	current rate
Revenues and SG&A	average rate	average rate
Cost of good sold	historical rate	average rate
Depreciation	historical rate	average rate
Net income	mixed*	average rate

* Net income is translated a "mixed rate" (i.e., a mix of the average rate and the historical rate) under the temporal method because (1) the FX translation gain or loss is shown on the income statement, (2) revenues and SG&A are remeasured at the average rate, while (3) COGS and depreciation are remeasured at the historical rate. Equity is "mixed" because the change in retained earnings (which includes net income) is posted to the equity accounts.

 Professor's Note: According to U.S. GAAP, nonmonetary liabilities are translated at the historical rate under the temporal method and at the current rate under the all-current method. However, the CFA curriculum provides no examples of nonmonetary liabilities, so I suggest that on the exam you treat all liabilities as monetary liabilities unless the question specifically tells you otherwise.

A very common question among Level 2 candidates is: *How can equity be translated at the current rate under the all-current method if common stock is translated at the historical rate and net income (and therefore retained earnings) are translated at the average rate?*

The answer is simple: the translation gain or loss that appears in the equity section under the all-current method is the "plug" figure that forces equity *as a whole* to be translated at the current rate.

Another way to look at this is to recognize the equity is equal to assets minus liabilities; if assets and liabilities are both translated at the current rate, the difference between them (equity) must also be translated at the current rate.

CHOICE OF APPROPRIATE METHOD

LOS 26.e: Distinguish whether the all-current or the temporal method is appropriate in various scenarios.

Now we can turn our attention to the issue of which translation method is appropriate to use for a given set of circumstances. The first step in determining which method should be used is to identify the functional currency. The choice of functional currency is based on management judgment and may not be completely objective. This choice determines whether the temporal method or the current rate method will be used.

The following rules govern the **determination of the functional currency**:

1. The results of operations, financial position, and cash flows of all foreign operations must be measured in the designated functional currency.

2. Treatment of subsidiaries:

   - Self-contained, *independent subsidiaries* whose operating, investing, and financing activities are primarily located in the local market will use the *local currency* as the functional currency.
   - Subsidiaries whose operations are *well integrated* with the parent (i.e., the parent makes the operating, financing, and investing decisions) will use the *parent's currency* as the functional currency.
   - Subsidiaries that *operate in highly inflationary environments* will use the *parent's currency* as the functional currency. A high inflation environment is defined as cumulative inflation that exceeds 100% over a 3-year period (see LOS 26.k at the end of this topic review).

3. If the functional currency is the local currency, use the *all-current method*. The use of the all-current method under SFAS 52 is called translation (see Column 1 of Figure 4).

4. If the functional currency is the parent's currency or some other currency, use the *temporal method*. The use of the temporal method under SFAS 52 is called remeasurement (see Column 2 of Figure 4).

5. Finally, a third currency may serve as the functional currency when a subsidiary is operating relatively independently in a market where the local currency, prices, and some costs are controlled or restricted. For example, if a subsidiary of the U.S. parent is operating in China, the Hong Kong dollar might be the functional currency (see Column 3 of Figure 4).

Figure 4 illustrates the three ways a local currency may be remeasured and/or translated into the reporting currency for the parent. Note the choice of the functional currency determines the methods used for conversion.

Figure 4: Three Methods for Remeasurement/Translation of Local Currencies

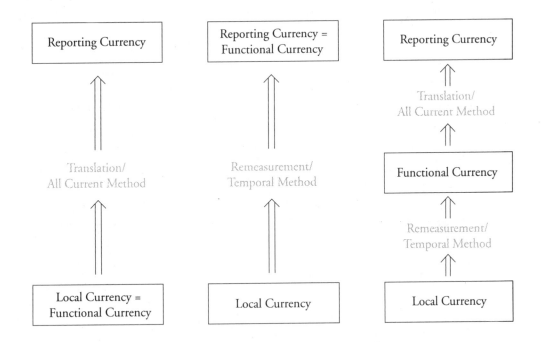

Example: Determining the appropriate method under SFAS 52, part 1

A U.S. multinational firm has a Japanese subsidiary. It has been determined that the Japanese yen (¥) is the functional currency. Determine which foreign currency translation method is appropriate.

Answer:

In this case, remeasurement is not needed, since the financial data is already expressed in the functional currency. Use the all-current method to translate the subsidiary's data to U.S. dollars.

Example: Determining the appropriate method under SFAS 52, part 2

A U.S. multinational firm has an independent Swiss subsidiary, and the Swiss franc is the functional currency. The subsidiary prepares its financial statements in Swiss francs but has receivables and payables denominated in euros. Determine which foreign currency translation method is appropriate.

Answer:

We have to answer this in two steps. First, look at just the Swiss subsidiary and its euro-denominated receivables and payables. The question says that the Swiss franc is the functional currency, so we remeasure from euros into the functional currency using the temporal method.

> Next look at the Swiss subsidiary and the parent company. The Swiss subsidiary's financials are now all in Swiss francs, and the Swiss franc is the functional currency (as stated in the question). To translate the functional currency into the reporting currency we now use the all-current method to translate Swiss francs into U.S. dollars.

TRANSLATION GAINS/LOSSES CALCULATION

LOS 26.f: Calculate the translation effects of the all-current and temporal methods of foreign currency translation.

Translation gains or losses result from gains or losses related to balance sheet accounts that are translated at the current rate (i.e., they are exposed to changes in exchange rates). We can use this insight to calculate the translation gain or loss under either the all-current or the temporal method by first calculating the net exposure under each method (the net assets exposed to changes in the exchange rate), and then calculating the flow effect and the holding gain/loss effect associated with that exposure.

Under the all-current method, all assets and liabilities are translated at the current rate, so the net exposure is assets minus liabilities, or total shareholders' equity:

exposure under the all-current method = shareholders' equity

Under the temporal method, only cash and marketable securities, accounts receivable, accounts payable, current debt, and long-term debt are translated at the current rate (remember that inventory and fixed assets are translated at the historical rate):

exposure under the temporal method
= (cash + accounts receivable) – (accounts payable + current debt + long-term debt)

 Professor's Note: In the original Level 2 CFA Program Curriculum, the only asset and liability accounts mentioned are cash, accounts receivable, inventory, accounts payable, current debt, and long-term debt. Therefore, these formulas reflect only those accounts. If the exam question includes other current items, you will have to be told whether they are monetary or nonmonetary accounts. In that case the calculation of exposure under the temporal method will have to include those additional accounts classified as monetary assets or liabilities.

The flow effect measured in dollars under both methods is equal to the change in exposure (ending exposure less beginning exposure) times the difference between the ending rate and the average rate (in $ per unit of local currency):

flow effect (in $) = change in exposure (in LC) × (ending rate – average rate)

The holding gain/loss effect measured in dollars is the beginning exposure times the difference between the exchange rate at the end of the year and the exchange rate at the beginning of the year (measured in $ per unit of local currency):

holding gain/loss effect (in $)
= beginning exposure (in LC) × (ending rate – beginning rate)

The total translation gain or loss measured in dollars is the sum of the two effects:

translation gain/loss (in $) = flow effect + holding gain/loss effect

Under the all-current method, the translation gains/losses are accumulated on the balance sheet in the equity section as part of comprehensive income in an account called the **cumulative translation adjustment** (CTA). Remember that this is a cumulative account—each year the translation gain for that year (or loss) is added to (or subtracted from) the CTA. For example, if the CTA at the beginning of the year is $100 and the translation loss for the year is $35, the CTA at the end of the year will equal $65.

Under the temporal method, the translation gain/loss appears on the income statement.

APPLYING THE ALL-CURRENT METHOD

LOS 26.g: Translate a subsidiary's balance sheet and income statement into the parent company's currency, using the all-current method and the temporal method.

Example: The all-current method

FlexCo International is a U.S. company with a subsidiary named Vibrant Inc. located in the country of Martonia. Vibrant was acquired by FlexCo on 12/31/2005. FlexCo reports its financial results in U.S. dollars. The currency of Martonia is the loca (LC). Vibrant's financial statements for 2006 are shown in the following two figures.

Vibrant December 31, 2005 and 2006 Balance Sheet

	2005	2006
Cash	LC100	LC100
Accounts receivable	500	650
Inventory	1,000	1,200
Current Assets	LC1,600	LC1,950
Fixed assets	800	1,600
Accumulated depreciation	(100)	(700)
Net fixed assets	LC700	LC900
Total assets	LC2,300	LC2,850
Accounts payable	400	500
Current debt	100	200
Long-term debt	1,300	950
Total liabilities	LC1,800	LC1,650
Common stock	400	400
Retained earnings	100	800
Total equity	LC500	LC1,200
Total liabilities and shareholders' equity	LC2,300	LC2,850

Vibrant 2006 Income Statement

	2006
Revenue	LC5,000
Cost of goods sold	(3,300)
Gross margin	1,700
Other expenses	(400)
Depreciation expense	(600)
Net income	LC700

The following exchange rates between the U.S. dollar and the loca were observed:

- December 31, 2005: LC2.00 = $1.00; $0.50 = LC1.00.
- December 31, 2006: LC2.20 = $1.00; $0.4545 = LC1.00.
- Average for 2006: LC2.10 = $1.00; $0.4762 = LC1.00.
- Historical rate for fixed assets, inventory, and equity: LC2.00 = $1.00; $0.50 = LC1.00.

The majority of Vibrant's operational, financial, and investment decisions are made at Vibrant headquarters in Martonia, although Vibrant does rely on FlexCo for information technology expertise.

Use the appropriate method to translate Vibrant's 2006 balance sheet and income statement into U.S. dollars.

Answer:

Vibrant is relatively self-contained, which means the loca is the functional currency and the appropriate method is the all-current method. The all-current method uses the current rate for all balance sheet accounts (except common stock, which is translated at the historical rate) and the average rate for all income statement accounts. The translation gain or loss appears in the CTA in the equity section as part of comprehensive income.

Let's first calculate the translation gain/loss for 2006.

ending exposure = LC1,200

beginning exposure = LC500

change in exposure = LC1,200 – LC500 = LC700 (which is equal to net income for 2006 in this example because the company doesn't pay dividends)

flow effect = LC700 × (0.4545 – 0.4762) = –$15.2

holding loss effect = LC500 × (0.4545 – 0.50) = –$22.7

translation loss for 2005 = –$15.2 – $22.7 = –$37.9

The cumulative translation adjustment for 2006 equals the beginning balance of zero plus the translation loss for the year: $0 + –$37.9 = –$37.9. Because Vibrant was acquired at the end of 2005, the CTA attributable to Vibrant was zero on that date.

Vibrant's translated 2006 income statement is shown in the following figure. Notice that we translate the income statement first with the all-current method to derive net income, which we then use to calculate retained earnings on the balance sheet.

Vibrant's 2006 Translated Income Statement Under the All-Current Method

	2006 (LC)	Rate	2006 ($)
Revenue	LC5,000	$0.4762	$2,381.0
Cost of goods sold	(3,300)	$0.4762	(1,571.5)
Gross margin	1,700		809.5
Other expenses	(400)	$0.4762	(190.5)
Depreciation expense	(600)	$0.4762	(285.7)
Net income	LC700		$333.3

Beginning (2005) retained earnings in U.S. dollars was LC100 × $0.50 = $50, so ending (2006) retained earnings are $50 + $333.3 = $383.3.

Vibrant's 2006 translated balance sheet is shown in the next figure.

Vibrant 2006 Translated Balance Sheet Under the All-Current Method

	2006 (LC)	Rate	2006 ($)
Cash	LC100	$0.4545	$45.5
Accounts receivable	650	$0.4545	295.5
Inventory	1,200	$0.4545	545.4
Current Assets	LC1,950		$886.4
Fixed assets	1,600	$0.4545	727.3
Accumulated depreciation	(700)	$0.4545	(318.2)
Net fixed assets	LC900		$409.1
Total Assets	LC2,850		$1,295.5
Accounts payable	500	$0.4545	227.3
Current debt	200	$0.4545	91.0
Long-term debt	950	$0.4545	431.8
Total liabilities	LC1,650		$750.1
Common stock	400	$0.50	200.0
Retained earnings	800	Calculated	383.3
Cumulative translation adjustment	—	Calculated	(37.9)
Total equity	LC1,200		$545.4
Total liabilities and shareholders' equity	LC2,850		$1,295.5

Now let's move on to the more difficult method: the temporal method. First we'll take a little detour to explain how inventory, cost of goods sold, fixed assets, and depreciation are actually calculated using the temporal method.

WARM-UP: CALCULATING INVENTORY, COST OF GOODS SOLD, FIXED ASSETS, AND DEPRECIATION UNDER THE TEMPORAL METHOD

Professor's Note: Although technically these calculations are part of the LOS, I think it's unlikely you'll have to do them on the exam. I recommend that you know how to calculate the translation gain/loss under the temporal method, and be able to remeasure all of the other balance sheet and income statement accounts besides inventory, COGS, fixed assets, and depreciation. Remember, however, that these accounts are translated at historical rates.

The exchange rates we use to remeasure inventory under the temporal method depend on whether the FIFO or LIFO inventory cost method is used. We'll assume Vibrant and FlexCo use the FIFO method, which is much more common than LIFO outside of the United States. The beginning inventory balance is remeasured at the historical rate of $0.50, while purchases and ending inventory are remeasured at the average rate during 2006 of $0.4762.

Let's start by calculating cost of goods sold (COGS) in dollars. We know that beginning inventory is LC1,000, ending inventory is LC1,200, and COGS is LC3,300. Therefore, purchases must be 3,300 + 1,200 – 1,000 = LC3,500.

Figure 5: Deriving Vibrant's 2006 COGS in U.S. Dollars Using the Temporal Method

	LC	Rate	$
Beginning inventory	LC1,000	$0.50	$500.0
+ Purchases	3,500	$0.4762	1,666.7
– Ending inventory	(1,200)	$0.4762	(571.4)
2006 COGS	LC3,300		$1,595.3

Remeasured inventory on the balance sheet in 2006 is $571.4, and remeasured COGS on the income statement is equal to $1,595.3.

> *Professor's Note: Remember, inventory and COGS are remeasured at the historical rate under the temporal method. The historical rate for inventory is, technically, the rate in effect when each individual purchase of inventory occurred. However, that is very impractical to implement, so instead the temporal method assumes that beginning inventory is remeasured at the rate from the end of the year, when Vibrant was acquired. Purchases are assumed to occur evenly throughout the year, so we approximate the "historical rate" for <u>each</u> inventory purchase using the average rate for the year. Then COGS is calculated as the plug figure, and it, too, represents the amount remeasured at the <u>approximate</u> "historical rate" for each separate piece of inventory sold.*
>
> *When we get all done it looks like we've violated the temporal method rules by remeasuring inventory and COGS at a "mixed rate" and not the "historical rate." However, we have applied the temporal method correctly: it is just a little complicated because we have had to make some educated guesses as to the historical rate for each individual inventory purchase.*

The second step is to derive net fixed assets and depreciation. Fixed asset investment (i.e., purchases of fixed assets during the year) is remeasured at the average rate, and beginning gross fixed assets are remeasured at the historical rate. The tricky part here is that depreciation on the income statement is remeasured at a "blended rate." We'll show you how it is calculated, but you'll probably be given the blended rate in the unlikely event that you're asked to remeasure depreciation under the temporal method on the exam.

$$\text{blended rate} = \left(\frac{\text{beginning fixed assets}}{\text{ending fixed assets}} \times \text{historical rate} \right) + \left(\frac{\text{fixed asset investment}}{\text{ending fixed assets}} \times \text{average rate} \right)$$

In the FlexCo example, the blended rate is calculated as follows:

$$\text{blended rate}(\text{in LC per \$}) = \left(\frac{800}{1,600} \times 2.00 \right) + \left(\frac{800}{1,600} \times 2.10 \right) = 2.05$$

$$\text{blended rate}(\text{in \$ per LC}) = \frac{1}{2.05} = 0.4878$$

Fixed asset investment for 2006 is equal to the difference between ending and beginning fixed assets: $1,600 - 800 = 800$. Fixed assets for 2006 in dollars are calculated in Figure 6.

Figure 6: Deriving Vibrant's 2006 Fixed Assets in U.S. Dollars

	LC	Rate	$
Beginning fixed assets	LC800	$0.5000	$400.0
+ Fixed asset investment	800	$0.4762	381.0
Ending fixed assets	LC1,600		$781.0

Accumulated depreciation for 2006 in dollars is calculated in Figure 7.

Figure 7: Deriving Vibrant's 2006 Depreciation in U.S. Dollars

	LC	Rate	$
Beginning accumulated depreciation	LC100	$0.5000	$50.0
+ 2006 depreciation	600	$0.4878	292.7
Ending accumulated depreciation	LC700		$342.7

Net fixed assets on the remeasured balance sheet for 2006 is $781 – $342.7 = $438.3. Remeasured depreciation on the 2006 income statement is $292.7.

> *Professor's Note: Just as with inventory and COGS, net fixed assets and depreciation end up being remeasured at the "historical rate." Once again, however, it is complicated by the fact that purchases of fixed assets occur throughout the year, so we have to make some educated guesses as to the "historical rate" for each transaction.*

APPLYING THE TEMPORAL METHOD

Now we're ready to apply the temporal method to the FlexCo example.

Example: The temporal method

Suppose instead that the majority of Vibrant's operational, financial, and investment decisions are made by corporate headquarters in the United States. All other information is the same.

Use the appropriate method to translate Vibrant's 2006 balance sheet and income statement into U.S. dollars, given the following information for 2006:

- COGS = $1,595.3.
- Inventory = $571.4.
- Fixed assets = $781.0.
- Accumulated depreciation = $342.7.
- Depreciation expense = $292.7.

Answer:

Now the U.S. dollar is the functional currency (because the subsidiary is well-integrated with the parent), and the temporal method applies.

Let's first calculate the translation gain/loss for 2006. Remember that with the temporal method, the exposure is equal to (cash + receivables) – (payables + current and long-term debt).

ending exposure = (100 + 650) – (500 + 200 + 950) = 750 – 1,650 = –LC900

beginning exposure = (100 + 500) – (400 + 100 + 1,300) = 600 – 1,800
= –LC1,200

change in exposure = –LC900 – (–LC1,200) = LC300

flow effect = LC300 × (0.4545 – 0.4762) = –$6.5

holding gain effect = –LC1,200 × (0.4545 – 0.50) = $54.6

translation gain for 2005 = –$6.5 + $54.6 = $48.1

Once again we'll start with the income statement. Remember that the translation gain appears on the income statement under the temporal method. Vibrant's remeasured income statement using the temporal method is shown in the following figure.

Vibrant's 2006 Remeasured Income Statement Under the Temporal Method

	2006 (LC)	Rate	2006 ($)
Revenue	LC5,000	$0.4762	$2,381.0
Cost of goods sold	(3,300)	Given	(1,595.3)
Gross margin	1,700		785.7
Other expenses	(400)	$0.4762	(190.5)
Depreciation expense	(600)	Given	(292.7)
Net income before translation gain	700		302.5
Translation gain	—	Given	48.1
Net income	LC700		$350.6

Beginning retained earnings in dollars was LC100 × $0.50 = $50, so ending retained earnings is $50 + $350.6 = $400.6.

Vibrant's 2006 translated balance sheet is shown in the next figure.

Vibrant 2006 Remeasured Balance Sheet Under the Temporal Method

	2006 (LC)	Rate	2006 ($)
Cash	LC100	$0.4545	$45.5
Accounts receivable	650	$0.4545	295.5
Inventory	1,200	Given	571.4
Current assets	LC1,950		$912.4
Fixed assets	1,600	Given	781.0
Accumulated depreciation	(700)	Given	(342.7)
Net fixed assets	LC900		$438.3
Total assets	LC2,850		$1,350.7
Accounts payable	500	$0.4545	227.3
Current debt	200	$0.4545	91.0
Long-term debt	950	$0.4545	431.8
Total liabilities	LC1,650		$750.1
Common stock	400	$0.50	200.0
Retained earnings	800	Calculated	400.6
Total equity	LC1,200		600.6
Total liabilities and shareholders' equity	LC2,850		$1,350.7

Why Do the Two Methods Report Significantly Different Results?

You should notice immediately that the two different methods report very different results, particularly related to the size and sign of the translation gain/loss, net income, and total assets. These comparisons for the FlexCo example are shown in Figure 8.

Figure 8: The FlexCo Example: All-Current vs. Temporal Method

	All-Current	Temporal
Net income before translation gain/loss	$333.3	$302.5
Translation gain/loss	–$37.9	$48.1
	(on the balance sheet)	(on the income statement)
Net income	$333.3	$350.6
Total assets	$1,295.5	$1,350.7

Notice that:

- Net income before translation gain/loss is different between the two methods. This is because COGS and depreciation are different.
- The translation gain/loss is different between the two methods; it's not even the same sign. The all-current method reports a translation loss, while the temporal method reports a translation gain. This is NOT an unusual occurrence.
- Net income is different between the two methods.
- Total assets are different between the two methods because inventory and net fixed assets are different.

The reason the two methods report such different results is because of the differing treatment of specific exchange rate asset and liability gain/losses, as shown in Figures 9 and 10.

Figure 9: Treatment of Exchange Rate Gains and Losses Under the All-Current Method

	Realized Gains/Losses	*Unrealized Gains/ Losses*
Monetary assets and liabilities	CTA on the balance sheet	CTA on the balance sheet
Nonmonetary assets (inventory and fixed assets)	CTA on the balance sheet	CTA on the balance sheet

Figure 10: Treatment of Exchange Rate Gains and Losses Under the Temporal Method

	Realized Gains/Losses	*Unrealized Gains/Losses*
Monetary assets and liabilities	Translation gain/loss on the income statement	Translation gain/loss on the income statement
Nonmonetary assets (inventory and fixed assets)	Included in COGS and depreciation expense on the income statement	Ignored

There are three key differences:

1. Exchange rate gains/losses appear on the balance sheet with the all-current method and the income statement with the temporal method, and the size and sign of the gain or loss are usually different.
2. Realized exchange rate gains and losses on inventory and fixed assets are included in COGS and depreciation expense under the temporal method.
3. Unrealized exchange rate gains and losses on inventory and fixed assets are ignored under the temporal method—they are not recorded on the income statement or the balance sheet.

Professor's Note: What does all this mean for the Level 2 CFA candidate? It means that the choice of method matters for reported financial results, and because management makes the decision on the functional currency and ultimately the accounting treatment of consolidated foreign subsidiaries, management can choose the method that reports the best financial results on the consolidated statements. Therefore, the analyst needs to understand how the choice of translation method affects financial ratios.

COMPARING SUBSIDIARY RESULTS TO TRANSLATED RESULTS UNDER THE ALL-CURRENT METHOD

LOS 26.h: Analyze how the translation of a subsidiary's financial statements will affect the subsidiary's financial ratios.

Next you are asked to compare:

- The subsidiary's financial statements and ratios before translation (this LOS).
- The subsidiary's translated financial statements and ratios using the all-current method (LOS 26.i).

For example, Figure 11 is a side-by-side comparison from the FlexCo/Vibrant example of Vibrant's original 2006 balance sheet and income statement and Vibrant's translated statements.

Figure 11: Vibrant LC and Translated Balance Sheet and Income Statement

	2006 (LC)	2006 ($) All Current Method
Cash	LC100	$45.5
Accounts receivable	650	295.5
Inventory	1,200	545.4
Current assets	LC1,950	$886.4
Fixed assets	1,600	727.3
Accumulated depreciation	(700)	(318.2)
Net fixed assets	LC900	$409.1
Total assets	LC2,850	$1,295.5
Accounts payable	500	227.3
Current debt	200	91.0
Long-term debt	950	431.8
Total liabilities	LC1,650	$750.1
Common stock	400	200.0
Retained earnings	800	383.3
Cumulative translation adjustment	—	(37.9)
Total equity	LC1,200	$545.4
Total liabilities and shareholders' equity	LC2,850	$1,295.5
Revenue	LC5,000	$2,381.0
Cost of goods sold	(3,300)	(1,571.5)
Gross margin	1,700	809.5
Other expenses	(400)	(190.5)
Depreciation expense	(600)	(285.7)
Net income	LC700	$333.3

Professor's Note: This LOS requires a detailed understanding of the all-current method. Fortunately, there are a few general rules (i.e., shortcuts) that may buy you some time on the exam, especially if you are only required to identify whether or not a change occurs and the direction of said change.

Pure Balance Sheet and Pure Income Statement Ratios

All pure income statement and pure balance sheet ratios are *unaffected* by the application of the all-current method. In other words, the local currency trends and relationships are "preserved." What we mean by "pure" is that the components of the ratio all come from the balance sheet, or the components all come from the income statement.

For example, the current ratio (current assets over current liabilities) is a pure balance sheet ratio because both numerator and denominator are on the balance sheet and translated at the current rate. If you multiply both numerator and denominator by the same exchange rate, the rate cancels, and you're left with the same ratio. All profit margin measures are pure income statement ratios because both the numerator (some measure of profit such as gross profit) and the denominator (sales) come from the income statement and are translated at the average rate.

Figure 12 shows a sample of typical pure balance sheet and pure income statement ratios and the actual ratio values for the FlexCo/Vibrant example. Notice that the all-current method preserves the original LC ratio in each case.

Figure 12: FlexCo/Vibrant Pure Balance Sheet and Pure Income Statement Ratios

Ratio	2006 (LC)	2006 ($) All Current Method
Pure Balance Sheet Ratios		
Current ratio	2.79	2.79
Quick ratio	1.07	1.07
LTD-to-total capital	0.44	0.44
Pure Income Statement Ratios		
Gross profit margin	34.0%	34.0%
Net profit margin	14.0%	14.0%

 Professor's Note: Interest coverage (EBIT divided by interest expense) is another example of a pure income statement ratio.

Mixed Balance Sheet/Income Statement Ratios

The all-current method results in small changes in **mixed ratios** that combine income statement and balance sheet items because the numerator and the denominator are almost always translated at different exchange rates. Don't expect the ratio to remain the same, but don't expect large changes either. The direction of the change will depend on the relationship between the exchange rate used to translate the denominator and the exchange rate used to translate the numerator.

Our analysis of mixed ratios isn't as clear-cut as the analysis of pure ratios, but we can make one definitive statement: *mixed ratios calculated from financial statements translated using the all-current method currency will be different than the same ratio calculated from the local currency statements before translation.* However, we can't make any definitive statements about whether specific ratios will be larger or smaller after translation unless we make the assumption that all mixed ratios are calculated using end-of-period balance sheet numbers. The analysis that follows does not necessarily apply for mixed ratios calculated using beginning or average balance sheet figures.

This is a very important point so we'll repeat it again: the conclusions drawn in the following section assume we're using end-of-period balance sheet figures.

Figure 13 shows a sample of typical mixed balance sheet/income statement ratios and the actual ratio values for the FlexCo/Vibrant example. Recall that the exchange rate went from $0.50 = LC1.00 in 2005 to $0.4545 = LC1.00 in 2006, which means the local currency (LC) was depreciating. The average rate in 2006 was $0.4762 = LC1.00.

Figure 13: FlexCo/Vibrant Mixed Balance Sheet/Income Statement Ratios (Depreciating LC)

Ratio*	2006(LC)	2006 ($) All Current Method
Return on assets	24.6%	25.7%
Return on equity	58.3%	61.0%
Total asset turnover	1.75	1.84
Inventory turnover	2.75	2.88
Accounts receivable turnover	7.69	8.06

* Ratios are calculated using end-of-period balance sheet numbers.

Notice that in each case the translated ratio is larger than the original ratio. This will always be the case when the LC is depreciating because the average rate is greater than the ending rate. Because the numerator of each of the ratios is on the income statement and is translated at the (higher) average rate, and because the denominator in each is on the end-of-period balance sheet and is translated at the (lower) ending rate, each translated ratio is larger than the original ratio. When the LC is appreciating, each of these ratios will decrease.

Professor's Note: In the Level 2 curriculum, we don't run across many mixed ratios with a balance sheet item in the numerator and an income statement item in the denominator. One example is receivables collection period. Just remember that if accounts receivable turnover increases, receivables collection period will decrease. The same is true for inventory processing period.

On the exam, remember these key points regarding the original versus the translated financial statements and ratios:

- Pure balance sheet and pure income statement ratios will be the same.
- If the LC is depreciating, translated mixed ratios (with an income statement item in the numerator and an end-of-period balance sheet item in the denominator) will be larger than the original ratio.

- If the LC is appreciating, translated mixed ratios (with an income statement item in the numerator and an end-of-period balance sheet item in the denominator) will be smaller than the original ratio.

COMPARING RESULTS USING THE TEMPORAL AND ALL-CURRENT METHODS

LOS 26.i: Compare and contrast the effect of using the temporal method and the all-current method on the parent company's financial ratios.

Next you are asked to compare:

- The remeasured financial statements and ratios using the temporal method.
- The translated financial statements and ratios using the all-current method.

For example, Figure 14 is a side-by-side comparison from the FlexCo/Vibrant example of Vibrant's 2006 remeasured financial statements (using the temporal method) and translated financial statements (using the all-current method).

Figure 14: Vibrant LC and Remeasured Balance Sheet and Income Statement

	2006 ($) Temporal Method	2006 ($) All Current Method
Cash	$45.5	$45.5
Accounts receivable	295.5	295.5
Inventory	571.4	545.4
Current assets	$912.4	$886.4
Fixed assets	781.0	727.3
Accumulated depreciation	(342.7)	(318.2)
Net fixed assets	438.3	409.1
Total assets	$1,350.7	$1,295.5
Accounts payable	227.3	227.3
Current debt	91.0	91.0
Long-term debt	431.8	431.8
Total liabilities	$750.1	$750.1
Common stock	200.0	200.0
Retained earnings	400.6	383.3
Cumulative translation adjustment	—	(37.9)
Total Equity	600.6	$545.4
Total liabilities and shareholders' equity	$1,350.7	$1,295.5
Revenue	$2,381.0	$2,381.0
Cost of goods sold	(1,595.3)	(1,571.5)
Gross margin	785.7	809.5
Other expenses	(190.5)	(190.5)
Depreciation expense	(292.7)	(285.7)
Net income before translation gain	302.5	333.3
Translation gain	48.1	—
Net income	$350.6	$333.3

Please note that this analysis assumes we're using **end-of-period balance sheet figures**.

Analyzing the effect on the financial ratios of the choice of accounting method is a little more difficult in this case, but the basic procedure is as follows:

- Determine whether the local currency (LC) is appreciating or depreciating.
- Determine which rate (historical rate, average rate, or current rate) is used to convert the numerator under both methods. Determine whether the numerator of the ratio will be the same, larger, or smaller under the temporal method versus the all-current method.
- Determine which rate (historical rate, average rate, or current rate) is used to convert the denominator under both methods. Determine whether the denominator of the ratio will be the same, larger, or smaller under the temporal method versus the all-current method.
- Determine whether the ratio will increase, decrease, stay the same, or if the effect is uncertain, based on the direction of change in the numerator and the denominator.

For example, let's analyze the fixed asset turnover ratio, which is equal to sales divided by fixed assets.

- Let's assume the local currency is depreciating.
- The numerator (sales) is converted at the same rate (the average rate) under both methods.
- The denominator (fixed assets) is converted at the historical rate under the temporal method and the current rate under the all-current method. If the LC is depreciating, the historical rate will be higher than the current rate, which means fixed assets will be higher under the temporal method.
- Fixed asset turnover will be lower under the temporal method.

Figure 15 outlines the effect on various balance sheet and income statement accounts of each method with an appreciating and a depreciating currency.

Figure 15: Effect of Translation Methods on Balance Sheet and Income Statement Items

	Appreciating LC		Depreciating LC	
	Temporal	All-current	Temporal	All-current
Income Statement Items				
Revenues	same	same	same	same
COGS*	lower	higher	higher	lower
Gross profit	higher	lower	lower	higher
Depreciation*	lower	higher	higher	lower
Other expenses	same	same	same	same
NI before translation gain/loss	higher	lower	lower	higher
Translation gain/loss	+/–	+/–	+/–	+/–
NI after translation gain/loss	uncertain	uncertain	uncertain	uncertain
Balance Sheet Items				
Cash	same	same	same	same
Accounts receivable	same	same	same	same
Inventory	lower	higher	higher	lower
Fixed assets	lower	higher	higher	lower
Total assets	lower	higher	higher	lower
Liabilities	same	same	same	same
Equity	lower	higher	higher	lower

* COGS and depreciation are converted at the historical rate under the temporal method, so they experience the same relative effects as inventory and fixed assets, respectively.

The sign of the translation gain/loss is case-specific using either the temporal or all-current methods, because it depends on whether the exposure and the change in the exposure are positive or negative, and whether the LC is appreciating or depreciating. However, we can make some general observations if the effects are in the same direction, as shown in Figure 16.

Figure 16: Effect of Appreciating or Depreciating Currency on Translation Gain/Loss for Temporal and All-Current Methods

	Appreciating LC	*Depreciating LC*
Beginning exposure > 0 Change in exposure > 0	translation gain	translation loss
Beginning exposure > 0 Change in exposure < 0	uncertain	uncertain
Beginning exposure < 0 Change in exposure > 0	uncertain	uncertain
Beginning exposure < 0 Change in exposure < 0	translation loss	translation gain

We can use Figure 15 to determine the effect on a selected set of common ratios, as shown in Figure 17. In some cases the effect on the ratio is uncertain because the change in the numerator and denominator are in the same direction, or the change in one component is uncertain. All ratios in Figure 17 are calculated using end-of-period balance sheet numbers.

 Professor's Note: We've tried to be as comprehensive as possible in our treatment of all the possible ratios you might see on exam day. However, be prepared to analyze the effect on ratios not listed in Figure 17. You should be able to apply the procedure we've discussed to the analysis of any financial ratios.

Figure 17: Effect of Translation Methods on Selected Financial Ratios

	Appreciating Local Currency		Depreciating Local Currency	
	Temporal	All-Current	Temporal	All-Current
Liquidity Ratios*				
Current ratio (assuming subsidiary has inventory)	lower	higher	higher	lower
Quick ratio	same	same	same	same
A/R turnover	same	same	same	same
Inventory turnover	uncertain	uncertain	uncertain	uncertain
Operating Efficiency Ratios*				
Fixed asset turnover	higher	lower	lower	higher
Total asset turnover	higher	lower	lower	higher
Profitability Ratios*				
Gross profit margin	higher	lower	lower	higher
Net profit margin	uncertain	uncertain	uncertain	uncertain
ROE	uncertain	uncertain	uncertain	uncertain
ROA	uncertain	uncertain	uncertain	uncertain
Financial Leverage Ratios*				
Interest coverage	higher	lower	lower	higher
LTD-to-total capital	higher	lower	lower	higher

* Ratios are calculated using end-of-period balance sheet numbers.

Professor's Note: To keep our example as simple as possible, we provided a one-period illustration. Be aware that changing exchange rates may result in what appears to be trends over multiple periods in the translated data. These trends may simply be an artifact of the changing rates and not due to changes in product markets and profitability trends for the subsidiary. Furthermore, ratios calculated from statements translated using the all-current method versus the temporal method will not only differ in terms of absolute value but may also show different trends (e.g., the current ratio may be increasing with one method and decreasing with the other).

Effect on Parent Company Ratios

When parent firms and their foreign subsidiaries experience different trends and ratio characteristics, changing exchange rates will distort trends and ratios calculated from the consolidated financial data. If a local currency is appreciating, the foreign subsidiary's performance will have a greater impact on the consolidated data. When the local currency is depreciating, it will have a diminished impact. Even if there are no changes in the underlying ratios, changes in exchange rates will result in changes in the consolidated ratios. When the parent has many subsidiaries operating under separate functional currencies, trends and ratios from the consolidated data may become very difficult to interpret without isolating the data by functional currency or by subsidiary.

Effect on the Statement of Cash Flows

SFAS 95 is intended to isolate the statement of cash flows from the effects of changing exchange rates. It requires that cash flows in the parent (reporting) currency replicate cash flows in the local currency. Thus, in theory the cash flow statement should be unaffected by the translation method used. However, while reported cash flows exclude the effects of changing exchange rates on assets and liabilities (holding effects), flow effects from changing rates are present and do have an impact on reporting currency cash flows.

ANALYZING FOREIGN CURRENCY FOOTNOTE DISCLOSURES

LOS 26.j: Analyze foreign currency disclosures in the footnotes to financial statements.

Professor's Note: For you returning Level 2 candidates, this LOS is new for 2008, so spend some extra time studying it as you review multinational operations and currency translation.

Up to this point we have analyzed a multinational parent company with only one subsidiary. That made the analysis easier (although it sure doesn't seem that way!) because we could link the effect on the consolidated financial statements resulting from the choice of translation method directly to that specific subsidiary.

However, in practice, multinationals have many foreign subsidiaries, which means that the cumulative translation adjustment (CTA) on the balance sheet, the translation gain or loss on the income statement, and the parent company ratios all reflect the effects of the consolidation of several different subsidiaries. SFAS 52 does not have very extensive disclosure requirements, so it is very difficult for the analyst to get information on what currencies the firm conducts business in and how much exposure it has to each of these currencies. In some cases it is even difficult to determine what accounting method (temporal or all-current) the firm uses for its various foreign operations and what functional currencies it uses.

What little information there is available is found in the footnotes to the parent company's financial statements. Therefore in this section we will discuss how the analyst can use the limited information available to analyze a large multinational's foreign operations.

Balance Sheet Exposure

A multinational's balance sheet exposure depends on the choice of functional currency and the composition of the subsidiary's balance sheet.

Choice of functional currency. Remember that the choice of functional currency determines which method is applied and the foreign currency exposure. If the local currency is the functional currency, the all-current method is applied and exposure is net assets. If the parent currency is the functional currency, the temporal method is applied and exposure is equal to net *monetary* assets. The choice is based almost completely on management's discretion, so there is very little consistency across U.S. multinationals in the method used. So what conclusions can we draw if the choice of functional currency is not disclosed?

- If the firm has a CTA on the balance sheet, the all-current method is used for at least some of its subsidiaries.
- If the firm does not have a CTA on the balance sheet, then the parent currency must be the functional currency for all subsidiaries and the temporal method is used exclusively.

Composition of the subsidiary's balance sheet. Subsidiaries with few liabilities face significant foreign currency exposure. For example, if the all-current method is used exposure is the subsidiary's net assets (total assets minus total liabilities), and a firm with small liability balances will have a very large balance sheet exposure. One way to reduce this exposure is for the subsidiary to borrow in the local currency.

Once we have determined the functional currency and have some information on the subsidiary's balance sheet composition, we can estimate the effect of changes in the value of the functional currency on the consolidated financial results. We use a similar method as we used in calculating the foreign currency translation gain or loss in LOS 26.f: calculate the holding effect and the flow effect separately, and then add them up to determine the total effect. In the following example, because we only know identifiable assets, and not exposure (as defined under either the temporal or all-current methods) we estimate a "holding effect" and "flow effect" for identifiable assets only.

Example: Analyzing a subsidiary's balance sheet exposure

Jim Bowerman is an analyst with The Prestigious Group. Bowerman is analyzing the South African operations of Global Holdings, a U.S.-based conglomerate. He has found the following information in the footnotes related to the identifiable assets of Global's South African operations.

South African Operations	2006	2007
Identifiable assets (in millions of $)	$500	$638

He has also collected information on the U.S. dollar/Rand exchange rate.

	2006	2007
Year-end exchange rate	$1 = 10.0	$1 = 8.0
Average exchange rate	$1 = 11.0	$1 = 9.0

Determine how much of the 2007 increase in identifiable assets resulted from the appreciation of the Rand and calculate the translation gain or loss on the identifiable assets.

Answer:

As shown in the following figure, the increase in identifiable assets was almost entirely due to the appreciation of the Rand during 2007 and not growth in Rand-denominated assets.

South African Operations	2006	2007	% change
Identifiable assets (in millions of $)	$500	$638	+28%
× year-end exchange rate	10.00	8.00	
= Identifiable assets (in millions of Rand)	5,000	5,104	+2%

The translation gain on the identifiable assets is equal to the sum of the "holding effect" and the "flow effect":

$$\text{"holding effect"} = \$5,000 \times \left[\frac{1}{8} - \frac{1}{10} \right] = \$125.00$$

$$\text{"flow effect"} = (\$5,104 - \$5,000) \times \left[\frac{1}{8} - \frac{1}{9} \right] = \$1.44$$

$$\text{translation gain on identifiable assets} = \$125.00 + \$1.44 = \$126.44$$

Income Statement Exposure

Recall that most of the items on the income statement are translated at the average exchange rate under both the temporal and all-current methods. Therefore, the major effect on the income statement of exchange rate changes is the flow effect on changes in revenues and expenses.

The income statement flow effect is composed of an *exchange rate effect* and an *operational effect*:

exchange rate effect = income statement item × Δ average rate

operational effect = Δ in income statement item × previous period average rate

The exchange rate effect is the effect of changes in the exchange rate on the subsidiary's translated income statement. The operational effect is the effect of changes in the subsidiary's operating results.

Example: Analyzing a subsidiary's income statement exposure

Bowerman also gathers segment information from the footnotes on the operating results of South African operations.

South African Operations	2006	2007	$ change	% change
Net sales (in millions of U.S.$)	$1,000	$1,300	$300	+30%
Operating income (in millions of U.S.$)	$150	$150	$0	+0%

Analyze the South African operating results for 2007, and calculate the exchange rate effect and the operational effect.

Answer:

In the following figure, the net sales and operating income amounts in U.S. dollars are converted into Rand at the average exchange rate for the year (11.0 in 2006 and 9.0 in 2007.)

South African Operations	2006	2007	% change
Net sales (in millions of Rand)	11,000	11,700	6%
Operating income (in millions of Rand)	1,650	1,350	–18%
Operating margin	15%	11.5%	

It appears that the South African operations suffered a significant decline in operating margins while sales were essentially flat. We can confirm that observation by calculating the exchange rate and operational effects on sales and operating income.

The increase in dollar denominated sales was primarily due to the effect of the appreciating Rand:

$$\text{exchange rate effect (sales)} = (11,700) \times \left(\frac{1}{9} - \frac{1}{11} \right) = \$236$$

$$\text{operational effect (sales)} = (11,700 - 11,000) \times \left(\frac{1}{11} \right) = \$64$$

$$\text{total effect (sales)} = \$236 + \$64 = \$300$$

The flat dollar-denominated operating income was due to the appreciating Rand offsetting declining Rand margins:

$$\text{exchange rate effect (operating income)} = (1,350) \times \left(\frac{1}{9} - \frac{1}{11} \right) = \$27$$

$$\text{operational effect (operating income)} = (1,350 - 1,650) \times \left(\frac{1}{11} \right) = -\$27$$

$$\text{total effect (operating income)} = \$27 - \$27 = \$0$$

TRANSLATION METHODS IN HYPERINFLATIONARY ECONOMIES

LOS 26.k: Illustrate and analyze alternative accounting methods for subsidiaries operating in hyperinflationary economies.

SFAS 52 defines a hyperinflationary economy as one that experiences a cumulative 3-year inflation rate of more than 100%. In a hyperinflationary economy, the foreign currency will be rapidly depreciating against the reporting currency because the extremely high inflation rate will quickly deteriorate the purchasing power of the foreign currency. In this case, using the current rate to translate all balance sheet amounts will result in very low values for all assets and liabilities after translation into the reporting currency.

In reality, the real value of nonmonetary assets and liabilities is typically not affected by hyperinflation because the local currency-denominated values increase to offset the impact of inflation (e.g., real estate values rise with inflation). As a result, the temporal method is more appropriate in this situation. Recall that under the temporal method, all nonmonetary accounts are remeasured at the historical rate.

For exam purposes, if you are given an inflation rate for one year, extrapolate that rate for a cumulative 3-year effect. For example, any annual inflation rate above 26% will result in a 3-year cumulative inflation rate greater than 100%. This assumes compounded inflation ($1.26^3 - 1$ is approximately equal to 1.00 or a 100% increase).

KEY CONCEPTS

1. Flow effects are the impact of changes in the exchange rate on income statement items such as revenue. Holding gain/loss effects are the impact of changes in the exchange rate on assets and liabilities on the balance sheet, such as cash balances.

2. Some important definitions:
   - The functional currency is defined as the primary currency of the economic environment in which the firm operates. This can be the currency in which the firm operates or some other currency.
   - The reporting currency is the currency in which the multinational firm prepares its final, consolidated financial statements.
   - The local currency is the currency of the country in which the foreign subsidiary is located.
   - In foreign currency translation, it is possible to have another foreign currency that is different from the local currency.
   - The current rate is the exchange rate as of the balance sheet date.
   - The average rate is the average exchange rate over the reporting period.
   - The historical rate is the rate that existed when a particular transaction was conducted.

3. Under the temporal method, cash, accounts receivable, accounts payable, and long-term debt are translated using the current rate. All other assets and liabilities are translated at the historical rate. Revenues and expenses are translated at the average rate. COGS and depreciation are translated by applying the historical rate to inventory and fixed asset purchases. The translation gain or loss is shown on the income statement.

4. Under the all-current method, all income statement accounts are translated at the average rate. All balance sheet accounts are translated at the current rate except for common stock, which is translated at the appropriate historical rate that applied when the equity was issued. Dividends are translated at the historical rate that applied when they were issued. The foreign currency adjustment is included on the balance sheet in the equity section. Pure balance sheet financial ratios and pure income statement financial ratios will be unaffected by an all-current method translation.

5. The rules that govern the determination of the functional currency under SFAS 52 are:
   - The results of operations, financial position, and cash flows of all foreign operations must be measured in the designated functional currency.
   - Self-contained, independent subsidiaries whose operations are primarily located in the local market will use the local currency as the functional currency.
   - Subsidiaries whose operations are well integrated with the parent will use the parent's currency as the functional currency.
   - If the subsidiary operates in a highly inflationary environment, use the parent's currency as the functional currency. A high inflation environment is defined as cumulative inflation that exceeds 100% over a 3-year period.

- If the functional currency is the local currency, use the all-current method. The use of the all-current method under SFAS 52 is called translation.
- If the functional currency is the parent's currency ($) or some other currency, use the temporal method. The use of the temporal method under SFAS 52 is called remeasurement.

6. Translation gains or losses result from gains or losses related to balance sheet accounts that are exposed to changes in exchange rates. Rates are in $/LC.
   - Exposure under the all-current method = shareholders' equity
   - Exposure under the temporal method = (cash + accounts receivable) – (accounts payable + current debt + long-term debt)
   - Flow effect (in $) = change in exposure (in LC) × (ending rate – average rate)
   - Holding gain/loss effect (in $) = beginning exposure (in LC) × (ending rate – beginning rate)
   - Translation gain/loss (in $) = flow effect + holding gain/loss effect

7. There are three reasons the temporal and all-current methods report significantly different results.
   - Translation gains/losses appear on the balance sheet with the all-current method and on the income statement with the temporal method.
   - Realized gains and losses on nonmonetary inventory and fixed assets are included in COGS and depreciation expense under the temporal method.
   - Unrealized gains and losses on inventory and fixed assets are ignored under the temporal method.

8. On the exam, remember these key points regarding the original versus the financial statements translated using the all-current rate.
   - Pure balance sheet and pure income statement ratios will be the same.
   - If the LC is depreciating, translated mixed ratios (with an income statement item in the numerator and an end-of-period balance sheet item in the denominator) will be larger than the original ratio.
   - If the LC is appreciating, translated mixed ratios (with an income statement item in the numerator and an end-of-period balance sheet item in the denominator) will be smaller than the original ratio.

9. To analyze the effect on the financial ratios of the choice of accounting method (temporal versus all-current):
   - Determine whether the local currency is appreciating or depreciating.
   - Determine which rate (historical rate, average rate, or current rate) is used to convert the numerator under both methods. Determine whether the numerator of the ratio will be the same, larger, or smaller under the temporal method versus the all-current method.
   - Determine which rate (historical rate, average rate, or current rate) is used to convert the denominator under both methods. Determine whether the denominator of the ratio will be the same, larger, or smaller under the temporal method versus the all-current method.
   - Determine whether the ratio will increase, decrease, stay the same, or if the effect is uncertain, based on the direction of change in the numerator and the denominator.

10. If the firm has a CTA on the balance sheet, the all-current method is used for at least some of its subsidiaries. If the firm does not have a CTA on the balance sheet, then the parent currency must be the functional currency for all subsidiaries and the temporal method is used exclusively.

11. To estimate the balance sheet effects of changes in the value of the functional currency on consolidated financial results, calculate the holding effect and the flow effect separately, and then add them up to determine the total effect.

12. The major effect on the income statement of exchange rate changes is the flow effect on changes in revenues and expenses. The income statement flow effect is composed of an *exchange rate effect* and an *operational effect*:

$$\text{exchange rate effect} = \text{income statement item} \times \Delta \text{ average rate}$$

$$\text{operational effect} = \Delta \text{ in income statement item} \times \text{previous period average rate}$$

CONCEPT CHECKERS

1. Which of the following statements is *most accurate* regarding foreign currency translation? Under the:
   A. temporal method, the monetary asset accounts of a foreign subsidiary are translated using the current rate.
   B. temporal method, the nonmonetary asset accounts of a foreign subsidiary are translated using the current rate.
   C. all-current method, all balance sheet accounts of a foreign subsidiary are translated using the average rate.
   D. all-current method, dividends of a foreign subsidiary are translated at the current rate.

2. Which of the following is *least likely* a condition that requires the use of the temporal method for a U.S. parent that reports results in U.S. dollars?
   A. The subsidiary's functional currency is the euro, while its local currency is the Swiss franc.
   B. The functional currency is the local currency.
   C. The foreign subsidiary is operating in a highly inflationary economy.
   D. The functional currency is some currency other than the local currency or the U.S. dollar.

3. Subsidiary XYZ operates in the United Kingdom, and the functional currency is the British pound (£). XYZ's income statement shows £400 of net income and a £100 dividend that was paid on October 31 when the exchange rate was $1.60 per £. The current exchange rate is $1.70 per £, and the average rate is $1.55 per £. Translate the dividends at the appropriate historical rate. The change in retained earnings for the period in U.S. dollars under the provisions of SFAS 52 is *closest* to:
   A. $460.
   B. $465.
   C. $480.
   D. $510.

4. Which of the following ratios may be larger in the reporting currency versus the local currency when translated with the all-current method?
   A. Current ratio.
   B. Return on assets.
   C. Net profit margin.
   D. Debt equity ratio.

5. Mazeppa Inc. is a multinational firm with its head office located in Toronto, Canada. Its main foreign subsidiary is located in Paris, but the primary economic environment in which the foreign subsidiary generates and expends cash is in the United States (New York). The:
   A. local currency is the U.S. dollar.
   B. functional currency is the euro.
   C. reporting currency is the U.S. dollar.
   D. reporting currency is the Canadian dollar.

6. A Swedish firm owns a foreign subsidiary in Hong Kong. This year, sales of the foreign subsidiary were HK$10 million, and the HK$/SEK average exchange rate was 1.05. Last year, sales were also HK$10 million and the HK$/SEK average exchange rate was 0.94. Based on this information, which of the following statements is *most accurate*?
    A. Reported sales in SEK increased by 1.1 million over last year.
    B. Reported sales in SEK decreased by 11.7% over last year.
    C. The HK$ has appreciated relative to the SEK over the past year.
    D. Reported sales in the SEK decreased this year due to the depreciation of the HK$.

7. In translating inventory and COGS under the temporal method, if the local currency is appreciating and LIFO is being used, which of the following combinations of COGS and ending inventory should result compared to FIFO?

	COGS	Ending inventory
A.	Lower	Higher
B.	Lower	Lower
C.	Higher	Lower
D.	Higher	Higher

8. Which of the following statements about the temporal method and the all-current method is *least accurate*?
    A. The choice of functional currency is completely at management's discretion.
    B. Net income is generally more volatile under the temporal method than under the all-current method.
    C. Subsidiaries that operate in highly inflationary environments will generally use the temporal method.
    D. Subsidiaries whose operations are well integrated with the parent will generally use the all-current method.

9. Under the temporal method, realized exchange rate gains and losses on inventory are:
    A. a component of the translation gain or loss on the income statement.
    B. a component of the cumulative translation adjustment on the balance sheet.
    C. included in cost of goods sold on the income statement.
    D. not recorded anywhere in the financial statements.

10. If beginning currency exposure is negative, the change in currency exposure is positive, and the local currency is depreciating, the flow effect will be:
    A. negative, and a holding gain will result.
    B. negative, and a holding loss will result.
    C. positive, and a holding gain will result.
    D. positive, and a holding loss will result.

CHALLENGE PROBLEMS

Use the following information to answer Questions 11 through 15.

This information is a continuation of the FlexCo/Vibrant example from the topic review. Suppose it is now the end of 2007, and Vibrant reports the operating results shown in the following figure.

Vibrant December 31, 2006 and 2007 Balance Sheet

	2006	2007
Cash	LC100	LC150
Accounts receivable	650	800
Inventory	1,200	1,400
Current assets	LC1,950	LC2,350
Fixed assets	1,600	2,500
Accumulated depreciation	(700)	(1,500)
Net fixed assets	LC900	LC1,000
Total assets	LC2,850	LC3,350
Accounts payable	500	500
Current debt	200	100
Long-term debt	950	1,150
Total liabilities	LC1,650	LC1,750
Common stock	400	400
Retained earnings	800	1,200
Total equity	LC1,200	LC1,600
Total liabilities and shareholders' equity	LC2,850	LC3,350

Vibrant 2007 Income Statement

	2007
Revenue	LC5,500
Cost of goods sold	(3,800)
Gross margin	1,700
Other expenses	(500)
Depreciation expense	(800)
Net income	LC400

The following exchange rates between the U.S. dollar and the loca were observed:

- December 31, 2006: LC2.20 = $1.00; $0.4545 = LC1.00.
- December 31, 2007: LC2.50 = $1.00; $0.40 = LC1.00.
- Average for 2007: LC2.33 = $1.00; $0.4292 = LC1.00.

The CTA for 2006 was equal to –$37.9 under the all-current method.

11. Assume for this question only that management determines Vibrant is well-integrated with FlexCo. For 2007 FlexCo *most likely* will report a translation:
   A. loss on the consolidated income statement of $52.0 related to Vibrant.
   B. gain on the consolidated income statement of $46.2 related to Vibrant.
   C. loss on the consolidated balance sheet of $46.2 related to Vibrant.
   D. gain on the consolidated balance sheet of $52.0 related to Vibrant.

12. Assume for this question only that management determines Vibrant operates relatively independently from FlexCo. For 2007, FlexCo *most likely* will report a cumulative translation loss on the consolidated:
   A. income statement of $77.1 related to Vibrant.
   B. income statement of $115.0 related to Vibrant.
   C. balance sheet of $77.1 related to Vibrant.
   D. balance sheet of $115.0 related to Vibrant.

13. The gross profit margin and the return on assets from Vibrant's 2007 U.S. dollar financial statements translated using the all-current method are *closest* to:

Gross profit margin	Return on assets
A. 22.7%	12.8%
B. 22.7%	11.9%
C. 30.9% ✓	12.8%
D. 30.9% ✓	11.9%

14. The gross profit margin from Vibrant's 2007 U.S. dollar financial statements remeasured using the temporal method is *closest* to:
   A. 28.5%.
   B. 30.9%.
   C. 32.7%.
   D. 41.8%.

15. Accounts receivable turnover from Vibrant's 2007 U.S. dollar financial statements (calculated using ending balance sheet numbers) remeasured using the temporal method is *closest* to:
    A. 3.1.
    B. 5.6.
    C. 7.4.
    D. 9.2.

16. Bob Haskell, CFA, is analyzing the financial statements of a U.S.-based company called Seriev Motor. Seriev has a foreign subsidiary located in Japan. Seriev translates the subsidiary results using the all-current method. Haskell determines that the following four ratios will remain the same after translation from yen into U.S. dollars:
    • Gross profit margin.
    • Interest coverage (EBIT/interest expense).
    • Return on assets.
    • Quick ratio.

    The dollar has depreciated against the yen during the most recent year. Haskell is correct in his analysis of:
    A. all four ratios.
    B. three of the four ratios.
    C. two of the four ratios.
    D. one of the four ratios.

17. How many of the following situations *might* result in a translation gain if the local currency is appreciating? Beginning currency exposure:
    • and change in currency exposure are positive.
    • is positive and change in currency exposure is negative.
    • is negative and change in currency exposure is positive.
    • is negative and the change in currency exposure is negative.
    A. None.
    B. One.
    C. Two.
    D. Three.

Use the following information to answer Question 18.

	Beginning of Year	Average	End of Year
Assets	LC6,000	LC7,000	LC8,000
Liabilities	LC3,000	LC3,800	LC4,600
Exchange rate (LC/$)	4.0	4.5	5.0

18. The translation gain or loss using the all-current method is *closest* to:
    A. –$158.89.
    B. –$141.11.
    C. $2,800.00.
    D. $3,200.00.

ANSWERS – CONCEPT CHECKERS

1. **A**   Monetary asset accounts of a foreign subsidiary are translated using the current rate under the temporal method.

2. **B**   If the functional currency is the local currency, the temporal method is not required.

3. **A**   Net income is translated using the average rate. Dividends are translated at the historical rate on the date the dividends were paid.

   ($1.55 × 400) – ($1.6 × 100) = $460

4. **B**   All pure income statement and balance sheet ratios are unaffected by the application of the all-current method. What we mean by "pure" is that the components of the ratio all come from the balance sheet, or the components of the ratio all come from the income statement. Return on assets is a "mixed ratio" because assets come from the balance sheet and are translated at the current rate and net income is translated at the average rate. Unless the exchange rate doesn't change during the year, the two accounts will be translated at different rates, and the local currency value of the ratio will change when translated into the reporting currency. The other ratios will *always* be the same using the all-current method.

5. **D**   As a multinational firm, the location of Mazeppa's head office would most likely determine the currency to be used to prepare its final, consolidated financial statements. That is the reporting currency, and in this case, it is the Canadian dollar. Based on the facts, the local currency is the euro and the functional currency is the U.S. dollar.

6. **D** $$\text{sales (this year)} = \frac{\text{HK\$10 million}}{1.05} = \text{SEK9.524 million}$$

   $$\text{sales (last year)} = \frac{\text{HK\$10 million}}{0.94} = \text{SEK10.638 million}$$

   decrease in reported sales = SEK1.1 million = 10.5%

   Last year it only cost 0.94 HK$ to purchase 1 SEK. This year it costs 1.05 HK$ to purchase 1 SEK. Therefore, the SEK is relatively more expensive, so the SEK has appreciated relative to the HK$, or the HK$ has depreciated relative to the SEK. Since the HK$ has depreciated relative to the SEK, the translation of HK$ sales into SEK will result in lower reported SEK values.

7. **C**   Under LIFO, the most recent prices are used to determine COGS, so if the local currency is appreciating, the highest prices are being used—this should result in relatively higher COGS amounts. Under LIFO, the oldest prices are used to determine ending inventory, so if the local currency is appreciating, the lowest prices are being used—this should result in relatively lower ending inventory amounts.

8. **D**   Subsidiaries whose operations are well integrated with the parent will generally use the parent's currency as the functional currency. Remeasurement from the local currency to the functional currency is done with the temporal method.

9. **C**   Realized exchange rate gains and losses on nonmonetary assets (like inventory) are included in operating expenses on the income statement under the temporal method.

Realized exchange rate gains and losses on inventory specifically are included in cost of goods sold.

10. **A**   Flow effect equals change in exposure times ending minus average rate. If the local currency is depreciating, ending rate will be less than the average rate. The positive change in exposure times the negative exchange rate difference will result in a negative flow effect.

Holding gain/loss effect equals beginning exposure times ending minus beginning rate. The negative beginning exposure times the negative exchange rate difference will result in a holding gain.

ANSWERS – CHALLENGE PROBLEMS

11. **B**   If management determines that Vibrant is integrated with FlexCo's operations, the functional currency is the U.S. dollar and the temporal method applies.

Remember that with the temporal method, the exposure is equal to (cash + receivables) – (payables + current and long-term debt).

ending exposure = (150 + 800) – (500 + 100 + 1,150) = 950 – 1,750 = –LC800

beginning exposure = (100 + 650) – (500 + 200 + 950) = 750 – 1,650 = –LC900

change in exposure = –LC800 – (–LC900) = LC100

flow effect = LC100 × (0.40 – 0.4292) = –$2.9

holding gain effect = –LC900 × (0.40 – 0.4545) = $49.1

translation gain for 2006 = –$2.9 + $49.1 = $46.2

Under the temporal method the translation gain is reported on the income statement.

12. **D**   If management determines that Vibrant operates independently from FlexCo, the functional currency is the loca and the all-current method applies.

Remember that with the all-current method the exposure is equal to shareholders' equity.

ending exposure = LC1,600

beginning exposure = LC1,200

change in exposure = LC1,600 – LC1,200 = LC400

flow effect = LC400 × (0.40 – 0.4292) = –$11.7

holding gain effect = LC1,200 × (0.40 – 0.4545) = –$65.4

translation loss for 2006 = –$11.7 – $65.4 = –$77.1

This is the translation gain for 2007, but the *cumulative* translation adjustment (CTA) is reported in the equity section of the balance sheet as part of comprehensive income under the all-current method. The CTA in 2006 was –$37.9, so the CTA in 2007 is –$37.9 – $77.1 = –$115.0.

13. **C** It might look like you have to construct the translated financial statements to answer this question, but you actually don't have to if you remember the relationships between the original subsidiary ratios measured in the local currency and the translated ratios measured in U.S. dollars.

Pure income statement ratios like gross profit margin will be the same. The gross profit margin measured in the local currency is LC1,700/LC5,500 = 30.9%; the gross margin measured in U.S. dollars must also be 30.9%.

Mixed ratios like ROA will be different, and in this case, because the local currency is depreciating, the translated ROA will be greater than the original. This occurs because net income (in the numerator) is translated at the higher average rate and assets (in the denominator) will be translated at the lower current rate. ROA measured in the local currency is LC400/LC3,350 = 11.9%. The ROA measured in U.S. dollars must be greater than 11.9%, which means 12.8% is the only possible answer.

If you did go through the process of calculating the translated ratios, you should have arrived at these numbers:

$$\text{translated gross margin} = \frac{1,700 \times 0.4292}{5,500 \times 0.4292} = \frac{\$729.6}{\$2,360.6} = 30.9\%$$

$$\text{translated ROA} = \frac{400 \times 0.4292}{3,350 \times 0.40} = \frac{\$171.7}{\$1,340} = 12.8\%$$

14. **A** The local currency is depreciating, so the gross profit margin remeasured in U.S. dollars using the temporal method will be lower than the gross profit margin translated into U.S. dollars using the all-current method. This is because cost of goods sold will be measured at the higher historical rate under the temporal method and at the lower average rate under the all-current method. With temporal method COGS greater than all-current COGS, temporal method gross margin will be less than all-current method gross margin. All-current gross margin is the same as in the original currency (30.9% from the previous problem), which means the only possible answer is 28.5%.

15. **C** Accounts receivable turnover is equal to sales divided by accounts receivable. Under the temporal method, sales are remeasured at the average rate ($0.4292 in 2007), and accounts receivable are remeasured at the current rate ($0.40 for 2007):

$$\text{A/R turnover} = \frac{5,500 \times \$0.4292}{800 \times \$0.40} = \frac{\$2,360.6}{\$320} = 7.4$$

16. **B** Gross profit margin and interest coverage are pure income statement ratios that will not change. Quick ratio is a pure balance sheet ratio that will not change. Return on assets is a mixed ratio (income statement item in the numerator and balance sheet item in the denominator), so it will change as long as the average and current exchange rates are different. Given that the dollar is depreciating against the yen, the current and average rates are likely to be different.

Therefore Haskell is correct in his analysis of three of the four ratios: gross profit margin, interest coverage, and the quick ratio.

17. **D**   In three of the four situations a translation gain *could* occur. Only in the case in which both beginning exposure and the change in exposure are negative would a translation gain *definitely not* occur.

If the local currency is appreciating and both beginning exposure and the change in exposure are positive, a translation gain will definitely occur. If the local currency is appreciating and both beginning exposure and the change in exposure are negative, a translation loss will definitely result. If the beginning exposure and change in exposure are of opposite sign, a translation gain or a translation loss *could* occur, although which one does occur depends on the specific situation.

18. **A**   Under the all-current method, exposure equals assets minus liabilities, or shareholders' equity. Notice that the exchange rate is quoted in LC per $, so to compute the flow and holding effects you must convert them into $ per unit of LC by taking the reciprocal.

beginning exposure = 6,000 – 3,000 = LC3,000

ending exposure = 8,000 – 4,600 = LC3,400

change in exposure = 3,400 – 3,000 = LC400

flow effect = LC400 × [(1/5.0) – (1/4.5)] = –$8.89

holding gain effect = LC3,000 × [(1/5.0) – (1/4.0)] = –$150.00

translation gain = –$8.89 – $150.00 = –$158.89

The following is a review of the Financial Statement Analysis principles designed to address the learning outcome statements set forth by CFA Institute®. This topic is also covered in:

ACCOUNTING SHENANIGANS ON THE CASH FLOW STATEMENT

EXAM FOCUS

This new reading for 2008 provides a brief discussion of several techniques used to manipulate operating cash flow. Management has several ways to manipulate operating cash flow, including deciding how to allocate cash flow between categories and changing the timing of receipt of cash flows. Know how lengthening the terms of accounts payable, financing accounts payable, securitizing accounts receivable, and repurchasing stock options to offset dilution can affect the categorization and timing of cash flows. Also keep in mind that not all increases in cash flow are sustainable. The material ties into the topic review on accounting for stock compensation in Study Session 6.

WARM-UP: ACCRUAL ACCOUNTING AND CASH FLOW MANIPULATION

Recall from Level 1 that most firms use the accrual method of accounting for financial reporting purposes. Accrual accounting is easily manipulated because of the many estimates and judgments that are involved. However, cash flow, particularly operating cash flow, is usually unaffected by estimates and judgments. However, firms can still manipulate users of financial information by creating the perception that operating cash flow is sustainable.

A number of techniques can be used to misrepresent a firm's cash generating ability by classifying financing activities as operating activities and vice versa. In addition, management has discretion over the timing of cash flows. An analyst should take care to investigate the quality of a company's cash flows and determine whether increases in operating cash flow are sustainable. Management also has discretion over where to report cash flows, and the analyst should be aware that the difference in treatment among companies may make comparisons of cash flow less useful, particularly for valuation.

LOS 27: Analyze and discuss the following ways to manipulate the cash flow statement: stretching out payables; financing of payables; securitization of receivables; and using stock buybacks to offset dilution of earnings.

STRETCHING ACCOUNTS PAYABLE

Transactions with suppliers are usually reported as operating activities in the cash flow statement. A firm can temporarily increase operating cash flow by simply stretching accounts payable; that is, by delaying payments to its suppliers. By delaying payment, the firm effectively receives no-cost financing. However, stretching payables is not a sustainable source of cash flow since the firm's suppliers may eventually refuse to extend credit because of the slower payments.

One way to determine whether a firm is stretching its payables is to examine the number of days in accounts payable. **Days-in payables** is calculated by dividing the average balance of accounts payable by cost of goods sold (COGS) and multiplying the result by the number of days in the period.

$$\text{days in accounts payable} = \left(\frac{\text{average accounts payable}}{\text{COGS}} \right) \text{number of days}$$

 Professor's Note: Source reading #27 from the CFA program curriculum uses ending accounts payable to calculate days in accounts payable. However, we recommend using average accounts payable on the exam if both beginning and ending accounts payable are provided in the question.

Example: Calculating days in accounts payable

At year-end, Silver Creek Company reported cost of goods sold of $250 million. Beginning accounts payable is $45 million, and ending accounts payable is $55 million. Assuming there are 365 days in a year, calculate the number of days on average it takes Silver Creek to pay its suppliers.

Answer:

$$\text{average accounts payable} = \frac{\$45 + \$55}{2} = \$50 \text{ million}$$

$$\text{days in accounts payable} = \left(\frac{\$50}{\$250} \right) \times 365 = 73 \text{ days}$$

 Professor's Note: At Level 1, we calculated the days in payables by dividing 365 by accounts payable turnover. Recall that accounts payable turnover is equal to COGS divided by average accounts payable. So, in the previous example, accounts payable turnover is equal to 5 ($250 million / $50 million) and days in accounts payable is equal to 73 (365 / 5). It is not necessary to remember both formulas; pick the one with which you are most comfortable. Be aware of terminology, however; you may see this ratio referred to as days sales in payables, (DSP).

FINANCING ACCOUNTS PAYABLE

Delaying the cash flows associated with payables can also be accomplished by entering into a financing arrangement with a third party, usually a financial institution. Such an arrangement allows the firm to manage the timing of the reported operating cash flows.

For example, suppose a manufacturing firm purchases raw materials from a supplier on credit. In the cash flow statement, the firm reports the increase in inventory as an operating outflow and the increase in accounts payable as an operating inflow. Total operating cash flow does not change.

When the account payable is due, a financial institution makes payment to the supplier on behalf of the firm, and the firm reclassifies the account payable to short-term debt. The decrease in accounts payable results in an operating outflow, and the increase in short-term debt results in a financing inflow. At this point, operating cash flow is lower, but total cash flow is still unaffected. Although operating cash flow is lower from the reclassification, the firm might time the arrangement so that the lower operating cash flow is offset by higher operating cash flows from other sources, such as seasonal cash flows or cash flows from receivable sales or securitizations. In effect, the firm times the operating cash outflow to occur when other operating cash inflows are higher, and as a result "hides" the decrease related to the financing.

Finally, when the firm repays the financial institution, the firm reports the outflow of cash as a financing activity and not an operating activity. Ultimately, the firm has delayed the outflow of cash. Of course, the financial institution will charge a fee (interest) to handle the arrangement.

SECURITIZING ACCOUNTS RECEIVABLE

Firms can immediately convert accounts receivable to cash by borrowing against the receivables, or by selling or securitizing the receivables. When a firm borrows against its receivables, the inflow of cash is reported as a financing activity in the cash flow statement.

When receivables are securitized, they are usually transferred to a bankruptcy remote structure known as a special purpose entity (SPE). The SPE pools the receivables together and sells securities representing an undivided interest in the pool. A securitization is treated just like a collection; that is, the inflow of cash is reported as an operating activity in the cash flow statement because the transaction is reported as a sale. So, by securitizing its accounts receivable, rather than waiting to collect from the customer, a firm can accelerate operating cash flow into the current period.

Accelerating operating cash flow by securitizing receivables is not sustainable because the firm only has a limited amount of accounts receivable.

Securitizing accounts receivable may also affect earnings. When the receivables are securitized, the firm can recognize a gain in some cases. This gain is the result of differences in the book value and fair value of the receivables at the time of securitization. The gain can be affected by a number of estimates including the expected default rate, the expected prepayment rate, and the discount rate.

GAAP is silent on where the gains from securitizations should be reported in the income statement. Some firms take a more aggressive approach and include the gains as revenue. Other firms reduce operating expenses by the amount of the gains. Some firms report the gains as a part of nonoperating income.

STOCK OPTION TAX BENEFITS

 Professor's Note: The reporting of stock option tax benefits is not specifically addressed in the LOS. However, we have included the information because it is necessary to understand some of the issues with using stock buybacks to offset dilution, which is specifically addressed in the LOS.

Firms are now required to report compensation expense for employee stock options in the income statement. Compensation expense from stock options, which is recognized when the options are granted, is not immediately deductible for income tax purposes; thus, a deferred tax asset is created.

 Professor's Note: Stock option compensation is discussed in more detail in the topic review of FAS 123R—Accounting for Stock-Based Compensation.

For nonqualified stock options, the issuing firm receives an income tax benefit when the options are exercised. The tax benefit is equal to the employee's profit (the difference in the market price and exercise price) multiplied by the firm's tax rate. The tax benefit related to compensation expense is reported as an operating activity in the cash flow statement. The *excess* tax benefits are reported as financing activities.

 Professor's Note: The excess tax benefits are the difference in the benefits related to compensation expense and the actual tax benefits when the options are exercised.

For firms that use a lot of stock options, analysts must decide whether the increase in operating cash flow from the tax benefits is sustainable and whether the benefits are the result of improved operations. As a firm's stock price increases, the tax benefits increase which implies cash flow growth. The higher stock price may also result in more stock option awards to personnel.

The income tax benefits from stock options can provide a significant source of cash flow. Analysts must examine the financial statements and footnotes to fully understand the effects.

REPURCHASING STOCK TO OFFSET DILUTION

When a firm's stock options are exercised, shares must be issued. The higher the stock price relative to the exercise price, the more shares that must be issued by the firm. As the shares are issued, dilution of earnings per share occurs.

Firms will often repurchase stock to offset the dilutive effects of stock option compensation. The cash received from the exercise of the option and the outflow of cash from the share repurchase are both reported as financing activities in the cash flow statement. As previously discussed, the tax benefits related to the recognition of compensation expense are reported as operating activities. This results in a mismatch of classifications.

For analytical purposes, the net cash outflow to repurchase stock should be reclassified from financing activities to operating activities to better reflect the substance of the transaction.

> **Example: Reclassifying stock option cash flows to operating activities**
>
> At the beginning of the year, Dillon Manufacturing Company issued 5,000 employee stock options. Recently, 2,000 of the options were exercised. To avoid dilution, Dillon repurchased 2,000 shares at an average price of $12 per share. If the exercise price was $10 per share, calculate the net cash outflow to be reclassified as an operating activity for analytical purposes.
>
> **Answer:**
>
> | | |
> |---|---|
> | Share repurchase | $24,000 ($12 average price × 2,000 shares) |
> | Less: Proceeds from exercise | 20,000 ($10 exercise price × 2,000 options) |
> | Net cash outflow | $4,000 |
>
> According to GAAP, Dillon will report the $4,000 net cash outflow as a financing activity. By reclassifying the outflow for analytical purposes, operating cash flow is lower by $4,000, and financing cash flows are higher by the same amount.

KEY CONCEPTS

1. Firms can manipulate operating cash flow by classifying operating activities as financing activities and vice versa.
2. Stretching accounts payable by delaying payment is not a sustainable source of operating cash flow. Suppliers may refuse to extend additional credit because of the slower payments.
3. Stretching accounts payable can be identified by increases in the number of days in payables.
4. Another form of delaying cash flows associated with accounts payable is to finance the payables through a third party. This allows the firm to alter the timing of payment as well as treat the payment as a financing activity in the cash flow statement.
5. Securitizing accounts receivable accelerates the operating cash flow into the current period, but the source of cash is not sustainable. Securitizing receivables may also allow the firm to immediately recognize gains in the income statement.
6. The analyst must determine whether the income tax benefits from employee stock options provide a sustainable source of operating cash flow.
7. Some firms repurchase stock to offset the dilutive effect of employee stock options.
8. For analytical purposes, reclassify the net cash outflow to repurchase stock from financing activities to operating activities.

CONCEPT CHECKERS

1. How is decreasing accounts payable turnover *likely* to affect cash flow from financing activities, and is the source of cash sustainable?

	Financing activities	Sustainable source
A.	Increase	Yes
B.	Increase	No
C.	No impact	Yes
D.	No impact	No

2. As part of its working capital management program, Rotan Corporation has an accounts payable financing arrangement with the First National Bank. The bank pays Rotan's vendors within 30 days of the invoice date. Rotan reimburses the bank 90 days after the invoice is due. Ignoring interest, which of the following *best* describes the effect on Rotan's operating cash flow and financing cash flow when the bank is repaid?

	Operating cash flow	Financing cash flow
A.	Decrease	Increase
B.	No effect	Increase
C.	Decrease	Decrease
D.	No effect	Decrease

3. In order to generate cash, Company A securitized its accounts receivable through a special purpose entity. Company B pledged its accounts receivable to a local bank in order to secure a short-term loan. Assuming Company A and Company B are identical in all other respects, which company has higher operating cash flow and which company has higher financing cash flow?

	Higher operating cash flow	Higher financing cash flow
A.	Company A	Company A
B.	Company A	Company B
C.	Company B	Company A
D.	Company B	Company B

4. Over the past two years, a firm reported higher operating cash flow as a result of securitizing its accounts receivable and from increasing income tax benefits from employee stock options. The tax benefits are solely the result of higher tax rates. Should an analyst conclude that these two sources of operating cash flow are sustainable?

	Securitizing receivables	Stock option tax benefits
A.	Yes	Yes
B.	Yes	No
C.	No	Yes
D.	No	No

©2008 Schweser

5.   The employees of Hi-Tech Inc. are compensated with a combination of salary and stock options. To avoid dilution of earnings per share, Hi-Tech repurchases its shares as the options are exercised. Recently, 12,500 options were exercised at a price of $5 per share. The average market price of the repurchased shares was $8 per share. What amounts should Hi-Tech report in its cash flow statement that *best* reflect the substance of the stock repurchase?

	Operating activities	Financing activities
A.	$0	$37,500 outflow
B.	$37,500 outflow	$0
C.	$62,500 inflow	$100,000 outflow
D.	$100,000 outflow	$62,500 inflow

ANSWERS – CONCEPT CHECKERS

1. **D**   Decreasing accounts payable turnover saves cash by delaying payments to suppliers. The result is an operating source of cash, not a financing source. Decreasing accounts payable turnover is not a sustainable source of cash flow because suppliers may eventually refuse to extend credit because of the slower payments.

2. **D**   When the bank is repaid, the cash outflow is reported as a financing activity. Operating cash flow is not affected when payment is made.

3. **B**   The cash received from securitizing receivables is reported as an operating activity. The cash received from borrowing against accounts receivable is reported as a financing activity.

4. **D**   Accelerating operating cash flow by securitizing receivables is not sustainable because the firm only has a limited amount of accounts receivable. An increase in tax benefits as a result higher of tax rates is not sustainable. Tax rates could also decrease in the future.

5. **B**   Under GAAP, Hi-Tech will report a $37,500 net outflow of cash from financing activities [12,500 options × ($8 average price – $5 exercise price)]. However, since the options are a form of compensation, the $37,500 outflow is more appropriately classified as an operating activity.

FINANCIAL REPORTING QUALITY: RED FLAGS AND ACCOUNTING WARNING SIGNS

Study Session 7

EXAM FOCUS

Earnings quality has been in the Level 2 curriculum for years in one form or another; however, this is a brand new reading. It is a broad, qualitative overview of the topic of earnings quality. The details of how to make the appropriate adjustments to the firm's financial statements are covered in the topic review of Reading 30 at the end of this Study Session. Focus on the techniques used by firms to manipulate earnings. Also, pay attention to the different risk factors that may lead to fraudulent financial reporting.

INCENTIVES TO OVERREPORT OR UNDERREPORT EARNINGS

LOS 28.a: Describe incentives that might induce a company's management to overreport or underreport earnings.

Earnings quality refers to the conservatism of a firm's financial reporting. Quality earnings should not be confused with predictable earnings. Predictable earnings are often the result of manipulation by the firm. Firms are under pressure to show predictable earnings and earnings growth, and they respond to that pressure by using various techniques to "smooth" reported earnings.

Much judgment is involved in financial reporting, particularly in the income statement. Firms are motivated to manage earnings because of the potential benefits.

Management may be motivated to overstate net income to:

- Meet earnings expectations.
- Remain in compliance with lending covenants.
- Receive higher incentive compensation.

Managing earnings can also involve understating net income. Management may be motivated to underreport earnings to:

- Obtain trade relief.
- Negotiate favorable repayment terms from creditors on transactions that have already occurred.
- Negotiate labor union contracts.

Firms may also be motivated to manage the balance sheet. For example, by overstating assets or understating liabilities, the firm appears more solvent. Conversely, a firm might understate assets or overstate liabilities to appear less solvent in order to negotiate concessions with creditors and other interested parties. A firm may also manage its balance sheet in order to enhance its ratios. For example, lower assets will result in a higher return on assets ratio and a higher asset turnover ratio.

ACTIVITIES THAT RESULT IN LOW QUALITY EARNINGS

LOS 28.b: Describe activities that will result in a low quality of earnings.

Generally accepted accounting principles (GAAP) can be exploited by a firm to achieve a specific outcome while meeting the letter, but not the spirit, of the standards; however, earnings quality may also be affected. Low quality earnings are the result of:

- Selecting acceptable accounting principles that misrepresent the economics of a transaction. For example, a firm might choose the units-of-production method of depreciation in periods when the consumption of the asset is better measured by the straight-line or accelerated methods. If the units-of-production method results in lower depreciation than the straight-line method early in the asset's life, earnings will be front-loaded in the early years of the asset's life.
- Structuring transactions to achieve a desired outcome. For example, a firm might structure the terms of a lease to avoid capital lease recognition, resulting in lower liabilities and lower leverage.
- Using aggressive or unrealistic estimates and assumptions. For example, lengthening the lives of depreciable assets or increasing the salvage value will result in lower depreciation expense and higher earnings.
- Exploiting the intent of an accounting principle. For example, some firms have applied a narrow rule regarding unconsolidated special purposes entities (SPE) to a broad range of transactions, because leverage is lower if the firm does not consolidate the SPE. See the topic review of VIEs in Study Session 5 for more details.

 Professor's Note: When fraud is involved, the earnings are considered to be "no quality" rather than "low quality." Fraudulent accounting practices are addressed in LOS 28.c through 28.g in this topic review.

FRAUD TRIANGLE

LOS 28.c: Describe the "fraud triangle."

Users of financial information should become familiar with the risk factors and warning signs of fraud. Statement on Auditing Standards No. 99, *Consideration of Fraud in a Financial Statement Audit* (SAS No. 99), issued by the American Institute of Certified Public Accountants (AICPA), identifies three conditions that are usually present when fraud occurs. These conditions, known as the **fraud triangle**, are illustrated in Figure 1. Note that not all of these conditions need to be present for fraud to occur.

Figure 1: "Fraud Triangle"

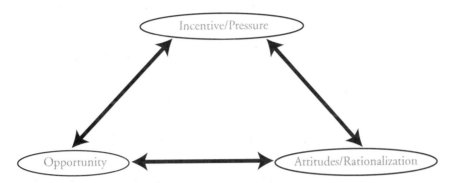

- **Incentive or pressure** is the motive that exists to commit fraud. For example, suppose a firm needs to meet earnings expectations because much of senior management's compensation is tied to the firm's stock price.
- **Opportunity** exists when there is a weakness in the internal control system.
- **Attitudes or rationalization** is a mindset that fraudulent behavior is justified. Each of these parts of the fraud triangle is discussed in the next three LOS.

INCENTIVE OR PRESSURE RISK FACTORS

LOS 28.d: Describe the risk factors related to incentives and pressures that may lead to fraudulent accounting.

SAS No. 99 identified four risk factors related to the incentives or pressures (motive) that may lead to fraudulent reporting.

1. *Threats to financial stability or profitability* as a result of economic, industry, or entity operating conditions such as:
   - Competition or market saturation, along with declining margins.
   - Vulnerability to rapid changes in technology, product obsolescence, or interest rates.
   - Declining customer demand or increasing business failures.
   - Operating losses that may result in bankruptcy, foreclosure, or a hostile takeover.
   - Recurring negative operating cash flow or inability to generate positive cash flow while reporting earnings or earnings growth.
   - Rapid growth or unusual profitability.
   - New accounting standards, laws, or regulatory requirements.

2. *Excessive third party pressures* on management from:
   - Aggressive or unrealistic profitability or trend expectations.
   - Debt or equity financing requirements in order to stay competitive.
   - Stock exchange listing requirements.
   - Debt covenants and repayment requirements.
   - Impact of real or perceived effects of poor financial performance on pending transactions such as a business acquisition.

3. *Personal net worth of management or the board of directors is threatened* because of:
   - A significant financial interest in the firm.
   - A significant amount of contingent compensation based on achieving aggressive targets such as stock price, operating profit, and cash flow. See the discussion of performance-based awards in the topic review of stock-based compensation in Study Session 6.
   - Personal guarantees of the firm's debt.

4. *Excessive pressure on management or operating personnel to meet internal financial targets*, including sales and profitability.

OPPORTUNITY RISK FACTORS

LOS 28.e: Describe the risk factors related to opportunities that may lead to fraudulent accounting.

SAS No. 99 identified four risk factors related to the opportunities to commit fraud in financial reporting.

1. The *nature of the firm's industry or operations* involve:
   - Significant related party transactions, particularly when those parties are unaudited or audited by another firm.
   - Ability to dictate terms and conditions to suppliers and customers that may result in transactions that are not at arms length.
   - Significant estimates and judgments in accounting for assets, liabilities, revenues, and expenses.
   - Unusual or complex transactions, especially near year-end, such as transactions that present "substance over form" issues.
   - Operations that exist or transactions that occur internationally where cultures and business practices may differ.
   - Bank accounts or operations located in tax-havens without clear business justification.

2. *Ineffective management monitoring* as a result of:
   - Management being dominated by a single person or small group.
   - Ineffective oversight by the board of directors or audit committee.

3. *A complex or unstable organizational structure* as evidenced by:
   - Difficulty in determining who is in control.
   - Organizational structure that involves unusual legal entities or unusual lines of authority.
   - High turnover among management, legal counsel, or board members.

4. *Deficient internal controls* that can result from:
   - Inadequate monitoring controls.
   - High turnover rates of accounting and information technology personnel.
   - Ineffective accounting and information systems.

Professor's Note: The last three factors relate to corporate governance. In firms with more effective corporate governance systems, the opportunities to commit fraud are limited. See the topic review of corporate governance in Study Session 9 for more details.

ATTITUDE AND RATIONALIZATION RISK FACTORS

LOS 28.f: Describe the risk factors related to attitudes and rationalizations that may lead to fraudulent accounting.

SAS No. 99 identified the following risk factors related to attitudes and rationalization to justify fraudulent behavior:

1. *Inappropriate ethical standards* or failure to effectively communicate or support a firm's ethical standards.

2. *Excessive participation by nonfinancial management in the selection of accounting standards* and the determination of estimates.

3. Known history or allegations of *violations of laws and regulations by management or board members.*

4. *Management's obsession with maintaining or increasing the firm's stock price or earnings trend.*

5. *Making commitments to third parties to achieve aggressive results.*

6. *Failing to correct known reportable conditions* in a timely manner.

7. *Inappropriately minimizing earnings for tax purposes.*

8. Management's continued *use of materiality as a basis to justify inappropriate accounting.*

9. *A strained relationship between management and the current or previous auditor* as evidenced by the following:
   - Frequent disputes on accounting, auditing, and reporting issues.
   - Unreasonable demands on the auditor, such as unreasonable time constraints.
   - Restricting the auditor's access to people and information.
   - Limiting the auditor's ability to effectively communicate with the board of directors and audit committee.
   - Domineering management behavior toward the auditor.

WARNING SIGNS

LOS 28.g: Describe common accounting warning signs and methods of detecting each.

Aggressive revenue recognition. The most common earnings manipulation technique is aggressively recognizing revenue; that is, recognizing revenue *too soon*. Recall from Level 1 that revenue is recognized in the income statement when it is earned and payment is assured. Usually revenue is recognized at delivery but, in some cases, revenue can be recognized before delivery takes place. Firms are required to report their revenue recognition policies in the financial statement footnotes. It is imperative for analysts to understand when revenue recognition takes place.

Some examples of aggressive recognition include:

- Bill and hold arrangements whereby revenue is recognized before the goods are shipped.
- Holding the accounting period open past year-end.
- Sales-type leases whereby the lessor recognizes a sale, and profit, at the inception of the lease, especially when the lessee does not capitalize the lease.
- Recognizing revenue before fulfilling all of the terms and conditions of sale.
- Recognizing revenue from swaps and barter transactions with third parties.

Different growth rates of operating cash flow and earnings. Over time, there should be a fairly stable relationship between the growth of operating cash flow and earnings. If not, earnings manipulation may be occurring. A firm that is reporting earnings growth, but operating cash flow is negative or declining, may be recognizing revenue too soon or delaying the recognition of expense.

The relationship of operating cash flow and earnings can be measured with the cash flow earnings index (operating cash flow/net income). An index that is consistently less than one or that is declining over time is suspect.

Abnormal sales growth as compared to the economy, industry, or peers. Abnormal growth may be the result of superior management or products, but may also indicate accounting irregularities. Receivables that are growing faster than sales [as evidenced by an increasing average collection period (days in receivables)] may be an indication of aggressive revenue recognition.

Abnormal inventory growth as compared to sales growth. Increasing inventory may be an indication of obsolete products or poor inventory management. Also, by overstating inventory, cost of goods sold is lower and thus gross profit and net profit are higher. This can be detected by looking for declines in inventory turnover.

 Professor's Note: Recall from Level 1 that ending inventory is equal to beginning inventory plus purchases minus cost of goods sold (COGS). If ending inventory is too high, COGS will be too low, all else equal.

Study Session 7

Cross-Reference to CFA Institute Assigned Reading #28 – Financial Reporting Quality: Red Flags and Accounting Warning Signs

Boosting revenue with nonoperating income and nonrecurring gains. Some firms try to reclassify nonoperating income and nonrecurring gains as revenue, in effect, moving these items "up" the income statement. Net income is the same but revenue growth is higher.

Delaying expense recognition. By capitalizing operating expenditures, the firm delays expense recognition to future periods. Watch for an increase in assets with unusual sounding names such as "deferred marketing charges" or "deferred customer acquisition costs."

Abnormal use of operating leases by lessees. Operating leases are common in most firms. However, some firms use this off-balance sheet financing technique to improve ratios and reduce perceived leverage. Analysts should compare the firm's use of leasing, as a financing source, to its industry peers. For analytical purposes, consider treating operating leases as capital leases.

Hiding expenses by classifying them as extraordinary or nonrecurring. The result is to move expenses "down" the income statement and boost income from continuing operations.

LIFO liquidations. When a LIFO firm sells more inventory than it purchases or produces, it penetrates the lower cost layers of inventory. The result is lower cost of goods sold and higher profit, although taxes are higher as well. However, the profit is not sustainable because the firm will eventually run out of inventory. A declining LIFO reserve is usually an indication of a LIFO liquidation. Firms should disclose the effects of a LIFO liquidation in the financial statement footnotes.

Abnormal gross margin and operating margin as compared to industry peers. Abnormal margins may be the result of superior management or cost controls; however, they may be an indication of accounting irregularities. Determine the firm's conservatism by comparing the firm's accounting principles, as disclosed in the footnotes, to its industry peers.

Extending the useful lives of long-term assets. Depreciating or amortizing the cost of an asset over more periods results in higher earnings. Compare the useful lives of the firm's assets with its industry peers.

Aggressive pension assumptions. Aggressive assumptions such as a high discount rate, low compensation growth rate, or high expected rate of return will result in lower pension expense and higher earnings. Compare these assumptions with industry peers.

 Professor's Note: See LOS 24.b in Study Session 6 for a discussion of the effect of changing pension assumptions on reported earnings.

Year-end surprises. Higher earnings in the fourth quarter that cannot be explained by seasonality may be an indication of manipulation.

Equity method investments with little or no cash flow. Equity method investments are not consolidated. However, the pro-rata share of the investee's earnings are included in net income. Without dividends (cash flow), these earnings are low quality. Watch for frequent use of nonconsolidated special purpose entities.

 Professor's Note: See LOS 21.d for information on the equity method, and 23.b for consolidation rules for SPEs.

Other off-balance sheet financing arrangements including debt guarantees. Firms must disclose these arrangements in the financial statement footnotes. For analytical purposes, consider adjusting the balance sheet for these arrangements.

 Professor's Note: Keep in mind that these are warning signs of low quality earnings. They are not necessarily indications that fraud has occurred or will occur.

ENRON ACCOUNTING SCANDAL: WARNING SIGNS

LOS 28.h: Describe the accounting warning signs related to the Enron accounting scandal.

A study of Enron indicates numerous warning signs to investors, analysts, and creditors. Following is a brief discussion of some of the red flags disclosed in Enron's financial statements for the fiscal year 2000.

- **Insufficient operating cash flow.** Although Enron's operating cash flow exceeded net income, certain transactions were classified as operating activities when, in substance, the transactions were more like financing activities. In addition, Enron did not generate sufficient operating cash flow to fund its investing activities. Financing activities made up the difference.
- **Pressure to support stock price and debt ratings.** If Enron's stock price declined by a certain amount, or if Enron's debt rating dropped below investment grade, additional collateral in the form of Enron stock was required by its lenders. These provisions provided an incentive for Enron to manipulate earnings in order to boost its stock price and debt ratings. We mentioned in LOS 28.a that a motivation for overreporting earnings is to remain in compliance with lending covenants.
- **Revenues reported using mark-to-market accounting.** Mark-to-market revenue accounting is allowed in very limited situations, mostly involving commodities. Enron applied this accounting method to a number of different types of contracts. In some cases, there were no established market prices to value the underlying contract; thus, market value was simply estimated by Enron. As a result, Enron could recognize revenue before the contracts were even operational.
- **Amount of revenues reported in the last half of the year.** Revenues reported in the third and fourth quarters were disproportionate with Enron's seasonal trend from previous years.
- **Inflated sales to SPEs.** Enron securitized assets and sold the securitizations at inflated values to special purposes entities. In some cases, Enron protected the SPE investors from the risks involved in the transactions.

Study Session 7

Cross-Reference to CFA Institute Assigned Reading #28 – Financial Reporting Quality: Red Flags and Accounting Warning Signs

- **Use of mark-to-market accounting for equity method investments.** Recall that equity method investments are not consolidated; rather, the pro-rata earnings of the investee are reported in net income. In some cases, Enron reported these investments at fair value.
- **Use of barter transactions.** In some cases, Enron would sell cable capacity to a party and simultaneously purchase capacity from the same party.
- **Significant use of related party transactions.** Probably the most egregious irregularities occurred using limited partnerships whereby an Enron employee served as general partner. The limited partnerships engaged in billions of dollars in derivatives transactions with Enron. The primary assets of the partnerships included receivables from Enron and Enron securities.
- **Senior management compensation and turnover.** Senior management's compensation was based mostly on bonus and stock awards. In addition, during the year 2001, several key top managers resigned.

SUNBEAM ACCOUNTING SCANDAL: WARNING SIGNS

LOS 28.i: Describe the accounting warning signs related to the Sunbeam accounting scandal.

As previously discussed in this topic review, the most common earnings manipulation technique is recognizing revenue too soon. Sunbeam Corporation's 1996 and 1997 financial statements provide an excellent case study in earnings manipulation through revenue recognition. Sunbeam was a financially distressed company and, as part of Sunbeam's turnaround, management engaged in a number of questionable transactions. Following is a brief discussion of some of the warning signs found in Sunbeam's financial statements:

- **Created "cookie jar" reserves.** As a part of its turnaround, Sunbeam recognized restructuring charges and created reserves by recognizing losses in its 1996 income statement. For example, writing-off inventory results in a loss; however, this loss turns to profit when the inventory is sold in subsequent periods.
- **Receivables increased faster than sales.** In 1997, Sunbeam's receivables increased faster than sales. Sales without collections may be an indication that both sales and receivables are poor quality.
- **Generated negative operating cash flow.** In 1997, Sunbeam reported a record level of earnings but operating cash flow was negative. The negative cash flow was primarily the result of increasing inventories and receivables.
- **Engaged in bill and hold sale arrangements.** In 1997, Sunbeam changed its revenue recognition policy and began recognizing some sales under bill and hold arrangements, whereby revenue was recognized before the goods were shipped.
- **Lowered bad debt expense.** In 1997, bad debt expense related to receivables decreased even though sales and receivables increased significantly.
- **Increased fourth quarter revenues.** The financial statement footnotes indicate that Sunbeam's products are not seasonal, yet the footnotes reveal that Sunbeam initiated an early buy program for certain products. Accordingly, the percentage of Sunbeam's total revenue was highest in the fourth quarter. The increase in fourth quarter revenue of a nonseasonal business is suspect.

KEY CONCEPTS

1. Management may be motivated to overstate or even understate its earnings.
2. Low earnings quality is the result of:
   - Selecting accounting principles that misrepresent the economics of the transaction.
   - Structuring transactions to achieve a desired outcome.
   - Using aggressive or unrealistic estimates and assumptions.
   - Exploiting the intent of an accounting principle.
3. Incentive/pressure, opportunity, and attitudes/rationalization form the fraud triangle.
4. Incentive/pressure is the motive to commit fraud.
5. Opportunities to commit fraud exist when the firm has a weak internal control system.
6. Attitude/rationalization is the mindset that fraud is justified.
7. Common warning signs of earnings manipulation include:
   - Aggressive revenue recognition.
   - Different growth rates of operating cash flow and earnings.
   - Abnormal comparative sales growth.
   - Abnormal inventory growth as compared to sales.
   - Moving nonoperating income and nonrecurring gains up the income statement to boost revenue.
   - Delaying expense recognition.
   - Excessive use of off-balance sheet financing arrangements including leases.
   - Classifying expenses as extraordinary or nonrecurring and moving them down the income statement to boost income from continuing operations.
   - LIFO liquidations.
   - Abnormal comparative margin ratios.
   - Aggressive assumptions and estimates.
   - Year-end surprises.
   - Equity method investments with little or no cash flow.

Study Session 7

Cross-Reference to CFA Institute Assigned Reading #28 – Financial Reporting Quality: Red Flags and Accounting Warning Signs

CONCEPT CHECKERS

1. Which of the following is *least likely* to be a motivation to overreport net income?
   A. Meet earnings expectations.
   B. Negotiate labor union contracts.
   C. Remain in compliance with bond covenants.
   D. Higher incentive compensation.

2. Which of the following is *least likely* to be an activity that will result in low quality earnings?
   A. Using aggressive pension assumptions.
   B. Structuring a lease transaction to avoid capitalization on the balance sheet.
   C. Booking revenue from a fictitious customer.
   D. Selecting an acceptable depreciation method that misrepresents the economics of the transaction.

3. Are motive and rationalization usually present when fraud occurs within a firm?

	Motive	Rationalization
A.	Yes	Yes
B.	Yes	No
C.	No	Yes
D.	No	No

4. Are third party pressures and a deficient internal control system motive risk factors that may lead to fraudulent accounting?

	Third party pressures	Deficient internal control system
A.	Yes	Yes
B.	Yes	No
C.	No	Yes
D.	No	No

5. According to Statement on Auditing Standards No. 99, Consideration of Fraud in a Financial Statement Audit, which of the following is *least likely* to be a risk factor related to opportunities to commit fraudulent accounting?
   A. High turnover among senior management, legal counsel, or board members.
   B. Significant related party transactions.
   C. High turnover among accounting and information systems personnel.
   D. Aggressive or unrealistic profitability expectations from third parties.

6. Are inappropriate ethical standards and frequent disputes with auditors examples of attitude and rationalization risk factors that may lead to fraudulent accounting?

	Inappropriate ethical standards	Frequent disputes with auditors
A.	Yes	Yes
B.	Yes	No
C.	No	Yes
D.	No	No

7. Which of the following actions is *least likely* to immediately increase earnings?
    A. Using aggressive pensions assumptions such as a higher discount rate.
    B. Selling more inventory than is purchased or produced.
    C. Lowering the salvage value of depreciable assets.
    D. Holding the accounting period open past year-end.

8. There were many red flags about the accounting irregularities at Enron that were disclosed in the firm's financial statement footnotes. Did Enron use bill and hold arrangements and related party transactions to manipulate its earnings?

	Bill and hold arrangements	Related party transactions
A.	Yes	Yes
B.	Yes	No
C.	No	Yes
D.	No	No

9. Which of the following actions was *not* a warning sign of potential earnings manipulation disclosed in Sunbeam's financial statement footnotes?
    A. A record level of earnings, yet operating cash flow was negative.
    B. Sales were increasing, but bad debt expense was decreasing.
    C. Higher fourth quarter revenues even though Sunbeam's products were nonseasonal.
    D. Significant use of barter transactions.

CHALLENGE PROBLEM

10. MSH Corporation manufactures high-volume copy equipment used primarily by large printing companies. In some transactions, MSH leases equipment to customers. Ignoring income taxes, what is the immediate effect on MSH's net income and total cash flow if the lease is treated as a sales-type lease as compared to an operating lease?

	Net income	Total cash flow
A.	Higher	Higher
B.	Higher	No difference
C.	Lower	Higher
D.	Lower	No difference

ANSWERS – CONCEPT CHECKERS

1. **B**   Negotiating labor union contracts would be a reason to underreport, not overreport, earnings. The other three choices are motivations to overreport earnings.

2. **C**   Booking revenue from a fictitious customer is fraud. Fraud provides no quality of earnings.

3. **A**   The fraud triangle identifies three conditions that are usually present when fraud occurs: Incentive/pressure (motive), opportunity, and attitudes/rationalization.

4. **B**   A deficient internal control system relates to the opportunity to commit fraud. It has nothing to do with incentives or pressure.

5. **D**   Unrealistic profitability expectations from third parties is a risk factor related to motive. The other choices are risk factors related to management's ability to commit fraud.

6. **A**   Inappropriate ethical standards and frequent disputes with auditors are both examples of attitude and rationalization risk factors.

7. **C**   Lowering the salvage value will result in higher depreciation expense, and thus, lower earnings. The other three choices will immediately increase earnings. A higher discount rate will reduce pension expense and increase earnings. Selling more inventory than is purchased or produced will increase revenue without increasing cost of goods sold, which will increase earnings. Holding the accounting period open past year-end is an aggressive revenue recognition method that will boost earnings.

8. **C**   Enron engaged in significant related party transactions. Bill and hold arrangements were used by Sunbeam, but not Enron.

9. **D**   Sunbeam was not involved in barter transactions. The other three choices are all warning signs related to Sunbeam's accounting scandal.

ANSWER – CHALLENGE PROBLEM

10. **B**   In a sales-type lease, all of the profit from the sale is reported up front. In an operating lease, the profit is recognized over the term of the lease. Thus, immediate net income is higher with a sales-type lease. The lease payment is the same under both methods; therefore, total cash flow is the same.

The following is a review of the Financial Statement Analysis principles designed to address the learning outcome statements set forth by CFA Institute®. This topic is also covered in:

THE LESSONS WE LEARN

EXAM FOCUS

This new topic review provides a brief discussion of the lessons learned from recent accounting scandals and how transparency should help keep analysts from repeating past mistakes. Also, accounting for derivatives used for hedging purposes is introduced. Make sure you know where the gains and losses are reported for each type of hedge.

WARM-UP: TRANSPARENCY IN FINANCIAL REPORTING

As a result of recent accounting scandals, users of financial information have called for more transparency in financial reporting. When applied to financial reporting, transparency involves disclosures that are understandable and reliable.

Generally accepted accounting principles (GAAP) require a minimum amount of disclosure, and many firms are now choosing to provide even more information than is required. Consequently, the management discussion and analysis section of the financial statements has expanded significantly in recent years.

Even though the quantity of information has increased, it is still necessary for users to evaluate the quality of information. That said, a number of important lessons have been learned from past accounting scandals.

FIRST LESSON: READ IT ALL

There is more to an annual report than just the financial statements. The financial footnotes and the management discussion and analysis (MD&A) section are where most of the detail and explanations are found.

The footnotes provide information about the firm's accounting principles, estimates, and assumptions, as well as other details. MD&A provides information about the firm's liquidity, capital resources, and results of operations. Also, some firms use this section to voluntarily provide a discussion of their critical accounting policies.

Unfortunately, there are no standards as to the format and readability of the footnotes and MD&A. This is where transparency adds value. When the footnotes and explanations are not understandable, analysts should move to a higher level of alert.

SECOND LESSON: BE SKEPTICAL

If the financial results are too good to be true, they probably are. Although there are some exceptions, be skeptical when a firm's earnings are growing faster than the industry and the economy over the long-run.

Also, earnings growth is not sustainable in the long-run without growth in operating cash flow. Over the short-run, earnings growth can be financed with debt; however, the debt markets can quickly dry up without the support of internally generated cash flow. This was one of the many problems experienced by Enron.

THIRD LESSON: EVALUATE THE DISCLOSURES

LOS 29.a: Distinguish among the various definitions of earnings (e.g., EBITDA, operating earnings, net income, etc.).

Some disclosures are required in accordance with GAAP, while other disclosures are related to pro-forma information.

Disclosures often refer to the firm's earnings or the components of earnings. In accounting jargon, the terms "earnings" and "net income" are often used synonymously. However, the terms are not necessarily the same. Thus, it is critical to understand the firm's definition of earnings.

Recall from Level 1 that a multi-step income statement includes subtotals. Each subtotal can be considered a measure of earnings. Following are some common earnings measures.

- **Earnings before interest, taxes, depreciation, and amortization** (EBITDA). EBITDA is often used as a proxy for operating cash flow although it is still an earnings based measure. EBITDA does not consider the changes in operating accounts on the balance sheet and is subject to the many estimates and judgments involved with accrual accounting.

 Professor's Note: In LOS 47.i in Study Session 12, you are required to critique the use of EBITDA as a proxy for cash flow.

- **Operating earnings** or **earnings before interest and taxes** (EBIT). EBIT is often referred to as operating income, or operating profit. It excludes the effects of financing and taxes.
- **Income from continuing operations.** This subtotal is equal to the firm's earnings before any "below the line" items are considered. Recall from Level 1 that discontinued operations and extraordinary items are reported "below the line," net

of tax. Without any "below the line" items, income from continuing operations and net income would be the same.

Professor's Note: The cumulative effect of a change in accounting principle is no longer reported "below the line" in the income statement. A change in accounting principle is now reported retrospectively in accordance with SFAS No. 154, "Accounting Changes and Error Corrections." Accordingly, all of the prior period financial statements presented are restated to reflect the change.

Net income. Net income is the bottom line of the income statement. Net income includes all revenues, expenses, gains, losses, and "below the line" items.

In pro-forma disclosures, some firms have created their own measures of income (usually called pro-forma earnings) whereby they strip away certain nonoperating and nonrecurring transactions. For example, a firm might remove a restructuring charge from pro-forma earnings, treating the charge as nonrecurring. In some firms, however, restructuring charges seem to continue to occur every few years. Therefore, it is necessary to examine the footnotes and other disclosures in order to evaluate whether these transactions should be removed for analytical purposes.

FOURTH LESSON: CHECK FOR CASH FLOW

LOS 29.b: Illustrate how trends in cash flow from operations can be more reliable than earnings trends.

Operating cash flow is generally more reliable than earnings because it is less subject to estimates and judgments. However, over time there should be a fairly stable relationship between the growth of operating cash flow and earnings. If not, the firm may be engaging in earnings manipulation. Also, earnings growth is not sustainable without the support of operating cash flow over the long-run.

In the case of Enron, there were wide differences in operating cash flow and operating income. Operating cash flow was often negative while operating income was positive. Also, earnings growth significantly exceeded the growth in operating cash flow.

Professor's Note: For the warning signs related to the Enron accounting scandal, see LOS 28.h in the previous topic review.

FIFTH LESSON: UNDERSTAND THE RISKS

LOS 29.c: Provide a simplified description of the accounting treatment for derivatives being used: to hedge exposure to changes in the value of assets and liabilities; to hedge exposure to variable cash flow; and to hedge a foreign currency exposure of an investment in a foreign corporation.

Firms face a multitude of business and financial risks. Analysts must be able to identify the risks and understand how the firm manages the risks. Of course, not all firms face the same risks, but some of the more common risks include:

- Interest rate risk.
- Foreign exchange risk.
- Accounts receivable risk.
- Price risk of raw materials and other inputs.

Firms often use derivatives to manage these risks. Generally, these transactions involve some type of hedge whereby the firm will use the fair values or cash flows from derivative instruments to offset the changes in fair values or cash flows of the at-risk assets or liabilities.

Derivatives are reported on the balance sheet at fair value. If the firm is using a derivative to speculate, all gains and losses (both realized and unrealized) from the derivative are recognized in the income statement. If the derivative is used for hedging purposes, gain or loss recognition depends on the type of hedge (fair value, cash flow, and net investment of a foreign subsidiary).

- **Fair value hedge.** In a fair value hedge, the firm uses derivatives to hedge exposure to changes in the fair value of recognized assets or liabilities. For example, a firm might use a put option to hedge an equity investment. If perfectly hedged, the gain or loss on the derivative will exactly offset the gain or loss of the hedged asset or liability. The firm reports both the derivative and the hedged asset or liability on the balance sheet at fair value. In addition, the unrealized gains and losses from the derivative and from the hedged asset or liability are recognized in the income statement.
- **Cash flow hedge.** In a cash flow hedge, the firm uses derivatives to hedge exposure to variable cash flows. For example, a firm might use a forward contract to hedge the future cash flows of an anticipated transaction. Like a fair value hedge, the firm reports the derivative instrument at fair value on the balance sheet. However, the unrealized gains and losses from the derivative bypass the income statement and are reported in shareholders' equity as a part of other comprehensive income. The accumulated gains and losses are eventually recognized in the income statement when the anticipated transaction affects earnings.
- **Net investment hedge of a foreign subsidiary.** A firm with a foreign subsidiary may enter into foreign exchange contracts and other transactions in order to offset the effects of fluctuating foreign currency on its net investment in the subsidiary. The gains and losses from the foreign currency transactions bypass the income statement and are reported in shareholders' equity as a part of other comprehensive income. This treatment offsets the gain or loss recognition in equity from translating the financial statements of the foreign subsidiary using the all-current method.

 Professor's Note: If the foreign subsidiary's financial statements are remeasured using the temporal method, the gains and losses from the hedge are recognized in the income statement along with the remeasurement gains and losses. The all-current method and the temporal method are covered in the topic review on the analysis of multinational operations in Study Session 6.

The three types of hedges are summarized in Figure 1.

Figure 1: Summary of Hedge Types

	Purpose	*Recognition*
Fair value hedge	Offset exposure to changes in fair value of an asset or liability.	Gains and losses are recognized in the income statement.
Cash flow hedge	Offset exposure to variable cash flows from anticipated transactions.	Gains and losses are reported in equity. The gains and losses are eventually recognized in the income statement once the anticipated transaction affects earnings.
Net investment hedge of a foreign subsidiary	Offset exposure from an existing investment in a foreign subsidiary.	Gains and losses are recognized in equity along with translation gains and losses.

An effective hedge is one in which the change in fair value, cash flow, or net investment is exactly offset by changes in the hedging instrument. If the change in the hedging instrument is more or less than the change in value, cash flow, or net investment, the "extra" change is referred to as the portion of the hedge that is not effective.

In all three hedge types, any portion of the hedge that is not effective is recognized in the income statement.

KEY CONCEPTS

1. It is critical to understand the firm's definition of earnings:
   - EBITDA is not an appropriate proxy for cash flow.
   - Operating earnings are also referred to as EBIT, operating income, and operating profit.
   - Income from continuing operations is earnings before extraordinary and nonrecurring items.
2. It is necessary to examine the footnotes and other disclosures in order to evaluate whether nonoperating and nonrecurring transactions should be removed for analytical purposes.
3. Over time, there should be a fairly stable relationship between the growth of operating cash flow and earnings. Earnings growth is not sustainable without the support of operating cash flow growth over the long-run.
4. Firms often use derivatives to manage risk.
5. In a fair value hedge, the gains and losses from the derivative and from the hedged asset or liability are recognized in the income statement.
6. In a cash flow hedge, the gains and losses from the derivative bypass the income statement and are reported in shareholders' equity.
7. In a net investment hedge of a foreign subsidiary, the gains and losses are recognized in equity along with the translation gains and losses.

CONCEPT CHECKERS

1. Which of the following statements about earnings before interest, taxes, depreciation, and amortization (EBITDA) is *least accurate*?
    A. It is sometimes used as a proxy for operating cash flow.
    B. It is an earnings based measure.
    C. It is calculated without regard to working capital changes on the balance sheet.
    D. It is based on the cash basis of accounting.

2. BHG Corporation provides goods and services to its customers on credit. Customer payments are due 30 days from invoice date. Ignoring taxes, what is the *likely* impact on net income and operating cash flow if BHG recognizes revenue too soon?

	Net income	Operating cash flow
A.	Higher	No effect
B.	Higher	Higher
C.	No effect	No effect
D.	No effect	Higher

CHALLENGE PROBLEMS

3. At the beginning of this year, KSG Company issued a $10 million, 8% coupon bond maturing in five years. KSG is concerned that if interest rates decrease, the fair value of its liability will increase. Consequently, KSG enters into an interest rate swap whereby it will receive payments at a fixed rate and make payments at a floating rate. KSG designates the swap as a fair value hedge. If interest rates decline at the end of the year, is the holding gain from the swap recognized in net income and other comprehensive income?

	Net income	Other comprehensive income
A.	Yes	Yes
B.	Yes	No
C.	No	Yes
D.	No	No

4. RGH Corporation is a coffee distributor. Next year, RGH anticipates purchasing 100 tons of coffee beans. Concerned that coffee bean prices will increase next year, RGH immediately purchases a futures contract and designates the contract as a cash flow hedge. At the end of this year, the price of coffee beans is higher than today. Next year, when the contract is settled, the price of coffee beans has increased even more. If all of the coffee beans are consumed next year, where in the financial statements are the gains on the futures contract recognized this year and next year?

	This year	Next year
A.	Net income	Other comprehensive income
B.	Net income	Net income
C.	Other comprehensive income	Net income
D.	Other comprehensive income	Other comprehensive income

5.   Frankfurt Company, located in Germany, is a wholly owned subsidiary of New
        York Company. New York uses the all-current method to translate the financial
        statements of Frankfurt into U.S dollars. New York wants to hedge its net asset
        position in Frankfurt by issuing euro denominated bonds. If the hedge is
        effective, would a gain on the bond hedge be recognized in New York's income
        statement and as a direct adjustment to New York's equity?

Income statement	Direct adjustment to equity
A. Yes	Yes
B. Yes	No
C. No	Yes
D. No	No

ANSWERS – CONCEPT CHECKERS

1. **D** EBITDA is a measure of earnings that is based on the accrual method of accounting. The other choices are correct.

2. **A** Recognizing revenue too soon will result in higher net income. Operating cash flow is only affected when payments are received. Net income will increase by the amount of the revenue increase (because we're ignoring the income tax impact), but accounts receivable will increase by the same amount. Operating cash flow is equal to net income plus noncash charges plus increases in working capital, so the two effects will offset each other and operating cash flow won't change.

ANSWERS – CHALLENGE PROBLEMS

3. **B** Since the swap was designated as a fair value hedge, the holding gain on the swap is recognized in net income. Other comprehensive income is not affected.

4. **C** Since the futures contract is designated as a cash flow hedge the unrealized gain at the end of this year is reported in shareholders' equity as a component of other comprehensive income. All of the gains from the futures contract are recognized in net income next year when the coffee beans are consumed.

5. **C** Since New York uses the all-current method to translate the financial statements of Frankfurt, the gains and losses from effective foreign currency hedges bypass the income statement and are reported in shareholders' equity as a part of other comprehensive income.

ANALYSIS OF FINANCIAL STATEMENTS: A SYNTHESIS

Study Session 7

EXAM FOCUS

This is a key topic review in Study Session 7, and perhaps in all of the financial statement analysis material. Here you put everything together by making the appropriate adjustments to the balance sheet and computing normal operating earnings and comprehensive income, based on your analysis of management's choice of accounting methods and assumptions. Make sure you can determine and interpret the effects of these choices on the reported financial results and ratios.

BALANCE SHEET ADJUSTMENTS

LOS 30.a: Analyze and evaluate the balance sheet for assets and liabilities that are not recorded, and for assets and liabilities for which the amounts shown on the balance sheet differ from their current values.

Professor's Note: A detailed example of financial statement adjustments is the best way to address all of the LOS presented in this topic review. For illustration purposes, we will use the J.C. Penney Company 10-K[1] (JCPenney) reports from 2006. The adjustments and the adjusted financial statements are presented with the original financial data in Figures 1, 2, and 3 of this topic review. Please note that some of the data used in the calculation of adjustments are taken from the actual 10-K but are not otherwise presented separately in Figures 1, 2, and 3.

Two problems are commonly encountered in the analysis of a firm's balance sheet: (1) some assets and liabilities are not recorded, and (2) the book values of the assets and liabilities may differ significantly from their market values. Recall that when adjusting financial statements, an analyst is attempting to more accurately represent the underlying economic condition of the firm.

Professor's Note: As you are making adjustments to the balance sheet, remember that assets equals liabilities plus equity. The balance sheet has to balance after you make the adjustments, so your entries have to offset each other. For example, if you increase an asset account, you have to increase liabilities and/or equity by the same amount.

---

1. http://www.sec.gov/Archives/edgar/data/1166126/000095013407007548/ d44721e10vk.htm (August 2007)

ADJUSTMENTS FOR UNRECORDED ITEMS

Variable Interest Entity

Special purpose entities (SPEs) were discussed in the topic review of variable interest entities in Study Session 5. Recall that companies create SPEs to move assets and liabilities off the balance sheet into an SPE, which is a separate legal entity created for a specific purpose, such as to securitize loans or purchase receivables. In 2003, U.S. accounting standards were changed by defining a specific type of SPE called a variable interest entity (VIE) and making VIEs subject to consolidation and additional disclosure requirements.

The appropriate adjustment for SPEs that are not consolidated is to increase the current and/or long-term assets and liabilities of the primary beneficiary by the amount of the current and/or long-term assets and liabilities held in the SPE. The effect is to increase the reported leverage of the primary beneficiary since liabilities increase but equity does not change.

JCPenney is not a party to any off-balance sheet or special purpose entity; thus, no adjustment is required.

Adjustment #1: Leases

Financial leases result in a capitalized asset and liability, whereas operating leases require only footnote disclosure of rental commitments. The existence of operating leases is essentially off-balance sheet financing. To adjust the balance sheet for operating leases (i.e., capitalize them), increase the assets and liabilities by the present value of the lease payments. This results in higher leverage and lower asset turnover. The interest rate in this present value computation is the lower of the firm's financing rate or the interest rate that is implicit in the lease.

JCPenney's future minimum operating lease payments total $1,948 million and the present value is $944 million discounted at a weighted-average interest rate of 7.9%. Thus, we will increase both long-term assets and long-term liabilities by this amount (adjustment #1).

Adjustment #2: Guarantees, Commitments, and Contingencies

Guarantees and commitments represent liabilities that are not reported on the balance sheet. The analyst should adjust the balance sheet by adding the present value of the transaction to both assets and liabilities if sufficient information is available in the footnotes.

JCPenney has entered into a number of off-balance sheet purchase agreements for exclusive merchandise, fixtures, royalty obligations, and obligations for professional services, energy services, and software maintenance and network services. JCPenney's contractual obligations total $317 million. We will increase current assets and current liabilities by the estimated present value of $285 million (adjustment #2).

Next, we will consider the contingencies that are reported in the financial statement footnotes. Recall from Level 1, if a liability is probable and can be reasonably estimated, it must be reported on the balance sheet. Since judgment is involved in applying these criteria, the analyst must be aware of the potential to keep liabilities off the balance sheet.

JCPenney discloses a number of legal and governmental proceedings involving insurance products offered by a former subsidiary, environmental considerations, and guarantees. JCPenney indicates that reserves have been established as appropriate and the potential exposure would not have a material effect on the firm's financial statements. Without more information about the specific facts of the contingencies, no adjustment is justified.

ADJUSTMENTS FOR RECORDED ITEMS

LOS 30.b: Analyze and evaluate the balance sheet for the current value of assets and liabilities.

Cash and Equivalents

JCPenney's cash and equivalents consist of highly liquid debt instruments, eurodollar time deposits, and money market funds with original maturities of three months or less. No adjustment is necessary since the carrying value approximates fair value.

Accounts Receivable

Accounts receivable are reported on the balance sheet at net realizable value; that is, the firm's estimate of collectibility. JCPenney did not separately disclose its allowance for doubtful accounts. However, JCPenney reports no significant concentrations of credit risk. Without more information, no adjustment is warranted.

JCPenney does not sell receivables to enhance liquidity. If JCPenney did sell its receivables "with recourse," we would adjust the balance sheet by adding the receivables sold back to current assets and increasing current liabilities by the amount received from the receivable sale. In addition, the proceeds received from the sale should be reclassified from operating cash flow to financing cash flow.

Adjustment #3: Inventories

Under the **first-in, first-out** (FIFO) inventory cost flow assumption, the first costs incurred (beginning inventory and early purchases) are assigned to cost of goods sold (COGS) for the period, and the most recently incurred costs are assigned to ending inventory. Therefore, the FIFO measure of inventory amount on the balance sheet is a good approximation of the current cost of the inventory, but FIFO understates COGS reported in the income statement in an inflationary environment.

Under the **last-in, first-out** (LIFO) method, the most recently incurred costs are assigned to COGS, and the costs of beginning inventory and earlier purchases are assigned to ending inventory. In an inflationary environment, LIFO inventory understates the current cost of the inventory but LIFO COGS is a good approximation of current cost. The LIFO reserve is the difference between the LIFO and FIFO inventory values and is required disclosure in the footnotes.

For analytical purposes, FIFO is preferred on the balance sheet since FIFO is a better approximation of replacement cost. The appropriate balance sheet adjustment is to add the LIFO reserve to inventory and shareholders' equity.

JCPenney accounts for inventory using LIFO. As of February 3, 2007, the LIFO reserve was $8 million. Therefore, we add $8 million to inventory and shareholders' equity (adjustment #3).

Property, Plant, and Equipment

The mark-to-market of non-financial assets such as real estate and equipment should be performed if fair value can be reasonably estimated. Unfortunately, fair value is rarely made available. In some cases, the analyst can extrapolate fair value using gains (difference in cost and market value) of recent transactions. For example, suppose a timberland firm reports recurring gains from land sales. These gains could be used to estimate the fair value of the remaining property.

The fair value of JCPenney's property and equipment (P&E) is unknown. The firm reports its P&E at cost and uses straight-line depreciation. P&E is periodically tested for impairment. Accordingly, JCPenney recognized impairment losses totaling $2 million in 2006 and $7 million in 2005. Without additional disclosure, there is no basis for further adjustment to P&E.

Intangible Assets including Goodwill

Goodwill is recorded on the balance sheet as a result of applying the purchase method of accounting to acquisitions. Goodwill has no separate value apart from the firm. Therefore, goodwill should be eliminated by reducing assets and shareholders' equity for analytical purposes. All of JCPenney's goodwill was written-off during 2004. Therefore, no goodwill remains on its balance sheet.

U.S. GAAP does not permit the upward revaluation of intangible assets, so the carrying value of intangible assets may not reflect the assets' economic value. For analytical purposes, it may be beneficial to revalue the intangible assets to reflect fair value. No fair value data is made available for JCPenney's intangible assets; thus, no adjustment is made.

Adjustment #4: Long-Term Debt

For purposes of analysis, market values of long-term debt are more appropriate than book values. If long-term debt is adjusted to fair value, the appropriate offsetting entry is to shareholders' equity. For example, firms that issue debt when interest rates are low are relatively better off when interest rates increase, and this increase should be reflected in a higher value of equity and a lower value of debt.

If interest rates rise, the firm's debt is adjusted downward to market value with an offsetting increase to equity. The adjusted balance sheet liability now represents the amount that must be paid to retire the debt. As a result, the adjusted debt-to-equity ratio at current market values is lower (lower numerator and higher denominator). If interest rates decline, the opposite effects will occur from adjusting debt upward to its fair value.

Both U.S. and IAS GAAP require disclosures about the fair value of outstanding debt based on year-end or quarter-end prices. These disclosures are made in the notes to the financial statements.

On February 3, 2007, the fair value of JCPenney's outstanding long-term debt, excluding capital leases and equipment financing, was $3.6 billion. Long-term debt was reported on the balance sheet at $3.4 billion. Therefore, we need to adjust long-term debt upward by $200 million (adjustment #4). JCPenney has no convertible debt or preferred stock outstanding, so no other debt adjustments are necessary.

Pensions

Pension accounting may affect several items on the balance sheet. The most likely items affected are prepaid pension cost (an asset) and/or accrued pension cost (a liability). The appropriate balance sheet adjustment is to replace the net pension asset or liability with the actual economic status of the plan (the funded status). The offsetting entries are to equity and deferred taxes as follows:

- An increase in a pension liability (or decrease in a pension asset) will result in an offsetting declines in equity and deferred tax liabilities.
- A decrease in a pension liability (or increase in a pension asset) will result in an offsetting increases to equity and deferred tax liabilities.

 Professor's Note: For more detail on the appropriate pension adjustments, see the topic review on pension accounting in Study Session 6.

As of February 3, 2007, JCPenney adopted the provisions of SFAS No. 158, "Employers Accounting for Defined Benefit Pension and Other Postretirement Benefit Plans" whereby the funded status of the pension and other postretirement benefit plans are recognized on the balance sheet. As a result of the implementation of SFAS No. 158, JCPenney's assets decreased $525 million, liabilities decreased $291 million, and equity decreased $234 million. No further adjustment is required for the most recent balance sheet. However, JCPenney did not retroactively restate the prior balance sheets. Therefore, it will still be necessary to make the pension adjustment to the prior balance sheets for comparison purposes.

Stock-Option Plans

When considering the balance sheet impact of option-based compensation plans, recall that there are only rare exceptions that merit adjustments. Recognition of these contracts may affect assets, primarily deferred taxes. The more important issue is the impact on net income as stock option compensation is expensed in the income statement. See the topic review of stock-based compensation in Study Session 6 for a complete discussion.

Adjustment #5: Deferred Income Taxes

Deferred tax liabilities may be treated in one of two ways by the analyst:

- If the liabilities are likely to be reversed in the future, they should be discounted to present value and treated as liabilities. The difference between the reported value and the present value should be reclassified as equity. The adjustment would cause a decrease in the debt-to-equity ratio (lower numerator and higher denominator).
- If the liabilities are unlikely to reverse, they should be treated as equity (without discounting). This adjustment would lower the debt-to-equity ratio, sometimes significantly.

Deferred tax assets that are unlikely to be reversed are offset by a valuation allowance, which effectively reduces equity. Increases in the valuation allowance increase the debt-to-equity ratio (lower denominator).

JCPenney's net deferred tax liabilities have been volatile over the past five years (data not presented). This volatility has resulted primarily from pension and other retiree benefits, discontinued operations, depreciation, and leveraged leases.

JCPenney expects to open more stores in the future. This would suggest that deferred tax liabilities may not reverse as property and equipment increase. Therefore, we will assume zero net deferred tax liabilities on the adjusted balance sheet and increase equity $1,206 million (adjustment #5).

Some firms do not make tax provisions for undistributed earnings of certain foreign subsidiaries if the earnings are considered permanently reinvested. If the analyst feels that the earnings are likely to be repatriated, liabilities would be increased to reflect the taxes associated with the foreign subsidiary's income.

Accumulated Other Comprehensive Income

In addition to all of the adjustments we have already made to shareholders' equity, it may be necessary to adjust the accumulated other comprehensive income account. This account may show a gain or loss. Specifically, this account contains transactions related to minimum pension liability, unrealized gains and losses from available-for-sale securities, deferred hedging gains and losses, and the cumulative translation adjustment of a foreign subsidiary.

For the year ended February 3, 2007, JCPenney reported an accumulated other comprehensive loss of $176 million. The loss is primarily the result of the implementation of SFAS No. 158 whereby the funded status of the JCPenney's pension and other postretirement benefit plans were recognized on the balance sheet.

Professor's Note: If the analyst decides to remove the accumulated other comprehensive income account from the balance sheet, the appropriate offsetting adjustments are to the asset and liability accounts affected by the specific items that make up the comprehensive income account. To identify each specific offsetting adjustment would require more time and effort than is necessary for the Level 2 exam.

©2008 Schweser

Another way to look at the accumulated other comprehensive income account is that it makes the balance sheet equation balance. If the accumulated other comprehensive income account is removed, an equity adjustment may be necessary to force the balance sheet equation to balance.

Adjusted Balance Sheet

JCPenney's reported and adjusted balance sheets are presented in Figure 1.

Figure 1: JCPenney 2006 Consolidated Balance Sheet with Adjustments

As of February 3, 2007	Reported	Adjustments	Adjusted
(in millions of dollars)			
Assets			
Current assets:			
Cash and cash equivalents	$2,747		$2,747
Accounts receivable	263		263
Merchandise inventories *(adjustment #3)*	3,400	8	3,408
Prepaid expenses and other *(adjustment #2)*	238	285	523
Total current assets	6,648		6,941
Property and equipment, net *(adjustment #1)*	4,162	944	5,106
Prepaid pension	1,235		1,235
Other assets	628		628
Total Assets	**$12,673**		**$13,910**
Liabilities and Stockholders' Equity			
Current liabilities:			
Trade payables	$1,366		$1,366
Other current liabilities *(adjustment #2)*	1,692	285	1,977
Current maturities of long-term debt	434		434
Total current liabilities	3,492		3,777
Long-term debt *(adjustment #4)*	3,010	200	3,210
Capital leases *(adjustment #1)*	-	944	944
Deferred income taxes *(adjustment #5)*	1,206	(1,206)	-
Other liabilities	677		677
Total Liabilities	**8,385**		**8,608**
Shareholders' Equity			
Common stock	112		112
Additional paid-in capital	3,430		3,430
Reinvested earnings	922		922
Accumulated other comprehensive income (loss)	(176)		(176)
LIFO Inventory (adjustment #3)	-	8	8
FV of Long-term debt (adjustment #4)	-	(200)	(200)
Eliminate Deferred tax liability (adjustment #5)	-	1,206	1,206
Total Stockholders' Equity	**4,288**		**5,302**
Total Liabilities and Stockholders' Equity	**$12,673**		**$13,910**

INCOME STATEMENT ADJUSTMENTS

LOS 30.c: Compute a company's normal operating earnings and comprehensive income.

The goal of financial statement analysis is to restate the reported results to reflect the economic character of the firm's operations. In the case of the income statement, this means that the analyst wants to determine the **earning power** of the firm. The earning power of the firm is the income that results from ongoing operations. That is, the earning power is the income of the firm without all the noise that is included in most income statements (e.g., differences due to accounting changes, one-time charges, and restructurings). It is the job of the financial analyst to filter out the noise inherent in net income and restate income in terms of earning power. This process is called normalization and the result is called **normal operating earnings**.

 Professor's Note: In our topic review of price multiples in Study Session 12, normal operating earnings are referred to as underlying earnings.

Examples of nonrecurring items reported in net income that may require adjustment include:

- Discretionary accounting changes (inventory, depreciation, pension plan assumptions, capitalized versus expensed items).
- Regulated accounting changes (impairment, derivatives).
- Realized capital gains/losses.
- Gains/losses on the repurchase of debt.
- Catastrophes such as natural disasters or accidents.
- Insurance settlements.
- Strikes.
- Impairment or restructuring charges.
- Litigation or government actions.
- Discontinued operations.

Some of these items are included in the income statement as separate line items. Other items require the analyst to glean the information from the financial statement footnotes or from management's discussion and analysis. The analyst must be alert for (1) whether items are reported on a pre-tax or after-tax basis and (2) changes made on other statements that need corresponding changes on the income statement as well. Once earnings are normalized, they can be used to discern trends in operating income and valuation.

Income normalization of non-U.S. firms is somewhat complicated by varied accounting treatments, including different inventory accounting methods (FIFO is more common outside the United States), use of capitalization versus expensing, different lease accounting rules, and different depreciation methods. Nevertheless, income needs to be normalized for comparability purposes.

A REVIEW OF NECESSARY ADJUSTMENTS TO NET INCOME

At Level 1 you mastered a number of adjustments to net income related to important accounting issues with the intent of estimating normal operating earnings. The following section reviews two of the most important adjustments that you should be aware of and be able to implement on exam day.

Adjusting FIFO COGS to LIFO

As we discussed earlier in this topic review, LIFO will provide the most useful estimate of current cost COGS; FIFO understates COGS in an inflationary environment. Therefore, the appropriate adjustment for firms that use FIFO is to adjust reported COGS to reflect LIFO.

Use the following formula to convert FIFO COGS to LIFO COGS:

LIFO COGS = FIFO COGS + (beginning FIFO inventory × inflation rate)

The inflation rate should be an inflation rate appropriate for that firm or industry, not a general inflation rate for the economy. It can be determined by two methods:

1. Industry statistics.

2. The increase in the LIFO reserve for a similar firm in the same industry divided by that firm's beginning inventory level converted to a FIFO basis.

Declining LIFO Reserve

The preceding analysis assumed that prices and inventory were stable or rising. Stable or rising prices and stable or increasing inventory quantities are a typical situation for a business. In these cases, the LIFO reserve will not decline (the LIFO reserve is the difference between the value of the inventory under FIFO and the value under LIFO). However, the LIFO reserve will decline if either the inventory balance or prices are falling.

- *Declining inventory quantity.* A LIFO liquidation refers to a declining inventory balance for a company using LIFO (sales exceed production for the period; thus, ending inventory is less than beginning inventory). In this case, COGS does not reflect current cost and can be many years out of date. This would make COGS appear lower and gross profit and net profit to be artificially high. An analyst must adjust COGS and pre-tax income for the decline in the LIFO reserve that is caused by the decline in inventory quantity. This amount is typically listed in the footnotes of the financial statements.
- *Declining prices.* If prices decline, the difference in the values of inventory and COGS under LIFO and FIFO are opposite of what was stated earlier. Specifically:
  - If prices are declining, the value of inventory under FIFO will be lower than the value of inventory under LIFO (most recently purchased goods have a lower value relative to goods purchased earlier).
  - If prices are declining, the COGS under LIFO will be lower than the COGS under FIFO.

However, even when prices decline, FIFO still provides a more accurate estimate of the economic value of inventory, and LIFO still provides a more accurate estimate of the economic COGS. The decline in the LIFO reserve does not have to be adjusted if it occurs because of a price decline.

Capitalizing Operating Leases

Let's briefly discuss the difference between an operating lease and a capital lease from the point of view of the lessee (the company that pays to use the asset). The company must classify a lease as a capital lease if it meets any of four criteria (the specific criteria are not part of the Level 2 curriculum, so you don't need to worry about it). A lease not meeting any of the criteria is classified as an operating lease.

Accounting for an operating lease (by the lessee) is relatively straightforward. At the inception of the lease, no entry is made. During the term of the lease, rent expense (the lease payment) is charged to income and to cash flow from operations. Footnote disclosure of the lease payments in total and for each of the next five fiscal years is required.

Accounting for a capital lease is somewhat more complicated. At the inception of the lease, the present value of the minimum lease payments is recognized as an asset and as a liability on the lessee's balance sheet. During the term of the lease, the lessee recognizes depreciation expense on the asset and interest expense on the liability. The interest expense is equal to the lease liability at the beginning of the period multiplied by the interest rate. Depreciation expense is recognized over the term of the lease unless title is transferred at the end of the lease or there is a bargain purchase option. In the case of a title transfer or bargain purchase option, the leased asset is depreciated over its useful life.

The lease payment is separated into interest expense and principal payment on the lease liability (the lease payment less the interest expense).

- Cash flow from operations is reduced by the interest expense and cash flow from financing is reduced by the principal payment on the lease liability.
- All else held constant, operating income will be higher for companies that use capital leases relative to companies that use operating leases. This is because the interest expense for a capital lease is not included in the calculation of operating income. Under operating leases, the entire rental payment is subtracted in arriving at operating income.

Total expense over the life of the lease will be the same for operating and capital leases because the sum of the depreciation and interest expense will equal the total of the lease payments. Although the lease payments and depreciation are constant, the interest expense is higher in the early years (this behavior of interest expense is typical of an amortizing loan) and lower in the later years of the lease. Consequently, net income in the early years of the lease will be lower for firms with capital leases because the sum of depreciation and interest expense exceeds the lease payment. In the later years, the reverse is true; net income will be higher for firms with capital leases.

Making the appropriate adjustment to capitalize operating leases for firms that consistently use operating leases will:

- Increase interest expense and depreciation expense.
- Increase operating income.
- Decrease net income in the early years.

CALCULATING NORMALIZED INCOME

Figure 2 contains the adjustments and calculations for JCPenney's normalized income. Notice that in calculating normalized income, we are eliminating nonrecurring transactions that increased net income by subtracting them from reported net income and transactions that originally decreased net income are added back to reported net income.

Figure 2: JCPenney's Normalized Income

For the fiscal year ended	2006	2005	2004
(in millions of dollars)			
Reported net income	$1,153	$1,088	$524
Items reported pretax			
LIFO credit	(16)	(1)	(18)
Impairment losses and other closing costs	4	12	19
Management transition costs	7	-	29
Debt retirement charges	-	18	47
Net gains on asset sales	(8)	(27)	(8)
Total pretax adjustments	(13)	2	69
Effective tax rate	36.7%	32.3%	34.6%
After-tax adjustments	(8)	1	45
Items reported after tax			
Stock-based compensation	-	-	(11)
Release of income tax reserves	(32)	-	-
Discontinued operations	(19)	(111)	133
Total adjustments	(51)	(111)	122
Combined total adjustments	(59)	(110)	167
Normalized income	$1,094	$978	$691
Percent of unadjusted income	95%	90%	132%

In both cases, JCPenney's reported net income and normalized income have increased since 2004. However, normalization resulted in a smoother income measure over the three year period. As compared to reported net income, normalized income was only 5% lower in 2006. However, normalized income was 10% lower than reported income in 2005 and 32% higher than reported income in 2004. The differences in normalized income are primarily the result of eliminating the gains and losses from discontinued operations.

Comprehensive income is an income measure that includes all changes in equity (other than owner contributions and distributions). That is, comprehensive income is an income measure that aggregates all the valuation changes to assets and liabilities in a component of shareholders' equity. A few of the more common transactions reported as direct adjustments to equity include:

- Funded pension status in accordance with SFAS No. 158 (see the topic review of pensions in Study Session 6).
- Unrealized gains and losses from available-for-sale securities in accordance with SFAS No. 115 (see the topic review of intercorporate investments in Study Session 5).
- Cumulative foreign currency translation adjustments related to SFAS No. 52 (see the topic review of analysis of multinational operations in Study Session 6).

JCPenney's reported comprehensive income is presented in Figure 3. Note all of these adjustments are reported on the balance sheet as "accumulated other comprehensive income (loss)." The largest component in 2006 was the adoption of the provisions of SFAS No. 158, which required the firm to recognize the funded status of its defined benefit pension and postretirement plans directly to the balance sheet.

Figure 3: JCPenney's Components of Comprehensive Income

For the fiscal year ended	2006	2005	2004
(in millions of dollars)			
Net income	$1,153	$1,088	$524
Unrealized gain on investments	48	44	14
Minimum pension liability	(6)	-	(20)
Reclassification for currency translation loss	-	83	-
Other comprehensive income from discontinued operations	-	21	12
Application of SFAS No. 158	(234)	-	-
Comprehensive income	$961	$1,236	$530

While comprehensive income is an interesting concept, the focus of the analyst is on measuring the future earning power of a firm. Comprehensive income is inherently volatile because of its dependent relationship with valuation changes and, as such, it is not a reliable measure of the firm's earning power. Moreover, the comprehensive income adjustments prescribed by U.S. GAAP do not include many of the adjustments we have discussed so far. These include adjustments:

- From FIFO COGS to LIFO COGS in the income statement.
- To capitalize operating leases.
- To deferred tax assets and liabilities.
- For marking-to-market long-term assets.
- For marking-to-market long-term debt.
- For capitalized interest.
- For other off-sheet transactions (e.g., purchase commitments).
- For pension plan funded status prior to the issuance of SFAS No. 158.

An expanded version of the comprehensive income measure for JCPenney, which includes a number of these adjustments, is provided in Figure 4. The adjustment to long-term debt is found in Figure 4. The deferred tax adjustment is in the Income Tax footnote of JCPenney's 2006 10-K (detail not shown). On the exam, any deferred tax adjustment you would be required make will be given to you. As previously discussed, it is not necessary to adjust for the pension and postretirement funded status for 2006.

Figure 4: Calculation of Expanded Definition of Comprehensive Income

For the fiscal year ended	2006
(in millions of dollars)	
Reported comprehensive income	$961
Adjustment for change in net deferred tax liabilities	(41)
Adjustment for long-term debt mark-to-market	(200)
Comprehensive income (expanded definition)	$720

These additional adjustments result in an expanded comprehensive income measure of $720 million, $433 million less than reported net income of $1,153 million. Even though this measure is more volatile than the GAAP definition (which itself is volatile), it more accurately reflects the economic changes that are excluded from the GAAP net income and comprehensive income measures. Note the adjustments are calculated as changes in each measure from the previous year.

FINANCIAL STATEMENT ADJUSTMENTS: EFFECT ON FINANCIAL RESULTS AND RATIOS

LOS 30.d: Analyze and interpret: the effect on reported financial results and ratios of a company's choices of accounting methods and assumptions; the effect on reported financial results and ratios of changes in accounting methods and assumptions; the effects of balance sheet modifications and earnings normalization on a company's financial statements, financial ratios, and overall financial condition.

Figure 5 contains three sets of financial information for JCPenney: the reported income statement and balance sheet, a normalized income statement and adjusted balance sheet, and a comprehensive (expanded) income statement and adjusted balance sheet.

Up to this point, we have discussed many of the effects related to the adjustments to the income statement and balance sheet. In this section, we examine several financial ratios from the three sets of financial data as a means of gaining some additional insight into the effects of the adjustments and comparing the three measurement methods. Ratios were calculated using end-of-year balance sheet figures because we only have the 2006 adjusted balance sheet.

Figure 5: Effects on Financial Statements and Ratios

Selected Income Statement Data (in millions of dollars)	Reported	Normalized	Expanded Comprehensive
Revenue	$19,903	$19,903	$19,903
Operating profit	1,922	1,909	1,984*
Interest expense	130	130	205*
Net income	$1,153	$1,094	$720

Selected Balance Sheet Data (in millions of dollars)	Reported	Adjusted	Adjusted
Current assets	$6,648	$6,941	$6,941
Total assets	12,673	13,910	13,910
Current liabilities	3,492	3,777	3,777
Total liabilities	8,385	8,608	8,608
Equity	4,288	5,302	5,302
Selected Ratios			
Operating margin	9.7%	9.6%	10.0%
Net profit margin	5.8%	5.5%	3.6%
Current ratio	1.9	1.8	1.8
Times-interested earned	14.8	14.7	9.7
Total debt-to-total capital	66.2%	61.9%	61.9%
ROA	9.1%	7.9%	5.2%
ROE	26.9%	20.6%	13.6%

* Professor's Note: The appropriate adjustment associated with capitalizing the operating lease involves eliminating the rental payment from operating profit and replacing it with depreciation expense. In addition, interest expense is increased by the imputed interest from the operating lease. For simplicity, we added the imputed interest of $75 million ($944 million × 7.9%) to operating profit and added the same amount to interest expense.

Effect on Profitability Ratios

Operating profit margin is virtually the same under all three measures since the largest adjustments to the normalized and expanded comprehensive measures are found below operating profit. Expanded comprehensive operating profit margin is slightly higher because of the reclassification of imputed interest from the operating leases.

Not surprisingly, the reported financial statements show the highest net profit margin. Normalized income is lower because of the LIFO credit totaling $16 million, the release of income tax reserves totaling $32 million, and the income from discontinued operations totaling $19 million have all been removed. Similarly, expanded comprehensive income is also lower. Expanded comprehensive income is also lower due to the increase in long-term debt to fair value and the removal of the decrease in the net deferred tax liability.

Effect on Liquidity Ratios

Reported current assets are lower than adjusted current assets; however, the current ratio is higher. This is because the percentage increase in the adjusted current liabilities is greater than the percentage increase in adjusted current assets. A larger percentage increase in current liabilities results in a lower current ratio. The largest adjustment included the $285 million contractual obligations added to both current assets and current liabilities.

Effect on Leverage Ratios

We measured leverage using the total-debt-to-capital ratio and the times-interest-earned ratio. Leverage was higher in the reported balance sheet. Adjusted debt was increased by the operating lease adjustment and mark-to-market adjustment. However, these two adjustments were more than offset by the reclassification of the net deferred tax liability to equity. The times-interest-earned ratio is lower using expanded comprehensive income because the imputed interest associated with the capitalization of the operating leases was added to interest expense.

As discussed, the funded status of JCPenney's pension and postretirement benefit plans were already included on the reported balance sheet, so no adjustment was required. For purposes of the exam, watch for adjustments for operating leases and pensions.

Effect on ROA and ROE

Finally, we consider return on assets (ROA) and return on equity (ROE). ROA based on the reported financial data is the highest. This is because reported net income (numerator) is the highest of the measures and reported total assets (denominator) is the lowest of the measures. Recall that the adjustment for off-balance sheet financing (operating leases) resulted in higher assets as well as higher liabilities. Therefore, ROA is usually lower after the lease adjustment. Likewise, ROE based on the reported data is the highest. This is because reported net income (numerator) is the highest of the measures and reported equity (denominator) is the lowest of the measures. Adjusted equity was higher because of the reclassification of the net deferred tax liability from debt to equity.

Effect of Changes in Accounting Methods and Assumptions

Analysts must also be aware of changes in accounting methods and assumptions. Firms can change accounting methods and assumptions to manipulate net income.

In the case of JCPenney, the changes in accounting methods were all mandated under U.S. GAAP. The most significant accounting change that applied to JCPenney was the adoption of the recognition and disclosure provisions of SFAS No. 158, which required the company to recognize the funded status of its defined benefit pension and postretirement plans directly in its balance sheet. The new standard did not affect the income statement.

JCPenney has lowered the discount rate used in its pension calculations. A lower discount rate results in a higher projected benefit obligation (lower funded status) and higher pension expense. The expected rate of return has remained steady at 8.9%; however, the actual return has been significantly higher over the past four years. The higher actual return has resulted in higher pension assets (higher funded status) and lower pension expense.

KEY CONCEPTS

1. There are two problems commonly encountered in the analysis of a firm's balance sheet: (1) some assets and liabilities are not recorded, and (2) the book values of assets and liabilities may differ significantly from their market values.

2. Examples of assets and liabilities that may not be recorded on the balance sheet include operating leases, assets and liabilities of unconsolidated affiliates, take-or-pay contracts, and effects of lawsuits or environmental obligations.

3. Examples of adjustments to assets include converting LIFO inventories to FIFO, marking-to-market nonfinancial assets such as real estate, revaluation of operating assets or intangible assets, and adjusting for a pension plan value in excess of the projected benefit obligation.

4. Examples of adjustments to liabilities include the restatement of deferred income taxes to reflect the probability of reversal and the revaluation of debt to reflect changes in interest rates or risk.

5. Extraordinary or nonrecurring items may require adjustments to the income statement. Adjusting net income for nonrecurring items results in an estimate of normal operating income. Examples of income statement items requiring adjustment include accounting changes, one-time charges, and restructuring charges.

CONCEPT CHECKERS

Use the following data to answer Questions 1 through 5. Consider each question independently of information contained in the other questions.

Dot.Com Company Balance Sheet
(in millions of $)

Assets	
Cash	$10
Marketable securities	5
Accounts receivable	20
Inventories	40
Total current assets	**$75**
Net property, plant, & equipment	$115
Intangible assets	10
Total assets	**$200**
Liabilities & Owners' Equity	
Accounts payable	$15
Notes payable	5
Total current liabilities	**$20**
Long-term debt	$60
Common stock (10 million shares)	20
Retained earnings	100
Total stockholders' equity	**$120**
Total liabilities & equity	**$200**

Dot.Com has 10 million shares of common stock outstanding.

The footnotes to Dot.Com's financial statements provide the following information:
- Inventories are valued at cost as determined by the last-in, first-out (LIFO) method. The LIFO reserve is $5 million.
- Additional operating facilities and equipment are financed with operating leases that have a present value of $10 million.
- Intangible assets include $2 million of goodwill from previous acquisitions.
- Due to a decrease in interest rates, Dot.Com's long-term debt has a current market value of $75 million.

1.   The long-term debt-to-equity ratio based on the historical balance sheet bears what relationship to the ratio based on the adjusted balance sheet? The long-term debt-to-equity ratio:
     A. based on the historical balance sheet is the same as that based on the adjusted balance sheet.
     B. based on the historical balance sheet is greater than that based on the adjusted balance sheet.
     C. based on the historical balance sheet is less than that based on the adjusted balance sheet.
     D. cannot be determined for the adjusted balance sheet.

2.   In addition to the information already presented in the question, assume that the tax basis of net property, plant, and equipment is $100 million and that the capital expenditures are expected to grow indefinitely in the future. The applicable tax rate is 30%. The required adjustment to Dot.Com's equity balance to account for deferred taxes is *closest* to:
     A. $0.
     B. –$4.5 million.
     C. +$4.5 million.
     D. +$15.0 million.

3.   In addition to the information already present in the question, assume that the current allowance for doubtful accounts is $5 million and that sales for the year were $100 million. The analyst subsequently discovers that a more reasonable estimate for allowance for doubtful accounts should be 6% of sales. Dot.com's adjusted current assets balance based on all the available information is *closest* to:
     A. $74 million.
     B. $76 million.
     C. $79 million.
     D. $81 million.

4.   The amount of the adjustments to equity necessary to arrive at an adjusted balance sheet for Dot.Com is *closest* to:
     A. –$12 million.
     B. $12 million.
     C. $18 million.
     D. $30 million.

5.   Dot.com's total liabilities and equity balance after any necessary adjustments is *closest* to:
     A. $203 million.
     B. $213 million.
     C. $215 million.
     D. $225 million.

Use the following data to answer Questions 6 through 11.

XYZ Company Balance Sheet
(in thousands of dollars)

Assets	
Cash	$5,000
Marketable securities	3,000
Accounts receivable	20,000
Inventories	10,000
Deferred taxes	5,000
Total current assets	**$43,000**
Net PP&E	80,000
Prepaid pension cost	6,000
Intangible assets	12,000
Total assets	**$141,000**
Liabilities & Owners' Equity	
Accounts payable	$18,000
Notes payable	7,000
Total current liabilities	**$25,000**
Long-term debt	24,000
Deferred taxes	8,000
Preferred stock (200 thousand shares)	10,000
Common stock (2 million shares)	40,000
Retained earnings	34,000
Total stockholders' equity	**$84,000**
Total liabilities & equity	**$141,000**

The following information is obtained from footnotes to XYZ's financial statements and other sources:

- One of XYZ's major customers that accounts for $5,000 of receivables has just filed for bankruptcy protection.
- Inventories are valued at cost as determined by the LIFO method. The LIFO reserve is $3,000.
- The deferred tax asset and liability are unlikely to reverse in future periods.
- Additional operating facilities and equipment are financed with operating leases that have a present value of $15,000.
- The value of XYZ's pension plan assets in excess of the projected benefit obligation is $8,000.
- Intangible assets represent $12,000 of goodwill from previous acquisitions.
- Due to a decrease in interest rates, XYZ's long-term debt has a current market value of $26,000.
- The current market price of XYZ's preferred stock is $40 per share.
- XYZ is expected to incur expenses with a present value of $5,000 to settle a legal claim related to a workmen's compensation case.

6. XYZ's adjusted inventory based on the FIFO method is *closest* to:
   A. $7,000.
   B. $10,000.
   C. $13,000.
   D. $16,000.

7. XYZ's current ratio after any necessary adjustments is *closest* to:
   A. 1.44.
   B. 1.64.
   C. 1.72.
   D. 1.84.

8. XYZ's long-term assets balance after any necessary adjustments is *closest* to:
   A. $101,000.
   B. $103,000.
   C. $113,000.
   D. $115,000.

9. XYZ's long-term liabilities balance after any necessary adjustments is *closest* to:
   A. $34,000.
   B. $46,000.
   C. $49,000.
   D. $54,000.

10. XYZ's ratio of long-term debt to common and preferred equity based on the historical cost balance sheet is:
    A. 0.17.
    B. 0.29.
    C. 0.58.
    D. 0.68.

11. XYZ's ratio of long-term debt to common and preferred equity based on the adjusted balance sheet is *closest* to:
    A. 0.29.
    B. 0.58.
    C. 0.60.
    D. 0.68.

12. Which of the following is the *best* indicator of high earnings quality?
    A. Straight-line depreciation method is used. ✗
    B. Interest is capitalized on an on-going basis. ✗
    C. LIFO inventory costing is used in a rising-price environment.
    D. High expected return on assets assumption is used for employee benefit plans. ✗

CHALLENGE PROBLEMS

13. Penguins Inc. uses the temporal method to translate foreign currency amounts. During the year, it reported net income of $5,000,000, an unrealized gain on available-for-sale securities of $150,000, an extraordinary loss of $200,000, a gain from discontinued operations of $175,000, and a foreign currency translation loss of $250,000. Penguins' comprehensive income and normal operating income, respectively, are *closest* to:

	Comprehensive income	Normal operating income
A.	$4,875,000	$5,025,000
B.	$4,875,000	$5,125,000
C.	$5,150,000	$5,125,000
D.	$5,150,000	$5,025,000

14. Ben Knowlin is also analyzing the financial statements of another construction equipment manufacturing company, Ridgeway Equipment. Ridgeway uses the LIFO method of inventory accounting. Knowlin calculates inventory turnover and gross profit margin without making the proper adjustments to the financial statements. Ridgeway's LIFO reserve increased from $1,000 to $1,200 during the year. What has been the effect of Knowlin's analysis on his estimates of adjusted inventory turnover and adjusted gross profit margin?

	Inventory turnover	Gross profit margin
A.	Underestimated	Properly estimated
B.	Underestimated	Overestimated
C.	Overestimated	Properly estimated
D.	Overestimated	Overestimated

Use the following information for Questions 15 through 17.

Jonorton Inc. uses the LIFO method of accounting for its inventories. Arnold Van Braun, CFA, has adjusted the statements from LIFO to FIFO, and compiled the following financial ratios for Jonorton Inc. using both the original LIFO based financial statements, and the adjusted FIFO financial statements.

	LIFO	FIFO
Current ratio	1.23	1.48
Inventory turnover	3.11	2.08
Gross margin	30.0%	37.5%

15. The most meaningful current ratio number that Van Braun should use for comparative analysis purposes is:
  A. 1.23.
  B. 1.48.
  C. the average of 1.23 and 1.48.
  D. current assets from the LIFO statements divided by current liabilities from the FIFO statements.

16. The most meaningful inventory turnover number that Van Braun should use for comparative analysis purposes is:
   A. 3.11.
   B. 2.08.
   C. cost of goods sold from the LIFO statements divided by inventory from the FIFO statements.
   D. cost of goods sold from the FIFO statements divided by inventory from the LIFO statements.

17. The most meaningful gross margin number that Van Braun should use for comparative analysis purposes is:
   A. 30.0%.
   B. 37.5%.
   C. the average of 30.0% and 37.5%.
   D. gross margin from the FIFO statements divided by sales from the LIFO statements.

18. An analyst determines that a firm's capital expenditures will likely grow indefinitely. The firm has recorded a deferred tax liability solely as a result of utilizing accelerated depreciation methods for tax purposes. After the analyst makes the appropriate adjustments, what are the *likely* effects on:

	D/E ratio?	ROE?
A.	Decrease	Decrease
B.	Decrease	Increase
C.	Increase	Decrease
D.	Increase	Increase

19. An analyst is reviewing a company with a large deferred tax asset on its balance sheet. In reviewing the company's performance over the last few years, the analyst has determined that the firm has had cumulative losses for the last three years and has a large amount of inventory that can be sold only at sharply reduced prices. Which of the following adjustments should the analyst make to account for the deferred tax assets?
   A. Record a deferred tax liability to offset the effect of the deferred tax asset on the firm's balance sheet and decrease earnings by the amount of the valuation allowance.
   B. Recognize a valuation allowance to reflect the fact that the deferred tax asset is unlikely to be realized.
   C. Do nothing. The difference between taxable and pretax income that caused the deferred tax asset is likely to reverse in the future.
   D. Decrease tax expense by the amount of the deferred tax asset unlikely to be realized.

ANSWERS – CONCEPT CHECKERS

1. **C** The long-term debt to equity ratio is calculated as:

$$\text{based on historical balance sheet} = \frac{\$60}{\$120} = 50\%$$

$$\text{based on the adjusted balance sheet} = \frac{\$85}{\$108} = 78.7\%$$

2. **A** If capital expenditures are expected to grow indefinitely in the future, then any temporary differences would not be expected to reverse. Therefore, no deferred taxes should be recorded. Since there are no deferred taxes recorded on the balance sheet, no adjustment is required.

3. **C** The current allowance for doubtful accounts balance (a contra-asset account) of $5 million is already incorporated in the accounts receivable balance. Since a more reasonable balance for allowance for doubtful accounts is $6 million ($100 million × 6%), we should reduce the accounts receivable balance by $1 million. We also have to increase the inventory balance by the LIFO reserve of $5 million to reflect the use of the FIFO method. The net change as a result of these two adjustments is a $4 million increase in current assets and an adjusted balance of $79 million.

4. **A** Equity adjustments:
$ 5 million	(from inventory adj.)
– 2 million	(from goodwill adj.)
– 15 million	(from long-term debt adj.)
–$12 million	(total)

   Note that you have to ignore the allowance for doubtful accounts information from Question 4 because the instructions say "consider each question independently of information contained in other questions."

5. **B** See detail in the adjusted balance sheet for Dot.com Company in the following table.

Dot.Com Company Adjusted Balance Sheet
(in millions of $)

Assets	
Cash	$10
Marketable securities	5
Accounts receivable	20
Inventories	45
Total current assets	**$80**
Net property, plant, & equipment	$125
Intangible assets	8
Total assets	**$213**
Liabilities & Owners' Equity	
Accounts payable	$15
Notes payable	5
Total current liabilities	**$20**
Long-term debt	$85
Common stock	$20
Retained earnings	100
Equity adjustment	−12
Total stockholders' equity	**$108**
Total liabilities & equity	**$213**

The footnotes to Dot.Com's financial statements provide the following information:

Item	Adjustment
Inventories are valued at cost as determined by the LIFO method. The LIFO reserve is $5 million.	Adj. inventory = $40 + 5 = $45 million. Also, add $5 million to equity.
Additional operating facilities and equipment are financed with operating leases that have a present value of $10 million.	Add $10 million to net property plant and equipment and to long-term debt.
Intangible assets represent $2 million of goodwill from previous acquisitions.	Reduce intangibles by the $2 million goodwill. Also reduce equity by $2 million.
Due to a decrease in interest rates, Dot.Com's long-term debt has increased in value by $15 million.	Add $15 million to long-term debt. Reduce equity by $15 million.

6. **C** LIFO inventory of 10,000 + LIFO reserve of 3,000 = FIFO inventory of $13,000

7. **A** Current ratio = $\dfrac{\text{Current assets}}{\text{Current liabilities}}$

Current assets:

Cash	$5,000	
Marketable securities	$3,000	
Accounts receivable	$15,000	(20,000 – 5,000)
Inventories	$13,000	(10,000 + 3,000)
Deferred taxes	$0	(5,000 – 5,000); see detail in the summary
Total current assets	$36,000	
Current liabilities:		
Accounts payable	$18,000	
Notes payable	$7,000	
Total current liabilities	$25,000	

Current ratio = $\dfrac{\$36,000}{\$25,000} = 1.44$

8. **B** Long term assets = net PP&E + prepaid pension cost + intangible assets;
(80,000 + 15,000) + (6,000 + 2,000) + (12,000 – 12,000) = $103,000
See detail in summary.

9. **B** Long term liabilities = long-term debt + capitalization of operating leases + deferred taxes + workman's compensation expense;
(24,000 + 2,000) + (0 +15,000) + (8,000 – 8,000) + (0 + 5,000) = $46,000
See detail in the summary.

10. **B** Long-term debt-to-equity (unadjusted) = $\dfrac{24,000}{84,000} = 0.29$

11. **D** Long-term debt-to-equity (adjusted) $= \dfrac{24,000+15,000+2,000+5,000}{68,000} = 0.68$

See detail in the summary.

Summary of adjustments—adjusted balance sheet for XYZ.

Assets

Cash	$5,000
Marketable securities	3,000
Accounts receivable[1]	15,000
Inventories[2]	13,000
Deferred taxes[3]	0
Total current assets	**$36,000**
Net PP&E[4]	$95,000
Prepaid pension cost[5]	8,000
Intangible assets[6]	0
Total assets	**$139,000**

Liabilities & Owners' Equity

Accounts payable	$18,000
Notes payable	7,000
Total current liabilities	**$25,000**
Long-term debt[7]	$26,000
Capitalization of oper. leases[4]	15,000
Deferred taxes[3]	0
Legal claim[9]	5,000
Total long-term obligations	**$46,000**
Preferred stock[8]	$8,000
Common stock (1 million shares)	40,000
Retained earnings	34,000
Net adjustments to equity[10]	(14,000)
Total stockholders' equity	**$68,000**
Total liabilities & equity	**$139,000**

Notes:

1. A/R declined to $15,000 due to the bankruptcy of a customer. Equity will be reduced by this amount as well.

2. Recognition of the LIFO reserve will increase inventory by $3,000 and equity by $3,000.

3. The deferred tax asset and deferred tax liability have been eliminated because the tax timing differences are unlikely to reverse in future periods. $5,000 tax asset is eliminated, reducing equity by $5,000. $8,000 tax liability is eliminated, increasing equity by $8,000. The net equity adjustment is a $3,000 addition.

4. Operating leases are capitalized by adding $15,000 to PP&E and $15,000 to long-term debt.

5. The current balance sheet valuation of the pension plan is $6,000. Since the plan surplus is actually $8,000, a $2,000 addition to prepaid pension cost is posted. Equity rises by this

same amount. No adjustment was made to deferred taxes resulting from the adjustment to the funded status because all deferred tax assets and liabilities were eliminated and reclassified as equity, as discussed in Note 3.

6. Intangible assets are eliminated. Equity is reduced by $12,000.

7. LTD is adjusted to market value. An increase of $2,000 is posted to LTD, and a decrease of $2,000 goes to equity.

8. The preferred stock valuation is reduced to $8,000 = $40 (200). The offset is a $2,000 increase to equity.

9. The legal claim contingency is a liability. The offsetting adjustment is to equity of $5,000.

10. The net adjustments to equity are (5,000) + 3,000 + 3,000 + 2,000 + (12,000) + (2,000) + 2,000 + (5,000) = ($14,000) respectively for items 1-9.

12. **C** High earnings quality generally refers to reporting a more conservative (i.e., lower) level of earnings. LIFO inventory costing (when prices are rising) generally results in a more conservative level of reported earnings. The other three items result in less conservative (higher levels of) reported earnings.

ANSWERS – CHALLENGE PROBLEMS

13. **D** Comprehensive income

Net income	$5,000,000
Unrealized gain on available-for-sale securities	$150,000
Total	$5,150,000

Normal operating income

Net income	$5,000,000
Add back: Extraordinary loss	$200,000
Deduct: Gain from discontinued operations	($175,000)
Total	$5,025,000

Penguins uses the temporal method, so the foreign currency translation loss, which is recorded on the income statement, is already incorporated in net income. The unrealized gain on available for sale securities is recorded directly to equity.

14. **C** LIFO cost of goods sold (COGS) is greater than FIFO cost of goods sold (by the change in the LIFO reserve, or $200), and LIFO inventory balance is less than FIFO inventory by the amount of the LIFO reserve ($1,200). The proper analysis is to use LIFO COGS and FIFO inventory balance to calculate financial ratios. Knowlin has used LIFO COGS and LIFO inventory, so he has properly estimated gross profit margin, but he has overestimated inventory turnover (COGS divided by inventory) because he used the correct figure in the numerator (LIFO COGS) but the incorrect, lower LIFO inventory figure in the denominator.

15. **B** For comparative ratio analysis the analyst should use the FIFO inventory figure and the LIFO cost of goods sold figure. The appropriate current ratio number is FIFO current assets divided by current liabilities, which is 1.48 from the figure. Notice that current liabilities are the same under LIFO and FIFO.

16. **C** For comparative ratio analysis the analyst should use the FIFO inventory figure and the LIFO cost of goods sold figure. The appropriate inventory turnover number is cost of goods sold from the LIFO statements divided by inventory from the FIFO statements.

17. **A**   For comparative ratio analysis the analyst should use the FIFO inventory figure and the LIFO cost of goods sold figure. The appropriate gross margin number is LIFO gross profit divided by net sales, which is 30.0% from the figure. Notice that sales are the same under LIFO and FIFO.

18. **A**   Based on the facts, there is no likelihood of reversal of the deferred tax liability. Therefore, it should be reclassified as equity. The increase in the equity base will cause both the D/E ratio and ROE to decrease.

19. **B**   The valuation allowance is used to offset deferred tax assets if it is unlikely that those assets will be realized. Because the company has a history of losses and inventory that is unlikely to generate future profits, it is unlikely the company will realize its deferred tax assets in full. Income tax expense will increase, and earnings will decrease, by the amount of the valuation allowance.

Use the following information to answer Questions 1 through 6.

Susan Alverson is a senior research analyst covering the pharmaceutical industry for McCool Asset Management. One of the major holdings at McCool is Vandon Pharmaceuticals, a manufacturer and distributor of drugs for rare, life-threatening diseases. Recently, Vandon's stock price has dropped by 15%, and according to the rules that govern security positions held at the firm, the stock must have an extensive review, including a reaffirmation of the investment thesis for holding the stock.

As McCool's senior analyst for the pharmaceutical industry, it is Alverson's responsibility to review Vandon's financial condition and make a recommendation as to whether or not the firm's portfolio managers should continue to hold the stock. One of Alverson's major concerns is that Vandon's financial statements do not accurately reflect Vandon's financial condition. Alverson analyzes the following information:

Figure 1: Vandon Pharmaceuticals Consolidated Balance Sheet for 2007 (in 000's of $)

Assets

Cash and Equivalents	$22,400
Receivables	412,600
Inventories	564,800
Total Current Assets	**$999,800**
Gross Property Plant, & Equip.	$892,500
Accumulated Deprecation	(184,600)
Net Property, Plant & Equip.	707,900
Goodwill	322,000
Total Assets	**$2,029,700**

Liabilities

Payables	$364,100
Short Term Debt	157,000
Current Portion of LT Debt	60,000
Total Current Liabilities	**$581,100**
Long Term Debt	$596,980
Common Stock	$400,000
Additional Paid in Capital	200,000
Retained Earnings	251,620
Common Shareholder's Equity	$851,620
Total Liabilities and Equity	**$2,029,700**

Figure 2: Vandon Pharmaceuticals Income Statement for 2007 (in 000's $)

Revenues	$3,600,500
Cost of Goods Sold	2,780,600
Gross Profit	819,900
Operating Expenses	653,800
Operating Income	166,100
Interest Expense	24,300
Depreciation	52,600
Earnings Before Taxes	89,200
Taxes (40%)	35,680
Net Income	$53,520 — 10,500 = 43,020
Dividends Paid	10,700

Figure 3: Vandon Pharmaceuticals Footnotes to 2007 Financial Statements:

- In 2007, Vandon sold $50 million of receivables with full recourse to a qualified special purpose entity. The SPE was not consolidated.
- The firm has outstanding operating leases for research facilities. The present value of the leases is $225 million.
- Due to an increase in market interest rates during the year, the fair market value of all outstanding long term debt is $616,980,000.
- Vandon is the defendant in a patent litigation suit with a court date in June 2006. The amount of the lawsuit is $300 million. Vandon's attorneys believe the lawsuit is without merit and have lab journals and other documents detailing Vandon's original production of the drug in question.
- Vandon has a take-or-pay contract commitment to purchase $25 million of chemical compounds each year for the next eight years. The interest rate on the contract is 7% and the present value of this commitment is $150 million. The commitments are in an unconsolidated SPE and are not recognized on the balance sheet.
- $322 million of goodwill is associated with Vandon's acquisition of a consumer products company five years ago.
- Vandon uses the LIFO inventory accounting method. The LIFO reserve in 2007 was $60 million. In 2006, the LIFO reserve was $40 million.

Using this information, Alverson decides to recalculate important financial ratios for Vandon and report her findings to the McCool Asset Management investment committee. For all items, assume that inventory has been to a FIFO basis, where appropriate.

To adjust the income statement for the take-or-pay contract, Alverson increases interest expense by the present value of the commitment times the explicit interest rate on the contract. She increases EBIT by the same amount. Assume these are the appropriate adjustments.

↳ take or pay

1. The percentage change in Vandon's current ratio after Alverson makes the appropriate adjustments is *closest* to:
   A. an increase of 0.6%.
   B. an increase of 1.8%.
   C. a decrease of 2.2%.
   D. an increase of 2.4%.

2. The percentage change in Vandon's receivables turnover ratio after Alverson makes the appropriate adjustments is *closest* to:
   A. no change.
   B. a decrease of 10.8%.
   C. an increase of 12.1%.
   D. an increase of 13.8%.

3. The percentage change in Vandon's total asset turnover ratio after Alverson makes the appropriate adjustments is *closest* to:
   A. an increase of 6.9%.
   B. a decrease of 7.4%.
   C. a decrease of 13.8%.
   D. a decrease of 19.2%.

4. Alverson is aware that any change to net income is likely to be small, so she wants to focus her attention on the balance sheet. The percentage change in Vandon's return-on-equity (ROE) ratio (using end-of-period equity) after Alverson makes the appropriate adjustments is *closest* to:
   A. an increase of 34.9%.
   B. a decrease of 25.9%.
   C. a decrease of 10.7%.
   D. an increase of 19.2%.

5. Alverson is interested in the financial situation implied by Vandon's long-term liabilities. The percentage change in Vandon's long-term debt to equity ratio after Alverson's adjustments is *closest* to an:
   A. increase of 19.2%.
   B. increase of 24.8%.
   C. increase of 39.7%.
   D. increase of 111.1%.

6. After Alverson makes the appropriate adjustments, how will the gross profit margin and interest coverage ratios change? (*Note*: No calculations are required).

	Gross profit margin	Interest coverage ratio
A.	Increase	Decrease
B.	Increase	Increase
C.	Decrease	Decrease
D.	Decrease	Increase

Use the following information to answer Questions 7 through 12.

Gotham Pharmaceuticals wants to jump-start its sales growth, which has sagged in recent quarters, by boosting its research and development budget with the intention of purchasing a smaller company that lacks the resources to market its ground-breaking osteoporosis treatment. Operating cash flow alone will not provide the cash Gotham wants to spend, so the company decides to sell some of its assets.

Bonds and other income investments comprise the bulk of Gotham's investment portfolio. Below is a list of Gotham's financial assets, most of which the company has owned for a decade or more.

Securities	Carrying Value at End of Most Recent Fiscal Year	Estimated Market Value Six Months Into Current Year
HTM Corporate Bonds 6.25%	$75,000,000	$74,000,000
Available Treasury Bonds 6.75%	$125,000,000	$128,000,000
Available S&P 500 Index Fund	$35,000,000	$41,000,000
Trading General Electric Preferred Stock	$13,000,000	$12,500,000
Available Package of Residential Mortgages →cost why	$42,000,000	$43,000,000

Frank Caper, Gotham's CFO, is unsure how to approach the security sales, so he assigns Julia Ward, director of the company's accounting division, to handle the record keeping. When Ward asks Caper which securities he plans to sell, Caper responds that he has not yet decided, but he expects the purchase of the smaller drug company will require between $190 million and $240 million.

Ward begins her review of Gotham's securities holdings and learns the following:

- The corporate bonds are classified as held-to-maturity.
- The preferred stock is classified as a trading security.
- The Treasury bonds, package of mortgages, and index fund are classified as available-for-sale.

A review of the balance sheet left Ward with several questions. She called Caper for clarification, who made the following statements:

- The package of mortgages is carried at cost because such securities are not commonly traded, and no market value is available.
- We know the market price for the corporate bonds, but record their value at cost anyway.
- We intend to reclassify the Treasury bonds as trading securities because they mature in less than a year.
- Because the index fund has the most appreciation potential, we intend to reclassify it as held-to-maturity.

Confused by Caper's statements, Ward tries a new tactic and looks at the securities from an income-statement perspective. She prepares a table showing how the securities have performed over the last year, and then reviews the income statement and balance sheet for the year to see how Gotham handled the accounting.

Securities	Dividends/Interest, Last Fiscal Year	Unrealized Gains/Losses, Last Fiscal Year	Realized Gains/Losses, Last Fiscal Year
Corporate Bonds 6.25%	$4,500,000	$2,500,000	
Treasury Bonds 6.75%	$8,500,000	−$6,000,000	
S&P 500 Index Fund	$630,000	$4,000,000	$500,000
General Electric Preferred Stock	$740,000	$1,200,000	
Package of Residential Mortgages	$2,200,000	−$3,600,000	$3,000,000

After reviewing Gotham's accounting for its securities, Ward realizes she does not have enough information to recommend reclassification for the securities.

While preparing to call Caper for more information, Ward comes across one additional investment not included in the original list. Gotham owns 35% of the Klesten Research Center, a laboratory that provides preclinical-testing services. That stake is not represented on the income statement or balance sheet. Last year, Klesten Research Center lost $150 million, increased its debt load by $400 million to $2.1 billion, saw its market value fall by $100 million to $4.85 billion, and paid $40 million in dividends.

7. The effect of Gotham's investment portfolio on corporate income in the last fiscal year was *closest* to a gain of:
   A. $15,670,000.
   B. $18,170,000.
   C. $19,270,000.
   D. $21,270,000.

8. Under Gotham's current accounting system, which securities are *least accurately* classified?
   A. Preferred stock.
   B. Treasury bonds.
   C. Package of mortgages.
   D. Corporate bonds.

9. Caper has not provided enough information for Ward to reclassify the securities. She needs more details regarding:
   A. when the securities were originally purchased.
   B. which securities have the poorest return potential.
   C. how much Gotham intends to spend on the purchase.
   D. which securities Gotham plans to sell to raise the money.

10. Gotham, which purchased 35% of Klesten Research Center in 2002, restates the last three years of financial statements to account for the purchase. In the fiscal year ended December 2005, what effect would the *most likely* effect of the Klesten investment have on Gotham's financial statements?

	Income	Assets
A.	Decrease	Decrease
B.	Increase	Decrease
C.	Increase	Increase
D.	Decrease	Increase

11. Which of Caper's statements reflects the *best* understanding of security classification?
    A. Because the index fund has the best appreciation potential, we intend to reclassify it as held-to-maturity.
    B. We know the market price for the corporate bonds, but record their value at cost anyway. *amortized cost is really what they should do*
    C. We intend to reclassify the Treasury bonds as trading securities because they mature in less than a year.
    D. The package of mortgages is carried at cost because such securities are not commonly traded, and no market value is available.

12. After reviewing Gotham's financial statements and reconsidering Caper's statements, Ward suspects Caper wants to use accounting classifications to change the company's financial picture. Caper's proposed changes would *most likely*:
    A. reduce current and deferred taxes.
    B. increase return on equity.
    C. increase interest coverage.
    D. increase revenues.

SELF-TEST ANSWERS: FINANCIAL STATEMENT ANALYSIS

Refer to the following sheet for adjustments to Vandon's financial statements for the year 2007.

		Adjustment	Comment	New Value
Assets				
Cash and Equivalents	$22,400			$22,400
Receivables	412,600	+50,000	Receivables with recourse	462,600
Inventories	564,800	+60,000	LIFO Reserve	624,800
Total Current Assets	**$999,800**			**$1,109,800**
Gross Property Plant, & Equip.	$892,500	+225,000	Leases	1,117,500
Accumulated Deprecation	(184,600)			(184,600)
Net Property, Plant & Equip.	707,900			932,900
Supply agreement		+150,000	Take or pay contract	150,000
Goodwill	322,000	−322,000		0
Total Assets	**$2,029,700**			**$2,192,700**
Liabilities				
Payables	$364,100			364,100
Receivables recourse		+$50,000	New liability for recourse on receivable	50,000
Short Term Debt	$157,000			157,000
Current Portion of LT Debt	$60,000			60,000
Total Current Liabilities	**$581,100**			**$631,100**
Long Term Debt	596,980	+225,000, −40,000 +150,000	Leases, FMV debt, take or pay contract	931,980
Common Stock	400,000			
Additional Paid in Capital	200,000			
Retained Earnings	251,620			
Common Shareholder's Equity		+40,000, −	FMV debt, goodwill,	
	$851,620	322,000, +60,000	LIFO reserve	**$629,620**
Total Liabilities and Equity	**$2,029,700**			**$2,192,700**

Notes:
- To calculate the change to LTD, first take the total of LTD and the current portion of LTD, since the footnotes say the value of 617,080 applies to all outstanding LTD. The change to LTD is 616,980 - (60,000 + 596,980) = -40,000.
- Not necessary to make adjustments for the pending lawsuit since the likelihood of the liability being realized is low.

1. **C** The current ratio is calculated as current assets / current liabilities. Prior to Alverson's adjustments, the current ratio was $999,800 / $581,100 = 1.721, but since Vandon sold $50 million in receivables, Alverson adjustments change the current ratio to 1,109,800 / 631,100 = 1.759. The percentage change is (1.759 / 1.721) − 1 = 0.022, or 2.2%.

2. **B** The receivables turnover ratio is calculated as sales / receivables. Prior to Alverson's adjustments, the receivables turnover ratio was $3,600,500 / $412,600 = 8.726. The first footnote states Vandon sold $50 million of receivables with full recourse, so Alverson's will adjustment the receivables turnover ratio to $3,600,500 / $462,600 = 7.783. The percentage change is (7.783 / 8.726) − 1 = −0.10807, or a 10.8% decrease.

3. **B** The total asset turnover ratio is calculated as sales / total assets. Prior to Alverson's adjustments, the total asset turnover ratio was $3,600,500 / $2,029,700 = 1.773. Alverson's adjustments alter the total asset turnover ratio to $3,600,500 / $2,192,700= 1.642. The percentage change is (1.642 / 1.773) − 1 = −0.073886, or a 7.4% decrease. Refer to the table for adjusted total assets.

4. **A** The return on equity ratio is calculated as net income / total equity. Prior to Alverson's adjustments, the total Net Income/Equity ratio was $53,520 / $851,620 = 0.063. Alverson will adjust the Net Income/Equity ratio to $53,520 / $629,620 = 0.085. The percentage change is (0.085 / 0.063) − 1 = 0.3492 or a 34.9% increase. Refer to the table for adjusted total equity.

5. **D** The LTD/Equity ratio is calculated as LTD / total equity. Prior to Alverson's adjustments, the total LTD/Equity ratio was $596,980 / $851,620 = 0.701. After Alverson's adjustments, the LTD/Equity ratio was $931,980 / $629,620 = 1.480. The percentage change is (1.480 / 0.701) − 1 = 1.1113, or a 111.1% increase. Refer to the table in the final answer for adjusted LTD and total equity.

6. **A** As a result of converting the financial statements from LIFO to FIFO, COGS will decline by the amount of the change in the LIFO reserve. Since COGS decreases, gross profit increases, so the gross profit margin will increase. The interest coverage ratio declines as a result of the take or pay contract. On the income statement, the proper adjustment is to increase interest expense by the product of the present value obligation times the explicit interest rate on the contract. EBIT should also be increased by the same amount as interest expense to reflect income on the contract. Since the EBIT/ interest expense ratio is greater than one, adding the same amount to the numerator and denominator will decrease the ratio.

7. **D** To calculate the income effect, we begin by looking at how each security is classified. The corporate bonds are classified as held-to-maturity, preferred stock is a trading security, and the Treasury bonds, package of mortgages, and index fund are classified as available-for-sale. For trading securities, dividends, interest, and both realized and unrealized losses count toward income. For securities classified held-to-maturity or available-for-sale, only dividends, interest, and realized gains count toward income.

Securities	Dividends/Interest	Unrealized Gains/Losses	Realized Gains / Losses	Accounting	Income Effect
Corporate Bonds 6.25%	$4,500,000	$2,500,000		Held-to-Maturity	$4,500,000
Treasury Bonds 6.75%	$8,500,000	–$6,000,000		Available-for-Sale	$8,500,000
S&P 500 Index Fund	$630,000	$4,000,000	$500,000	Available-for-Sale	$1,130,000
General Electric Preferred Stock	$740,000	$1,200,000		Trading	$1,940,000
Package of Residential Mortgages	$2,200,000	–$3,600,000	$3,000,000	Available-for-Sale	$5,200,000
Total					$21,270,000

8. **A** There is nothing wrong with how Gotham classifies the bonds and mortgages, as the available-for-sale classification leaves plenty of flexibility. However, until recently, Gotham appeared to have no intention of selling securities. As such, no investments should have been classified as a trading security.

9. **D** Ward must know which securities Gotham will sell so she can correctly classify the securities. The purchase date of the securities is irrelevant, and even if Ward knew how much Gotham intended to spend, it would not tell her which securities to reclassify. Return potential may have an effect on which securities the company chooses to sell, but that return information will not help Ward change the accounting policy.

10. **A** The equity method appears to be the best way to account for Gotham's 35% stake in Klesten Research Center. Under the equity method, the proportional share of Klesten's operational loss is included in Gotham's income, which will decrease Gotham's total income. This decrease would also reduce the carrying value of the Klesten stake on the balance sheet, and the dividend would reduce it still further. Market value is irrelevant in this case, as is the increase in Klesten's debt level.

11. **B** Securities held-to-maturity like the corporate bonds are supposed to be carried at cost basis on the balance sheet even if a market price is available. The remaining statements reflect a lack of understanding. The mortgages are classified as available-for-sale, and must be carried at market value. Gotham must either determine a market value for them or classify them as held-to-maturity. The maturity of a bond has nothing to do with its classification. Furthermore, the classification of a trading security has do with intent to sell, not marketability. Equity securities cannot be classified as held-to-maturity.

12. **B**   Caper expects the value of the index fund to rise sharply, and reclassifying the index fund as held-to-maturity rather than available-for-sale will result in the future unrealized gains not being added to equity. That would result in a lower equity balance and most likely increase ROE. Reclassifying the Treasury bonds as trading securities would require any unrealized gains to be reported as income. The bonds increased in value during the first six months of the year, and the reclassification would not reduce taxes. Caper's proposed changes would not directly affect interest coverage or revenues.

FORMULAS

ECONOMICS

annualized forward premium/discount:

$$\text{forward premium/discount} = \left(\frac{\text{forward rate} - \text{spot rate}}{\text{spot rate}}\right)\left(\frac{360}{\text{number of days forward}}\right)$$

relative PPP: $\dfrac{E(S_1)}{S_0} = \dfrac{1 + E(i_{FC})}{1 + E(i_{DC})}$, where S is FC/DC

international Fisher relation:

exact methodology: $\dfrac{1 + r_{FC}}{1 + r_{DC}} = \dfrac{1 + E(i_{FC})}{1 + E(i_{DC})}$

linear approximation: $r_{FC} - r_{DC} \approx E(i_{FC}) - E(i_{DC})$

uncovered interest rate parity:

exact methodology:

$$\frac{E(S_1)}{S_0} = \frac{1 + r_{FC}}{1 + r_{DC}}$$

or

$$\frac{E(S_1) - S_0}{S_0} = \%\Delta S = \left(\frac{1 + r_{FC}}{1 + r_{DC}}\right) - 1 = \frac{r_{FC} - r_{DC}}{1 + r_{DC}}$$

linear approximation:

$$\frac{E(S_1) - S_0}{S_0} = \%\Delta S \approx r_{FC} - r_{DC}, \text{ or } E(S_1) \approx S_0\left[1 + (r_{FC} - r_{DC})\right]$$

foreign exchange expectation relation:

$$F = E(S_1)$$

$$\frac{F - S_0}{S_0} = E(\%\Delta S)$$

interest rate parity:

exact methodology:

$$\frac{F}{S_0} = \frac{1 + r_{FC}}{1 + r_{DC}}$$

forward premium or discount $= \dfrac{F - S_0}{S_0} = \left(\dfrac{1 + r_{FC}}{1 + r_{DC}}\right) - 1 = \dfrac{r_{FC} - r_{DC}}{1 + r_{DC}}$

linear approximation:

forward premium or discount $= \dfrac{F - S_0}{S_0} \approx r_{FC} - r_{DC}$

---

expected domestic currency return:

unhedged $E(R_{DC}) = E(R_{FC}) + E(\%\Delta S) = E(R_{FC}) + \dfrac{E(S_1) - S_0}{S_0}$

hedged $E(R_{DC}) = E(R_{FC}) + \dfrac{F - S_0}{S_0}$

real exchange rate:

real $S = S \times \left(\dfrac{P_{FC}}{P_{DC}}\right)$

$\%\Delta$ in real $S = \%\Delta$ in nominal $S - (i_{DC} - i_{FC})$

foreign currency risk premium:

$$FCRP = \dfrac{E(S_1) - S_0}{S_0} - (r_{DC} - r_{FC})$$

$$FCRP = \dfrac{E(S_1) - F}{S_0} \text{ , assuming IRP holds}$$

FINANCIAL STATEMENT ANALYSIS

funded status of the plan: funded status = fair value of plan assets − PBO

adjusted pension expense = service cost + interest cost − actual return on plan assets

---

translation gain/loss:

exposure under the all-current method = shareholders' equity

exposure under the temporal method = (cash + accounts receivable) − (accounts payable + current debt + long-term debt)

flow effect (in $) = change in exposure (in LC) × (ending rate − average rate)

holding gain/loss effect (in $) = beginning exposure (in LC) × (ending rate − beginning rate)

translation gain/loss (in $) = flow effect + holding gain/loss effect

---

Professor's Note: Not all of these ratios are used in this book. However, this list includes most of the common ratios that you are likely to encounter on exam day.

$$\text{current ratio} = \frac{\text{current assets}}{\text{current liabilities}}$$

$$\text{quick ratio} = \frac{\text{cash} + \text{marketable securities} + \text{receivables}}{\text{current liabilities}}$$

$$\text{cash ratio} = \frac{\text{cash} + \text{short-term marketable securities}}{\text{current liabilities}}$$

$$\text{receivables turnover} = \frac{\text{net annual sales}}{\text{average receivables}}$$

$$\text{average receivable collection period} = \frac{365}{\text{receivables turnover}}$$

$$\text{inventory turnover} = \frac{\text{cost of goods sold}}{\text{average inventory}}$$

$$\text{average inventory processing period} = \frac{365}{\text{inventory turnover}}$$

$$\text{payables turnover} = \frac{\text{cost of goods sold}}{\text{average payables}}$$

$$\text{average payables payment period} = \frac{365}{\text{payables turnover}}$$

$$\text{total asset turnover} = \frac{\text{net sales}}{\text{average total net assets}}$$

$$\text{fixed asset turnover} = \frac{\text{net sales}}{\text{average net fixed assets}}$$

$$\text{equity turnover} = \frac{\text{net sales}}{\text{average equity}}$$

$$\text{gross profit margin} = \frac{\text{gross profit}}{\text{net sales}}$$

$$\text{operating profit margin} = \frac{\text{operating profit}}{\text{net sales}} = \frac{\text{EBIT}}{\text{net sales}}$$

$$\text{net profit margin} = \frac{\text{net income}}{\text{net sales}}$$

$$\text{return on assets} = \frac{\text{net income}}{\text{average total assets}}$$

$$\text{return on total invested capital ratio} = \frac{\text{net income} + \text{interest expense}}{\text{interest bearing debt} + \text{shareholders' equity}}$$

$$\text{return on total equity} = \frac{\text{net income}}{\text{average total equity}}$$

$$\text{interest burden rate} = \frac{\text{interest expense}}{\text{total assets}}$$

$$\text{tax retention rate} = 1 - \left(\frac{\text{dividends declared}}{\text{operating income after taxes}} \right)$$

$$\text{financial leverage ratio} = \frac{\text{total assets}}{\text{total equity}}$$

$$\text{long-term debt-to-equity ratio} = \frac{\text{total long-term debt}}{\text{total equity}}$$

$$\text{debt - equity ratio} = \frac{\text{total debt}}{\text{total equity}}$$

$$\text{debt - to - capital ratio} = \frac{\text{short-term debt} + \text{long-term debt}}{\text{short-term debt} + \text{long-term debt} + \text{total equity}}$$

$$\text{interest coverage} = \frac{\text{EBIT}}{\text{interest expense}}$$

$$\text{payout ratio} = \frac{\text{dividends paid}}{\text{net income}}$$

$$\text{retention ratio} = 1 - \text{payout ratio}$$

$$\text{earnings per share} = \frac{\text{net income} - \text{preferred dividends}}{\text{average common shares outstanding}}$$

$$\text{book value per share} = \frac{\text{common stockholders' equity}}{\text{total number of common shares outstanding}}$$

INDEX

S

T

U

V